Oded Yisraeli
Temple Portals

Studia Judaica

Forschungen zur Wissenschaft des Judentums

Begründet von
Ernst Ludwig Ehrlich

Herausgegeben von
Günter Stemberger, Charlotte Fonrobert
und Alexander Samely

Band 88

Oded Yisraeli
Temple Portals

Studies in Aggadah and Midrash in the Zohar

Translated by
Liat Keren

DE GRUYTER   MAGNES

ISBN 978-3-11-060745-1
e-ISBN (PDF) 978-3-11-043255-8
e-ISBN (EPUB) 978-3-11-043276-3
ISSN 0585-5306

Library of Congress Cataloging-in-Publication Data
A CIP catalog record for this book has been applied for at the Library of Congress.

Bibliografische Information der Deutschen Nationalbibliothek
Die Deutsche Nationalbibliothek verzeichnet diese Publikation in der Deutschen Nationalbibliografie; detaillierte bibliografische Daten sind im Internet über http://dnb.dnb.de abrufbar.

© 2018 Walter de Gruyter GmbH, Berlin/Boston
& Hebrew University Magnes Press, Jerusalem
This volume is text- and page-identical with the hardback published in 2016.
Satz: Konrad Triltsch, Print und digitale Medien GmbH, Ochsenfurt
Druck und Bindung: CPI books GmbH, Leck

♾ Gedruckt auf säurefreiem Papier
Printed in Germany

www.degruyter.com

Preface

A well-known zoharic parable depicts Torah-study as a love story between the Torah and those who study it, likening the Torah to a beautiful maiden imprisoned in a remote, concealed palace. Desiring to be seen by her lover who walks around and around it seeking his beloved, she makes a small opening through which he can glimpse her for a brief moment before she disappears once again. Having pondered this parable for many years, I have concluded that the palace represents the *Zohar*'s self-image, through which it opens up its multifaceted features to those who immerse themselves in it. In this volume—dedicated to lovers of both the midrash and the *Zohar*—I have endeavoured to examine the *Zohar* as a midrashic work, forming part of the long history of aggada and midrash reaching back to the ancient world.

Approaching the *Zohar* as midrash combines two of my primary fields of study—the broad and rich body of aggadic and midrashic literature and the *Zohar* with all its literary qualities and profound religious sensitivities. In the central chapters of this book, I have sought to open twelve windows on its midrashic world, the introduction addressing the conceptual and methodological elements that underpin it and the conclusion outlining some general characteristics and directions for future study.

The fruit of many years of labour, the material first saw the light of day in the Hebrew edition, published by Magnes in 2013. In this English version, I hope to make its insights available to the wider English-speaking world.

The final text also reflects the rewarding and thought-provoking input of a number of colleagues whom I wish to take this occasion to thank (and, of course, absolve from any responsibility for errors or mistakes, which remain my alone). First and foremost, my thanks go to Proprietor of the palace, who planted a love of studying in general and of aggada, midrash, and the *Zohar* in particular, in me, also providing me with the tools and environment in which I could engage in such research. Secondly, I wish to thank my faithful guides through corridors of the palace—my teachers Yehuda Liebes and Moshe Idel, who taught me to read the *Zohar* closely and sensitively with an open mind and intellectual boldness from many and diverse perspectives. A special thanks to Zeev Gries, who not only made me privy to his prodigious store of knowledge but also initiated, encouraged, and helped crystalise my thoughts. Special thanks also to Ronit Meroz and Daniel Matt for their generosity in sharing their yet-unpublished insights with me, giving me access to the most accurate and faithful renderings of the zoharic homilies available to date. I also wish to thank my colleagues in the Department of Jewish Thought at Ben-Gurion University for their community spirit, support, and collaboration, as well as to my students, many of whose ideas are to be found within these pages.

During the years in which I was engaged in writing this book, I made extensive use of the treasures of the Jewish National Library, Jerusalem, receiving greatly-appreciated assistance from its librarians and staff. In particular, I wish to thank the staff of the Scholem Collection, which became my home from home, and the staff of the Institute of Microfilmed Hebrew Manuscripts who were ready with help, guidance, and advice.

I wish to thank the director of Magnes Press, Hai Tzabar, for his initial assistance. The Walter de Gruyter *Studia Judaica* series staff encouraged me to translate the Hebrew edition into English, Sophie Wagenhofer, project editor of Theology & Religious Studies section, in particular contributing towards transforming the idea into reality. Particular thanks go to Liat Keren for her elegant translation.

The English edition was also made possible by the Harry Walsh, Q.C., Career Development Chair in Jewish Law and Morality, the Foundation of the Dean of Humanities and Social Sciences at the University of Ben-Gurion, as well as the Foundation the University's Rector. It also benefitted from the bequest fund of the late Zelig Slutzki. To all these I extend my deep gratitude.

I owe a deep debt of thanks to my beloved family, who have and still fill my life with the light and inspiration so necessary for a life of study and creativity. My thanks to my mother, Sarah Yisraeli, my wife Rivki, and my beloved children for their support, counsel, and help all along the way. In sorrow and yearning, I pay my respects to my late father, Chaim Yisraeli, a multifaceted bibliophile who championed the Hebrew version, encouraging me to publish it as soon as possible. Although he saw its bones taking on flesh, he died before it was published. May his memory be blessed.

I hope the volume will be of interest both to those in the field of midrash and aggada and those whose preoccupied with the *Zohar*, making a modest contribution to promoting the study of the latter from a perspective that to date has remained relatively neglected and spurring others to take up the labour and lend their shoulder to the task of opening up further windows in the palace through which we can glimpse the beloved of our hearts.

Oded Yisraeli
Ben-Gurion University of the Negev, February 2016

Table of Contents

Chapter One: The *Zohar* as Midrash — 1
    Why midrash? — 5
    The *Zohar*'s homiletic methodology — 11

Chapter 2: The Zoharic Homilies: General Outlines — 16

Chapter 3: From the Rabbinic to Zoharic Aggada: Preservation, Reworking, and Alteration — 20

Chapter 4: "The Light Hidden for the Righteous": For Whom is it Reserved? — 33
    "The light reserved for the righteous": The early traditions — 33
    The "hidden light" and the "light of thought" — 37
    The "world to come" and the "future" — 40
    The "hidden light" in the *Zohar* — 43
    The "hidden-present": In the wake of the *Zohar* — 48
    Conclusion — 49

Chapter 5: Adam's Sin: Its Meaning and Essence — 50
    The meaning of Adam's sin: Polemical residues in nascent kabbalistic thought — 51
    "He entered in tranquility and departed in terror": Original sin in the writings of R. Moses de Léon — 57
    "Many accounts": Original sin in the Zohar — 60
    Exegetical tendencies and the exegete — 64
    Conclusion — 65

Chapter 6: Enoch and Elijah: From Angel to Man, Man to Angel — 67
    The ancient traditions about Enoch and Elijah — 67
    Enoch and Elijah's ascents in medieval philosophy — 74
    Elijah's ascent: Nahmanides' view — 77
    Enoch's and Elijah's ascents in the zoharic circle and later works — 79
    Conclusion — 85

Chapter 7: "He failed": The Story of Abraham's Origins — 87
    The zoharic homily: The exegetical context — 87
    The story of Abraham's origins in medieval Jewish literature — 90

The activist approach and its early roots —— 93
The *Zohar*, Maimonides, and *Sefer Yetzira* —— 97
The various versions in the *Zohar* —— 101
The *Zohar*, Philo, and *Genesis Rabbah* —— 103
Conclusion —— 106

Chapter 8: The *Aqeda:* From Test to Experience —— 108
What did God really want? —— 109
The essential view of the *aqeda* and its manifestations in midrash and *piyyut* —— 112
The essentialist approach in Nahmanides commentary on the Torah —— 117
The zoharic aggada: The "completion" of the aqeda —— 119
The zoharic aggada: The *aqeda* as an incense offering —— 121
The *aqeda* as the "binding of *Din*" in early kabbalistic writings and the *Zohar* —— 123
The *aqeda* in the *Zohar*: From theosophic to a personal-existential midrash —— 127
Conclusion —— 132

Chapter 9: The Birthright and the Blessing: Esau's Suppressed Cry —— 134
'That wicked one': Esau as archetype —— 134
The literary roots of the archetypal image —— 140
Esau and Edom in the zoharic myth —— 145
Esau's cry: The wronging of evil and its vengeance —— 149
Conclusion —— 155

Chapter 10: The Exodus and the Liberation of the Kabbalistic Spirit —— 157
From the deliverance of the people to the deliverance of the spirit —— 158
From national enterprise to mythical struggle —— 160
From mythic struggle to personal-spiritual freedom —— 163
Conclusion —— 167

Chapter 11: The War Against Amalek: Human vs. Divine Needs —— 168
"Did Moses' hands wage war?": The *Zohar* and *Roš. Haš.* 3:7 —— 168
The war against Amalek: A double and triple war —— 175
Moses' hands and Amalek's defeat —— 178
Conclusion —— 185

Chapter 12: Nadab and Abihu's Sin as a "Holy Revolt" —— 186
    Early and earlier traditions —— 186
    Nadab and Abihu's sin in the *Zohar* —— 191
    Nadab, Abihu, and Phinehas —— 196
    The meaning of the homily in its historical context —— 199
    Conclusion —— 201

Chapter 13: "But Amongst the Nations of the World There Did Arise One Like Moses": Moses and Balaam —— 202
    Prophet or diviner: From the ancient aggadah to the early Kabbalah —— 203
    Moses and Balaam: An aggadic tradition and its meaning —— 207
    Balaam's and Moses' prophecies in the *Zohar* and R. Moses de Léon's Writings —— 209
    Criticism of the dualist view of prophecy —— 215
    The dualistic view of prophecy: Exegetical and ideological aspects —— 218
    Conclusion —— 220

Chapter 14: "Then Moses, the Servant of the Lord, Died There": Did Moses Really Die? —— 222
    Moses' death in the pre-zoharic literature —— 223
    "Death by a kiss" —— 226
    Moses' death in the *Zohar* —— 228
    The relationship between the *Zohar* and the early aggada —— 235
    Moses' light and soul in the *Tiqunim* literature —— 239
    Conclusion —— 243

Chapter 15: Elijah the Zealot —— 244
    Elijah's origin and identity —— 245
    Zeal and Elijah in rabbinic thought —— 250
    Elijah and Phinehas in the zoharic tradition —— 254
    Elijah's zeal: Between earth and heaven —— 256
    Conclusion —— 259

Epilogue —— 261

Bibliography —— 266

Chapters first published elsewhere —— 283

Index of Zoharic Sources —— 284

Index of subjects —— 286

Index of persons —— 289

Chapter 1:
The *Zohar* as Midrash

First appearing in Spanish Catalonia at the end of the thirteenth century, the *Zohar* has become one of the most important and revered books in the Jewish canon. Forming one of the central pillars of kabbalistic thought, it has left a deep imprint on Jewish texts, customs, and halakhah, its extensive circulation witnessing to its acceptance across broad sectors of the Jewish world. Its various sections were first published during the second half of the sixteenth century, subsequently seeing dozens of further editions.[1]

Contra the prevalent, traditional opinion that ascribes the *Zohar* to the second-century Sage R. Simeon bar Jochai, scholars and sages over the generations have demonstrated that its central sections were in fact penned at the end of the thirteenth and beginning of the fourteenth century.[2] The circumstances of its composition and identity of its author(s) nonetheless remain obscure. The dominant scholarly view up until the 1980s is represented by Gershom Scholem who, despite early uncertainty, ultimately concluded that it should be attributed (with the exception of *Raya mehemna* and *Tiquney zohar*) to the kabbalist R. Moses de Leon (Scholem, 1941).[3] This was challenged by Yehuda Liebes in 1988 in an article in which, based on a close examination of parallels and comparison of the expositions belonging to the zoharic corpus with those cited in the works of contemporary Castilian mystics—such as R. Joseph Gikatilla, R. Joseph of Shushan, R. David ben Judah Hehasid, and, of course, R. Moses de Leon—he argued that: "The *Zohar* is the fruit of a whole group that together dealt with the Kabbalah on the basis of a common tradition and ancient texts" (1988: 5). This broader perspective "breaks the bounds of the *Zohar*'s pages," admitting a far wider corpus into what we know as the "zoharic literature."

---

[1] *Sefer tiquney zohar* was published in Mantua in 1558. *Sefer ha-zohar al-ha-torah* was also published, in three volumes, in Mantua in 1558–1560—the edition that subsequently became the basis of all those that followed. Another edition of *Sefer ha-zohar al ha-torah* was published in Cremona in 1559–1560. *Sefer zohar chadash* was first published in Salonica in 1597. For the first printed editions of the *Zohar*, see Tishby and Lachower (1989), 97–99. Unless otherwise noted, quotations follow the Pritzker edition.

[2] For the history of the critique of the traditional view, beginning with R. Elijah del Medigo in the fifteenth century through R. Judah Aryeh of Modena in the seventeenth century and R. Jacob Emden in the eighteenth century, to the modern scholarly opinion of the nineteenth and twentieth centuries, see Tishby and Lachower (1989: 30–55); Huss (2008: 284–358).

[3] For the history of the study of this question up until Scholem and a survey of Scholem's own work in this regard, see Abrams (2010: 264–293).

In the wake of Liebes' argument, Boaz Huss (2008) asserted that the zoharic corpus was formed over a lengthy period, the fourteenth-century mystics having at their disposal diverse collections. The compilation thus process stretched from this early material through to the printing of the book in Mantua, Cremona, and Salonica in the sixteenth century. Ronit Meroz (2001, 2002a, 2006) takes a different direction, positing that the book embodies the literary activity of various—at times rival—groups over several generations through the eleventh to fourteenth centuries, distinct sections being discernible within the book.[4] Addressing the complexity of the compositional process via a study of R. Joseph Angelet, she asserts that three aspects of his work can be determined: he continued and maintained the path of the *Zohar*, he interpreted it, and he authored parts of it (2007: 311). The most innovative approach is that adopted by Daniel Abrams (2010: 224–428), who disputes the notion of the *Zohar* as a "book" in the modern historical sense of the term, contending that the zoharic corpus is rather the fruit of a "textual community"—an artifact that represents a series of treatments of an idea (or systems of ideas) by diverse figures not necessarily familiar with one another or individually with the whole text (ibid: 369). Although the notion of a group of authors remains controversial, it has now become prevalent, forming the underlying premise of the current contribution.

The *Zohar* has attracted the interest of mystics and scholars alike. The former have generally focused on its kabbalistic content, the latter also addressing historical-bibliographical questions—the circumstances of its composition, the identity of its author(s), the relationship between its various sections, its language and canonical status, etc. Very few have examined its literary nature and genre. This field only began to burgeon during the last decades of the twentieth century, Daniel Abrams (2003), Michal Oron (1986, 1989a, 1994), Moshe Idel, Shifra Asulin (2006), Amos Goldreich (1994), Pinchas Giller (2001), Arthur Green, Boaz Huss (2008), Melila Hellner-Eshed (2009), Joel Hacker, Elliot Wolfson (1986, 1988b, 1988c, 1993a), Naomi Tene (1986), Oded Yisraeli (2005), Yehuda Liebes (1993d, 1994, 1995, 2000), Mati Meged (1963), Dorit Cohen Aloro (1987), Daniel Matt (1989), Ronit Meroz (2001, 2002a, 2006), Haviva Pedaya, Mordechai Pachter (1989) and others all investigating the literary expressions of the zoharic myth and the poetic features of the framing story.

This volume focuses on a specific aspect of this discipline—namely, the zoharic aggadah. The aggadic tradition stretches back to rabbinic midrashim if not the biblical text itself, constituting an exegesis of the biblical narrative by way of

---

4 For an extensive discussion of these issues, see Meroz (forthcoming).

interpretation, expansion, and elaboration.⁵ While the rabbinic aggadah have been extensively studied, however, those in the *Zohar* have largely escaped scholarly attention to date.⁶ I hope herein to open a window on the book from a defined and delimited perspective that is nevertheless significant and important. Rather than discussing the poetic features of the zoharic aggada or its cultural links in medieval Spain I wish to examine the links between the zoharic aggada and the ancient talmudic-midrashic aggada and their kabbalistic exegesis during the Middle Ages. I shall analyze a selection of aggadot that play a major role in the *Zohar*, reading each of the zoharic passages in light of its ancient sources and discussing the affinities and disparities that developed as the aggada found its way into the zoharic corpus.⁷

The distinctive way in which aggadic stories are reworked in the *Zohar* reflects in great part the vicissitudes the aggadic tradition experienced across the centuries and the changes that occurred within it prior to the thirteenth

---

5 For "inner-biblical interpretation, see Fishbane (1985: 399–400); Zakovitch (2009: 15–20); Menn (2003).

6 See Frankel (1991: 287–321); Levinson (2005: 6–27 and the bibliography cited therein). One of the few exceptions is Segal (1992), who primarily raises preliminary questions. For a more specific aspect, see Gruenwald (1989). Yehuda Liebes has examined the figures of Abraham and Moses in his discussion of other issues (2000: 74–75; 2007b: 2656–264).

7 Nineteenth- and early-twentieth-century aggada scholars who laid the foundations of the modern field failed to recognize the zoharic aggada as part of the aggadic corpus. While Zunz (1974: 189–192), for example, devoted space to kabbalistic writing and the *Zohar*, he did so merely in order to demonstrate that this literature "took the place to a certain extent of the aggada" (p. 192). In their monumental *Book of Legends*, Bialik and Rawnitzki (1948) brought no examples from the *Zohar*. While they cite late midrashim, such as *Shocher Tov*, *Midrash Proverbs*, and *Midrash Samuel*, in their list of literary sources in the introduction, even apologizing for not including medieval works of the ilk of *Sefer Hayashar*, *Josippon*, and *Sefer ma'asiyyot le'rabbeinu nissim*, they make no mention of the *Zohar*. Joseph Heinemann followed a similar path, quoting from *Sefer Hayashar* and even *Midrash Hagadol* but not from the *Zohar*. The attitude of such scholars towards the zoharic aggada appears to reflect their well-known reservations towards Kabbalah in general. One of the few exceptions to this rule was Ginzberg, who included material from the *Zohar* in his *Legends of the Jews*: "The works of the older Kabbalah are likewise treasuries of quotations from lost Midrashim, and it was among the Kabbalists, and later among the Hasidim, that new legends arose. The literatures produced in these two circles are therefore of great importance for the present purpose" (2003: 1:XXXI). This view seems to have derived from his folkloristic approach to the study of aggada. In this context, we must also note the collection of folk tales made by Micha Josef Berdyczewski (1939–1945), which also contains material from the *Zohar*. My thanks go to Zeev Gries for bringing this latter fact to my attention.

century.⁸ At the same time, however, the zoharic aggadot betray clear traces of their kabbalistic authors, reflecting the world of the *Zohar* and its compilers. An analysis of the manner in which the aggadic tradition made its way into the zoharic literature in light of its zoharic reworking thus sheds light on the *Zohar*'s authors. The novel and creative way in which the zoharic narrator chose to implant the ancient story into the zoharic exposition reveals much about his mystical orientation and religious interest, spiritual difficulties, and self-awareness in a Jewish world in which recognition of the status of the Kabbalah and its practitioners was far from self-evident.⁹ Although a long road stretches ahead of us before we shall be able to draw solid historical conclusions—facing several serious methodological issues on the way—there is no doubt that identification of subterranean streams in the zoharic exposition will help to illuminate the figure who stands behind it. In a scholarly context in which the identity of the zoharic authors remains far from clear, this constitutes a valuable tool.

In order to understand the "expanded biblical story" in the *Zohar*, let us first avail ourselves of the definition of aggada as a "homiletic story"—i.e., a narrative whose starting point lies in a scriptural text.¹⁰ This definition requires examination not only of the character of the story but also of the nature and significance of the homiletic method.¹¹ The introductory chapters herein will thus be devoted to a theoretical analysis of the homily and the elements of the homiletical story in the *Zohar*. The discussion will focus firstly on the midrashic writing in the *Zohar* and its features, then turning to the aggadic story itself and the various ways in which the blending of tradition and creativity find expression in the zoharic aggada. Finally, we shall address the validity of the historical deductions that may be drawn from the literary aspects elucidated by the analysis.

---

8 The history of the rabbinic midrashim within the talmudic-midrashic corpus has been extensively investigated, most prominently by Isaac Heinemann (1974), to whose methodology I am greatly indebted herein.
9 For the history of the acceptance of the *Zohar* within medieval Judaism and subsequent generations, see Huss (2008).
10 "The homiletic story is both homily and story. As homily, its starting point lies in the biblical text—a word, statement, verse, or passage—to which new meaning it attributes new meaning. As story, it contains characters, a plot, and meaning" (Meir, 1987: 63). For the homiletical story as a genre, see ibid: 66–70; Frankel (1991: 1:287–321); Levinson (2005: 6–27).
11 I am using the terms "aggada" and "midrash" in the sense they customarily bear in the study of aggada: aggada is a non-halakhic utterance, midrash the exegesis of a biblical passage that imbues the text with new meaning: see Frankel (1991: 1: 11–16).

Why midrash?

The midrashic nature of the homiletical story in the *Zohar* and its meaning forms part of a broader issue—namely, midrashic writing as a whole in the book. On the one hand, the *Zohar* is the only medieval text—with the possible exception of *Sefer Habahir*—written in midrashic style. On the other, it is also the only midrash—again with the possible exception of *Sefer Habahir*—whose content is kabbalistic. We must therefore ask why the zoharic authors chose precisely this genre.¹²

This question is sharpened by the fact that during this period methods of biblical exegesis—in particular of the *pshat* (literal meaning)—were developing in Western Europe that gradually replaced the midrashic discourse.¹³ When the Kabbalah emerged in Provenance and Spain—at the end of the twelfth and during the thirteenth century—midrashic texts were thus in serious decline, being replaced by the *yalqut* anthologies—*Yalqut Shimʿoni* in Ashkenaz and *Midrash Hagadol* in Yemen.¹⁴ The spirit that heralded the ending of this period was also exemplified in the work of such mystics as R. Ezra, R. Azriel, and R. Todros Abulafia who, like others amongst their contemporaries, helped create the genre of talmudic aggadot exegesis.¹⁵ Midrashic writing thus already appears to have been largely regarded as a "closed" field from which one could not deviate— nor add. At the same time, mystics and kabbalists were increasingly adopting

---

12 The midrashic character of *Sefer Habahir* has yet to be fully investigated and in my opinion is not self-evident: see Scholem (1948: 102–118); Dan (1986; 1997: 87–107). Its midrashic quality nonetheless differs from that of the *Zohar*, which is far fuller, riper, and rooted. For the view that the *Zohar* comprises the first (and only) medieval kabbalistic midrashic text, see also Idel (1993: 54–55; 2008: 330–331); Liebes, (2001: 7). I hope to address the revolution that occurred in medieval kabbalistic mysticism when the focus of attention shifted from the visual experience of the temple/palace, *pardes*, and garden in the upper realms to the secret hidden and concealed within the Torah. This new trend helps to explain why Simeon bar Jochai was chosen as the *Zohar*'s principal protagonist rather than the classical heroes of ancient and talmudic mysticism and *hekhalot* literature—R. Akiba, R. Ishmael, R. Nechunia b. Haqana, etc. Here, I shall address not only the attentiveness to the biblical text but also the specific midrashic method adopted whereby the zoharic homily demonstrates its interest in the biblical passage under discussion.
13 See Zunz (1974: 176–177); Grossman (2001: 462–468); Touitou (2003: 11–47); Mack (2010: 97). For the kabbalistic contexts of these processes, see Pedaya (2003: 47–77).
14 For the distinctive nature of this genre, see Zunz (1974: 144–150); Frankel (1991: 841–844); Elboim (2004).
15 For the literary genre of aggadic exegesis in the period under discussion and kabbalistic aggadic exegesis in particular, see Elboim (2000: 13–251). For the early kabbalists' attitude towards aggada, see Wolfson (1989b: 154 n. 143, 156–157 and the bibliography cited therein).

radical, non-semantic exegetical methods (exchanging/combining letters, etc.).[16] The revival of midrashic writing at the height of a supremely "a-midrashic" period thus poses a conundrum. The burst of Spanish and Provençal Jewish creativity cannot help explain the emergence of a type of literature that had long since become passé. Whence, then, did this cultural renaissance (or regression, depending on one's point of view) develop?[17] The idea of mere cultural imitation—pseudepigraphy—seems too easy and facile, the literary quality of the zoharic midrash and the poetic heights it reaches reflecting profound midrashic motivations and an authentic identification with the genre.[18]

I suggest that the *Zohar*'s authors choice of midrash should be understood in light of the exegetical rejuvenation that occurred in the thirteenth century—a period of great significance in the history of the Jewish scriptural exegesis. The rise in status of the *pshat* posed a complex hermeneutic challenge to exegetes, philosophers, and mystics alike—namely, how to adopt broad, traditional, philosophical, or kabbalistic ideas without compromising the accepted literal meaning of the text. As early as Maimonides' *Guide for the Perplexed*, scholars had attempted to deal with this problem, the Rambam formulating it in his now well-known dictum (on the basis of Prov 25:11: "A word fitly spoken is like apples of gold in vessels of silver"): "Now see how marvellously this dictum describes a well-constructed parable. For he says that in a saying that has two meanings—he means an external and an internal one—the external meaning ought to be as beautiful as silver, while its internal meaning ought to be more beautiful than the external one, the former being in comparison to the latter as gold is to silver" (p. 12 [7a]).

The "apples of gold" are philosophical truths—visible to the eye but only discernible by those capable of observing and understanding them. This hermeneutic strategy was subsequently adopted by the kabbalists, including R. Moses de Leon and R. Joseph Gikatilla.[19] Maimonides not providing any further methodo-

---

16 For these exegetical methods, see Idel (2008: 354–384).
17 Pedaya regards the innovation as lying precisely in kabbalistic exegesis, perceiving the zoharic midrash as a "traditional model": "In terms of the types of writing associated with mysticism, we may say that the *Zohar* chose a traditional model—that of revelation ... Nahmanides, in contrast, turned towards presenting mysticism via providing an 'exegesis' of the Torah ... this approach places him in contexts that may be identified precisely as innovative" (2003: 74). In my opinion, however, as long as a historical continuum of midrashic-mystical writing has yet to proved, the *Zohar*'s resumption of this genre—however "traditional" it may be—remains unexplained.
18 See, for example, Dan (1986: 138).
19 See Moses de Leon (n.d.; 1993: 64–65); Joseph Gikatilla (1989: 3a). For the origins of this view amongst the thirteenth-century kabbalists, see Tishby (1989: 2:363–365); Scholem

logical insights beyond this theoretical idea, however—neglecting to explain precise how the "apples of gold" are to be identified with the "vessels of silver"—he appears to have regarded the way to decipher the secrets of the Torah (if indeed such existed) as part of the secret itself. It could therefore only be grasped by those competent to do so.

One of the early Spanish kabbalists—Nahmanides—espoused a similar hermeneutic paradigm, proposing a method for revealing its secrets in his commentaries on the Torah. According to this methodological scheme, Scripture must be read in a dual sense: "Know that in the way of the truth Scripture tells about the lower creatures and alludes to the higher ones" (to Gen 1:1; cf. on 3:22). Perhaps the earliest kabbalistic-hermeneutical system, this method enables him to render difficult verses both literally and "by way of the truth." In this way, the kabbalist can understand both the *pshat* of the biblical text and the secret it contains.[20]

The zoharic adoption of midrash seems to be a continuation and development of Nahmanides' hermeneutic method.[21] While Nahmanides himself regarded the straightforward meaning of Scripture as a simile for transcendent metaphysical entities, however, the *Zohar* posits the existence of far more complex concealed sphere. In contrast to the theosophical picture we find in Nahmanides' largely static kabbalah, the *Zohar* presents us with a dynamic, vigorous version, torn between left and right and engaged in a dramatic struggle between the pure and impure, the poem of creativity and the catastrophe of destruction.[22] Rather than sufficing with a "painting" or paradigmatic picture, the *Zohar* seeks to discover a concrete plot beyond the text.[23] In order to reveal this within the

---

(1976a: 52–55); Idel (1981); Yisraeli (2005: 210–213). This trend can be seen as continuing in the *Zohar* and its surroundings in the first appearances of the "fourfold system," according to which the Torah contains four layers of meaning: see Yisraeli (2005: 213–215). The most well known version of this methodology is that of PaRDeS–*pshat*, *remez*, *drash*, and *sod*. The *Zohar* itself, however, also contains methods that relate to another aspect of the layers of meaning in the Torah. Thus, for example, in one of its most well-known expositions (3, 152a), it defines the biblical narratives (the most accessible, exterior stratum), the commandments, the secrets, and the secret of secrets respectively as the clothing in which the Torah is garbed, its body, its soul, and its inmost soul.

20 For the "dual reading" system and "similes," see Yisraeli (2010: 279–286 and the bibliography cited therein).
21 The zoharic hermeneutic may also be viewed, of course, not only as a continuation of Nahmanides' method but also as a alternative to it—a reflection of the power struggle between the two Spanish kabbalistic centres: see Huss (2008: 11–83).
22 This aspect of the zoharic exposition was identified early on by Idel (1990a: 235–236).
23 This disparity between Nahmanides and the *Zohar* can also be seen, for example, via a comparison of the way in which each describes the tree of life in the Garden of Eden: see Yisraeli

biblical text—to "set in motion" the static portrait of the divine world—its authors required a far more complex method than "similes." They found it in midrash—a more open, flexible, and "freer" approach than Nahmanides' hermeneutic model.

Heinemann defines the blank aspect of the midrashic system as the eradication of the Logos and the dissolution of sentences into single words in order to link them in a different order—i.e., the breakdown of the biblical verse into atomic units while stripping them of their semantic meaning, charging them with new significance, and reassembling them.[24] While this "surgical" delineation also corresponds in striking fashion to the expositional act carried out in the *Zohar*, here the explication crafts the elements of the verse—its "atomic units"—into a full, new kabbalistic "story." The kabbalistic midrash thus seeks to go behind the biblical texts, in varying levels of resolution, to reach the upper, turbulent dramas of the divine world.

The midrashic writing of the *Zohar* must also be examined from another perspective. Much of the study of the classic midrash is devoted to the question of the character of the midrashic consciousness. Here, we are faced with the question of its driving force: is midrash primarily interested in exegeting the biblical text and providing answers to hermeneutic problems or does it merely seek the idea—the religious sentiment—the verse thus simply serving as a rhetorical-didactic means for conveying this thought?[25] Scholars are divided over this issue. Despite their essential differences, both Isaac Heinemann (1974: 9–11) and Joseph Heinemann (1993: 4–6) regarded the midrashic act as one of indoctrination—a medium for bequeathing cognitive content. Frankel (1991: 287–295) and Levinson (2005), on the other hand, view it as the fruit of creative activity within the tension between textual exegesis and the cultural values within which the latter is conducted: "The goal [of the exegetical reading] is to solve problems that arise from the encounter between two distinct semantic systems: the biblical text and rabbinic culture. These problems are both exegetic and ideological" (Levinson, 2005 :37). Boyarin takes another approach, perceiving midrash to be a "portrayal of the reality which the rabbis perceived in the Bible

---

(2010: 279–288). R. Moses de Leon's writings (1996: 80) also betray Nahmanides' influence: see Yisraeli (2010: 285–286 and n. 61).

24 Heinemann (1974: 109). Cf. Frankel: "The verse is in its very essence a complex entity—i.e., it consists of different parts that are not only juxtaposed but also constructed within one another, each influencing the other. Even the shortest verse can be dissected into its elements to reveal their relationship. The exposition of the verse thus generally yields a new meaning in line with its complexity" (1991: 139).

25 For a survey of the various views, see Levinson (2005: 29–59); Boyarin (1994: 1–19).

through their ideologically colored eyeglasses ... a development ... of the intratextual interpretive strategies which the Bible itself manifests" in an attempt to "understand how a committed reading of the holy and authoritative text works in the rabbinic culture" (1994: 15).²⁶

The question also arises in relation to the biblical aggadot in the *Zohar:* do they represent the endeavour to comprehend the biblical text in a world saturated by a kabbalistic consciousness—or a calculated bid to convey kabbalistic truth in the garb of the ancient midrashic form?²⁷ In a certain sense, we are standing on firmer ground here, the *Zohar*—in contrast to rabbinic literature—being quite frank about this issue. On a number of occasions, it elaborates on the nature of the interpretive act via conceptual statements or *ars poetica* expressions, which provide an answer as to why its authors chose the midrashic genre. The most well-developed and overt delineation of the *Zohar*'s interpretive consciousness occurs in the section known as *Saba de-mishpatim*.²⁸ This intersperses various hermeneutic insights into its text (Yisraeli: 226–231). One of these—which I have called "active hermeneutics"—regards exegesis as way of revealing and making manifest. According to this view, the secret is hidden in the Torah's "garb," those who are "full-sighted" being responsible for "casting their gaze" upon it and grasping it in the moment of grace in which it flashes for an instant before vanishing again.²⁹

Alongside this exegetical manifesto the author also sets another, more far-reaching approach. This "hermeneutics of love" (ibid: 231–246) makes use of the well-known parable of the maiden at the window, which likens the secret concealed in the Torah to a beloved imprisoned within a palace—the Torah in which the secret is buried. The one who studies the Torah encircles the palace, seeking a glimpse of his beloved, who hides behind its walls so as only to be seen by her beloved. She thus only allows herself to be seen for a brief moment—the blink of an eye—by him alone. In this way only he, whose "loins of

---

26 Although Boyarin specifically discusses the midrash in the *Mekilta* herein, his observations in this regard appear to represent his view of midrash in general: see ibid: 11–19.
27 This issue was addressed early on by Scholem, who wondered whether "the biblical text serves as the impetus for the mystical interpretation or whether the latter is in fact merely only an artificial means whereby new ideas, completely dissociated from Scripture, can be introduced into it or developed out of it" (1976a: 37). For the question of the "high" purpose of hermeneutic activity—i.e., why the kabbalist engages in biblical exposition—see Idel (cf. 1990a: 200–249). My interest here lies rather in the way in which the zoharic author practices his craft.
28 See Yisraeli (2005: 191–266).
29 As I have demonstrated therein, although this hermeneutical method exhibits strikingly Maimonidean features, it nonetheless differs widely in several respects from the hermeneutics of the *Guide*.

the heart and soul follow her," can drink in the fleeting image she presents to him.

Beyond the innovative move of basing the interpretive act on love rather than wisdom, as in Aristotelian circles, the parable also contains another exceptional and paradoxical insight into the nature of the exegetical-homiletic act. As I have shown (ibid), the beloved can only be someone who already knows and is familiar with the secret hidden in the palace: "But when she reveals herself from her sheath and quickly hides, she does so only for those who know and recognize her" (*Zohar*, 2, 99a). The exegete who seeks the secret must thus already be aware of it before he sets out to find it. His desire lies not in the revelation or discovery of something new but in the renewed and refreshing encounter with an old, familiar truth. Just as the lover only longs for his beloved because he already knows and recognizes her, so the homilist only finds in the Torah truths which he has long held dear.

The parable of the maiden at the window exemplifies a profound, authentic reflective consciousness in relation to the kabbalistic exegetical act. The homilist is well aware of the fact—noting it expressly at the outset—that when he engages in a kabbalistic reading of the Torah he already knows his goal. The fruit of the homiletical act already being laid before him, his focus lies upon grasping it from another angle as he studies a new verse, thereby making a new "breach" in the fortified wall of the palace of the Torah.

The challenge faced by the biblical exegete, for whom both the starting point and goal are clear, is to draw a homiletical line between the two. Within this hermeneutic link, the drama of the exegetical act lies not in the theosophical innovation but in the route that led to it. Such a consciousness is heavily dependent upon the varied exegetical options that only the midrashic "tool box" can offer. Only the variation embedded within the homiletic method can enable the lover to see his beloved's face and satisfy the longings of his heart. The homiletic medium was thus almost the only option available.

Use of the parable of the maiden at the window to understand the zoharic midrash must be made with great caution, both because (as noted above) the treatise itself presents alternative hermeneutic models, and because (as I have shown in a previous volume) the *Saba de-mishpatim* section represents a relatively later stratum. Belonging to the transitional stage between the body of the *Zohar* and the *tiqunim*, it thus does not necessarily represent the early spirit of the work.[30] This may nonetheless constitute at the very least a trace of the zoharic "unconscious" that characterizes other parts of the books.

---

30 See Yisraeli (2005: 271–272).

The *Zohar*'s homiletic methodology

Analysis of the zoharic homily requires a discussion of the nature of its homiletic deductions, the tools with which it forms and develops the homily, the channels through which it flows, and the status of the biblical text. These questions may be addressed in both practical and conceptual terms. The first (lower) level relates to the homiletic techniques: what "tool box" do the homiletic expositions use, do they conform to the rules of the rabbinic homily, are they regarded as a consistent, systematic method or do they ignore the rules of biblical exegesis?

This subject requiring examination in and of itself, it lies beyond my present scope.[31] Even if the *Zohar* does not always conform to the rules of the halakhic midrash or ancient aggada, however, its various authors generally take great care not to stray from the classic homiletic methodology. Although stretched to breaking point, the midrashic method is still preserved. Thus, for example, we find the morphological technique of the school of R. Akiba, of which the *Zohar* great use, at times turning it into a broad and many-branched "alphabetic midrash." The ancient talmudic practice of *heqesh* (juxtaposition) and free association—frequently constructed on the basis of syntax or assonance—also serve the *Zohar* on numerous occasions. Overall, the homily is constructed in a way that closely resembles that of the rabbinic homily—a traditional *petichta* opening, the raising of the key question that creates the tension, linkage and discussions generated between homilies via substantive or associative links, and the circular "closure" by means of joining up again with the starting point.[32] The techniques characteristic of the central sections of the *Zohar* can thus be understood as representing a "soft," dynamic conservative approach.[33]

---

[31] See Gruenwald (1989). In this context, we should note the affinities between the zoharic literature and the literary world of Hasidei Ashkenaz and the possible influence of the latter on the *Zohar*. For the homiletic practices of Hasidei Ashkenaz, see Dan (1997: 87–107). The fact that no trace of most of their "gates of wisdom" appears in the *Zohar*, however, suggests that they did not penetrate the *Zohar* from this source.

[32] This rule does not apply, of course, to the *Tiquney zohar*, the latest stratum of the zoharic corpus, which deviates not only from conventional kabbalistic homiletic rules but also from all methodological frameworks. For the distinctively associative nature of the homily in *Tiquney zohar*, see Tishby and Lachower (1989: 3:1089–1090); Goldreich (2010a: 56–64). As I have discussed elsewhere (2005: 219–226, 255–259), this trend is already evident in *Saba de-mishpatim*, which represents the transitional stage between the earlier layers of the *Zohar* and the *tiqunim*.

[33] The *Zohar*'s attitude towards ancient homiletic practices may be compared with its attitude towards the halakhic tradition. While here, too, the *Zohar* reflects a deeply-entrenched conser-

The *Zohar* appears to take a far less conformist approach to the explicit or implicit fundamental midrashic view that the biblical text constitutes the legitimate source and ultimate foundation of all proper religious utterances, however, its religious world being far broader than the parameters covered by the biblical text even on a free, midrashic reading. It does not always possess sufficient virtuosic homiletic power to demonstrate the way in which its desired point is reflected in Scripture, not every idea easily finding its place within the biblical source even when crafted by sophisticated midrashic tools. In such cases, the zoharic homilist frequently spurns the traditional homily, basing his authority on other, less well-known literary forms.

One of the techniques closest to the classical homily is one whose theoretical grounds are laid out in *Saba de-mishpatim*. This makes the radical claim that no search for a "new interpretation of the complexity of the verse" (Frankel, 1991: 139) is necessary, the smallest biblical peg being sufficient to allude to a great secret, even when the latter deviates from the original context.[34] Here, while the verse remains the origin of the idea, its link becomes increasingly tenuous. Thus, for example, the author of *Saba de-mishpatim* understands the verse "you know the heart of an alien" (Exod 23:9) to refer to the soul in which the dead are garbed in the Garden of Eden—irrespective of the fact that this idea has link to the continuation of the verse "for you were aliens in the land of Egypt." Similarly, the phrase "If he takes another wife to himself" (Exod 21:10) is said to transmigration, despite the fact that the reset of the verse—"he shall not diminish the food, clothing, or marital rights of the first wife"—then becomes unintelligible. The context is redundant in the eyes of the *Saba*, serving simply as a sophisticated disguise behind which the secrets alluded to in the first half of the verse can be hidden. This radical hermeneutic method offers completely new exegetical possibilities, allowing the biblical text to be imbued with a vast array of homiletic meanings that go far beyond those accessible via the ancient homiletic methodology.

Despite stamping its imprint on several homilies, this hermeneutical resolution of the gap between the *Zohar*'s rich spiritual world and the narrow biblical scope appears in practice to have been infrequently adduced.[35] Generally speak-

---

vatism, it is also willing to "stretch" the borders of traditional halakhic in order to bring it into line with the kabbalistic worldview: see Yisraeli (2012).

34 For an elaboration of this technique, see Yisraeli (2005: 251–255). For radical exegetical techniques in medieval Kabbalah in general, see Idel (2008: 354–384).

35 This circumstance may be linked to the fact that, as noted above, *Saba de-mishpatim* represents a relatively late stage in the *Zohar*'s compilation, the radical approach not yet being evident in the earlier sections.

ing, the *Zohar* prefers an alternative solution, which may be regarded as an "expansion" of the biblical text. As is well known, the *Zohar* takes no pains to hide the fact that its homilies are based on earlier literary strata. As part of its attempt to highlight the traditional nature of its contents, it thus frequently stresses the ancient and well-known foundation that lies at the heart of its expositions—even if in practice it conceals the identity of its sources. In addition to the canonical texts it adduces, however, it also relies heavily on unknown works that do not represent the familiar talmudic tradition.[36] Various traditions are attributed, for example, to the "Book of Adam," the "Book of Enoch," and the "Book of Solomon."[37]

In other cases, it ascribes sayings or traditions to obscure talmudic figures, who take on mythic proportions in the *Zohar—Sifra de-rav hamnuneh saba, Sifra de-rav yeiva saba*, or *Sifra de-rav yeissa saba*.[38] The willingness to accept esoteric books as sacred is undoubtedly an bold and daring innovative move that significantly impacted the medieval traditional consciousness. The fact that the *Zohar* takes such an unusual step in "expanding" the rabbinic library indicates just how essential an act it regards this as being and the price it was willing to pay for breaking with the homiletical norm of generating new ideas from the narrow and circumscribed (in this context) framework of the biblical and talmudic text. By means of this new esoteric "library," the zoharic homilist ploughs fresh bibliographic furrows, finding for himself expanses that provide him with the prooftexts requisite for those cases in which the biblical text does not meet his needs or echo his truths.

This reliance on obscure books to establish kabbalistic innovations is, in fact, only one of the literary reflections of the motif of mystical revelation as a source of knowledge independent of the canonical text. The claim that the Torah contains secrets that were revealed by Elijah the prophet or other mythical figures recurs throughout all the layers of the book, primarily in the later strata,

---

36 For this "library," see Scholem (1993: 170–171); Tishby and Lachower (1989: 1:81–82); Matt (1989: 126).
37 For the "Book of Adam" and the "Book of Enoch" in the *Zohar*, see Liebes (2011: 66–95). For the "Book of Enoch," see 1, 47b; 3, 7b, 55b (*Sifra de-bey rab yibba saba*). It goes without saying that none of the zoharic quotations resemble the extant text of the apocryphal book.
38 For *Sifra de rav hamenunah saba*, see 1, 245a; 2, 6v, 48a. On occasion, the *Zohar* also cites the *Aggadata de-vei rav hamenunah saba* or *Hanei braitei de-vei rav hamenunah saba*: see 3, 287a, et al. For *Sifra de-rav yeiva saba*, see 1, 47b; 3, 7b, 55b (*Sifra de-aggadata de-bei rav yeiva saba*); et al. For *Sifra de-rav yeissa saba*, see 1, 79a, 226b (*Praqin de-rav yeissa saba*); 2, 76a (*Razey de-rav yeissa saba*); 3, 34b; et al. For the nature of the *Saba* in the *Zohar* and the concrete features of this and similar figures, see Yisraeli (2005: 69–76).

however.³⁹ This phenomenon is not unique or original to the *Zohar*. As Scholem has demonstrated (1976a: 25; 1987: 35–39), in the period close to the *Zohar*'s compilation "Elijah's revelations" had already been attributed to the early kabbalists—R. Abraham b. David of Posquières and his son R. Isaac Sagi-Nahor.⁴⁰ The significance of this tradition lies, of course, in the fact that core of the Kabbalah derives from "Elijah's revelations." In his zoharic guise, R. Simeon bar Jochai also largely represents intuitive insight, numerous kabbalists thus adducing him as the author of the *Zohar*, having received its contents via divine revelation.⁴¹

As we shall see below, the notion of the intuitive reception of the secrets of the Torah is also exemplified in the mythic status ascribed to Moses, primarily in *Raya mehemna* and *Tiquney zohar*. Herein, Moses shines the light of his teaching on the hearts of the sages of the generation rather than explicating biblical verses in order to generate new intuitive Torah insights.⁴² As Wolfson has demonstrated (1988), most of the cases in which the innovations come from Elijah or are presented as having been given to R. Simeon bar Jochai are not detached from the biblical context, the content generally serving as a new and novel way of understanding the verse.⁴³ The fact that the revelation is mystical, however, allows the *Zohar* greater freedom in its homilies on many occasions.⁴⁴

The conventional homiletic material in the *Zohar* thus (usually) conceals a much more dynamic, creative view. The "hanging by a thread" homilies that depend on esoteric sources outside the biblical text and the recognition of mystical-intuitive revelations of various types as legitimate sources of esoteric knowledge are characteristic of the *Zohar*'s homiletics, laying the foundation for its "manoeuvring space" and allowing it a creativity and innovativeness that go far be-

---

39 In addition to Rab hamenunah, Rav Yeiva, and Rav Yeissa, anonymous personages such as Saba, Tayah, and Yenuqa also appear, frequently being presented as other-worldly figures.
40 For Elijah's revelations in the early kabbalistic period, see Scholem (1987: 238–243). For the status of revelation in the *Zohar*, see Wolfson (1988). For revelation as one of the sources of authority in the history of religions, alongside scriptural exegesis and tradition, see Baine Harris (1976: 135).
41 See Huss (2008: 66–71, 78–81). For the possibility that the *Zohar* or the *tiquney* literature were penned via autonomous writing or "in the name of the writer," see Goldreich (2010a: 43–94. For other magical techniques for acquiring knowledge in the ancient and medieval worlds, see Harari (2005).
42 See below, Chapter 14.
43 For a broad analysis of the affinities between revelation and exegesis in the *Zohar*, see Wolfson (1988).
44 Although this phenomenon is most prominent, of course, in the *tiquney* literature, it also occurs in the earlier strata, such as the *idrot*.

yond the anchorage provided by the biblical text, frequently even flatly contradicting its plain meaning.[45]

The zoharic midrash exemplifies its authors' virtuosic capacity to engender the new from within the traditional and to represent the book's contents as forming an additional link in the chain of Jewish homiletics. In the following chapter, I shall examine this tension as it finds expression in various historical and methodological aspects. The remaining chapters will focus on particular homilies on selected biblical texts, examining the *Zohar*'s distinctive method and contrasting it with the early midrash. I hope that these contributions, and the book as a whole, will shed greater light on the *Zohar* and its study, first and foremost in relation to its unique and elusive spirit.

---

[45] For the features of zoharic creativity, see Liebes (1994); Hellner-Eshed (2009); Yisraeli (2005: 260–266 and the bibliography cited therein).

Chapter 2:
The Zoharic Homilies: General Outlines

As with the methodological aspects of the zoharic homilies, their "high" literary features also tend to seek to maintain continuity with the ancient homiletic form on the one hand and diverge strikingly in terms of religious context on the other. While zoharic homily initially adopts the literary style of the classic homily, it then broadens its horizons and climbs to other heights.

As is well known, the fundamental goal of the talmudic-midrashic homily is to "fill in the gaps" in the biblical story. Levinson defines these as "the silences in the text that must be filled in by the reader in order to created optimal coherence and meaning" (2005: 44). Rabbinic midrashim seek to "get these silence to talk," filling them in with biblical aggadic material.[1] Thus, for example, the early aggadic midrash displays great interest in what is left out of the account of the *aqeda*, the resulting story explaining the precise circumstances and motives behind the three-day journey.[2] Hereby, the inner thoughts and feeling of the two protagonists, the difficulties they encounter, and the way in which Satan attempts to prevent the trial from taking place are revealed. The narrative of Abraham's origins is also explicated in such a way as to solve the riddle of why he was the person whom God chose—a question the biblical text leaves unanswered.[3]

The aggadic story in the *Zohar* likewise constructs itself around the gaps in the biblical text and the attempt to fill them in. On occasion, its subjection of the literal meaning of a passage to in-depth scrutiny brings to light additional gaps and difficulties in the biblical account beyond those addressed in rabbinic literature. The way in which it chooses to fill in the gaps and rework the biblical material is completely different, however. While in classic aggada the story is customarily of a real, religious, or ethical nature, the zoharic homily explicates the biblical plot in theosophical, mythological, and mystical terms, exemplifying the new epistemological horizon the kabbalistic world introduces and the literary trend of anchoring kabbalistic truths in the biblical plot. The *Zohar* in effect regards Scripture as a prism or mirror (*aspeklaria*) through which a view of the kabbalistic universe may be glimpsed. Here, the *aqeda* is not merely an incident involving Abraham and Isaac but also a drama played out in the divine world

---

1 See Levinson (2005: 44–58) and the bibliography cited therein.
2 See below, chapter 8.
3 See below, chapter 7.

between God's attributes of mercy (represented by Abraham) and judgment (represented by Isaac).[4] In similar fashion, Abraham's journey to Canaan is not merely a chronicle of clan wanderings or a national epic but the tale of his mystical search for the *Shekhina*—the latter representing (the heavenly) Eretz Israel in the *Zohar*.[5]

The theosophical and mystical trends of the zoharic homily fall into three modes—the mythical-symbolic, the mythical-historical, and the psychological-existential.[6] The first model regards the human-historical biblical plot as reflecting another, higher, metaphysical plot populated by the upper theosophic entities, the *sefirot* and *sitra achra* lying at its centre. Thus, for example, the twisting plot of Judah and Tamar is interpreted as representing the mythical relationship between the Holy One (*Tiferet*)—and the bride (*Malkut*).[7] Joseph's demand that Benjamin remain hostage when his brothers return home to bring Jacob to Egypt—which is prefaced by the prefatory statement: "Then Judah went up to him" (Gen 44:18)—is portrayed in the *Zohar* as constituting an ideal portrait of the union of *Yesod* (represented by Joseph) and *Malkut* (represented by Judah) (*Zohar* 1, 208a–b). The account of Eve's creation in Genesis is similarly shrouded in the Idrot literature in mythical guise and interpreted as the "secret of the detachment" of the female from the male in the divine world (*Zohar* 3, 142b–143a [*Idra rabbah*]).

The mythical-historical model adduces a plot that involves both the upper and lowers realms, preserving the biblical protagonists' human-historical nature but transferring to the divine sphere, the shift in location changing the way they act. Aggadot of this type blur and obscure the gap between the real and theosophic spheres, human protagonists acting in the metaphysical world. This model has two sub-types—the theurgic-magical and the mystical. In the first, the biblical figure's involvement in the theosophical drama is exemplified by theurgic influence—in the repairing or corrupting of the upper realms. Thus, for example, Adam's sin in the Garden of Eden is understood in the *Zohar* as "cutting down the shoots," the tree from whose fruit he ate not (only) being a real tree

---

4 See below, chapter 8.
5 See below, chapter 7.
6 The question of the nature of the symbol in theosophical Kabbalah in general and the *Zohar* in particular falls beyond our presents scope. For a summary of the various views regarding this issue and a discussion of its diverse aspects, see Idel (2008: 385–439). For the distinction between symbol and allegory and the kabbalistic use of the latter, see Huss (1996: 158–159).
7 *Zohar* 3, 71b–72b. At various points in this homily, Tamar—a historical-human figure—appears to act as she does within the family, in line with the goal of influencing the upper theosophic plot. This move brings the homily closer to the mythical-historical model (see below).

but also that of the *sefirot*.⁸ Jacob's cheating of Esau out of his birthright similarly symbolizes the removal of the *sitra achra*'s dominance over the *sefirot*, gained in the wake of Adam's sin.⁹ Moses' withdrawal from his wife is likewise linked to his need henceforth to become one with the *Shekhina*.¹⁰ In the mystical model, the biblical protagonist pursues revelation and knowledge of the divine realm—or union with the sefiric divine entities. Abraham's journey to Canaan is regarded as an attempt to ascend the ladder of the *sefirot* in order transcend his human status—apparently to reach the upper *sefira* of *Hesed*.¹¹ His descent into Egypt correspondingly symbolizes his familiarity with the *sitra achra*—a necessary stage of mystical ascension.¹² Similarly, Isaac's digging of the wells represents his link with the *sefirot* (the wells) so that he can achieve the proper "full faith." The bread in the Exodus is likewise understood as reflecting the Israelites' ascension from their association with leaven (symbolizing the *sitra achra*) to matza—i.e., *Malkut*—and thence to manna, the "heavenly bread" (*Tiferet*).¹³ In all these cases, none of the protagonists of the plot shed their historical personages. In contrast to the stories of the mythical-symbolic type, Abraham plays himself, his activities being transferred to another realm and context, however.

While the first model focuses its attention on the upper divine realm and the second combines the mythic/real and divine/human, the third—the psychological-existential—is interested in the field of human relationships: the protagonist's mental state, his tensions, storms, and psychological dramas. These are interpreted on the basis of the subjective affinity between the human figures and upper Sefirot. Isaac's baffling love for Esau is thus explained as due to their innate psychic kinship, "each species loving its own" (1, 137b). Their kindred feeling is embedded in the well-known affinity between *Din* and the *sitra achra*. It thus comes as no surprise that Isaac's soul, hewn from the attribute of judgment, goes out to Esau, whose soul derives from the dark reaches of the "dross of

---

8 Cf. *Zohar* 1, 237a. For the roots of this interpretation, the traditions associated with it, and their affinities, see below, chapter 5.
9 Cf. *Zohar* 1, 35b. Another feature of zoharic aggada is evident in this homily, namely, the recurrent motif of twins. Jacob represents Adam here, Esau the serpent. Jacob's deception is thus a righting of the early wrong brought about by the serpent.
10 Cf. *Zohar* 1, 148a. It is not always possible to distinguish between the real and symbolic/mythic representations. Moses, for example, can appear in the very same homily as a historical-human figure and a mythic personage alike. For the relationship between symbol and myth in the *Zohar* and Moses in this context, see Liebes (1995). The theurgic-magical and mystical subtypes are based on the general models proposed by Idel (1995b: 92–115).
11 *Zohar* 1, 77b–80a (passim). See also below, chapter 7.
12 *Zohar* 1, 81b–83b (passim). See below, chapter 5.
13 Cf. Zohar 2, 61b–62a. See below, chapter 10.

gold." In similar fashion, the *Zohar* depicts the mental upheaval Phineas experienced when he kills Zimri, taking on Isaac's form in order to confuse the "harsh judgment of Isaac" that was destroying the people (3, 236b–237a). The most impressive example of this model is the homily on the *aqeda* (1, 119b), which I shall discuss at length below.[14] Here, the whole story is interpreted as a psychological drama pertaining to the struggle between mercy and judgment in Abraham's soul, the *aqeda* being intended to imprint a measure of judgment onto his soul of mercy.

This type of homily still remains to be properly investigated, not being self-evident. Although the *Zohar*'s interest in human psychology is well known, the most prevalent interpretive trend within kabbalistic doctrine in the thirteenth century—including the *Zohar* itself—was the mythic-symbolic or mythic-historical. In the majority of cases, the homilies in the *Zohar* are transferred into the realm of kabbalistic theosophy, whence they seek to draw the homiletic meaning of the biblical verse. The psychological-existential model—which penetrates not only the hidden upper realms but also the intricacies of the human soul—is far more unusual. Nonetheless, striking examples may be adduced within the zoharic literature, on occasion in the most surprising of places. These clearly evince that the principal focus of this type of homily—the human soul, perceived as a reflection of the kabbalistic upper world—does not lie in reviving Beshtian Hasidism. Its roots are rather embedded in the medieval zoharic literature.[15]

Like all typology, that presented here only identifies general trends and features. Not all the zoharic homilies fall into one of the three models or their subtypes. In many cases, it is difficult to identify and distinguish between the real and symbolic, the signifier and signified. In others, the homily appears to emerge in the space between them. Frequently, the *Zohar*'s poetic spirit and license cherishes precisely these equivocal, ambiguous, indeterminate spaces, not fitting any of the typologies adduced in the literature. The typological scheme can nonetheless help us recognize and understand this literary space and its rough outlines. Even if the typological definitions set forth here do not cover all the homily types we find in the *Zohar*, most can be categorized and classified on its basis.

---

14 See chapter 8.
15 Although this interest in the human soul is also characteristic of the prophetic Kabbalah of R. Abraham Abulafia, the zoharic orientation differs in its essence, being drawn to the knowledge (*gnosis*) of the hidden in the human psyche on the basis of its theosophical paradigm than to mystical-prophetic praxis.

Chapter 3:
From the Rabbinic to Zoharic Aggada: Preservation, Reworking, and Alteration

Having looked at the homiletic context of the biblical aggadic story within the *Zohar*, let us now turn to the story itself, its sources and distinctive features. As we have already noted, although the zoharic story differs from its talmudic predecessor in its spiritual and religious setting, on many occasions a common skeleton can be identified. In historical terms, the zoharic story made use of ancient talmudic and midrashic material, from which it fashioned—sometimes by disassembling and reassembling the elements—a new account designed to fill in the gaps in the biblical narrative according to the zoharic author's proclivities and purposes. The literary continuum between the early aggadic and zoharic aggadic stories provides a vantage point from which to examine the latter, the changes reflecting the medieval circumstances in which the Zohar was written and the spiritual and ideological developments that had occurred. The focus of this chapter lies on the way in which the *Zohar* reworks the early sources and stamps its own imprint upon them. Before we begin, however, we must elucidate some of our guiding premises with respect to the literary affinities between rabbinic and zoharic aggadot.

The *Zohar*'s dependence upon early talmudic and midrashic sources is self-evident and in need of no proof. Both Scholem (1941: 169–173) and Tishby and Lachower (1989: 1:74–83) have identified and discussed this genre, observing that analysis of the sources upon which the *Zohar* relies reveals the broad and rich rabbinic "library" that lay at its authors' disposal, stretching across an impressive expanse of talmudic and midrashic knowledge. *Inter alia*, this includes the Babylonian Talmud, the Midrash Rabbah, *Midrash Psalms*, the *Pesiqtot*, *Pirqe Rabbi Eliezer*, *Seder Eliyahu*, the *Alphabet of R. Akiba*, etc.[1] The literary link be-

---

1 As Scholem (1941: 169) noted early on, this was probably not an actual library but rather an extensive pool of knowledge. This conclusion is suggested by the fact that zoharic quotations of early sources are inaccurate and difficult to attribute to variant textual witnesses or chance errors. The phenomenon is most striking with respect to the citations of biblical verses that bear no resemblance to the Masoretic text. For another explanation, see Ta-Shma (1995: 50, 131– 132 n. 125). According to Tishby, the *Zohar* also makes use of the Palestinian Talmud. This appears to be very rare, however—not surprising in light of the status it held in medieval Spain. For *Seder Eliyahu*, see Yisraeli (2005: 67). No comprehensive study of the *Zohar*'s "library" has been conducted to date. Despite its importance, such an undertaking is beset with problems— from the fact that on many occasions the quotations appear to be cited from memory to the fact

tween the *Zohar* and talmudic and classical midrash takes on even greater scholarly significance as a working tool for understanding the spirit of the *Zohar* and its attitude towards diverse issues. Thus, for example, three articles devoted to the question of the figure and status of R. Simeon bar Jochai have made very fruitful use of the various links with the talmudic figure of R. Simeon bar Jochai in order to decipher the riddle of the choice of this talmudic Sage as the *Zohar*'s principal protagonist (Liebes, 1993d, 2007a; Huss, 2008: 11–42).

Today, the depth and extent of the affinities between the zoharic and the ancient talmudic-midrashic corpora is clearly evident due to two sets of comments written during the previous generation, both of which in their own way provide a broad and detailed picture. The first is Scholem's *Zohar* (1992), a treasury of references to Jewish sources from the whole spectrum of Jewish history, including the Talmuds, midrashic literature, apocrypha, Jewish mystical works, and early kabbalistic writings prior to the appearance of the *Zohar*.[2] The second is the collection of notes made R. Reuvein Margolies known as *Netzotzey zohar*.[3] As rich and important as these lists are, however, they only point to literary contexts, not explicating the nature of the relationship between the two corpora.

The fact that the *Zohar* is linked to talmudic literature not merely historically but also substantively was established by Liebes (1993a). Focusing primarily on identifying talmudic legends in the *Zohar*, he argued against Scholem (1976a: 87) that: "Kabbala is not a new creation but a reformulation, in different form, of the same myth that has been the very heart of the Torah since time immemorial" (1993a: 1). Not confining his claim to aggada, Liebes defines the relationship between the *Zohar* and early talmudic-midrashic sources *in toto* as representing a linear development.

While this view lies at the heart of the present volume, it does not contend that the two versions are identical. The aggadic and midrashic traditions have undergone various changes during the "development" during the Middle Ages of which Liebes speaks. The *Zohar* itself is also a distinctively medieval artifact. While the variations derive in many cases from linguistic and stylistic differences

---

that in most instances it is very difficult to ascertain whether a specific sources reached the *Zohar*'s authors directly or via another literary source, such as the Yalqutim, Rashi's commentary on the Torah, etc.

2 For the nature of these notes, see Liebes in his introduction to this edition.

3 Margolies taking a conservative approach, in principle he presents the *Zohar* as the source of the rabbinic statements, identification of the link usually lacking any significance. Alongside *Netzotzey zohar* we must also note his supplementary volume, *Sha'arey zohar*, which also adduces parallels (which he defines as "sources") to the talmudic and midrashic material in the *Zohar*. Also worthy of mention is Daniel Matt's edition of the *Zohar* (2003–2014), whose margins also include numerous additional references to midrashic and kabbalistic works.

or divergent literary tastes, they also represent new spiritual, theological, ideological, and aggadic trends. Tensions and conflicts between the *Zohar*'s faithfulness to the talmudic tradition and the new spiritual orientation that is characteristic of its vibrant world are frequently evident. The difficulty of pouring new wine into old wineskins we noted above in relation to the homiletic framework arises most forcefully in the philosophical context. Here, the dilemma pertains not only to methodological principles and homiletic practices but also to substantive questions. How can Abraham the Hebrew be depicted as a mystic and kabbalist while remaining loyal to his rabbinic garb? How is the story of Nadab and Abihu—which according to the ancient aggada conveys the lesson of discipline and submission to authority—to be understood in a world in which institutional values form no integral part? What does a medieval author do when the spirit of an aggada responsible for establishing traditional consciousness in a particular passage is no longer relevant in his society?

The *Zohar* demonstrates no compunction in expressing its objection to early aggadic traditions. Thus, for example, like the Sages it perceive Moses' words to Pharaoh—"Thus says the LORD: Toward midnight I will go forth among the Egyptians" (Exod 11:4)—as a form of hesitancy, Moses not adducing the precise hour but only indicating an approximate time (towards v. at midnight). The *Zohar* engages here with the amora R. Zera, who rebuffs the possibility that Moses might not have been sufficiently well-versed in astronomy to know the precise point of "midnight" and arguing instead that "Moses thought that the astrologers of Pharaoh might make a mistake, and then they would say that Moses was a liar" (*b. Ber.* 4a). The *Zohar* responds to this, in a homily attributed to Simeon bar Jochai, in its explication of *Parashat Bo:* "And if, as our colleagues have said: So that Pharaoh's astrologers would not say, 'Moses is a liar!'—then the difficulty persists ..." (2:37a). "Our colleagues" here are the amoraim of the Talmud, and the words with which they are polemicizing here are those of R. Zera. The *Zohar* does not regard this as a sufficient answer (for reasons they lay out in the homily but are not our concern here), thus proposing an alternative, kabbalistic explanation.

Elsewhere, the *Zohar* discusses the laws relating to houses afflicted by eruptive plague, addressing the Sages' opinion that they only afflicted the Israelites so that the treasures that the original inhabitants of Canaan had hidden therein might be discovered. As Rashi says: "... because the Amorites concealed treasures of gold in the walls of their houses during the whole forty years the Israelites were in the wilderness ... and in consequence of the plague they would pull down the house and discover them" (on Lev 14:34). As in the previous example, here, too, the *Zohar* rejects this explanation out of hand, adducing a decisive rebuttal: if indeed this section of the Torah is designed to bring about the razing of the walls in order to find the treasure buried therein, why does Scripture prohibit the remnants of the wall from being restored? It thus concludes that the portion must deal with another issue, proceeding to explain it according to its own method. This type of polemics occurs quite frequently in the *Zohar*.⁴

In other places, the *Zohar* confronts the disparity between the Sages' world and its own by adopting a compartmentalizing tactic that allows it to recognize the validity of diverse, sometimes even contradictory, interpretations without rejecting any of them. On the basis of the exegetical principle of multiple meanings, it can thereby hold a kabbalistic interpretation without necessarily dismissing old and familiar traditions out of hand, merely relegating them to the sidelines.⁵ It customarily employs this exegetical method by means of the well-known formula:אבל [אוקמינן] הא אוקמוה.⁶ Hereby, it skillfully demonstrates its faithfulness to early traditions and well-known and familiar answers to its question at the same time using the word "but" to arouse expectations of a "higher" response—i.e., a kabbalistic interpretation.

On occasion, the *Zohar* is even more open and expansive regarding its methodology, stating: "Come and see: Although we should look at the garment, now this verse is explained as follows ..." (3:155b). The reference here is to the well-known parable (quoted elsewhere) of the *pshat* as forming the garb in which the *sod* is clothed. By this means, an alternative answer can be offered to that given in the Talmud. While its superiority is established, it does not impinge on the status of the talmudic interpretation—which is in fact relegated to the "margins" of the interpretive consciousness.

Transitioning from the old traditional perspective to the new zoharic one, neither of these methods entails any essential spiritual watershed, occurring

---

4 I hope to investigate the nature of these in a forthcoming article. A preliminary examination suggests that the tradition against to which the *Zohar* objects is most likely according to the version transmitted by Rashi in his commentary on the Torah rather than the original midrashic or talmudic source.

5 According to Idel (1995a), the very adoption of this "multiple," compartmentalizing method within the kabbalistic environment must be understood as an attempt to relegate old truths to a secondary status in order to ensure the establishment of the new kabbalistic interpretation within the Jewish spiritual world without shaking its foundations: see also Yisraeli (2005: 213–216) and Huss (2000)—who maintains that the interpretive stratum serves to rank and compartmentalize diverse kabbalistic schools of thought.

6 The old interpretation relegated to the "margins" via this is not always or necessarily a talmudic one. As Scholem's notes make clear, it may also be a kabbalistic or earlier zoharic utterance dismissed in favour of that preferred by the homilist. For this structure of the zoharic homily, see Hellner-Eshed (2009: 172–175); Matt (1989). For examples of this approach in the works of Moses de Léon, see Matt (1993: 182–186).

for the most part in an interpretive context that is closely tied to the biblical text and not relating to essential ideas. In general, the *Zohar* only appeals to them when the textual base it requires for its homily is already "taken" by the rabbinic homily and it needs space for the new zoharic innovation. The compartmentalization/ relegation thus customarily pertains to methodology rather than substance.

The spiritual and religious "crossroads"—the points at which the literary continuum between the rabbinic and zoharic aggadot is broken—are therefore only indicated by more covert literary formulae. Paying attention to the sensitive and subtle conversation between the zoharic and early rabbinic aggadot, we can identify the changes and metamorphoses that take place. This method is commonly adopted by scholars of rabbinic aggada, for whom it serves as a way of distinguishing between Palestinian and Babylonian sources, tannaitic and amoraic sayings, and early and late midrashic traditions. These reflecting changes in the religious, ideological, or educational climate, thereby enabling a deeper understanding of the spirit of the period (Yisraeli, 2005: 67), I suggest that the same principle can be fruitfully applied to the *Zohar*. An attentive comparative and critical reading of the zoharic aggada in light of the rabbinic aggada, taking the differences in time and place into account, can illuminate the world of the *Zohar* from new and novel directions.

The aggadic traditions to be discussed also have their own biography in the broadest sense, the talmudic version already being a second or third cousin of a more ancient source from the Second Temple period or early Greek and Christian writings. The later zoharic story also contains traces of what will evolve into the ethical literature and Hasidic aggada of the following centuries. As instructive and fascinating as they may be, however, these chapters in the history of the aggada lie beyond the scope of our present interest, only being adduced if and when required by the talmudic-zoharic discussion.

Before discussing the *Zohar*'s distinctive imprint on various aggadic traditions, it is important to note that the dynamism and evolution the aggadic stories it contains exhibit not only relates to earlier strata but also reflects intra-zoharic processes. Frequently, we come upon an aggadic tradition that appears in various guises that cannot be attributed solely to transmission or copying errors. A case in point is the question of Adam's sin. As we shall see below, the *Zohar* cites the classical kabbalistic view that this consisted of "cutting down the shoots"—i.e., the sundering of the upper coupling between the tree of knowledge and the tree of life, the *sefirot* of *Malkut* and *Tiferet* (see Chapter 5). This tradition also occurs in another version, however, according to which Adam preferred the free-standing tree of knowledge over the upper tree of life, his sin thus being that of choosing to spend his time under the shade of the tree of the knowledge of good and evil—to which death was attached—rather than the eternal life (physical and spiritual) hidden under the branches of the tree of life. Another example, is the evolution of the kabbalist tradition concerning the *aqeda*. Although all the diverse zoharic circles regard this event as an account of the struggle between the *sefira* of *Hesed* (represented by Abraham) and the *sefira* of *Din* (represented by Isaac), significant differences exist between them. In some, the story is viewed as depicting the subjection of *Din* via its "binding" by *Hesed*. In others, it is perceived as an act whereby *Din* becomes part of *Hesed* as a way of correcting *Hesed* and bringing it into proper balance. While in most zoharic sources the *aqeda* is regarded as a drama taking place within the realm of the godhead, some—as we shall see in later chapters—conceive of it as a drama played out between the attributes of judgment (*din*) and mercy (*hesed*) within Abraham's soul.[7] These variants appear to reflect the fact that not all the homilies were composed by the same author.[8]

This multi-vocality is of great methodological importance for a comparative analysis of the zoharic and talmudic aggada. The plethora of versions appears to reflect a very broad range of affinities and disparities, making clear-cut distinctions difficult. When focusing on a particular zoharic tradition, it will almost always be noted that this does not represent "the" zoharic version—the "official" version, as it were—but the version found in the *Zohar*, sometimes one amongst many. Herein lies the great importance of identifying general trends in the zoharic aggada beyond the simple decipherment of each saying in its own right. The discernment of spiritual directions within such a turbulent climate as that of the *Zohar* is directly relevant for understanding the zoharic world. I shall thus discuss, for example, the way in which the zoharic homilies relating to Moses' death, while differing in purpose, consistently adopt a view that is marginal in the Talmud—namely, that he did not die (see Chapter 14). Similarly, while the *Zohar* adopts the tradition that Nadab and Abihu rebelled against authority, it seeks to soften the crime, all the while exhibiting diverse tones and levels of literary sophistication and ideological tension (see Chapter 12).

In what way, then, does the *Zohar* rework the biblical aggada within the medieval kabbalistic-zoharic context? Here, too, three models or types of creative continuity can be adduced: clarification, radicalization, and synthesis. The first is represented by those zoharic aggadot that seek to explicate what is hid-

---

7 See below, chapter 8.
8 In this respect, no difference exists between the zoharic and rabbinic corpora, both comprising a vast and varied mosaic in which diverse voices engage upon an erudite dialogue. For the implications of the multiple-author theory and in particular that which rejects the very notion of a "book," see Abrams (2010: 224–428).

den in early aggada.⁹ It is exemplified by three prominent texts. The first is the account of Abraham's origins in *Parashat Lekh-lekha* (see Chapter 7). Here, the drama of the divine revelation and Abraham's encounter with God is depicted in the *Zohar* as a bi-directional event motivated by the human party. In other words, God's revelation of Himself to Abraham comes as a response (אתערותא דלעילא) to Abraham's yearning to discover and approach Him (אתערותא דלתתא). As we shall see below, this watershed in the divine-human relationship is already intimated in the brief and succinct midrashic description in the Palestinian midrash: "*Now the* LORD *said to Abram: Get thee out of thy country...* Said R. Isaac: This may be compared to a man who was travelling from place to place when he saw a building in flames [i.e., Abraham saw the world being destroyed by vice and wrongdoing]. Is it possible that the building lacks a person to look after it? he wondered. The owner of the building looked out and said, 'I am the owner of the building'" (*Gen. Rab.* 29:1). Although the spiritual climate is different, of course, the model remains the same, contravening other versions—ancient and medieval—of the story of Abraham's origins.

The second example is that of the enigmatic aggadic tradition that "Moses did not die" (see Chapter 9). Warmly embraced by the zoharic authors, in particular the *Tiqunim* literature, it is enlisted in service of the idea that when Moses reappears the Torah will be renewed. Here, too, this meaning is already latent in the talmudic account—leading to rejection of this view. This trend also finds expression in the chapter on Balaam's prophecy: "But amongst the nations of the world [a prophet like Moses has arisen]: Balaam." Like their other medieval counterparts, the zoharic authors questioned the comparison between Balaam's and Moses' prophecies, asking what the two could possibly share in common. The *Zohar*'s answer—that Moses' prophecies come from a different divine source than Moses'—appears to be a novel interpretation from the school of Moses de León. As we shall see, however, it is in fact a clarification in theological kabbalistic language of the full formulation found in the rabbinic aggada (the "baker's parable"). While their spiritual language differs, Moses de León and the *Zohar* thus both reflect the spirit of the ancient midrash.

The second trend is that of radicalization. While the texts that exemplify this direction preserve the spirit of the early source they "stretch" it far beyond its original scope, at time radically expanding its parameters. Here, the creative endeavour to apply the ancient literary motif or myth to foreign theological or eth-

---

9 Early on, Liebes (1993a: 244) noted that the talmudic story frequently receives systemic formulation in the kabbalistic literature, being reworked into rigid frameworks. At the same time as sharpening the contours of the talmudic legend, the kabbalistic metamorphosis also weakens it, restraining its vitality.

ical contexts may at times empty out the original content—or, alternatively, reconstitute it as a new story. The most prominent example of this trend relates to the figure of Esau. (see Chapter 9). In the early aggada, Esau represents the essence of human evil—whose apotheosis in the Second Temple, mishnaic, and talmudic periods was Rome, responsible for the destruction of the Temple. In the *Zohar*, Esau takes on mythic proportions, thenceforward symbolizing not only the fount of human evil but also that of cosmic, mythic evil—the very embodiment of the *sitra achra*. While this demonization of Esau did not occur in a vacuum, undoubtedly originating in a talmudic aggada, his portrayal as the human villain *par excellence* in the Talmud is radicalized in the *Zohar*, where he becomes an actual demon.

As we shall see in Chapter 10, the early aggada similarly understands the "gods of Egypt" whom God afflicted—"I will mete out punishments to all the gods of Egypt" (Exod 12:12)—as a description of fetishistic delusion or, at most, a designation of lower theosophic entities, the "princes of Egypt" (i.e., the higher theosophic power appointed over the fate of Egypt). In the *Zohar*, they are presented as symbolizing the source of impurity in the upper world— the *sitra achra*, God's struggle against them thus constituting an attempt to deliver Israel from the forty-nine gates of impurity of the *sitra achra*. Here, the shift is not from the human to the demonic but from the (neutral) theosophic to the theosophic-demonic.

Another example is that of Nadab and Abihu (see Chapter 12). In this case, the *Zohar* adopts the prevalent rabbinic view that the brothers rebelled against authority—that Moses and Aaron (separately and together). In the eyes of the *Zohar*, however, they rebelled against the authority of *Malkut* by circumventing it and approaching God (there YHWH, who represents *Tiferet*) directly in order to worship Him without *ishe* (on the basis of the recurring phrase 'אִשֶּׁה לה in the chapters devoted to the sacrifices)—i.e., *Malkut*.

Finally, in relation to the *aqeda* (see Chapter 8), the *Zohar* "completes" the early aggadic story by asserting that Abraham did in fact sacrifice Isaac. As we shall see below, the *Zohar*'s proposal here is original and daring, going far beyond the parameters of the talmudic aggada.

The third trend is that of synthesis. The origin of this method can already be seen in the tension between the *Zohar*'s faithfulness to the ancient aggadic tradition—primarily its spirit—and its identification with (near-)contemporaneous interpretive and spiritual approaches marked by a medieval kabbalistic tone. In these cases, the zoharic homilist finds a way to bridge the gap by blending and merging the diverse explanations, generally in such as a way as to moderate the talmudic orientation.

Before we look at some examples of this trend, we must address the issue of the interpretive traditions known and used by the pre-zoharic medieval mystics. The exegetical activity of the first kabbalists in Provence and Spain was not merely the heir of rabbinic creativity but first and foremost formed the literary medium through which they sought to disseminate kabbalistic knowledge (Scholem, 1976a: 37). Although not many wrote extensive commentaries on the Torah, their other works adduce numerous interpretive traditions. Amongst the most important figures in this respect are R. Asher b. David, the members of the Gerona school—headed by R. Ezra b. Solomon, R. Azriel, and R. Jacob bar Sheshet— and the Castilian mystics, particularly R. Isaac Hacohen and R. Jacob Hacohen, R. Moses of Burgos, and R. Todros Abulafia. While not clearly belonging to any of these corpora or bearing any striking affinity to them, many additional works also contain important and valuable interpretive traditions for understanding the origins of the Kabbalah in general and the *Zohar* in particular.

The majority of this material falls into three distinct "canonical" bodies of work that constitute the beginnings of the Kabbala—*Sefer Habahir*, the traditions ascribed to R. Isaac Sagi-Nahor, and Nahmanides' commentary on the Torah. The first kabbalistic work to be written, *Sefer Habahir* comprises in large part a midrash on the Torah, thus containing a vast store of interpretive traditions relating to the biblical text.[10] While no orderly remnants of R. Isaac Sagi-Nahor's works have survived apart from his commentary on *Sefer Yetzira*, the writings of his disciples—R. Ezra, R. Azriel, R. Jacob bar Sheshet, and their colleagues—are replete with traditions transmitted in his name (frequently in the name of the "great *hasid*"). The writings of the Castilian mystics (particularly those of R. Todros Abulafia) and works from a slightly later period, such as the exegeses of Nahmanides' secrets, the writings of R. Joshua ibn Shuaib, and others, also contain traditions attributed to him. Nahmanides' commentary on the Torah provides an organized system of kabbalist interpretations that follows the order of the biblical text.[11]

To these must be added the kabbalistic literature composed by the mystics of the "zoharic circle"—R. Moses de Léon, R. Joseph Gikatilla, R. Bahya b. Asher, R. David b. Judah Hehasid, R. Joseph b. Shalom Ashkenazi, etc. (Liebes, 1988). Even if the relationship between these work and the *Zohar* remains unclear, they belong to the same "family" (in the Wittgensteinian sense), containing remnants of traditional kabbalistic exegesis alongside new interpretations. While not know-

---

10 See Scholem (1986); Pedaya (1990); Meroz (2002b); Abrams (2010: 118–197).
11 Some of the important recent studies on Nahmanides also deal with his kabbalistic interpretations: see Idel (1983, 1995); Wolfson (1989b); Funkenstein (1993); Berger (1983); Halbertal (2006); Pedaya (2003).

ing the extent to which the zoharic authors were familiar with this body of literature, in general terms it may be presumed to form the soil out of which the zoharic homiletic outlook sprouted and blossomed. The homilies in the *Zohar* certainly reflect the interpretive views known to us from its kabbalistic environs, either earlier or contemporaneous. When the zoharic authors treat the ancient talmudic-midrashic aggada, they do so in many cases through the lens early medieval kabbalistic exegesis. Frequently, they adopt this view, ignoring the talmudic version of the story. On other occasions, they reject it in favour of the talmudic-midrashic tradition. As noted above, they very often find a way to include both approaches, exhibiting reservations towards both and thus stamping their own imprint on the homily.

The story of the war against Amalek provides a good example of this circumstance (see Chapter 11). In interpreting this episode, the tannaim sought to downplay any magical element in Moses' raised hands, asserting that: "So long as Israel turned their thoughts above and subjected their hears to their father in heaven, they prevailed, but otherwise they fell" (*m. Roš. Haš.* 3:8). The *Sefer Habahir*, however, proposes that in lifting his hands Moses established and corrected the sefiric system, charging it with the necessary force for Israel to win the war. Here, the *Zohar* synthesizes the two approaches into a single view by positing that while Moses had to lift his hands (an apparently magical ritual), the act drew its power from the prayers of Israel.

Another example relates to the theme of the "light reserved for the righteous to come" (see Chapter 4). In this case, the ancient midrashic tradition sought to transfer the revelation of the light hidden for the righteous during the six days of creation to the utopian future. Mystics such as R. Azriel of Gerona, on the other, maintained that it was also available in this world, "since even the righteous can use it and it is their lot." Here, too, the *Zohar* steers a cautious, balanced median position. While, like R. Azriel, it "makes room" for the hidden light within historical parameters in this world, it confine this use to concrete figure from the biblical past.

The *Zohar* treats the question of Elijah's status following his ascension to heaven in the whirlwind in a similar fashion (see Chapter 6). Medieval Judaism in general and early kabbalistic circles in particular found difficulty with the view that he joined the heavenly host. In this case, the *Zohar* deals with the issue by contending that Elijah was a human being who clothed himself with the whirlwind and cloud and thus attired himself in a transformative garb that allowed him to assume a form of celestial existence. It also suggests that Elijah was born as an angel, only temporarily taking on the form of a human being in order to fulfill his mission on earth.

Finally, while rabbinic literature disapproves of Elijah's zeal, other circles regarded in a far more favourable light (see Chapter 6). Here, the zoharic homilist had to call upon all his ingenuity to bridge this gap in opinion. Although, like the ancient midrash, the *Zohar* "removes" Elijah from the human realm, it does so by raising him to a higher level. While his zeal has no place in human society, it is praiseworthy in principle.

To these three typological examples we may add another that exemplifies the *Zohar*'s creative activity on those occasions on which no talmudic or midrashic aggada lay at its disposal. As we shall see in the discussion of Adam's sin (Chapter 5), the *Zohar* offers an original, novel, and daring interpretation that differs from all the classical kabbalistic explanations, even contravening them to a certain extent. While the non-conformist spirit emanating from this homily—and in effect from the chapters as a whole—cannot be said to characterize the *Zohar* as a whole, the zoharic literature not constituting a unitary composition, it was precisely from within the zoharic framework that this type of spirit sprang from and flourished. This circumstances appears not have been a coincidence.

What historical conclusions—of even most broad and wide nature—can we draw from the above? How much can we learn from the *Zohar* in general, and the way in which it reworks diverse aggadic traditions in particular, about the circumstances in which it was composed and its social and political background—not to speak of the psychological soil whence it sprang? To what extent can the zoharic literary creation add to our understanding of the period? To what degree does it offer a vantage point from which to analyze Jewish society and spiritual life in thirteenth-century Spain? These questions, which seek to set the *Zohar* within a concrete historical context, are some of the most difficult and intractable issues in the study of its world. Despite their originality and erudition the conclusions drawn from some of most prominent scholars in this field remain within the sphere of speculation, extra-zoharic evidence being unavailable.[12]

---

[12] The first to discuss the *Zohar* from a historical perspective was Baer (1940; 1961: 1:154–165). In addition to his numerous insights (particularly those relating to the book's later stratum)—which became the guiding principles of zoharic studies—he also drew far-reaching conclusions regarding the Castilian mystical circles of the end of the thirteenth century and the way in which the zoharic framing story reflects their way of life. Other attempts to decipher the book's literary framework and translate it into historical currency were made by scholars of the following generation, primarily with regard to R. Simeon bar Jochai and the status attributed to Moses. Liebes (1988: 68–71) thus suggested that the former represents the Castilian mystic R. Todros Abulafia. He (1977: 303) and Amos Goldreich (1994: 477–482) also proposed that in the *Raya mehemna*, Moses stands for the historical figure of R. Moses de Léon, an idea

I do not seek to provide answers to these historical questions, which are only tangential to my primary focus. The vantage point offered by the zoharic homiletics can, however, contribute greatly to our understanding of the historical personages behind them—i.e., the zoharic homilists. Knowledge of the mood, mystical trends, and social sensitivities of the period is invaluable for sketching a portrait of these figures, whose precise identity remains unknown. Their mystical orientation is reflected, for example, in their desire to make the "light reserved for the future righteous" accessible already in this world, as also in the insight that Moses' light illuminates the souls of the sages of Israel from generation to generation. The *Zohar*'s social context can be adduced from the sympathetic attitude it exhibits towards Nadab and Abihu in those very homilies in which their sin is regarded as a rebellion against institutional authority. The zoharic spirit is most strikingly reflected in the way in which Elijah's zeal is reevaluated, the reservations in the talmudic-midrashic literature being turned into a measure of sympathy and its firm stamping of Esau as oppressed. Here, we find traces of radical—even subversive—non-conformism. These character outlines cannot be sketched with a stroke of the pen, however, but must be drawn subtly carefully, and with a great degree of caution.

The method proposed herein is clearly not flawless. Here, too, the transition from the literary context to the historical inference is far from simple. Analysis of the use the zoharic homilists make of earlier sources and the transformation of ancient traditions into zoharic garb nonetheless focuses on less-consciously fashioned and thus authentic processes. Another problem—attendant upon the endeavour to attribute historical meaning to the zoharic text—is linked to the multiple-author theory. If the *Zohar* was in fact penned by several people, the number of historical figures it portrays must reflect this fact, each differing from and possibly contrasting with the other. At the same time, however, group features—spiritual and intellectual ideas—may be adducible. Taking all

---

already mooted by Tishby and Lachower (1989: 3:1120–1121 n. 93). Discussing the fact that the body of the text places R. Simeon bar Jochai on a far higher level than Moses, Huss (2008: 42) on the other hand argues that Moses serves as a front for Nahmanides. The fresh approaches to the *Zohar*, and in particular the "bands/circles" theories, opened up new avenues for research. Meroz (2001, 2002a) is a leading proponent of the historical approach that contends that the *Zohar* not only gives expression to the views of a historical mystical group but also that, to a large extent, the literary circle of the framing story forms an image of that band. Engaging in a close and erudite analysis of the epic stratum in the *Zohar*, she has sketched the outlines of what may be call the zoharic "meta-story," painting a picture of the Castilian mystic group, its history, hierarchic structure, inner politics, tensions and crises. Objecting to this direction, Abrams (2010: 369) posits that no such "band" existed and that we must rather speak of a "textual community."

due caution and recognizing the complexities involved, the portrait drawn in the following chapters may thus help form a concrete and reliable, if still rather vague and imperfect, profile.

As Scholem has demonstrated, the *Zohar* has stamped it imprint both explicitly and implicitly upon all the Jewish thought and literature that followed it and the key chapters of Jewish history. Its enchantment, power, and influence are not only linked to its kabbalistic significance but also to a great extent to its literary character. The latter is due in large part to its distinctive homiletic traditions and the aggadot it transmits. The following chapters examine some of the most important and central of these aggadot.

Chapter 4:
"The Light Hidden for the Righteous":
For Whom is it Reserved?

The idea of the primordial light that, once created then vanishes, is an ancient tradition whose roots lie in Isa 30:26: "Moreover the light of the moon will be like the light of the sun, and the light of the sun will be sevenfold, like the light of seven days, on the day when the LORD binds up the injuries of his people, and heals the wounds inflicted by his blow." The "light of seven days" alludes to the light that ruled supreme during Creation, whose power is far greater ("sevenfold") than that of the sun.[1] Although this tradition raises questions regarding the origin and nature of this light (Urbach, 1975: 208–210; Altmann, 1969); Goshen-Gottstein, 1996: 64–66), my focus in this chapter lies primarily on the notion that it will reappear—or, more accurately, on its accessibility in the unredeemed present. As we shall see, the medieval mystics exhibit a great interest in this issue, the *Zohar* also addressing it in various homilies. The kabbalistic discussion shedding light on the background of this early midrashic tradition, let me first examine the roots and evolution of the idea in talmudic and midrashic literature.

"The light reserved for the righteous": The early traditions

The earliest evidence for the midrashic concept appears to be *b. Hag.* 12a and the early Palestinian midrash *Genesis Rabbah*. The Babylonian version occurs in a discussion of the "Work of Creation":

> But was the light created on the first day? For, behold, it is written: *And God set them in the firmament of the heaven* [Gen 1:17], and it is [further] written: *And there was evening and there was morning a fourth day* [Gen 1:19]—This is [to be explained] according to R. Eleazar. For R. Eleazar said: The light which the blessed Holy One created on the first day, one could see thereby from one end of the world to the other; but as soon as the blessed Holy One beheld the generation of the Flood and the generation of the Dispersion, and saw that their actions were corrupt, He arose and hid it from them, for it is said: *But from the wicked their light is withholden* [Job 38:15]. And for whom did he reserve it? For the righteous in the

---

[1] Absent from the Septuagint (Zakovitch, 2003), the Sages undoubtedly inherited this motif from an earlier period, employing it as one of the prooftexts for the idea of the hidden light: see below.

> time to come, for it is said: *And God saw the light, that it was good* [Gen 1:4]; and "good" means only the righteous, for it is said: *Say ye of the righteous that he is good* [Isa 3:10]. As soon as He saw the light that He had reserved for the righteous, He rejoiced, for it is said: *He rejoiceth at the light of the righteous* [Prov 13:9]. Now Tannaim [differ on the point]: The light which the blessed Holy One created on the first day one could see and look thereby from one end of the world to the other; this is the view of R. Jacob. But the Sages say: It is identical with the luminaries; for they were created on the first day, but they were not hung up [in the firmament] till the fourth day. (*b. Hag.* 12a)

The context here is explicitly hermeneutical, the Sages attempting to resolve the textual difficulty of the creation of the light on the first day and that of the luminaries on the fourth day. This leads the homilist to conclude that the light created on the first day was not that belonging to the luminaries, which were only created on the fourth day, but another, mystical light. This exegetical crux—echoed in the tannaitic dispute in the *baraita*—is adduced and elucidated by the amoraim. Both talmudic layers explicate the nature of this light: "one could see and look thereby from one end of the world to the other." According to a literal understanding, its uniqueness lies in its power—and possibly also its physical quality, which grants human beings the ability to see ("one could see and look thereby") great distances ("from one end of the world to the other").

Although the tannaim do not explain why the light was hidden, the amora R. Eleazar understands their words as indicating that God concealed it when He saw the wickedness of the generations of the flood and dispersion. Whether this was punishment for their sins or whether God foreknew that this generation would be evil, the act is directly linked to human iniquity. This fact is even more pronounced in the second version of the tradition. Appearing in several places in the Palestinian midrash, this asserts that the light was concealed in response to Adam's sin, being hidden when he was expelled from the Garden of Eden.[2] *Genesis Rabbah*, however, preserves another version, according to which the light disappeared from the world for a much more essential reason:

> It was taught: The light which was created in the six days of Creation cannot illumine by day, because it would eclipse the light of the sun, nor by night, because it was created only to illumine by day. Then where is it? It is stored up for the righteous in the Messianic future, as it says: *Moreover the light of the moon shall be as the light of the sun, and the light of the sun shall be sevenfold, as the light of the seven days*" (Isa 30:26). (*Gen. Rab.* 3:6)

---

[2] *Gen. Rab.* 12:6. For the parallels, see the note *ad loc.* in the Theodore Albeck edition. A (probably later) midrash adduces a positive reason for its concealment: "*And God saw the light that it was good* [Gen 1:4]—this teaches that the Holy One, blessed be He, saw the generation of the messiah and his deeds before the creation of the world, hiding the light for the messiah and his generation under His throne of glory" (*Yal. Shim'oni*, Isaiah, §499 [p. 314]).

Here, the hiding of the light forms an integral part of creation. The space illumined by the primordial light has no room for the sun and moon. Since they God has designated them to rule day and night, the primordial light must be removed. Here we find the basis of a mythic paradigm very close in spirit to the Lurianic idea of *tzimtzum* (contraction) that would soon conquer the kabbalistic world in the sixteenth century.³ This Palestinian tradition differs significantly from those cited above. In contrast to the "historical" reasons for the light's concealment in the former, here it is a function of the structure of creation itself. The world containing no room for any "extra" light, the primordial light must be removed until a new creation is introduced.⁴

The difference between the two explanation does not lie merely on the philosophical level, however. Each starts from a fundamentally divergent point, exemplifying diverse attitudes towards the primordial light. The de-rationalizing approach of the second erects an impenetrable wall between it and human existence, its inaccessibility being a function of its very nature rather than the result of a divine decree. In medieval philosophical terminology, the existence of the primordial light within the created world is a necessity rather than an accidental phenomenon. On this understanding, it is self-evident no one can use it to see "from one end of the world to the other" as in the Babylonian version. The view that regards its removal as a historical-theological event tied to evil and wickedness (of whatever form), on the other hand, constitutes ready soil for the sprouting of dreams, longings, and yearnings for a purer form of human existence in which the light that has been concealed may once again manifest itself.

---

3 For pre-Lurianic midrashic traditions relating to the divine *tzimtzum*, see Huss (2000: 139). For the hidden light as the "doctrine of *tzimtzum*" in ibn Lavi's writings and environs, see ibid: 108–146.

4 The two may possibly represent Babylonian and Palestinian traditions. While the printed editions of *Gen. Rab.* based upon the 1544 Venice edition contain the Babylonian version in chapter 12, all the manuscripts and other printed editions lack this paragraph (see p. 103 and the textual variants there, line 4). It thus appears not to have formed part of the original text. This conclusion is strengthened by the fact that it interrupts the flow of the text, as evinced by a comparison with the midrashic parallel in chapter 11 (p. 88). The spirit of the homily also deviates from the immediate context, linking the light's concealment with the wickedness of the generations of the flood and dispersion rather than Adam's sin. Finally, the text in the printed editions is identical to that of the Babylonian version, the only difference being that it is transmitted in R. Eleazar's name in the Babylonian Talmud and in R. Judah b. R. Simon's in *Gen. Rab.* All these details suggest that the homily that states that the light was hidden because of the evil generations was taken from the Babylonian Talmud and did not form part of the original text of *Gen. Rab.*

The latter trend later produced real fruit with the emergence of the Kabbalah began to emerge—and even earlier. Traces of its can be found in *Sefer Habahir*, for example:

> Rabbi Yochanan said: There were two [types of] light, as it is written, "[Let there be light,] and there was light." Regarding both of them it is written (Gen 1:4), "[And God saw the light] that it was good." The blessed Holy One took one [of these types of light] and stored it away for the righteous in the World to Come. Regarding this it is written (Ps 31:20), "How great is the *good* that You have hidden away for those who fear You, that You have accomplished this for those who find shelter in You ..." We learn that no creature could look at the first light. It is thus written (Gen 1:4), "And *God* saw the light that it was good." (§147)

Here, it is explicitly stated that the light was concealed because "no creature could look at" it, it thus not being tolerable in the created world. While this homily may be interpreted in a more moderate fashion—namely, that the light was stored away because human beings do not know how to use it—this is not the case of another in the same book. This clearly sharpens the essentialist approach:

> We learned that before the world was created, it arose in thought to create an intense light to illuminate it. He created an intense light over which no created thing could have authority. The blessed Holy One saw, however, that the world could not endure [this light]. He therefore took a seventh of it and left it in its place for them. The rest He put away for the righteous in the Ultimate Future. (§160)

In contrast to the earlier passage, here the light was never actually created, merely "arising in thought." God did not put this thought into action because He knew that "the world could not endure" such light. He thus took a "tolerable" amount—a seventh of the original thought—and placed it therein. This version of the myth clearly reflects the essentialist view: the primordial light could not exist in the created world because of its intrinsically different nature.

Like other "Bahiric" traditions, this is developed in the *Zohar*: "Come and see: And [the light] that was concealed for the righteous is one sixty thousand seventy-fifth of the light that dwells with the blessed Holy One, and the light of the sun is one sixty thousand and seventy-fifth of the light that was concealed for the righteous—not to speak of that light" (*Zohar Hadash*, 15a).[5] The affinities between this homily and the second passage cited above from *Sefer Habahir* are self-evident. Both reflect the same idea with respect to the relationship between

---

[5] For a discussion of this passage in its broader context, see below. For a similar tendency in another zoharic homily, cf. *Zohar* 3, 204a.

the primordial light and the light of the sun, stressing that over the first light "no created thing could have authority." Despite the minor differences, they both share the same paradigm. The formulations sharpen the divergence between the Babylonian tradition—according to which human beings can see with this light "from one end of the world to the other"—and this one, which holds that "no one can look at it." Behind this approach, which completely excludes the primordial light from the human sphere, may lie Philo's philosophical exegesis, which identifies this light with the "idea" of the light:

> And it is a star above the heavens, the source of those stars which are perceptible by the external senses, and if any one were to call it universal light he would not be very wrong; since it is from that the sun and the moon, and all the other planets and fixed stars derive their due light, in proportion as each has power given to it; that unmingled and pure light being obscured when it begins to change, according to the change from that which is perceptible only by the intellect, to that which is perceptible by the external senses. (*Opif.* 31).[6]

Philo asserts that the hidden light is distinguished from the overt light in a profound and essential sense:

> the other he called light, because it is surpassingly beautiful: for that which is perceptible only by intellect is as far more brilliant and splendid than that which is seen, as I conceive, the sun is than darkness, or day than night, or the intellect than any other of the outward senses by which men judge (inasmuch as it is the guide of the entire soul), or the eyes than any other part of the body. (ibid, 30)

Despite the deep roots this essentialist exegesis developed, the circumstantial view was far more prevalent during the medieval period, gaining a central and dominant place amongst the early mystics and zoharic authors. Let us now examine the expressions of this approach in medieval kabbalistic writings and the *Zohar*.

The "hidden light" and the "light of thought"

As we have noted above, the midrashic tendency towards "preserving" the light within arm's reach may reflect the early Babylonian tradition that regards its re-

---

[6] For the way in which Philo makes use of the concept of the ideas in order to interpret the act of creation and the divergence between this Platonic notion and Philo's development of it here, see Daniel-Nataf (2000: *ad loc.*, 7–9); Baer (1955: 85–86).

moval as a punishment for sin. Its rise in popularity amongst the medieval mystics—for whom it seemed to express their covert spiritual longings—must be understood as part of the mystical interpretation of the idea of the primordial light, however. As early as R. Judah al Barceloni (later eleventh/early twelfth century Spain), the primordial light was associated with the visionary gifts through which the future righteous would be able to see the Shekhina:

> About this light it is written: "The brightness was like the sun" [Hab 3:4]—the light the Holy One, blessed be He, will add to the righteous will be like the light at the end of the light Moses our Master saw of the glory of the Shekhina ... that the Holy One, blessed be He, will take from His glory and give to those who fear Him, adding light upon light to them until the light of the righteous of heart will appear and resemble the end of the light visible from the glory of the Shekhina as a candle appears to a torch. (*Perush sefer ha-bahir*, p. 19)

Although al Barceloni here explicitly states that the light will only be revealed to the future righteous, the very notion of such a manifestation as an inner illumination of the heart and the spiritual attainment of "the end of the light visible from the glory of the Shekhina" transfers it to the realm of mystical experience within this world. The passage occurs, moreover, in a discussion of prophecy, the expression "end of the light visible from the glory of the Shekhina" being associated with the nature of the prophetic utterance: "After the great light passes, at its end sparks fly from it. A great light: at which the prophet can look at from afar ... Although at its beginning the one who wishes to look at it immediately dies, from its end the prophets see heavenly visions" (ibid, p. 18).

The manifestation of the hidden light to the future righteous is thus the realization of the prophet ideal in its limited, historical form—"you shall see my back; but my face shall not be seen" (Exod 33:23). This attribute of the light, which enables a person "to see from one end of the world to the other," appears to be interpreted here as a form of superior prophetic inspiration, the idea that the horizon of prophecy coincides with the "end of the light visible from the glory of the Shekhina" also seemingly being linked in this mystical consciousness to the parallel talmudic expression—"from one end of the world to the other." Mystical literature being replete with various images of light, the description of the prophetic experience in terms of light is not surprising. From a midrashic perspective, however, the apprehension of the primordial light as the "light of prophecy" represents a hermeneutic development pregnant with meaning.[7] Its traces can be discerned in the writings of one of the earliest and

---

7 The trend towards spiritualizing the light is also evident amongst medieval philosophers: cf. Gersonides' commentary on Gen 1:3: "See how all concur that this light is not tangible but re-

most well-known medieval mystics—R. Azriel of Gerona.⁸ In his commentary on the talmudic aggadot, he addresses the Babylonian tradition regarding the hidden light, providing a clear and unambiguous interpretation:

> In this chapter, R. Eleazar said: The light the Holy One, blessed be He, created on the first day, one could see thereby from one end of the world to the other. When He looked at the generation of the Flood and the generation of the Dispersion, however, He arose and hid it from them, as it is written: "Light is withheld from the wicked" [Job 38:15]. And for whom did He hide it? For the future righteous, as it is written: "And God saw the light, that it was good" [Gen 1:4]—and "good" means only the righteous, for it is said: "Say ye of the righteous that he is good" [Isa 3:10]. ... As soon as He saw the light that He had reserved for the righteous, He rejoiced, for it is said: "He rejoiceth at the light of the righteous" [Prov 13:9]. This first light is like the light of thought in which a man sees all he wishes to look at ... this is the light of wisdom that rested upon the prophets and crowned them with its light, and they saw visions by power, visions of whatever could be, from one end of the world to the other. As long as the soul is pure, it shows in her its power and increases, shining brighter and brighter. This light is set apart for the righteous, as they a possess pure and clean spirit, and this light is called the light of life. (*Perush ha-aggadot*, p. 111)

Here, the primordial light "is like the thought ... the light of wisdom that rested upon the prophets."⁹ According to this Aristotelian-Maimonidean-like interpretation, the spirit that rested on the prophets was the "light of wisdom" and the "light of thought." When prophecy is apprehended in intellectual-psychological terms, it is embedded in this world. If it nonetheless lies beyond human reach at this present time, this is only because God is still reluctant to make it manifest. This view thus opens up the possibility that the light will be made accessible in this world—if and when God so wishes. As other places in R. Azriel's writings

---

gard it as the light of the intellect." For the various views regarding the "light of creation" in medieval Jewish philosophy, see Sermoneta (1994: 343–360.

8 For the "hidden light" in his *Perush ha-aggadot* and the myth amongst the early mystics, see also Pedaya (1996: 151–156).

9 In the following generation of mystics, this idea becomes even more explicit. Thus, for example, in his commentary on Gen 1:4, Rabbeinu Bachya b. Asher observes: "A kabbalistic approach to our verse yields the following insight. The words את האור ['and the light'] were meant to include something that R. Akiva achieved when he 'descended' into the '*Pardes*,' reigions of enquiry into the mysteries of the universe. He was the only person to emerge intellectually unharmed and physically intact from such studies" (1998: 1: 23–24). R. Menahem Recanti similarly asserts: "Our masters the Sages said: By means of this light a man can see from one end of the world to the other—this refers to the chariot [*merkava*], through which they attain the truth of all creation: from one end of the world to the other" (*Perush ha-torah*, p. 20).

suggest, the mystic potential of the primordial light may be realized before the "world to come"—i.e., in the here and now.

The "world to come" and the "future"

Although R. Azriel cites the talmudic source at the beginning of his commentary, as is his wont, a close and sensitive reading reveals that he in fact subjects it to a dramatic revision, completely ignoring and eradicating the future tense. According to his exegesis, the primordial light has already been present in the world: it "*rested* on the prophets and crowned them with its light, and they *saw* visions by power, visions of whatever could be, from one end of the world to the other." If we listen closely, we can also discern the lightning "leaps" from the past to present tense: "it is like the light of thought in which a man sees all that he *desires* to see" and "*shows* its power in it, *increasing* and shining brighter and brighter." This "sliding" from the future into the past and present is, of course, not coincidental, reflecting the writer's tendency towards releasing the light from its hiding place and making room for it within the imperfect reality of this world.

R. Azriel also makes another "minor" but very significant change in the source: "When He looked at the generation of the Flood and the generation of the Dispersion, He arose and hid it from them, as it is written: "Light is withheld from the wicked" [Job 38:15]. And for whom did He hide it? For the future righteous." Hereby, he asserts that the light was reserved "for the future righteous" (לעתיד)—rather than the "future to come" (לעתיד לבוא) as in the talmudic source, which carries eschatological connotations. The phrase "future righteous," in contrast, gives the impression of a future within historical time and the righteous in this world. R. Azriel does not appear to have had a variant text before him, employing the same version that exists in our extant text when quoting this passage elsewhere in a different context (see below). Although drawing conclusions from the omission of a single word is a risky business, the general picture we have painted, linguistic phenomena, and R. Azriel's explicit statements all suggest that the omission was deliberate, representing an attempt to bring the light closer to human reach by making it accessible to the righteous in this world.[10]

If this interpretation does not remove all doubts, we need only look elsewhere in the same work, where R. Azriel makes the same claim clearly and un-

---

10 The caution necessary here is primarily due to the paucity of textual witnesses: see R. Azriel, *Perush ha-aggadot*, Editor's Introduction (Tishby), p. 1.

ambiguously. Seeking to demonstrate the same idea from a different perspective, he employs a parable from *Midrash Psalms*, which he then explicates:

> In the world's use, when a man carries about the light of a lamp inside his house, can he say: "Such-and-such a man who is my friend is free to use the light of the lamp but such-and-such a man who is my foe is not free to use the light of the lamp? [... *Mid. Ps.* 27:1]. The light that he divided for Himself was the light that had already emanated from the Name and will be in the world to come. Some say: even the righteous can use it and it is their portion—the light and salvation.[11]

R. Azriel introduces two innovations here. The first is that the light will be in the "world to come." This, of course, is not a new thought. The other, adduced with a measure of reservation ("some say"), is that "even the righteous can use it"—in this world. In this explicit statement, we can identify an invitation to an alternative reading of the talmudic midrash and its assertion that the hidden light is reserved for "the righteous and the world to come." Here, rather than deleting a word R. Azriel adds a *waw conjunctive*. Both interpretations lead to the same goal, however, of seeking an allusion in the talmudic midrash to the manifestation of the hidden light in this world.

Who lies behind the anonymous opinion R. Azriel cites in the name of "some say" and who are the righteous who are worthy in this world to receive the hidden light? While R. Azriel does not provide any answers to these questions, his hints in the former passage quoted above strongly suggest that he himself identified with it. The reserved fashion in which he chooses to present this idea only informs us of its innovative quality—and perhaps its unconventional and daring bold mystical connotation. Here, Azriel gives voice to the yearnings of the early mystics for the revelation of that primordial light and the place it holds within their spiritual world—seeds that will sprout and blossom in the *Zohar*.

Before turning to the *Zohar* and its treatment of the myth, let us first examine one of the thirteenth-century kabbalists who contributed to *Zohar*'s compo-

---

[11] R. Azriel, *Perush ha-aggadot*, pp. 85–86; *Mid. Ps.* Buber edition with minor variations. For the various versions of this text in the manuscripts and printed editions, see there, notes and emendations 3. As in many other cases, R. Azriel's comments are based on R. Ezra b. Solomon's *Perush ha-aggadot*: see Tishby (1945: Introduction, 1–19). In R. Ezra's parallel commentary (Vitkin ms., pp. 33a–33b), only the text from *Mid. Ps.* is cited, followed by a brief comment: "Henceforth you can trust the truth of the verses and God preceded them day and night in a pillar of cloud and a pillar of fire, and the angel moved ahead." We learn from this that R. Ezra regarded the pillars of cloud and fire as a form of manifestation of the primordial light in history. Although recalling the pillars of cloud and fire in this context, R. Azriel himself refrains from drawing this conclusion: see Tishby (1945: 85–86).

sition, R. Moses de León.¹² De León appears to be the first kabbalist to have given a literary label to this light, identifying with the *sefira* of *Hesed* (ibid: 31–32).¹³ Despite the high and lofty position occupied by *Hesed*, however, R. Moses de Léon does not drive the hidden light beyond the human horizon. On the contrary, in his *Sefer Ha-rimon* he draws it into the mystical centre of the spiritual life, asserting that the very yearning for it constitutes an exalted realization of the ideal of the love of God:

> For indeed the secret of love is that it is the desire for the light of the seven days—i.e., the light reserved for the righteous in the world to come. This is the desire and love that yearns and longs for its Creator, ascending to the place of the Great Light, which is the primordial light that is the yearning and longing for the Creator. Love being the highest attribute, it cleaves and clings to God's upper right hand. When a man ascends within the mystery of love and loves his Creator with all his soul, he cleaves so as to be illumined by the light in the hidden light and is found as one who pursues it more than all others. (Wolfson, 1988a: 40)

Love being the "right hand of the uppermost"—*Hesed*—its supreme transcendence and realization is the yearning for the hidden light that emanates from it. Bearing an existential nature, at the heart of this passage lies the longing for the light rather than its attainment. If the light cannot be "touched" is any real or attainable sense, what point exists in desiring it" Why should one strive to "cleave" to it if the light is only attainable in the "world to come"? The very longing for the hidden light as a religious and mystical ideal thus mitigates against the force of the talmudic midrash, which erects an iron wall between the human beings and the eschatological hidden light, seeking to channel religious fervor into conformist furrows, wherein the righteousness that gives access to the light to only attainable in the world to come.

In the medieval kabbalistic world, therefore, the light is not really hidden. While it is reserved, it is reserved for the righteous—rather than for the "world to come." Traces of the "hidden light" as present in this world can in fact be found in rabbinic literature itself (Liebes, 1990: 143–145). The idea is evident in the teachings of the tannaim themselves, the earliest source being transmitted in the name of R. Jacob. Here, however, the light is not said to be reserved, the *baraita* merely stating that: "The light which the blessed Holy One created on the first day Adam could see and look thereby from one end of the world to the

---

12 For a summary of the diverse views regarding R. Moses de Léon's links with the *Zohar*, see Idel's introduction in de Léon (1996: i-iii).
13 This view subsequently becomes prevalent in the *Zohar* and the literature around it: see below.

other" (*b. Hag.* 12a). According to Liebes, אדם here refers to all men, not just Adam. The tradition regarding the hidden light is only amoraic. Gries (personal communication) similarly conjectures that the talmudic myth that a light burns above the unborn foetus' head in the womb and it "looks and sees from one end of the world to the other" (*b. Nid.* 30b) also alludes to the hidden light. If so, this dictum calls for all human beings, in the spirit of the Platonic remembering, to seek out the hidden light they lost prior to being born.[14] These speculations suggest that there is "nothing new under the sun," all the manifestations of imperfection accompanying the hidden light having existed since the foundation of the world. They nevertheless do not diminish the force of the revolution reflected in the thirteenth-century Catalonian kabbalist's writings, whose starting point lies in its final, amoraic form (the version customarily cited by medieval kabbalists and non-kabbalists alike). Via a virtuoso display of speculative exegesis, he denuded the talmudic text of its literal sense in order to prevent it standing as an obstacle in the way of attaining the light that has been reserved.

The "hidden light" in the *Zohar*

When we come to examine the evolution of the myth in the *Zohar* and the latter's attitude towards the questions discussed above, we find a treasure of zoharic sources scattered throughout its various layers. It is a very popular motif, hinted at in the very name of the book, the light in its highest manifestation being identified with the "primordial" or "hidden light."[15] Not being able to survey all the relevant zoharic homilies, I shall examine three central ones that exemplify the longing for the manifestation of the light in this world.[16]

The first comes from *Midrash Ne'elam* on Genesis and appears to represent the early zoharic stratum.[17] This text—part of which we have discussed above—adopts a harmonistic approach to the early midrashic sources:

> We have taught that the light the blessed Holy One created, one could see thereby from one end of the world to the other. Come and see: the light of the sun is 1/60,075 of that light of the speculum of that light that was hidden. And even in the light of this sun no one can look at it—not to speak of that light. And have we not stated that a person can see thereby

---

14 For a similar interpretation of this talmudic saying amongst the early Hasidim, see Buber (2005: 210).
15 For the place of the appearance and radiance of the light as a type of revelation in medieval Jewish mysticism see Wolfson (1994) and passim.
16 In addition to those addressed here, cf. also 1:7a, 30b, 45b–46a, 3:93a–b.
17 For the dating of *Midrash Ne'elam*, see Oron (2011: 115–125).

> from the top of the world to the end of the world? But we have determined thus in our teaching, that through this light one can know and see by the light of wisdom everything that was and will be—from the top of the world to the end of the world. This is light that was reserved for the righteous in the world to come. (*Zohar Hadash*, 15b)[18]

The *Zohar* juxtaposes two early midrashic traditions here (representing, as we have noted above, two diverse approaches—the essentialist, which asserts that the light was hidden because "no creature could look at the first light" [àla *Sefer Habahir*], and the view that, while thereby one can look from one end of the world to the other, the light was hidden because of sin) and seeks to harmonize them. It thus proposes two divergent functional definitions of the light: its physical manifestation in the human world—and possibly even the world to come—is completely impossible vs. the claim that the talmudic statement that thereby "one could look from one end of the world to the other" must be understood as pertaining to perception via the "light of wisdom" (i.e., the attainment of everything that was and will be from one end of the world to the other rather than tangible, optical observation).

While, as we have already noted, R. Judah al Barceloni adduces the "light of wisdom" in this context, the *Zohar* makes this light the end of a speculative process, suggesting that this interpretation of the myth was not known in the zoharic homilist's environs—and certainly not self-evident. The *Zohar* is aware that it is introducing a fundamental change into the notion, possibly even—in its own fashion—polemicizing against the fundamentalist view that the primordial light constitutes a purely optical medium. This deliberate shift and homiletical-speculative move must undoubtedly be understood against the background of the zoharic authors' mystical yearnings—which become clearer in the following examples.

The second text, which in the printed editions appears in the body of the *Zohar* on Genesis, also presents a unique interpretation of the light. Here, however, the homilist goes several steps further:

> And God said, "Let there be light. And there was light" (Gen 1:3). This is the light that the blessed Holy One created at first. It is the light of the eye. It is the light that the blessed Holy One showed the first Adam; with it he saw from one end of the world to the other. It is the light that the blessed Holy One showed David; he sang its praise: "How great is Your good that You have concealed for those who fear you" (Ps 31:19). It is the light that the blessed Holy One showed Moses; with it he saw from Gilead to Dan. But when the blessed Holy One saw that three wicked generations would arise: the generation of Enosh, the generation of the Flood, and the generation of the Tower of Babel, He hid the light away so that they

---

18 For the change from "end" to "top," see Matt (1989: 133).

would not make use of it. The blessed Holy One gave it to Moses and he used it for the three unused months of his gestation, as it is said: "She concealed him for three months" [Exod 2:2]. When three months had passed, he was brought before Pharaoh and the blessed Holy One took it away from him until he stood on Mt. Sinai to receive the Torah. Then He gave him back that light; he wielded it his whole life long and the children of Israel could not come near him until he put a veil over his face, as it said: "They were afraid to come near him" (Exod 34:30). He wrapped himself in it as in a *tallit*, as it is written: "He wraps Himself in light as in a mantle" (Ps 104:2). (*Zohar*, 1:31b)

Right at the outset, the homilist makes it clear here that the primordial light is the "light of the eye." At this point, he thus presents it as an optical rather than cosmic phenomenon. This comment is necessary in light of what follows, the development of the myth as demonstrating the secret of Moses' ability to see from "one end of the land to the other" only being possible on the basis of this premise. It is nonetheless difficult to ignore its mystical character which, even if not being explicitly identified as the "light of wisdom," is associated with the rays of light that shone from Moses' face when he descended from Sinai, serving him as a type of "mantle."[19] The homily weaves together here a cluster of biblical and midrashic motifs associated with unusual occurrences of light, reflecting the view that the light is accessible not only in the pre-historical and eschatological periods but also within history itself. It identifies "points of light" within biblical chronology—flickering from their hiding place—both for the present and in specific circumstances and purely personal contexts.[20] Naturally, it is not in accord with the essentialist version of the early myth, which removes the light from human reach until the end of days.

While it is easy to regard the zoharic homily as a continuation of the trend towards making the primordial light accessible to all human beings we saw in R. Azriel's treatment of the myth, the linkage between these two sources must be carefully scrutinized. As is his wont, R. Azriel engages in a systematic presentation of the subject, equating the primordial light with the "light of wisdom" in his philosophic conceptualization. The *Zohar*, in contrast, describes rather than defines the light, depicting it and its history poetically as multi-dimensional—both the "light of the eye" and possessed of prophetic features, being revealed to the eyes of all in the rays shining from Moses' face and exhibiting mys-

---

19 The attribution of a mantle of light to Moses is a bold homiletical step, the early midrash stating that it was God who wrapped Himself in the light: see *Gen. Rab.* 3:4 and parallels.
20 The light manifests itself only to exemplary biblical figures, of course. This tendency also lies behind the passage in *Zohar*, 1:203b, which associate this light with the sun that arose upon Jacob when he departed limping from his struggle with God (Gen 32:32). Jacob can thus be added to the list of people who attained the hidden light during their lifetime.

tical aspects. The most important divergence between the two interpretations, however, lies in the fact that R. Azriel (in the guise of "some say") believes that the hidden light lies at the disposal of the "righteous"—a very broad category. The zoharic source, in distinction, is much more cautious, the illumination being attributed exclusively to concrete biblical figures. In its traditional context, moreover, the prophetical-mystical quality ascribed to Moses is beyond the reach of other mortals, medieval Judaism perceiving his prophecy as possessing unparalleled status. Despite these differences, however, in relation to the starting point of the early midrash—or at least to the way in which it was understood in the Middle Ages—this homily no less than R. Azriel's comment constitutes a significant watershed, making room for the hidden light within human history, accessible to all.

As in many other instances, the most revealing and thus most important homily is that which reflects diverse approaches and gaps within the "zoharic circle." At the centre of the third example, found in *parashat Teruma* in the printed editions, lies a homiletic discourse—in effect a sort of polemic—between R. Simeon and R. Judah:

> *God said, "Let there be light!" And there was light* (Gen 1:3). R. Shim'on said: "That light was treasured away, and it is reserved for the righteous in the world that is coming, as has been established, for it is written: *Light is sown for the righteous* [Ps 97:11]—לצדיק (*la-tsaddiq*), *for the righteous*, precisely, unspecified. That light never functioned in the world except for the first day; afterward it was hidden away and performed no more. R. Yehudah said: "If it were completely hidden, the world would not exist even for a moment! Rather, it is hidden and sown like a seed that give birth to seeds and fruit. Every single day, a ray of that light shines into the world and keeps everything alive, for with that ray the blessed Holy One feeds the world. And everywhere that the Torah is studied at night, one thread-thin ray appears from that hidden light and flows down upon those absorbed in her, as it is written: 'By day the YHVH will enjoin His love; in the night His song is with me' [Ps 42:8]. (*Zohar*, 2:148b–149a)[21]

In line with the prevalent discursive pattern in the zoharic homily, the opening position taken by R. Simeon represents the well-known convention—the official traditional view: namely, that the light was hidden and did not serve in the world. This opinion may be adduced here simply to sharpen the alternative notion—apparently that of the homily's author—transmitted here in the name of R. Judah.[22] The innovation in this view lies first of all in its starting point, which expresses essential reservations regarding R. Simeon's insistence that the light

---

21 For this passage, see Gottlieb (1976: 165–166); Hellner-Eshed (2009: 269).
22 R. Judah's view also serves as the foundation for the homiletical developments in the following sections of the homily (not cited herein): see *ad loc.*

has no place in this world. According to this stance, it is unthinkable that the light should remain hidden until the end of the world, the latter's existence being dependent on its perpetual appearance.[23] The light's mystical nature is indicated by the following passage in the homily, according to which the primordial light is the source of the "thread of *Hesed*" drawn by day on the faces of those study Torah at night.[24]

Despite its decisive and unambiguous nature, we should not be too quick to draw far-reaching conclusions from this homily. The position attributed to R. Judah here does not argue for the real existence of the primordial light, not rejecting the talmudic source out of hand. Although the light is hidden, R. Judah says, it produces seeds everyday whose fruit (and its alone) can be enjoyed, and whose power (and its alone) sustains the world. No unambiguous determination is made here: this dictum does not seek to make the light as it is part of the world, nor does it concede that it was totally concealed. The light undergoes no real concretization. It is not truly attainable, only some of it—a thread of *Hesed*—being accessible, the smallest measure possible for sustaining the world. An iota of it is drawn across the faces of those who study the Torah—the kabbalists, who occupy themselves with the Torah at night. Like the previous examples, this homily thus also represents a cautious and far more reserved view than that of R. Azriel, according to which the light is neither attainable nor attained but only for the "world to come." Only part of it—the "thread" that bursts out every day—maintains the world, pre-eminently the kabbalists' most hidden yearnings.

A comparison of the previous two examples is very instructive. Despite the divergences between them, which suggest that they derive from different hands, both seek to represent the light as simultaneously present and absent. In the first passage, it only manifests itself to prominent figures throughout the generations—Adam, Moses, David. In the second, it sustains the whole world yet we only have the faintest glimmer of it—seeds, fruit, a thread of

---

23 The midrashic notion that the primordial light nourishes and sustains the world also appears to rest on the identification of the light with *Hesed*: see, for example, de Léon (1996: 32): "The world does not exist solely upon this rung, because the whole world does not exist solely according to *Hesed*." The idea of the "hidden light" that creates fruit through which the world is sustained also appears elsewhere in the *Zohar*: cf. 2:220b, 147b, 166b–167a; *Zohar Hadash* (Ruth), 85a–b; et al.

24 Herein the *Zohar* alludes, of course, to Resh Laqish's dictum: "Whoever occupies himself with [the study of] the Torah by night, the Holy One, blessed be He, draws over him a chord of lovingkindness by day, for it is said: 'By day the Lord doth command His lovingkindness'? Because 'by night His song is with me' (Ps 42:8)" (*b. Hag.* 12b). The zoharic interpretation proposes a new meaning of חסדו, namely the source of this light lies in *Hesed*.

Hesed. The roots of this complex and cautious trend lie not only in its formal correspondence with the talmudic source and its reluctance to turn its back on a canonic text but also in the *Zohar*'s profound spiritual sensitivity to the complexity of the mystical life. The force—both sensitive and tortuous—that nourishes this view is the tension between a cautiousness that verges on the edge of banalizing the early, lofty myth and the refusal to accept any banalization of the mystical life cut off from the mystical light that is the mystics and kabbalists' heart's desire.

The "hidden-present": In the wake of the *Zohar*

When we follow the expressions and evolution of the tendency to embed the hidden light within the mystical life in this world, we arrive at the idea that the hidden light is buried within the Torah. As Idel (2003) has shown, this notion can be found amongst medieval kabbalists, primarily R. Abraham Abulafia. Although the identification of the hidden light with the Torah does not demand the light's manifestation, the fact that the "end of the thread" is within human reach serves the concretization tendency, to a certain extent even grounding it more firmly.

In Hasidic literature, the yearning for the hidden light becomes so strong that it becomes a call to reach out and touch it. As R. Elimelech of Lizhensk, one of the generation of the "founding fathers" of Hasidism, writes:

> It is written of the light of the seven days of creation: *He saw that [the world] was not worthy of it*, etc. and reserved it for the righteous in the world to come, as it is said: "Who forms light and creates darkness" [Isa 45:7]. It should have said: *formed light*, etc.—past rather than present tense. But the truth is that, in His great compassion, the Holy One, blessed be He, is always forming the light—i.e., the hidden light is made manifest and revealed to the righteous who walk in His paths in truth and uprightness. Every day the righteous ascends, the more light is revealed to him. And this is: *He saw that [the world] was not worthy of it*, etc. and hid it for the righteous in the world to come. In other words, the righteous will come to this hidden light that was revealed to them. (Parashat Re'eh, 92b)

Elimelech understands the expression "light hidden for the righteous in the world to come" as the light to which the righteous "will be"—i.e., are called to come and of which it is said, in the present tense, that God forms light and creates darkness. As we have noted, here the presence of the light comes to its fulfilment as a real challenge and concept. Neither a "thread" nor a "ray," it is "the light" in its full sense and form. We find a similar statement in R. Aaron of Karlin, a contemporary of R. Elimelech: "For the first light that was hidden was reserved within the righteous, according to the rabbinic dictum, "and hidden for the righteous in the future." The reference is not to the world to come but to the righteous of each generation who attain the light through their good deeds" (Perlov, 1875: 21d). According to this statement, God concealed the light within the righteous, who must achieve it through their good deeds. Herein, Elimelech of Lizhensk and R. Aaron of Karlin sum up a midrashic trend going back at least five centuries that regards the hidden light as the elixir of life, without which, in the words of the *Zohar* quoted above, "the world would not exist even for a moment!" and whose complete concealment is thus impossible.

Conclusion

Let me conclude this chapter with a passage that opens Buber's well-known anthology of Hasidic tales—*The Hidden Light*. Cited in order to elucidate the book's title and written in Buber's language, it exemplifies the Hasidic approach *par excellence* and the role the hidden light has played in the Hasidic and mystical worlds since time immemorial:

> R. Eleazar said: "The light the Holy One, blessed be He, created on the first day"—one sees thereby from one end of the world to the other. When He looked at the generation of the Flood and the generation of the Dispersion and saw their corrupt deeds, He arose and hid it from them. For whom did He reserve it? For the righteous in the world to come. Hasidim asked: "Where did He conceal it?" They were answered: "In the Torah." They asked: "If so, will the righteous/*Tzadikim* not find some of the light as they study the Torah?" They answered: "They will certainly find some." They asked: "If so, what will the righteous/*Tzadikim* do when they find some of the concealed light in the Torah?" They answered: "They will reveal it in the way they live." (Buber, 2005: 5)

Chapter 5:
Adam's Sin: Its Meaning and Essence

In many respects, during the medieval period the way in which Adam's sin was understood serves as window through which broad outlooks and schools of thought can be ascertained, the way in which specific authors treat it shedding light of their attitude towards existential questions such as the meaning of life, the nature of human life and its status, and the essence of sin. Differences in approach exhibited by close circles and generations can reflect dramatic shifts in religious interest and the focus of spiritual life.

Perhaps due to its sensitive nature and the fact that it touches the "raw nerve" of the Christian doctrine of "original sin," rabbinic literature devotes little space to Adam's sin, the sparse comments therein giving the impression that the early Sages viewed it primarily as the violation of a command (Urbach, 1975: 420–436); Shinan, 2003b) Hirschfeld, 2010).[1] Medieval Jewish scholars—both philosophers and mystics—began exhibiting a much greater interest in this subject, however.[2] In this chapter, I shall examine the *Zohar*'s distinctive understanding of this incident as part of the conceptualizations of Adam's sin that arose in the mystical circles that preceded and accompanied its emergence.[3] As in many other cases, the *Zohar*'s exegetical preferences, sources, and interpretive boldness exemplify not only a subtle literary and hermeneutical approach but also a radically different mystical orientation.

The fact that the biblical text provides no reason for the prohibition against eating of the tree of knowledge prompts the sense that the punishment does not befit the crime, the severity of the penalty calling for a serious, even catastrophic, sin. The kabbalistic environment being more than capable of providing the tools for the taking of such a hermeneutic step, the question of the nature of Adam's sin stamped its imprint on kabbalistic thought virtually from its inception.

---

[1] For the doctrine of original sin in the encounter between Christianity and Judaism, see Schechterman (1988: 65–68 and the bibliography cited therein); Rembaum (1983), and below.
[2] At the centre of the philosophic focus lay Maimonides' interpretation of Adam's sin in the *Guide for the Perplexed*. Maimonides' view and that of the philosophers who followed him has been extensively discussed in the literature and lies beyond the scope of my present brief. One of the most important contributions, however, is Klein-Braslavi (1986).
[3] For Adam's sin in the *Zohar* in general, see Scholem (1941: 231–233); Tishby and Lachower (1989: 1:373–376); Cohen Eloro (1989: 36–75).

The fact that we cannot attribute this move to the very beginnings of the Kabbalah is due to the lack of any treatment of the subject in the first extant kabbalistic document to have survived—*Sefer Habahir*. Although this work recounts the story, it offers no new interpretation of the reason for the commandment or the gravity of the sin, focusing rather on the mythic causes and circumstances of the fall. It is thus states that Adam was incited by Samuel, who conspired with all the heavenly host against his master because he refused to accept the power and authority given to Adam, thus seeking enticing him to sin and compromise his status. Finding himself a "kindred soul"—the serpent—he uses his lackey to seduce Adam and Eve.[4]

This account, with its strongly gnostic overtones, cannot be attributed to any kabbalistic hand or environment, constituting a literary elaboration of the version of Adam's sin known from *Pirqe Rabbi Eleazar* (Scholem, 1987: 65; Pedaya, 2005: 142–144).[5] Had the "Bahiric" author had in his hands a mystical tradition relating to the nature of Adam's sin, he would surely have referred to it. The exegesis *Sefer Habahir* thus transmits thus belongs to the tradition of the rabbinic midrashic interpretation.

The meaning of Adam's sin: Polemical residues in nascent kabbalistic thought

The first extant kabbalistic composition in our hands that contains a real discussion of Adam's sin and its nature appears to be *The Mystery of the Tree of Knowledge* of R. Ezra of Gerona, one of the leading spokesmen of the Gerona kabbalistic circles of the generation of the disciples of R. Isaac Sagi-Nahor (Scholem, 1961).[6] Herein, R. Ezra ascribes a catastrophic dimension to Adam's sin by arguing that it separated the human soul from the upper spiritual realm:

> The matter of the tree of knowledge from which Adam was commanded not to eat: Give your attention to what this is and why God singled out this tree. You will find that He did not warn Adam about touching, as it is written regarding taking—only about eating. For Adam did not take from the fruit or glean it but Eve gave it to him. Nor does Scripture say anything but "Have you eaten from the tree of which I commanded you not to eat?" ... The eating leads to sin. Thus it is that eating the fruit of the Garden is the food of the soul

---

4 *Sefer Habahir*, §141, pp. 223–225. For the mythical dimensions of the tree of life in *Sefer Habahir*, see Yisraeli (2010: 274–277 and the bibliography cited therein).
5 For the depiction of Adam's sin in *Pirqe R. El.*, see Stein (2004: 78–88).
6 For a discussion of this text and the Gerona kabbalists' interpretation of Adam's sin, see Gavrin (2005: 42–47).

and for this Adam was punished—for eating, in which both body and soul partake. But the taking of the fruit is not forbidden in the upper realms—only in the eating of the fruit is the soul implicated, being nourished by it. Although taking the fruit involves some separation below, the soul finds no pleasure in it. Nor does it cause damage in the upper realms as does the eating, in which the soul participates, thus causing damage because the fruit contains dangerous elements, inciting the evil inclination and detracting from greatness and health and diminishing the power in the upper realms. This was the sin: you already knew that the tree of life and the tree of knowledge were one for below, one for above, as it is said: the tree of knowledge from the north wind and the tree of life from the east wind served to illumine the world. Satan's power is there, and in the Yerushalmi what is Satan? This teaches us that the Holy One, blessed be He, has one attribute called evil and this is on His north side, as it is said: "Out of the north disaster shall break out on all the inhabitants of the land" [Jer 1:14] ... After he had eaten from the tree of knowledge, which is the evil side, and separated it from the tree of knowledge, the evil inclination ruled over Adam in his eating. He was immediately punished and introduced to death and the alienation of the soul. So it is clear that in his eating he cut down below and above and separated the forces of the tree of knowledge from the tree of life. This is the cutting of the shoots, that after he separated the tree of knowledge—the evil inclination—from the tree of life and increased its power and sated his soul from it, he dissociated himself from the upper soul and gave power to the branches of the [tree] of knowledge to do evil, separating the tree of knowledge from the tree of life. His soul was denuded of all the properties that lie in the good and was united with the evil inclination.[7]

According to R. Ezra, the sin of eating represents cleaving to evil and assimilating it within one's soul. It is not merely the physical act of eating at stake here but the ingestion of food unfit for the soul, Adam's pleasure from it causing him to increase the power of the evil inclination and thus unite with it.[8] The root of the fall thus lies in Adam's "dissociating himself from the upper soul and giving power to the branches of the [tree] of knowledge to do evil." The latter element—upon which he elaborates in the continuation, is the severing of the individual soul from the upper, theosophic soul, hereby also creating a split in his own soul and removing all its properties that "lie in the good."

This exposition reveals much about the history of this interpretation and the environs in which it emerged. It is self-evidently a novel interpretation, no parallel to which can be found prior to the flourishing of the Kabbalah at the end of the thirteen century. A close reading of the text nonetheless reveals a fuller picture of the contemporaneous interpretive "map" regarding the essence of Adam's

---

7 This version is taken primarily from the Parma-Palatina ms. 2430. The first sentence, which appears to be fragmented, is reconstructed according to the London ms., BL 15299.
8 The novelty of this spiritualizing exegesis of Adam's sin is also exemplified in the continuation: "Do not stumble over the fact that Adam's sin was not in the eating because the separation was in the thought, which is more powerful than the soul."

sin. The passage opens on a polemical note. The statement "You will not find that He warned Adam about touching as it is written regarding taking, but only about eating" and the cluster of assertions and proofs that follow it are undoubtedly aimed at another exegesis known to R. Ezra's readers—one that may even have been more prevalent in Spanish kabbalistic circles.

The broad hints R. Ezra supplies enable us to reconstruct this view, which transpires to be the well-known interpretive tradition of the "cutting of the shoots." As we shall see below, this refers to the separation of the tree of knowledge (*Malkut*) from the tree of life (*Tiferet*), common motif in the discourse of the early kabbalists. Nahmanides, for example, associates it with Adam's sin in his commentary on the Torah, for example. As is wont, in his commentary "by way of the truth," he writes very succinctly and enigmatically, only hinting that "Adam sinned with the fruit of the tree of knowledge below and on high, in deed and thought" (on Gen 3:22) (Yisraeli, 2010: 279–286 and the bibliography cited therein). In his commentary on the tower of Babel, however, where he identifies the sin of the generation of the Dispersion with Adam's sin, he explicitly notes with respect to both that "they mutilated the shoots" (on Gen 11:2).[9] As we noted above—and learn from R. Ezra himself—this concept signifies the theurgic or theological disruption of the harmonious unity between the *sefirot* of *Tiferet* and *Malkut*.[10]

---

9 Cf. also his comments on Lev 23:40. These remarks are well explicated by Bachya's exegesis of the same verse (1998: 1799–1811 [on Lev 23:40]): see also ibn Shuaib's commentary on Nahmanides (1985: 6b–7a). For another interpretation of Nahmanides' statements here, see Safran (1983).
10 The echoes of a divergent theurgic view, according to which Adam's sin lay in the fact that he impinged upon the sacred space of the sefiric system by giving a hold within it to the *sitra achra*, can be heard in thirteenth-century Castilian circles. R. Todros Abulafia alludes to this exegesis in an exaggeratedly esoteric tone in *Sha'ar ha-razim* (Oron, 1989: 132), transmitted in the name of "the great kabbalist sages who delve into good and evil"—a reference to his masters, the Castilian kabbalists (ibid: nn. 467–468). The latent buds of this mystery become direct and explicit in the writings of R. Isaac Hacohen and R. Moses of Burgos. The former, for example, states: "The sin caused both of them to come and mix everything together, the upper and lower worlds. Some of the feet of the throne were shorn off and a wind reached each, the north wind arising to the east wind" (Scholem, 1934: 194–195). See further the editor's references in the notes. For R. Isaac Hacohen's understanding of Adam's sin, see Dan (1998). In the following generation, this theurgic view found its way into the writings of R. Joseph Gikatilla (cf. the tenth gate of his *Sha'arei ora* [1981: 2: 128–129] and *The Mystery of the Serpent and Its Law* [1998: 5]) (Scholem, 1976a: 204–206). Elsewhere in *Sha'arei ora*, however, Gikatilla appears to affix the Castilian idea of Adam's sin to the early concept of "cutting of the shoots" (1981: 1:247, 2: 78 and the editor's comments therein). For this interpretation, see Pedaya (2005: 227–

As we have observed, R. Ezra himself polemicizes against the theurgic view of Adam's sin as "cutting the shoots," countering it with the mystical idea that the catastrophic separation was not between the upper bodies themselves but between Adam's soul and the theosophic entity he calls the "upper soul." His interpretation is far more complex and serpentine, however. While he agrees that Adam "cut below and above and separated the powers of the tree of knowledge from the tree of life," he does not regard this as constituting the essence of the sin. Although the mutilation of the shoots severs the power operating on the north side—i.e., the tree of knowledge—from the general cosmic harmony, thereby transforming it into evil, the crux of the sin lies in Adam's internalization of evil within his soul.[11]

A close parallel to R. Ezra's explanation occurs in another contemporaneous kabbalistic work known as the *Letter to Burgos*, attributed by Scholem (1927 233–240) to R. Azriel:

> All things created are called the *emunei amana omen* because the power of each of them is drawn from an *omen*. Adam was created alone, with three parts emanating from him: the power of the *omen* and the power of *emuna*, which are called *emun*, and the power of *imun*. It was proper that there should be one will and Adam's will was worthy of dominating first through the power of the *omen* and afterwards Eve's will—the power of *emuna omen* and afterwards the will of their issue, which is trust *imun* in the *emuna omen*. And these three are one will that for this were one entity, so that the supreme will might exist in all three equally in thought, speech, and action. And in accordance with the fact that there was one in whom there were many powers, the will of its parts could change whether in the commandment or in transgression. And from this will itself that was necessary, it would be meritorious if it was directed towards realizing unity. And this is as they said: If Adam was meritorious, he became the angel of life; if he was not, he became the angel of death.[12] In her lack of *emuna*, Eve made Adam stray from the path of the *omen* and Cain sinned in the way of *emun* and killed his brother. And because they sinned and separated their wills from one another in the severing of their parts, they immediately became deserving of being changed and renewed in order to become equal in their attributes. But if the will of all three was one, the prosecutor would not be manifest in their deeds

---

228). For the notion of "cutting of the shoots" and its evolution in the early and later writings of Joseph Gikatilla, see Gottlieb (1976: 284–286).

11 This idea can also be identified in several zoharic homilies (cf. *Zohar* 1, 35b, 36a).

12 This formulation does not appear in the talmudic literature, only existing as: "If he is meritorious it

becomes for him a medicine of life, if not, a deadly poison" (*b. Yoma* 72b). We may have here a kabbalistic interpretation that understood the term סם as designating an angel (an abbreviation of Samuel?). Another possible source is *Gen. Rabbati* 9:10: "Thus whoever is capable of the commandments and good works is an angel of life and whoever is incapable of the commandments and good deeds is an angel of death." Here, too, the intention differs, however.

and man would not have needed to behave in the remainder of the attributes but in accord with the concealed will that was his wont. And he would have deserved to exist without eating or drinking and even to live forever ... But because he sinned against the *omen* death was decreed upon him and his descendants and he was condemned in all the ways of variability. And after he had set himself upon these way, he was not worthy of conducting himself in *omen* until he had cleansed and purged himself of that sin. (Scholem, 1927: 234–235).[13]

Although Azriel pours his kabbalistic interpretation of Adam's sin into unusual containers here and despite the not-insignificant differences in content and form between the two texts, both regard the sin as lying in the separation and severing of human existence from God. Although at first glance, this idea appears to reflect the kabbalistic notion of "cutting the shoots," it actually propounds a quite different notion. In the harmony that existed before Adam's sin, the human will was held and enveloped within the upper—divine—will. Adam, Eve, and Cain all embodied the sin because they "separated their wills from one another in the severing of their parts." It was this individuation—i.e., the embodiment of the human will as independent and self-reliant—that impinged on the cosmic harmony, in which the upper will was intended to exist in its three parts of "thought, speech, and action." To a great degree, the division and distancing of human beings from one another caused a cosmic disturbance—a type of "cutting the shoots."

According to this text, Adam's sin lay in seeking to become autonomous, in precisely the same fashion as in *The Mystery of the Tree of Knowledge*—despite the absence of the element of the internalizing of evil and the fact that R. Ezra links the act of individuation more closely with the catastrophe that follows the sin than the transgression itself. We thus have here a common tradition that seeks to shift the focus of the drama from the theurgic break within the godhead itself to the severing of human existence from the divine world.

The idea of sin in the form of the individual human will that it separates itself from the divine world also rather surprisingly appears in Nahmanides, who transmits in the kabbalistic interpretation the conservative interpretive tradition of "cutting the shoots" (see above). In several places in his commentary on the Torah, Nahmanides distinguishes between pre-sin human existence, marked by a lack of freewill, and post-sin existence, characterized by freewill. Thus, for example, he observes on Gen 2:9:

---

13 See Tishby and Lachower (1989: 2:453); Safran (1983: 75–106). For the attribution, see also Scholem (1942: 202 n. 2).

> The proper interpretation appears to me to be that man's original nature was such that he did whatever was proper for him to do naturally, just as the heavens and all their hosts do, "faithful workers whose work is truth, and who do not change from their prescribed course" [*b. Sanh.* 42a], and in whose deeds there is no love or hatred. Now it was the fruit of this tree that gave rise to will and desire, that those who ate it should choose a thing or its opposite, for good or for evil. This is why it was called *etz hada'ath* (*the tree of the knowledge*) *of good and evil*, for *da'ath* in is used to express will. Thus in the language of the Rabbis: "They have taught this only with regards to one *sheda'ato* (whose will) is to return [to his own home during Passover]"; and "his will is to clear" [the produce in the storeroom in his house before Passover–in which case he must search for leaven]. And in the language of Scripture: "Eternal, what is man *vateida'ehu*", [Ps 144:3], meaning that "Thou shouldest desire and want him?" [Ps 8:4]; *yedaticha beshem* [Exod 33:12], meaning "I have chosen you of all people.[14]

Adam's sin thus incited will, desire, and the power of choice within the human soul—i.e., individual human beings.[15] This interpretive tradition of individuation as the core of Adam's sin is also found in the Gerona kabbalists discussed above. While R. Ezra and R. Azriel offer this exegesis, each in his own way, as a kabbalistic alternative to the tradition of the "cutting of the shoots," Nahmanides juxtaposes it with his "by way of the truth" explanation, according to which Adam's sin is the cutting of the shoots. Here, the kabbalistic understanding does not preclude other hermeneutical options—the *pshat* or *drash*, for example. We thus have here two different approaches to the link between the interpretive tradition and the creative form of exegesis. While the Gerona kabbalists exhibit a tendency towards harmonizing and synthesizing these two views, Nahmanides holds them side by side, preserving the kabbalistic interpretation "by way of the truth" and presenting other exegeses—of whatever nature—under other categories.

---

[14] For this passage in its exegetical and theological contexts, see Pines (1988: 121–126). Halbertal (2006: 121–126) cites further parallels to this idea in Nahmanides' writings, noting that "To date, we have found no text that posits that Adam had no freewill before the fall" (ibid: 161). If so, the *Letter to Burgos* constitutes an earlier parallel even if its direct influence upon Nahmanides cannot be demonstrated.

[15] In this context, nuances can be discerned between R. Ezra and Nahmanides, who perceive individuation as the result of sin, and R. Azriel, who contends that it is the separation of human wills from one another and God that constitutes the essence of Adam's sin.

"He entered in tranquility and departed in terror": Original sin in the writings of R. Moses de Léon

The watershed that occurred in the understanding of Adam's sin is well exemplified in the works of R. Moses de Léon. While in his relatively early writings, such as *Sefer shoshan edut* and *Sefer ha-rimon*, R. Moses still holds a view close to that of R. Ezra (with certain reservations regarding the idea *per se* that Adam's sin was that of "cutting the shoots"), in his later works—written only a few years after *Sefer ha-rimon*—a very different tone is already evident.[16] Thus, for example, in his discussion of the "north gate" in *Sefer sheqel ha-qodesh*, he states: "You must know that the mystery of the poisonous wine—the wine that intoxicates the person who enters into it to his misfortune, to the point where he cannot distinguish between left and right, the wine with which Adam sinned and Noah sinned" (1996: 36–37). The common denominator between Adam and Noah's sin after the Flood draws attention away from the focus, painting Adam's sin in a completely different colour—the red of wine, if you like. Wine is "evil," R. Moses claims, because it intoxicates the person who "enters into it," making him unable to "distinguish between left and right." The wine metaphor reflects a relatively moderate view of Adam's sin. Wine does not carrying any overtly negative connotations in traditional Jewish settings, the reservations expressed in this regard relating to the consequences of over-imbibing rather than the fermentation *per se*. In contrast to the Gerona kabbalists, R. Moses thus does not regard the eating from the tree of knowledge as leading to human subjugation to the evil inclination. It merely makes man unable to distinguish between left and right—i.e., a state of confusion, numbing of the senses, and loss of the power of judgment.

R. Moses' other works open a broader window upon the mystical context of these statements. Here, the "intoxicating wine" turns out to be nothing other than the object of Adam's knowledge. Thus, for example, he observes in *Sefer sheqel ha-qodesh:*

> He entered Paradise and gave the supernal wisdom to all those below. The more knowledgeable he became, the more he sought to enter into the depths of fermented wine and

---

[16] *Sefer shoshan edut* and *Sefer ha-rimon* were composed between 1286 and 1287. The works cited below, in contrast, where penned in the early 1290 s: see Wolfson (1988a). For *Sefer ha-rimon*, see Scholem (1976b: 345); Wolfson (1988a: 368–369). Although R. Moses de Léon also addresses this subject in his *Or zarua* (Altmann, 1980: 177–182), as his wont therein he makes no mention of the kabbalistic exegesis so prevalent in his other writings. For this work, its date, and the circumstances in which it was composed, see Altmann (1980: 219–244).

> drink from the grapes of asps' heads, imbibing and forgetting his head, being enticed by the sweetness [of its honey] until he departed, in terror, in haste, banished from his glory. He entered in tranquility and departed in terror. (Wijnhoven, 1964: 118)

Here, Adam's sin lies in his "knowledge" and the intellectual-mystical drive within him to encompass and know the "depths of fermented wine"—which R. Moses appears to identify in this passage with the serpent's lair ("asps' heads"), namely the *sitra achra*.[17] However strange it may seem (nowadays), this drive is not evil *per se*, its danger lying rather in its attendant risks and consequences. This complex view is also found explicitly in another passage in *Sefer sheqel ha-qodesh*, here in relation to Solomon's gentile wives:

> It is true that King Solomon in all his wisdom and association with the tree desired to complete his wisdom and when you know the mystery of his thousand [gentile] wives in the mystery of another reason, you will find that this is the case: the same evil is linked in that tree and the sum of levels of that tree a thousand gentile women were in the cause of another god and Solomon in all his wisdom desired to understand the mystery and the mystery of the radiance of wisdom and fully understand the mystery of the tree, thus being drawn after them, to know [and recognize] and achieve the level ... he was drawn greatly after this matter, more than necessary. And the Holy One, blessed he Be, held him guilty on this account, as Scripture says: "If you have found honey, eat only enough for you, or else, having too much, you will vomit it" [Prov 25:16]. It is thus *a duty and commandment* to know and seek this matter and discern between good and evil—but not to cleave to it. For in this many sinned in being drawn after and entering it, not knowing how to safeguard [their ways]. Adam came and the Holy One, blessed be He, tested him in his great wisdom and he entered into this matter without knowing how to protect himself from error and was enticed by it, causing him and all his descendants to die. And then came Noah, who entered into it and was drawn after it and was not preserved ... Then came Abraham our father and entered into it in peace and departed from it in peace, as it is written: "And Abraham went down to Egypt" (Gen 12:10) and "Abraham went up from Egypt" [Gen 13:1]. (Wijnhoven, 1964: 149–150)

This complex and surprising idea is exemplified par excellence in the *Zohar*. As in *Sefer ha-mishqal*, several homilies in the *Zohar* relating to Abraham's descent into Egypt (Gen 12:10–20) laud the yearning for the knowledge and recognition of evil—attributed, as by R. Moses, to Abraham the Hebrew. This story, juxtaposed with Abraham's going up to Canaan in obedience to God's command, baffles the zoharic authors, who associate Egypt with the "great monster"—i.e., the *sitra achra*.[18] One of the explanations proposed pertains to our discussion: "Once

---

17 This "smartness" appears to bear a positive connotation here. For the desire to know whose price is the loss of eternal life, see Cohen Eloro (1989: 285 n. 24).
18 For the history of the symbol of "Egypt," see below, chapter 10.

Abraham knew and entered in perfect faith, he sought to know all those rungs linked below, and ... went down to Egypt" (1, 81b). The desire to know the "rungs of evil" is not only not regarded as sin here but even perceived as part of Abraham's process of ascension and association with the Shekhina ("perfect faith").[19] Elsewhere, this desire is revealed as a true value: "For this is fitting for a human being: to know good, to know evil, and to restore oneself to good. This is the mystery of faith" (*Zohar* 2, 34a).

Finally, like the author of *Sefer ha-mishqal*, the *Zohar* also contrasts Abraham's mystical perfection with Adam's and Noah's temptation by the serpent and cleaving to the lower rungs:

> R. Shim'on said, "Come and see: All is a mystery of wisdom. Here beckons an allusion to wisdom and rungs below, to the depths of which Abraham descended, knowing them but not clinging, returning to vitality. He was seduced by the serpent like Adam, who upon reaching that rung was seduced by the serpent and inflicted death upon the world. He was not seduced like Noah, for when he [Noah] descended and reached that rung, what is written? *He drank of the wine and became drunk, and exposed himself inside* אהלה (*oholoh*) *his tent*" (Gen 9:21) ... But of Abraham, what is written? '*Abraham went up from Egypt*' [Gen 13:1], ascending, not descending, returning to his domain, the supernal rung he had grasped before." (*Zohar*, 1:83a)

Rather than regarding Adam's sin as the internalization of evil and its entrenchment within the human soul, R. Moses de Léon views it as consisting of an incautious—even if justified—degree of contact between Adam's knowledge and the dark aspects of the tree of the knowledge of good and evil. This lack of care—perhaps even of proper mystical training—led to his intoxication, confusion, and loss of discernment. In his *Mishkan ha-edut*, he describes the instinctual dimension of this yearning for the knowledge of evil:

> Because Adam entered the garden of his pleasures, he transgressed the commandment and laid aside the righteousness of the world, pursuing fermented wine and foolishness and became confused, as is it said they went far from me, and went after worthless things, and became worthless themselves [Jer 2:5]. (n.d.: 146b).

The instructive comparison between the *Zohar*'s homily on Abraham's going down to Egypt and R. Moses de Léon's words raises the possibility that the latter

---

[19] In close proximity to this passage, the *Zohar* transmits (in the name of another Sage) a critical opinion concerning Abraham's descent to Egypt in a spirit resembling that of Nahmanides' commentary (on Gen 12:10). It is not clear, however, whether this critique is directed towards the mystical interpretation of the sin (if so, thus reflecting a measure of reservation towards these mystical tendencies) or is independent and relates to the literal sense of the biblical text.

may in fact be the author of the former. Irrespective of this issue, this saying may exemplify an implicit warning against an even more radical mystical bent. This finds expression in another homily in the *Zohar*, according to which the way to individual transcendence and perfection passes through a real encounter—rather than a passing acquaintance—with evil. This idea is also adduced in connection with Abraham's going down to Egypt—to which the *Zohar* also links the meaning of Israel's descent to exile in Egypt and the Canaanites' historical possession of the land:

> Come and see the mystery of the matter: If Abram had not gone down to Egypt and been refined there first, he would not have become the share of the Blessed Holy One. Similarly with his children, when the Blessed Holy One wanted to make a unique and perfect people, to draw them close to Him: If they had not first gone down to Egypt and been refined there, they would not have become His unique nation. Similarly, if the Holy Land had not been given first to Canaan to rule, it would not have become the portion and share of the Blessed Holy One. It is all one mystery. (*Zohar*, 1:83a)

The verb "refine" of which the *Zohar* makes use here marks the innovation this exegesis introduces. According to this passage, Abraham and his descendants— the Israelites—and the Land of Israel must both go through the melting pot of the *sitra achra* as a necessary stage of purification and refinement. In the words of the sixteenth-century zoharic exegete R. Abraham Galanti: "It is impossible to become perfect and ascend in level, each person according to his deeds, before he has gone down to the outer reaches and come up again" (1881: 38b).[20] No need exists to elaborate or stretch the historical canvas towards Sabbateanism in order to understand the radical nature of this view and its ethical implications.[21] When we examine the path taken by R. Moses de Léon in interpreting Adam's sin we must thus take into account the fact that a stance that appears so novel and extreme may in fact transpire to be a moderate, cautious, conservative reaction to infinitely more "left-field" opinions.

"Many accounts": Original sin in the Zohar

The midrashic utterances relating to Adam's sin in the zoharic and *tiqunim* literature are dominated by the interpretive trend of the "cutting the shoots." In one passage, for example, the *Zohar* presents Adam's expulsion from the Garden of

---

[20] See Tishby and Lachower (1989: 2:457).
[21] For the complex dimension of the *Zohar*'s attitude towards evil, see also below, chapter 9.

Eden as being a form of "measure for measure"—i.e., because Adam caused the tree to be "banished" from its rightful place he himself was driven out of his natural home (*Zohar*, 1:237a). In another, it asserts that Adam's sin led to the extrusion of the Shekhina from the Holy One, blessed be He (*Tiqunei zohar, tiqun* 56, 81a; cf. *tiqun* 69, 103a, 115a–b). On occasion, it even alludes to the fact that Adam impinged upon the uppermost *sefirot* rather than merely that found between the Holy One, blessed be He, and His Shekhina.[22] It thus appears to exhibit reservations in several places with regard to deciphering the mystery of the original sin.[23]

The predominance of the "cutting the shoots" notion is even more striking in light of the rejection of the other interpretations discussed above. The exegesis propounded by the Gerona kabbalists—of the internalization of evil within the human soul—can scarcely be found in the *Zohar*. Similarly, while the interpretation proposed by the interpretive school of R. Moses de Léon has parallels in the *Zohar*, in general the latter are simpler and more primitive versions (cf. *Zohar*, 1:36a, 1, 75b–76a, 2, 267b). The affinities between the zoharic homilies of this type and R. Moses' writings in most cases takes the form of the very association between "drinking wine" (as an expression of meriting a severe punishment) and the punishment of death attendant upon Adam's sin. The vitality and complexity of the yearning to know and the profoundly tragic nature of the loss of knowledge that arises from R. Moses' view are completely missing from these homilies.[24]

---

22 Cf. *Tiqunei zohar, tiqun* 69, 115a. The awareness that this represents an extreme interpretation is exemplified in the following exchange between R. Simeon and R. Eleazar. In a number of places, the *Zohar* employs a simple, general theurgic model, without any resort to the "cutting of the shoots" discourse. Thus, for example, *Zohar hadash*, 48b states that: "In the original sin, the upper faces were lost and in the sin of the Calf the lower faces." In contrast, *Tiquney zohar, tiqun* 64, 85b indicates that: "Adam's sin was bound up the middle pillar and Eve's with the Shekhina."

23 Cf. *Zohar hadash, Midrash Ne'elam*, 18c: "R. Judah said: That which R. Beroka said 'It is forbidden to contemplate more than this in this passage, as I heard from my father and have just remembered his words." Cf. also ibid, 19a. For the *Zohar*'s esoteric attitude towards Adam's sin here and in general, see Scholem (1941: 231–232); Cohen Eloro (1989: 36–37, 282 n. 3). Cohen Eloro's suggestion that Paul's claim that sin is only known via the law may have influenced the *Zohar* in this respect is untenable in my opinion.

24 Cf. *Zohar*, 1:192a, 2, 267b; *Tiqunei zohar, tiqun* 24, 69a. For the relationship between the exegesis of Adam's sin in the *Zohar* and the pre-zoharic interpretation, see Scholem (1941: 232). The "flat" and shallow nature of this interpretive version in the *Zohar* in relation to R. Moses is not characteristic, in many instances the opposite being the case. It is difficult to determine whether the zoharic version forms the basis of R. Moses' exegesis or constitutes a poor paraphrase of them.

New nuances within the vibrant zoharic discourse concerning Adam's sin can nonetheless be found. The following homily reflects the maturation of the trend whose origins we encountered above in R. Moses de Léon:

> Come and see, for people do not know or consider or contemplate: When the Blessed Holy One created Adam, investing him with supernal glory, He asked him to cleave to him, so that he would be unique and single-hearted, in a place of single cleaving, never changing or reversing— in that bond of faith, to which all is bound, as is written: *and the Tree of Life in the midst of the Garden* (Gen 2:9). Afterward, they strayed from the path of faith—abandoning the unified tree, highest of all trees—and came to cling to a place that changes and turns from color to color, and from good to evil and evil to good. They descended from above to below and clung below to many changes, abandoning highest of all, who is One and never changing, as is written: *God made the human being upright, but they have sought many schemes* (Eccl 7:29), surely! Then their hearts changed in that very aspect: sometimes toward good, sometimes toward evils; sometimes to Compassion, sometimes to Judgment—according to that to which they clung, surely! *They sought many schemes* and clung to them. The Blessed Holy One said to [Adam], "You have abandoned life and clung to death. Life, as is written: *and the Tree of Life in the midst of the Garden*—a tree called *Life*, for whoever grasps it never tastes death. "And you clung to another tree—surely, death faces you … Then Adam changed into many aspects: sometimes good, sometimes evil; sometimes agitation, sometimes passion; sometimes life, sometimes death—never enduring constantly in any of them, because that place dominated him. (*Zohar*, 1:221a–b)[25]

According to this passage, Adam's sin lay in his refusal to cleave to the tree of life, choosing the tree of knowledge of good and evil instead. This decision reflects the choice of one form of life over another. Life in the shadow of the upper tree—the tree of life (*Tiferet*)—is permanent, perpetual, unchanging. The existential experience of the "tree of life" is not acquainted with the vicissitudes of good and evil, judgment and mercy, life and death. The selection of the tree of knowledge of good and evil is in effect the choice of ceaselessly changing life— growth and decay, life and death. Adam acquired death as his inevitable fate honestly, the *Zohar* asserts, merely being the necessary, inexorable consequence of the choice of the tree of the knowledge of good and evil over the tree of life.[26]

---

25 This passage also occurs in its broader context in *Zohar*, 3:107a–b. For the duplication, see Matt (2003–2007: 3:328 n. 152 and the references cited therein).

26 For this passage, see Cohen Eloro (1989: 38–39), who regards the lower entity Adam chooses as magical wisdom—*chokhma de-tarfei ilana*. While possible, this is not a necessary understanding: see below. Irrespective of this issue, it is difficult to find in the *Zohar* or kabbalists of the same generation any other expression of this exegesis. A certain resemblance may occur in *Midrash ha-ne'elam*, *Zohar hadash*, 18c, according to which Adam's sin lay in the fact that he changed the "unique name" with regard to which he was commanded for a "shared name." The innovative nature of this approach—even with the zoharic context—is indicated by a parallel homily in *Zohar*, 1:52a–b. Here, too, Adam's sin is associated with the passing over of the tree of

When we place the "anthropocentric" interpretations of R. Ezra and R. Moses on the one hand and the *Zohar* on the other side by side, a common denominator immediately becomes evident. All three understand Adam's sin as the choice of the tree of knowledge over the tree of life. This interpretive commonality—which is not obvious and contains a surprising element—places the three hermeneutical routes along a continuum, representing diverse expressions or different versions of the same tradition. As in many other cases, however, it is precisely the common denominator that sharpens the divergence between their perception of Adam's sin—i.e., their understanding of the object of the sin, the tree of knowledge. R. Ezra views it as the embodiment of evil, thus linking it with the story transmitted in *Sefer Habahir* (the "Yerushalmi") regarding the evil attribute whose name is Satan which comes from the north—even though *Sefer Habahir* itself does not associate this "attribute" with the tree of knowledge. The separation of the tree of knowledge from the tree of life means in effect that evil is released from the hand of holiness and established as an autonomous ontological entity. The story of Adam's eating of this tree thus exemplifies his assimilation of that evil within the human soul.

The tree's demonic nature is much less pronounced in R. Moses, in contrast, who regards it as the "mystery of the poisonous wine—the wine that intoxicates the person who enters into it to his misfortune, to the point where he cannot distinguish between left and right." In his opinion, the eating of its fruit only led to a numbing of the senses—a psychological state in which a person "cannot distinguish between left and right." Only because the borders are blurred and he loses the power to distinguish between good and evil is Adam tragically swept into the territory of evil.[27]

While R. Moses moderates the tree's demonic nature, the zoharic homily eradicates it altogether. Where R. Moses presents the tree as at the very least as an entity of "vanity" that endangers a person's powers of judgment, in this passage in the *Zohar* it possesses no evil attributes *per se*, rather constituting the embodiment of the lower and inferior spiritual option. Here, Adam's sin

---

life. Unlike the homily discussed above, however, where his exclusion from the tree of life is regarded as a punishment that comes upon him—in accordance with the literal meaning of the biblical text—here the sin is the very preference of the tree of the knowledge of good and evil over the tree of life.

27 The idea that the post-sin state is a cognitive one in which the boundaries between evil and good are blurred immediately calls to mind Maimonides' position in regard to this issue. R. Moses de Léon beginning his journey in spiritual circles influenced by Maimonides (Scholem, 1941: 190–191), we cannot rule out the possibility that the latter left his imprint on R. Moses' later writings.

lies in the fact that, contrary to God's intentions and commandments, he chose the lesser, changeable form of life that holds to the tree of knowledge over the—physical and spiritual—superior life to which man was destined.

Exegetical tendencies and the exegete

The shift from R. Ezra's version to that of R. Moses de Léon and thence to the *Zohar* may be characterized as that of moderating the identity and nature of the metaphysical entity represented by the tree of the knowledge of good and evil.[28] The contrast between R. Ezra's interpretation and the spirit of the *Zohar* evinces, however, that they reflect divergent views regarding the nature of Adam's sin and its causes.[29] The mystical failure described in R. Moses de Léon's writings derives from the mystic's unbridled desire to know and taste of forbidden and dangerous mystical realms: "The smarter he became, the more he sought to enter into the depths of fermented wine and drink from the grapes of asps' heads." The zoharic homily discussed above, in contrast, warns of a very different danger, understanding Adam's sin as not too high an aspiration but the opposite—i.e., a willingness to compromise on the quality of his mystical life, preferring the lower level of mystical existence in *Malkut* over the higher level of perfection found in cleaving to the uppermost *Tiferet*.

In seeking to trace the mystical context in which a homily of this type could emerge we are aided by another passage dealing with a subject very close in spirit to that discussed above. Although this addresses another sin—that of the Dispersion—these two transgressions were closely associated in early kabbalistic exegesis. The fact that it exhibits close affinities with the tendency of the homily under investigation at present allows us to make cautious use of it to elucidate our passage. According to this text, the generation of the Dispersion exchanged cleaving to God for a lower, inferior theurgic entity:

---

28 This does not, of course, necessarily reflect a linear development in which each interpretation builds on its predecessor. It is quite possible that R. Moses or the zoharic author (or both) are relating directly to the tradition of the "cutting down of the shoots," without having any knowledge of the trend that emerged amongst the Gerona kabbalists at the same time as exemplifying it in their own writings in various degrees and variations.

29 Some scholars suggest that R. Ezra's modification of the idea that Adam's sin constitutes the source of evil in the human soul represents a recoiling from its close resemblance to the Christian doctrine of original sin. While such a possibility cannot be denied, medieval Jewish polemics in this regard focused primarily on the nature of the punishment and its effect on future generations rather than on the nature of the sin itself. For a survey of the Jewish claims in this respect, see Rembaum (1983).

When they journeyed from the east (Gen 11:2)—journeying from above to below, journeying from the land of Israel and descending to Babel. They said: "Here is a site to embrace. *Let us make a name for ourselves* [Gen 11:4]: then sustenance from below will adhere to this site. For when judgment looms over the world, this site will resist; from here the world will derive pleasure and nourishment, since above is too remote. (*Zohar*, 1:75b)

The preference for the tree of knowledge derives from a utilitarian attitude and lack of fervor and imagination. When the *Zohar* seeks close by to understand the sinners' motives, it puts a pragmatic claim in their mouths (ibid: 75a): "Why ascend any higher, whence we cannot derive pleasure. Here is a perfect place."[30] The *Zohar* comes out here against a phenomenon that may perhaps be called a "mystical bourgeoisie-ism," exemplified by a yen for the near and familiar rather a striving for the lofty and exalted.[31]

Conclusion

The *Zohar*'s call here to transcend religious dogmatism, bourgeoisie-ism, and pretension is not foreign to its spirit in any way, its authors taking every possible opportunity to preach keeping one's eyes open and gazing deeply into the mystery of existence and the godhead. Here, however, its summons appears to be directed towards the world of the kabbalists rather than to outside circles—i.e.,

---

30 Cf. *Ketem Paz* ad loc.: "For they did not intend to rebel against the King of the world but thought that in worshipping a cause close to their thought would suffice them to meet their needs without needing a cause far from their thought. And this is "And they journeyed from Qedem"—they journeyed from the Primordial One of the world" (ibn Lavi, 1981: 189c).
31 Bahya provides us with a very similar exegesis: "When Adam sinned this was not a denial of the supremacy of God, an heretical act. Even though he had seen the tree of life next to the tree of knowledge, he did not consider the tree of life as essential but he considered the tree of knowledge the key to his existence. In as much as the tree of knowledge provided the key to all opposites in the universe and enabled those who had consumed its fruit to perform all kinds of activities both in the terrestrial as well as in the celestial regions, this is what he considerer as essential. This is why the verses describing the tree of knowledge and its allure (3:2–6) spoke of its fruit, whereas no mention of fruit is made in connection with the tree of life" (Bachya, 1998: 5: 94 [on Gen 2:9]). According to this interpretation, Adam was attracted by the tree of knowledge (*Malkut*) because of its practical benefits. Bachya appears to allude here to magical powers—as the *Zohar* in our passage may also. Although he links Adam's sin to the "cutting of the shoots," he maintains that his transgression lay in his cognitive "cutting down" from the tree of life ("and was drawn after it to believe that it was the prime thing") instead of cleaving to the tree of knowledge. In the *Zohar*, however, the sin lies in the very choice of the tree of knowledge over the tree of life. For the magical context of Adam's sin, see *Zohar* 1, 36b; Cohen Eloro (1989: 47–48, 289 n. 50).

those who know how to discern between the "upper" and "lower" realms and yet still frequently make do with the lower theosophist experience, failing to exhibit any yearning for the "mountain air." Hereby, it chooses to issue a completely contrary call to that of R. Moses de Léon, on the basis of a novel and daring reading of the very same biblical text. These changes in orientation—which exist within the *Zohar* itself to a certain extent—undoubtedly point to the bents, tensions, aspirations, fears, and, above all, the vibrant and complex inner world of its authors.

Chapter 6:
Enoch and Elijah: From Angel to Man, Man to Angel

Enoch's and Elijah's disappearances were the subject of much discussion during the medieval period, both figures being surrounded by an air of mystery. The biblical text says of Enoch: "Enoch walked with God; then he was no more, because God took him" (Gen 5:24). A similar report is given of Elijah: "As they continued walking and talking, a chariot of fire and horses of fire separated the two of them, and Elijah ascended in a whirlwind into heaven" (2 Kgs 2:11). In neither case does Scripture explain the precise details of the events. Familiar with the ancient traditions relating to their ascension, unusual experience, and roles, medieval scholars and mystics also sought to understand the riddle these posed—not always successfully.

This chapter examines the way in which the *Zohar* and kabbalists of the same period dealt with the midrashic tradition that the two men became angels. This idea, whose roots appear to lie deep in Jewish exegetical history, was warmly embraced by early Christian theologians, thereby putting several fundamental Jewish tenets to the test. The way in which the *Zohar* perceives the ascent to heaven and the transformation of human beings into angels points to a perspective that is not always self-evident or obvious—a particularly fact striking in the light of the more ancient views. Let me begin by reviewing the early traditions embedded in Second Temple and rabbinic texts and the *hekhalot* literature, following which I shall discuss the mystical interpretations and zoharic homilies in which, alongside well-known ancient accounts, we also find novel exegeses that open a further window on *Zohar*'s world.

The ancient traditions about Enoch and Elijah

Genesis says no more about Enoch's end than that "he was no more, because God took him," this apparently deliberate shroud of mystery suggesting that the text contains an enigmatic allusion. As in many other cases, this esotericism gave rise to a plethora of attempts to "fill in the gaps." Enoch thus becomes a central figure in Second Temple and later Jewish texts, including the apocrypha and pseudepigrapha, Qumran, and the *hekhalot* and *merkava* literature. Although space is too limited here to provide a full review of these, the overall picture they present is relatively clear. The clause "Enoch walked with God" is generally understood in terms of agency rather than merit, denoting the way in which heaven and earth are bridged and testifying to human sin. Thus, for example, *Jubilees* states:

> This one was the first who learned writing and knowledge and wisdom, from (among) the sons of men, from (among) those who were born upon earth. And who wrote in a book the signs of the heavens according to the order of their months, so that the sons of men might know the (appointed) times of the years according to their order, with respect to their months ... And he saw what was and what will be in a vision of his sleep as it will happen among the children of men in their generations until the day of judgment. He saw and knew everything and wrote his testimony and deposited the testimony upon the earth against all the children of men and their generations ... And he was therefore with the angels of God six jubilees of years. And they showed him everything which is on earth and in the heavens, the dominion of the sun. And he wrote everything ... And he was taken from among the children of men, and we led him to the Garden of Eden for greatness and honor. And behold, he is there writing condemnation and judgment of the world, and all the evils of the children of men. (*Jub.* 4:17, 19, 21, 23)

Sirach similarly notes: "Enoch pleased the Lord and was taken up, an example of repentance to all generations" (44:16). Other Second Temple texts call him the "scribe of righteousness" (*1 Enoch* 12:4) who sees, writes, and testifies of the heavenly spheres—the world of the angels, cherubs, seraphim, and chariots (thus preceding the time of Ezekiel and his vision), delivering detailed astronomical knowledge of the celestial realms to men inscribed in a "book of the course of the heavenly bodies" and "heavenly tablets (*1 Enoch* 81:1).

Generally speaking, these apocryphal sources do not explore the nature of Enoch's supernatural existence, focusing rather on the functional significance of his ascent to heaven. They thus highlight his role in the celestial spheres to which he has been transferred, paying little attention to its mode. He is thus not portrayed as being changed from a human being into an angel, the fact that he dwelt eternally in the Garden of Eden posing no ideational difficulty.

A dramatic shift occurs in the literary representation of Enoch in the *hekhalot* and *merkava* literature of the first centuries C.E., which identify him with Metatron, *Sar Hapnim*, the highest-ranked angel in the celestial hierarchy. According to *3 Enoch*, Enoch was taken from the society of men during the Flood generation on account of his great righteousness in order to testify of its sins, God placing him amongst the heavenly host and bestowing wisdom, might, and beauty upon him, elevating him and granting him fantastical physical dimensions. Being stripped of his human form, he becomes a celestial angel of such distinction that he is given God's apparel and crown, henceforth being known as the "Lesser YHWH" and as such becoming the shadow-figure of God himself.[61]

The early rabbinic sources not only virtually completely ignore Enoch's identification with Metatron but also transmit very little information regarding the biblical Enoch son of Jared.[62] This deafening silence disappears in the amoraic midrashim, which explicitly oppose the *hekhalot* tradition. The fifth or sixth-century *Genesis Rabbah* makes an unambiguous statement in this regard as part of a polemic against the "minim"—in this context, Christians:

> Some sectarians asked R. Abbahu: 'We do not find that Enoch died?' 'How so"' inquired he. '"Taking" is employed here, and also in connection with Elijah,' said they. 'If you stress the word "taking",' he answered, 'then "taking" is employed here, while in Ezekiel it is said, *Behold, I take away from thee the desire of thine eyes*,' etc. (Ezek 24:16). R. Tanhuma observed: He answered them well. A matron asked R. Jose: 'We do not find death stated of Enoch?' Said he to her: 'If it said, *And Enoch walked with God*, and no more, I would agree with you. Since, however, it says, *And he was not, for God took him*, it means that he was no more in the world, [having died,] *for God took him*. (25:1)

This is very sensitive and charged issue within Jewish-Christian polemics, Enoch's immortality and ascent into heaven forming a prototype of Jesus.[63] It is thus not surprising that the Letter to the Hebrews states that Enoch's faith enabled him to defy death: "By faith Enoch was taken so that he did not experience death; and 'he was not found, because God had taken him.' For it was attested before he was taken away that 'he had pleased God'" (Heb 11:5). The Sages' opposition to this exegesis led them to allege that God had taken him in order to punish him for his sins. In direct conflict with the literal sense of the biblical text—echoed in the parallel midrashic tradition—this passage in *Genesis Rabbah*

---

[61] For the Enoch-Metatron tradition, see Scholem (1965); VanderKam (1984, 1995); Idel (1990b); Orlev (2005). For references to Enoch in the apocrypha and pseudepigrapha, see Elior (2005: 32 n, 23, 35 n. 28).

[62] A latent polemic against this myth may possibly exist in the account of Metatron writing Israel's merits (a euphemism for their sins), for which he was punished "with sixty fiery lashes" in *b. Hag.* 15a. The motif of "writing Israel's merits" undoubtedly alludes to the tradition cited in *Jubilees:* "And behold, he is there writing condemnation and judgment of the world, and all of the evils of the children of men" (4:23). Metatron's lashing that appears to be meant to "lash" the *hekhalot* myth of Enoch-Metatron (Liebes, 1990: 29–50).

[63] R. Abbahu was known for his arguments with Christians, one of the most relevant for the present discussion being that transmitted in *y. Ta'anit* 2, 1, 65b: "R. Abbahu said: If a man says: "I am God," he is a liar. [If he says:] "I am a son of man," in the end people will laugh at him. [If he says:] "I will go up to heaven," he says but does not perform": see Irshai (1982 and the bibliography cited therein); Travers-Herford (1903: 62); Pick (1913: 29–32); Schäfer (2007: 107–109).

claims that "he was not inscribed in the roll of the righteous but in the roll of the wicked. R. Aibu said: 'Enoch was a hypocrite, acting sometimes as a righteous, sometimes as a wicked man.' Therefore the Holy One, blessed be He, said: 'While he is righteous, I will remove him.'"[64]

The view that Enoch died like all mortals did not emerge solely due to Jewish-Christian polemics but goes back to peripheral Jewish hellenistic writings from the end of the Second Temple period. Philo does not associate Enoch with immortality or transfiguration in any way, shape, or form, regarding the biblical notation that he walked with God and "was not" as pointing to his dramatic turn from vice to virtue, one involving a "change of location" so that he could devote himself to a life of seclusion and purity (Loader: 2011: 142–143).[65] A clear allusion to the tradition that Enoch died also occurs in the Wisdom of Solomon, even if he is not referred to by name:

> But the righteous, though they die early, will be at rest. For old age is not honored for length of time, or measured by number of years; but understanding is gray hair for anyone, and a blameless life is ripe old age. There were some who pleased God and were loved by him, and while living among sinners were taken up. They were caught up so that evil might not change their understanding or guile deceive their souls. For the fascination of wickedness obscures what is good, and roving desire perverts the innocent mind. Being perfected in a short time, they fulfilled long years; for their souls were pleasing to the Lord, therefore he took them quickly from the midst of wickedness. (Wis 4:7–14) (Kraft, 1978)

---

64 While Enoch's righteousness is commensurate with the literal meaning of the text and the fact that "walking with/before God" is a positive attribute in Scripture (cf. "Noah was a righteous man, blameless in his generation; Noah walked with God" [Gen 6:9]; "When Abram was ninety-nine years old, the LORD appeared to Abram, and said to him, 'I am God Almighty; walk before me, and be blameless'" [Gen 17:1]; and perhaps: "The God before whom my ancestors Abraham and Isaac walked, the God who has been my shepherd all my life to this day" [Gen 48:15]), this poses the question of why he suffered an untimely death. Rashi cites this tradition that he was sometimes righteous and sometimes wicked with a slight but significant alteration: "*And Enoch walked [with God]*—He was a righteous man, but his mind was easily induced to turn from his righteous ways and to become wicked. The Holy One, blessed be He, therefore took him away very quickly and made him die before his full time" (on Gen 5:24). According to this interpretation, Enoch was weak of mind rather than an actual sinner, thus being removed before he could transgress. In the *Zohar*, this trend takes on a deterministic hue, being formulated as the principle that God on occasion removes the righteous from the world because He knows that they will stray from their path: cf. *Zohar*, 1:56b, 2:10b.

65 Cf. *Abr.* 16–19; *Praem.* 16–17; *Post.* 40–43; *Mut.* 32–39. See Kraft (1978). This view of Enoch (and Elijah) finds expression during the medieval period in Judah Halevi's *Kuzari* (3.1): see below. In *QG* 1:86, Philo presents a different explanation, asserting that Enoch was he was "translated from a visible place, perceptible by the outward senses, into an incorporeal idea, appreciable only to the intellect": see Belkin (1989: 119). This approach is developed amongst various medieval rationalist commentators: see below.

The concluding statement appears to be a free translation of the verse "and was not because God took him." This interpretation closely resembles that of *Genesis Rabbah*, suggesting that as early as the hellenistic period some exegetes refused to accept the fact that a human being could be granted such an elevated status. In their polemic against early Christianity with regard to this issue, the Sages favoured the rationalistic hellenistic over the traditional *hekhalot* view.[66]

A different strategy for dealing with the *hekhalot* tradition is reflected in the tractate *Derekh Eretz* (chap. 1), which lists Enoch (and Elijah) as amongst those who won eternal life in the Garden of Eden.[67] This approach appears to seek to preserve the early apocryphal tradition and the essential uniqueness of Enoch's end without transforming him into an angel. *Jubilees* (in the passage cited above) already understanding his ascent into Paradise as taking place during his lifetime, we may identify a kind of "retreat" from the bold *hekhalot* myth to the more modest foundation provided by the apocryphal and pseudepigraphal writings. Enoch's inclusion amongst the seven "greats" of the world also blurs the element of his ascent, blunting its force.[68]

In later midrashic strata—such as the *Otiot de R. Akiba*—Enoch is once again associated with Metatron.[69] The medieval *Midrash Aggada* presents the *hekhalot* vs. midrashic view as a tannaitic controversy:

> It is only that God took him; since he was a righteous one, the Holy One, blessed be He, took him from humans and transformed him into an angel, who is Metatron. There is a disagreement between R. Akiba and his colleagues on this matter. And the Sages say: "Enoch

---

[66] In this context is it noteworthy that Moses appears to have linked to a similar tradition. According to a very early midrashic tradition—whose roots are embedded in a Qumran text but finds no expression in rabbinic midrashim or talmudic texts—Moses' original name (prior to being taken out of the Nile) was Malachia: see Kister (2012: 84–88). For the early Jewish-Christian debate over the relative status of Abraham, Moses, the angels, and the messiah in Hebrews, see Flusser (1988).

[67] Cf. also the midrashic tradition transmitted in *Midrash Hagadol* on Gen 5:24: "Three ascended and served on high and these are they: Enoch and Moses and Elijah" (p. 132).

[68] "The seventh is a favourite among the generations. Thus: Adam, Seth, Enosh, Kenan, Mahalalel, Jared, Enoch, and of him it is written, *And Enoch walked with God* (Gen 5:22) (*Lev. Rab.* 29:11) (cf. *Pesiq. Rab. Kah.* 23).The talmudic tradition according to which Enoch dies is aware of the possibility that he was "transferred" out of life without the mediation of the Angel of Death: cf. b. *B. Bat.* 17a. This seems to reflect another form of death rather than a death-defying existence. For the similar tradition relating to Moses' death, see below, chapter 14.

[69] Version B, p. 352. For the links between this work and the *hekhalot/merkava* literature, see Dan (2005: 11–15); Ketterer (2005: 132–147).

was righteous at times and wicked at times. The Holy One, blessed be He, said: While he is righteous, I will remove him from the world—i.e., I will kill him. (1894: 15)⁷⁰

The Targumim also reflect the disparity between the early and later midrash (Kahane, 1956: 20). While Onqelos translates the phrase ואיננו כי לקח אותו אלהים as "he was not because God killed him (ולתוהו ארי אמית יתיה ה')," the later Pseudo-Jonathan alludes to his "resurrection" as in the *hekhalot* account: "*Enoch worshiped in truth before the Lord, and behold he was not with the inhabitants of the earth* because he was taken away and *he ascended to the firmament at the command of the Lord, and he was called Metatron, the Great Scribe* (והא ליתוהי עם דייר ארעה, ארום אתנגיד וסליק לרקיעא במימר קדם ה', וקרא שמיה מיטטרון ספרא רבה)" (to Gen 5:24) (Maher, 1992: 36).⁷¹

The renewal of the Enoch-Metatron myth may be understood as a sign of the Arabic period in the Land of Israel, during which the Jewish-Christian polemic began to fade slightly. Alternatively, it may derive from the spirit and power of the suppressed story itself, which helped it burst out of its underground channels even centuries later. In the Middle Ages at least, the identification of Enoch with Metatron was the prevalent trend in kabbalistic circles in general and the *Zohar* in particular (Tishby and Lachower, 1989: 1: 606–610).⁷²

In contrast to Enoch, Elijah's ascension to heaven in the whirlwind aroused very little controversy amongst the talmudic Sages and early midrashists. This may reflect the fact that the biblical text explicitly states that he ascended to heaven in a whirlwind—or that Elijah never played as major a role in the apocryphal, pseudepigraphal, and *hekhalot/merkava* literature as Enoch.⁷³ The accepted view of the third-century Palestinian amoraim was that Elijah was still alive. Thus, for example, in a discussion of the incident as a source for determining whether the rents torn in mourning clothes should be restored, Resh Laqish

---

70 See Idel (1990b: 229). For the date of *Midrash Aggadah*, see the editor's preface. Wertheimer also suggests that traces of Rashi's exegesis can be discerned: see his comment (on the fourth note) that R. Akiba's *hekhalot* view rests on the *Otiot de R. Akiba*, which lay at the author's disposal.
71 The reading of *Tg. Onq.* here follows the most faithful mss.— Yemen and Sabbioneta. For the textual variants in this verse and their significance for this reading, see Posen (2014: 42–44). For the Christian adoption of the figure of Enoch-Metatron, see Liebes (1987: 178–179).
72 See also below.
73 For Elijah's absence in the apocrypha and pseudepigrapha and in particular the Qumran library and his appearances in the Gospels, see Gruenwald, (2006: 44–45).

retorted to the claim that Elisha irrevocably tore his garments asunder with the declaration: "Elijah is alive!" (*b. Mo'ed Qat.* 26a).[74]

The prevalent rabbinic approach to Elijah in the majority of the innocently-messianic talmudic sources is thus that, after his ascent into heaven Elijah served as an angel of the heavenly host alongside the other well-known angels—Michael, Gabriel, etc.[75] A baraita in *b. Ber.* 4a, for example, states: "A Tanna taught: Michael [reaches his goal] in one [flight], Gabriel in two, Elijah in four, and the Angel of Death in eight. In the time of plague, however, [the Angel of Death, too, reaches his goal] in one." Other texts denote Elijah's distinctive role within the heavenly host, his tasks including those explicitly associated with the angels. In *b. B. Meṣ.* 85b, he is portrayed as serving the patriarchs in the upper realms. In the well-known story of R. Joshua b. Levi's death, "Elijah heralded him proclaiming, 'Make room for the son of Levi, make room for the son of Levi'" after he eluded the Angel of Death (*b. Ketub.* 77a)—a motif that becomes standard in the description of the deaths of other Sages. Elijah's angelic status also accounts for the fact that he is responsible for revealing to the Sages the things determined in the upper realms (cf. *b. Ber.* 3a; *b. Ta'an.* 22a; *b. Giṭ.* 6b; *b. B. Meṣ.* 59a).[76]

The *hekhalot* literature provides us with a living and graphic account of the way in which the rabbinic Sages understood how a human being could be transformed into an angel and the ways in which they depicted such events. According to *3 Enoch:*

> R. Ishmael said: The angel Metatron, Prince of the Divine Presence, the glory of highest heaven, said to me: When the Holy One, blessed be He, took me to serve the throne of glory, the wheels of the chariot and all the needs of the Shekinah, at once my flesh turned to flame, my sinews to blazing fire, my bones to juniper coals, my eyelashes to lightning flashes, my eyeballs to fiery torches, the hairs of my head to hot flames, all my limbs to wings of burning fire, and the substance of my body to blazing fire. On my right—those who cleave flames of fire—on my left—burning brands—round about me, swept wind, tem-

---

[74] Resh Laqish's argument is that, Elijah appearing from time to time and communing with saintly men, his case cannot be adduced as the principle for a ruling on a loss by death. R. Jochanan disagreed with him regarding Elijah, however: "Since it is written there 'And he saw "him no more," he was as dead to him [Elisha]' (ibid).

[75] For Elijah's removal as depicted in aggadic literature, see Ish-Shalom (1902: 14–20).

[76] One of the exceptions to this rule is R. Jose b. Halafta's well-known dictum in a baraita cited in *b. Sukka* 5a, whose apologetic tone and intention is clear: "Neither did the Shekhina ever descend to earth, nor did Moses or Elijah ever ascend to Heaven, as it is written, 'The heavens are the heavens of the Lord, but the earth hath He given to the sons of men' (Ps 115:16)" (Gruenwald, 2014: 129).

> pest, and storm; and the roar of earthquake upon earthquake was before and behind me. (15:1–2)[77]

The above discussion evinces that the tradition of the biblical protagonists who ascend to heaven and become part of the heavenly host was known to the Sages. Despite polemicizing against it in certain periods and places, they never delegitimized it, allowing it to retain its place in other places and contexts. Its history in rabbinic literature further demonstrates that in later strata it gained a far greater measure of legitimacy. It is thus no wonder that medieval philosophers and kabbalists devoted attention to it and renewed engagement with it.

Enoch and Elijah's ascents in medieval philosophy

The thorny issue of a person's removal from the world without passing through death preoccupied many of the medieval rationalist commentators and thinkers —with whom, of course, the kabbalists came into the contact. One of the fiercest and sharpest was R. Levi b. Abraham, who lived and worked in Provençe in the second half of the thirteenth century, who may be regarded as representing the radical stream of the Jewish philosophy of this period. In his *Leviat chen*—a commentary on creation and other sections of Genesis, he observes:

> While it is known that everything composed from the fundamentals and assembled from the opposite must die and all the living is existed and nourished and dies ... and every limited creature's power has an end. There are three states: creator and not created—God; created and not subject to death—the soul; created and subject to death—man. (2004: 328–329)

In other words, there is no such thing as life without death. The same opinion is articulated in somewhat simpler language by Gersonides in his commentary on the Torah: "Elijah cannot have been taken up into heaven because no bodies ascend thereto" (on 2 Kgs 2:1). From this perspective, how is it possible to explain Elijah's ascent in the whirlwind or Enoch's being taken? Several answers were proposed to this question in R. Levi's Provençal environs. R. David Kimchi (Radak), for example, regards Elijah as merely having experienced a more elevated form of death:

---

[77] Charlesworth (1985: 2:267); Schäfer (1981: §19 [according to Munich ms. 40]).

The wind of the whirlwind lifted him up from the earth into the air. As it lifts light things, so it lifted him by God's will to the wheel of fire, where all his clothes, apart from his cloak, were burnt andhis flesh and bones destroyed. And the wind came from God who sent it. (to 2 Kgs 2:1)[78]

Enoch died a similar death:

> *Was no more*—for there was no sickness or pain at the time of his death. It did not occur to his contemporaries that he would die halfway through his life but that he would live long like his fellow creatures. They did not feel him until he died. That is what is meant by "was no more." *And God took him*—i.e., took his soul and brought it to the upper realms. (on Gen 5:24)

On both these occasions, Radak takes pain to note that "the opinion of our masses, as well as our sages, is that the Lord brought him [Elijah] into the Garden of Eden with his body—as Adam had been before the sin." He nevertheless maintains that Enoch and Elijah died like all human beings.

In his commentary on the Torah, Gersonides similarly asserts that the unusual account of Enoch's death in Gen 5:24 is intended to point to his perfection (*ad loc.*). He offers an even more daring exegesis in his commentary on Kings, however—namely, that Elijah neither died nor was actually taken up to heaven but was only lifted up in that direction: "God's wind lifted him up supernaturally to a yet-unknown place, where he lives" (on 2 Kgs 2:1).[79] Judah Halevi in the *Kuzari*, written in Spain in the first half of the twelfth century, also presents Enoch and Elijah as exemplary righteous men, ideal worshipers of God who chose lives of asceticism and renunciation and were taken out of this world:

---

[78] Cf. Ibn Ezra on Gen 5:24, Ps 49:16, 73:24. See also Abrabanel's criticism of Radak (without referring to him by name) in his commentary on 2 Kgs 2:2.

[79] The biblical text itself hints at the fact that Elijah was simply transferred to another (unknown) place on earth, appearing and disappearing during his lifetime. Thus, for example, Obadiah tells him: "As soon as I have gone from you, the spirit of the Lord will carry you I know not where; so, when I come and tell Ahab and he cannot find you, he will kill me" (1 Kgs 18:12). Similarly, after his ascension, the disciples of the prophets seek him, saying to Elisha: "'See now, we have fifty strong men among your servants; please let them go and seek your master [Elijah]; it may be that the spirit of the Lord has caught him up and thrown him down on some mountain or into some valley'" (2 Kgs 2:16). The impression gained is that they found nothing strange in this. The LXX translates the word שמים as "as it were into heaven." Josephus asserts: "Now at this time it was that Elijah disappeared from among men, and no one knows of his death to this very day ... And indeed, as to Elijah, and as to Enoch, who was before the deluge, it is written in the sacred books that they disappeared, but so that nobody knew that they died" (*Ant.* 9.2.2).

> According to our view a servant of God ... even reaches the degree of Enoch, concerning whom it is said: "And Enoch walked with God" (Gen 5:24); or the degree of Elijah, freed from worldly matters, and to be admitted to the realm of angels. In this case he feels no loneliness in solitude and seclusion, since they form his associates. He is rather ill at ease in a crowd, because he misses the divine presence which enables him to dispense with eating and drinking. (3.1)

This form of cleaving replaces human fellowship, not alluding in any way or shape to metamorphosis or transfiguration. The person who worships God chooses to focus all his attention upon the kingdom of heaven, thereby associating himself with the heavenly host who perpetually gaze upon God's glory.[80]

Space constrains us from addressing the numerous difficulties attendant upon the rationalist or realist views.[81] Whether due to these or not, R. Levi b. Abraham adopted a slightly divergent approach. Although this rests on Maimonidean principles, it argues that Elijah's ascent is of the same order as Moses' death, also unusual in form:

> For in both cases the issue is that of spiritual enlightenment and intellectual cleaving to the upper realms. And they said that they [Elijah and Moses] did not gain [the upper realms] during their lives because of their cleaving to the material ... but in their separation from the material they ascended to the upper realms in a completely spiritual ascent, cleaving and becoming one with the separate. (2004: 331)

This is an allusion to the "death by a kiss" experienced by Moses, Aaron, and Miriam as explicated by Maimonides:

> When a perfect man is stricken with years and approaches death, this apprehension increases very powerfully, joy over this apprehension and a great love for the object of apprehension becomes stronger, until the soul is separated from the body at that moment in this state of pleasure. Because of this the Sages have indicated with reference to the deaths of Moses, Aaron, and Miriam that "the three of them died by a kiss" ... in the pleasure of this apprehension due to the intensity of passionate love. (*Guide*, 3.51)[82]

The use of this notion to explain Elijah's ascent forms a staging post in the transition from the philosophers' interpretive "workshop" to the kabbalists' speculative study hall, forming a point of contact between the two worlds.

---

80 For the link between Judah Halevi and Philo in this respect, see above, n. 0. The notion of "seeing the kingdom of heaven" nevertheless contains some *hekhalot* features.
81 For an examination of this issue, see Abrabanel's commentary on Kings.
82 For the sources of this idea and studies of it, see the bibliography cited therein.

Elijah's ascent: Nahmanides' view

In his commentary on the Torah, Nahmanides—an older contemporary of R. Levi b. Abraham—offers what appears to be a similar exegesis of the stories of Enoch and Elijah, likewise based on the principle of ecstatic union:

> But those who abandon altogether the concerns of this world and pay no attention to it, acting as if they themselves were not creatures of physical being, and all their thoughts and intentions are directed only to their Creator, just as was the case with Elijah, [these people] on account of their soul cleaving to the Glorious Name will live forever in body and soul, as is evidenced in Scripture concerning Elijah and as is known of him in tradition, and as the Midrashim speak of Enoch and of those belonging to the world to come who will rise at the resurrection. (2005: 1:246 [on Lev 18:5])

The occurrence of the assertion that the soul remains due to intellectual cleaving to the upper realms in the writings of a prominent kabbalists should not surprise us. R. Simeon bar Jochai, the *Zohar*'s chief protagonist, himself leaves this world at the ecstatic height of a revelation of the mysteries of the *Idra zuta*, it being far from impossible that he was influenced in this regard—however paradoxical and strange this idea may seem—by Maimonides' mysticism in the *Guide*. It is precisely R. Levi b. Abraham's link with Nahmanides, however, that sharpens the divergence and disparity between these two figures. Apart from the natural differences between the cleaving to the "separate" in R. Levi and the "Glorious Name" in Nahmanides, the very nature of the continued existence of the soul differs. While R. Levi stresses the soul's release from the confines of the body, Nahmanides regards the lofty such as Elijah as living "forever in body and soul." For Nahmanides, the "kiss"—the ecstatic touch—is not death at all. Elijah's ascent is in effect the realization of the kabbalistic ideal of transcendence and union, through which a person gains—in his physical state—immortality. That which to the philosopher is *a priori* impossible is for Nahmanides the precise and natural meaning of Elijah's ascent to heaven in the whirlwind. In their very victory over death, Enoch and Elijah realize one of the utopian goals of the Jewish mystic—freedom from the Angel of Death.

Nahmanides elaborates on this understanding of Enoch and Elijah's ascent in the "Gate of Reward":

> The existence of the [human] soul when it is united with *a knowledge of the Most High* [Num 24:16] is comparable to the existence of the angels, which is made possible by [that comprehension]. The ascendancy of the soul over the body annuls the physical powers ... and causes the body to exist without food and drink just as the soul exists and as Moses was sustained on Mount [Sinai] for forty days. Should we seek to attribute this to a miraculous [and supernatural] act, let [the case of] Elijah prove [otherwise. In his living ascent to heaven,]

> he did not cast off the [physical] body and was not separated from the soul. Yet, he still exists since that time and forever. A similar case is that of Enoch, according to the Midrash of our Rabbis, of blessed memory. ... Moreover, the prophet states, *Behold, I will send you Elijah the prophet before the coming of the great and fearful day of the Eternal* [Mal 3:23]. This verse is proof that [Elijah's] soul has never departed from his sacred body and that it exists in the human sense [of the union of body and soul]. (Chavel, 1978: 2:532–533)[83]

Enoch's and Elijah's meriting of eternal physical life is thus not a miracle but a law of existence imprinted upon human experience—the outcome of a person's cleaving to the upper realms. Men of character conquer this height, thus ensuring that even when their soul resides within their physical body they are already "bound in the bond of life," as Nahmanides says elsewhere:

> *And to cleave unto Him* [Deut 11:22] ... It is possible that the term "cleaving" includes the obligation that you remember God and His love forever, that your thought should never be separated from Him *when thou walkest by the way, and when thou liest down, and when thou risest up* [v. 19] to such a degree that [a person] during his conversation with people by mouth and tongue, his [entire] heart will not be with them, but instead be directed towards God. With men of such excellence it is possible that even in their lifetime their being is a "residence" for the Divine Glory, as the author of the Book of the Kuzari alludes. (on Deut 11:22)[84]

This view has a broad and solid base in Nahmanides' mystical world that he lays out in the "Gate of Reward (Chavel, 1978: 2:531–551). In his opinion, human immortality was the natural pre-sin state of all human beings, also being one of the prominent features of the eschaton (the "world to come").[85] The fact that he chooses to explicate Enoch's and Elijah's disappearances in this context also represents a significantly anti-traditionalist watershed. If Enoch and Elijah lived "forever in body and soul" and their existence not undergone change, both remaining human in form, they were thus certainly not angels. As we noted above, this stance is far removed from the prevalent talmudic view of Elijah as the Angel of the Presence, also being exceptional in the medieval kabbalistic context. The distance at which he places himself from the aggadic tradition

---

[83] Closely corresponding statements can be found in Nahmanides' contemporaries and those after him: see Bar Sheshet (1968: 73 and p. 54 of the Introduction). For R. Isaac of Acre's position in *Otzar he-chaim*, see Gottlieb (1976: 237).

[84] Nahmanides attributes Moses' forty days on Mount Sinai without food or drink to the same factor. His cautious reference to the *Kuzari* is in place, Judah Halevi attributing to the "worshiper of God" first and foremost a tendency towards asceticism and seclusion and visual prophecy rather than ecstatic union.

[85] For eternal physical existence in Nahmanides' thought in its various aspects, see Halbertal (2006: 126–142).

and its roots and circumstances can only properly be understood by examining the writings of his fellow kabbalists at the beginning of the Kabbalah in Spain.

Enoch's and Elijah's ascents in the zoharic circle and later works

Here, we encounter the clear and self-evident position that Elijah became an angel—namely, Metatron. Thus, for example, the Zohar describes Elijah's ascent in the following terms:

> *Elijah ascended in a whirlwind to heaven.* Come and see what is written: *Suddenly a chariot of fire an horses of fire appeared* (2 Kgs 2:11). For then body stripped from spirit and he ascended, unlike the rest of the earth and endured as a holy angel, like other holy supernal beings. He carries out missions in the world. (*Zohar*, 1:209a)

In this respect, the early kabbalists continued the early aggadic tradition. As we shall shortly see, however, they also exhibit a sense of unease and reservation towards the literal meaning of this idea. This issue is adduced explicitly in another text:

> However, *Who has gone up to heaven?* (Prov 30:4). Elijah, of whom it is written *Elijah ascended in a whirlwind to heaven* (2 Kgs 2:11). Now, how could Elijah ascend to heaven, when all the heavens cannot bear even as much as a mustard seed of a body of this world? Yet you say, *Elijah ascended in a whirlwind to heaven!* (*Zohar*, 2:197a)

The question the kabbalists are addressing here is not the philosophic problem of whether Elijah died or not.[86] The *Zohar* has no difficulty accepting Elijah's immortality, as inferred by the biblical text itself. What is at stake here is his transference to the upper realms. While the zoharic homilist accepts the figure of Elijah as immortal, appearing and disappearing amongst men, as reflected in Nahmanides' statement, he takes issue with the idea that he actually ascended into heaven.

In this text, the *Zohar* presents several solutions to this issue. One is based on the well-known zoharic principle of "clothing"—namely, that when it appears in a foreign context, an entity, be it physical or metaphysical, will appear in a

---

[86] Traces of attempts to deal with the issue of immortality are discernible in the *Zohar*, such as the aggada relating to Elijah's struggle with the Angel of Death (*Zohar hadash*, 76a), which betrays the direct influence of the ancient tradition of Moses' struggle with that Angel before his death. Cf. also *Zohar*, 1:209a.

garb befitting that environment. Thus, for example, when angels come down to earth they take the form of human beings—this also being the reason for Adam's need for "garments of skin" (or "garments of light" according to a later interpretation). The Torah likewise descended into the world in the "garment of sackcloth" of the *pshat*, as befitting this world, the holy soul descending in various forms (Cohen Eloro, 1987):

> However, like this: *YHVH came down upon Mount Sinai* (Exod 19:20), and it is written *Moses entered within the cloud and went up the mountain* (Exod 24:18). Now, the Blessed Holy One was on Mount Sinai, and it is written *The sight of YHVH's glory was like consuming fire at the mountain top* (Exod 24:17); so how could Moses ascend to Him? Well, of Moses it is written *Moses entered within the cloud*—entering the cloud as one dons a garment; thus he donned the cloud, entering it. In the cloud he approached the fire and was able to draw near. Similarly, of Elijah is written *Elijah ascended in a whirlwind*—entering that whirlwind and donning it and thereby ascending. (*Zohar*, 2:197a)

Although this interpretation satisfied the zoharic homilist, for our purposes the very raising of the issue and solution proposed reflects the watershed the mythic consciousness of the kabbalists of the zoharic circle represents. The question "so how could Moses ascend to Him?" indicates an essential unease with the idea that men can become angels and the boundaries of this myth in the thirteenth-century kabbalistic world. What was simply and innocently acceptable in the Talmud and classic midrash turns into something complex and problematic within the kabbalistic context.

Other thirteenth-century kabbalists, primarily in Spain, also addressed the difficulty of Elijah's angelic form. In addition to the "clothing" interpretation, first and foremost is Nahmanides' view (discussed above). While the *Zohar* "garbs" Elijah with the whirlwind in order to grant him existential status in the upper realms, Nahmanides seeks to preserve his physical existence, arguing that this does not change in any way, shape, or form. Here, the righteous of the ilk of Elijah live forever "in body and soul," his ascent thus merely signifying his cleaving—while still in his physical body—to the upper realms.

Bachya ben Asher—a kabbalist close to the time, place, and spirit of the *Zohar*—offers a type of paraphrase of the *hekhalot* tradition relating to Enoch's ascent in his commentary on the Torah—without identifying or revealing its roots, of course—that is pregnant with meaning. Herein, he depicts Enoch as seeking to know Metatron:

> For he endeavoured to know him and understand him, until he achieved this and clove to him. And when he clove to him, his body and name were changed, because his body became a fiery torch and his name was called Metatron. Because he clove to him, he was

called after the thing to which he clove, because he become as though he and it were one. (1998: 1:152 [on Gen 5:24])

Traces of the *hekhalot* tradition are discernible in these passage, Enoch's transfiguration here being virtually identical in form to that described in *3 Enoch*. The comment Bachya adds here, however, turns the myth on its head. According to him, Enoch did not turn (or strip off) his skin to become Metatron but only clove to him and became "as though he and it were one." In order not to allow anyone to be misled, he stresses that "because he clove to him he was called by the name of the thing to which he clove"—i.e., the name change was representative rather than essential.

Moshe Idel has adduced a parallel to this in a text called *Sod ve-yesod ha-qadmoni*:

> And this attribute was transmitted to Enoch, son of Jared, and he kept it, and would attempt to know the Creator, blessed be He, with the same attribute. And when he adhered to it, his soul longed to attract the abundance of the upper [*sefirot*] from the [*sefirah* of] wisdom, until his soul ascended to and was bound by the [*sefirah* of] discernment, and the two of them became as one thing. (1990b: 235)

Idel regards this passage and similar ones as a reworking of the idea of the transfiguration of the body when the soul ascends—a manifestation of the kabbalistic turn (even beyond the borders of R. Abraham Abulafia's prophetic Kabbalah) towards the *unio mystica* (Idel, 1990b: 235–237; 1990a: 60; 1996; 1998: 151–160).[87] For our present purposes, however, this explanation is insufficient. In contrast to this description of the classic ecstatic experience, Bachya's statement crosses the boundary of consciousness, the field of activity of the ecstatic mystic. He does not relinquish the idea of transfiguration—"because his body became a fiery torch"—his reservations only being related to the notion that Enoch became, in his very being, the angel Metatron. The kabbalistic exegete's attachment to the *hekhalot* tradition as the *pshat* and his adoption of the reductivist interpretation of Enoch's identity with Metatron suggest, in my opinion, that his distinctive approach must be understood first and foremost in the hermeneutical context. In other words, the problematic nature of the human-angel concept prompted him to impart a minimalist representative meaning to it.

Another kabbalist attempt to evade the simplistic conception of the Enoch-Metatron identification occurs in the writings of the kabbalist R. Joseph ben Sha-

---

[87] A comparison of the sources demonstrates that these expressions are linked to ecstatic elements in R. Abraham Abulafia's writings.

lom Ashkenazi, who lived and worked in Spain in the first half of the fourteenth century. In his kabbalistic commentary on *Genesis Rabbah*—which transmits a tradition that shuns this idea—he also briefly adduces the latter and comments upon it: "In the *Ma'aseh Merkava*, you find that Enoch is Metatron and transformed his flesh into torches, as it is written: *And Enoch walked with God* ... and God made a throne for him like His own and see there—i.e., *be-sod aliyat ha-sholeach ve-din benei chalof*" (Hallamish, 1984: 265).

The "*sod aliyat ha-Shelach*" and the "*din benei chalof*" allude to R. Joseph's developed version of the kabbalistic concept of transmigration. This is a unique and very broad view that regards the latter as a type of universal natural law according to which all human beings share a wide and inclusive changing of form. Created entities—from the upper reams of the *sefirot*, through to the angels, men, and fauna and flora—shed one form and take on another, whence they return to be reincarnated and turn upwards (Scholem, 1976a: 336–337). According to R. Joseph, Enoch's transformation into the angel Metatron is of the same order. While this brief allusion does not indicate how Enoch's end differed from the remainder of the created entities, who are also subject to the "*din benei chalof*," the answer to this question may lie in Metatron's high-ranking status. In other words, in distinction to all other human beings, who become ordinary angels, Enoch took on the form of the head of the whole heavenly host.

The kabbalists we are discussing here did not all adopt the same style, each developing his own particular interpretive approach. Nahmanides sought to preserve the status of the physical body within the ecstatic experience. The *Zohar* employs the "clothing" principle. Bachya takes a representative, non-essentialist path, R. Joseph speaking of the "*sod aliyat ha-sholeach*." All address the same question, however: how can a human being become an angel?[88]

Other thirteenth-century kabbalists offered another, far more far-reaching solution to this enigma. This is found, for example, in the *Zohar*'s second answer to the question it raised in the homily cited above, the fact that it is transmitted in the name of the "Book of Adam" indicating the special weight the homilist attributed to it:

> I found a secret in the Book of Adam describing the generations of the world: "There will be a great spirit that will descend to the world, on earth, and don a body, and Elijah is his name. In that body he will ascend, and his body will persevere and remain in the whirlwind, and another body—of light—will be prepared for him among the angels. When he descends, he will don that body, remaining in the whirlwind, and in that body he will man-

---

88 For another attempt to deal with this issue in later medieval kabbalistic thought, see R. Menahem Recanati (2003: 17.3); ibn Gabbai (1883: 2:31).

ifest below, while in the other body he will manifest above. This is the mystery of *has gone up to heaven and come down* (Prov 30:4). (*Zohar*, 1:107a)

Here, the *Zohar* alludes to the fact that Elijah's ascent and angelic status are a matter of primordial existence, a state not granted to human beings. Additional support for the mystery referred to here may be found in the *Zohar*'s exegesis of Gen 1:20, wherein it understands the birds as being the celestial angels:

> *And let birds fly above the earth* (Gen 1:20). The verse should read: יָעוּף (*ya'uf*), let fly. Why יְעוֹפֵף (*ye'ofef*)? R. Shim'on said: It is a mystery. וְעוֹף (*ve-of*), *And a bird*—Michael, as is written: *One of the seraphim* וַיָּעָף (*va-ya'af*), *flew, to me* (Isa 6:6). יְעוֹפֵף (*ye'ofef*), *Let fly*—Gabriel, as is written: *The man Gabriel whom I had previously seen in the vision* מוּעָף בִּיעָף (*mu'af bi'af*), *was flown in flight* (Dan 9:21). עַל הָאָרֶץ (*al ha-arets*), *Upon the earth*—Elijah, appearing continually on earth, not from the aspect of father and mother ... (*Zohar*, 1:47a)

According to this text, Elijah was one of the angelic creatures created on the fifth day of creation—a fact that should not bewilder us, the homilist asserts, because, unlike other mortals, he did not spring from the loins of a father and mother.

What remains obscure in this passage is elucidated by R. Moses de Léon in one of his responses relating to the Kabbalah published by Isaiah Tishby. Herein, he discusses the length of Elijah's angelic existence:

> You should know that in the mysteries of the Torah I saw a very great and wonderful mystery. You do not find a father or mother for Elijah or that he was the son of x but Elijah the Tishbite of Gilead. And they said that before then he descended from heaven and was an angel, whose name is known in the mysteries of the Torah. Moreover, subsequently he appeared to the Sages in many places and in many guises ... His appearance and image are in many matters. So do not be astonished by the fact that Elijah has a higher status than all other men. (1993: 61–62)

In other words, the fact that a man becomes an angel is not surprising because right from the beginning Elijah was not a man but an angel who took on the form of a man, his ascent into heaven thus merely being a return to his original status. This solution also occurs in a similar version in *Sefer ha-pli'ya*, which goes even further, perceiving in Enoch a remnant of the early *shemitta*—the *shemitta* of *Hesed*—during which all creatures were greater than angels:

> You should know that in the past *shemitta*, the physical Enoch was on a high level. He did not see evil and judgment in his time and the Holy One, blessed be He, brought him in this sabbatical year to sustain the world and be a supreme example, judgment and mercy, to test the creatures. They failed the test because they chose death over life. Enoch arose and said to God: This generation are all wicked and corrupt, they have no faith, and I know that you will destroy them. So why have you brought me amongst them when I

was the greatest of my generation and now I have no part of their evil deeds? Master of the Universe, I am worthy of being like one of the ministering angels because the generation of the past sabbatical year of mercy whence I have come were all greater than angels and I, too, was great amongst them. Is it not right that I should be greater than the angels on account of punishment, for I have seen wicked men with my own eyes. So let me be like the angels and I shall be amongst them, and do not let me be amongst this despised and rebellious people. So his flesh was transformed into a fiery torch like Elijah and he was placed amongst the angels, as it is written: *And Enoch walked with God.* (1997: 639–640)[89]

The tradition relating to Enoch and Elijah's angelic nature while they were still in the flesh also appears slightly later in the writings of the fourteenth-century kabbalist R. Menachem Zioni:

And the Re'ach wrote that Enoch and Elijah had an angelic aspect while they were flesh and blood, as we found in the midrash in relation to Phineas and his concealment that Phineas had an angelic aspect. It is possible in a real miracle that just as there are women who blossom in the world by night and become spirits in some cases, people become wolves. (1882: 7a)[90]

Surprising as it may seem, this solution offered by the *Zohar* and other kabbalists is of great import for understanding the kabbalistic rejection of the tradition of the prophets who become angels, since it undercuts the premise that the discussion as a whole reflects an anti-Christian polemic.[91] As we have seen above, the Letter to the Hebrews states that Enoch "did not experience death." The understanding of Elijah's ascent adduced by Zioni and the *Zohar*, however, seems to deny this possibility out of hand, the speculation regarding an angel who took the form of a man and then returned to his angelic status sounding more Christian than anti-Christian. Such an explanation would surely be the last to be adduced against Christian dogma.

---

89 According to the conventional *shemitta* system, prevalent in several medieval kabbalistic circles, the world was created and destroyed in seven periods of seven thousand years—i.e., *shemittot*. Each was governed by one of the lower *sefirot*, who determined its nature, form of life, and rules of creation. According to an accepted kabbalistic version of this doctrine (followed by the author of the *Sefer ha-pli'ya* here), the world in which we life belong to the *shemitta* of *Din*, the preceding seven-year period thus being that of *Hesed*. For this concept, see Scholem (1948: 176–193; 1987: 460–475); Pedaya (2003: 11–43).
90 It is unclear in whose name R. Menachem is transmitting this tradition. It may be Judah the Pious, who greatly influenced the Hasidei Ashkenaz: see Dan (1968: 259); Yuval (1988: 286–291).
91 Moses ben Jacob Cordovero cites this tradition in the name of Moses de Léon, vehemently dismissing it: "But to say that he took the form of an angel—no one will agree to this" (1962: 24,14).

The kabbalistic shunning of the human-angelic figure thus appears to represent a profound and essential repudiation of the myth that blurs the borders between heaven and earth beyond recognition. It is precisely the kabbalists—who elaborated and enriched the early story, painting it in bright and bold colours—who sought to preserve awareness of its perimeters. As amongst other kabbalists of the period, in the world of the *Zohar* the upper and lowers realms are tied together by isomorphic and symbolic bonds, as well as those of dependence and mutual influence, constituting a fertile bed for theurgical and magical outgrowths. The kabbalistic worldview itself, moreover, undermines the dichotomous separation of the diverse worlds by allowing both the upper and lower realms—human beings and angels—to appear in the same story. As we saw in Chapter Two, the zoharic drama is played out by key figures that can operate in the upper realms and possess a rich and complex relationship with various celestial beings. When the ontological distinction human beings and the world above them is blurred, however, the fundamental religious distinction between Creator and created—which, perhaps intuitively, the zoharic authors perceive as constituting the essential difference between Jewish and non-Jewish thought—is at risk of being eradicated. The kabbalists thus made great efforts on the one hand to present a multifaceted myth and on the other to preserve its boundaries.

Conclusion

In this chapter, I have sought to trace the evolution of the aggadic tradition relating to Enoch and Elijah's ascent, commencing from its initial literary appearances in antiquity through to its medieval philosophical and kabbalistic forms. This picture may also help us understand the Kabbalah's spirit and tendencies at the beginning of its emergence. The creative and mythic fervor of the early Kabbalah and *Zohar* is not devoid of footsteps. When the kabbalistic homilist makes use of an ancient tradition, he sometimes turns to complex and foreign speculations that create real theological problems. The questions asked here, implicitly and explicitly, regarding the doctrine of the early kabbalists strengthen Liebes' identification of the talmudic aggada as the more authentic and freer mythic core of the Kabbalah than its younger kabbalistic sister (1993a: 56).

The reflective spirit revealed to us in the *Zohar* and contemporaneous kabbalistic writings also demonstrates the extent to which the zoharic creation was infused with the spirit of its time. Right at the outset, the influence of scholastic thought upon aggada is evident, the latter losing its freshness and innocence. Here again, we find the kabbalistic pretension (found principally within the *Zohar*) of forming a continuation of the ancient midrash and aggada an impossibility, every work—wittingly or unwittingly—being anchored in its own time and place. Despite and with all this, however, there can be no doubt that its insistence upon holding fast to the talmudic traditions in the face of the difficulties attendant upon such an act also reflects its fundamentally traditionalist tendency. The fact that, unlike the philosophers, the kabbalists did not refrain from or shun the early midrashic traditions of Enoch as Metatron and Elijah as an Angel while directly addressing these traditions indicates that the ancient mythic aggada still lies at the core of the zoharic aggada.

Chapter 7:
"He failed": The Story of Abraham's Origins

In the history of religious thought in Israel (as also outside it), Abraham is regarded as the father of the believers—a prototype of the perfect believer who walks with God. The covert literary polemics over the figure of Abraham is thus of great religious import, relating not only to the patriarch but also the religious *tupos*. This is especially true with respect to the aggadic story of his origins, an account that pertains to religious beginnings and the nature of divine revelation and election. It thus not surprising that diverse versions of this narrative are found in various circles. In Maimonidean circles, Abraham is as an Aristotelian philosopher, for the kabbalists he is a kabbalist. The story of his origins as recorded in Jewish literature in general and the *Zohar* in particular also serves as the archetype of the intimate, unmediated encounter between human beings and God.[1]

The zoharic homily: The exegetical context

The various traditions regarding Abraham's origins are diverse and rich, primarily due to the lacunae within the biblical text. Not only do the narratives in Genesis fail to provide a convincing explanation of why *Abraham* was chosen to be the father of the believers but no account is given of his early life. He is 75 years old when he enters the stage, everything preceding that point apparently being of no interest to the biblical author. In the early literature (and midrashic literature in general), these two gaps are interlinked. Henceforth, the two questions are thus customarily formulated as one: what does Abraham's pre-written biography contain that may shed light on the reason for his election by God? This is the exegetical framework within which the various traditions regarding his pre-election period must be examined. Let us start with the aggada cited in a zoharic homily on Gen 12:5:

---

[1] Ginzberg (2003: 2:185–217); Sandmel (1971); Liebes (2005: 73–110). Liebes' remarks and innovations (see esp. pp. 73–79) relate directly to our subject here. Although I acknowledge his influence, my starting point and purpose herein differ from his. My interest in the links and associations between the various sources also takes a different direction, as will become clear below.

As they set out, what is written? *To go to the land of Canaan*. Their desire was to go there. From here we learn: Whoever arouses himself to purity is assisted. Come and see it is so, for as soon as he set out *to go to the land of Canaan*, immediately: *YHVH said to Abram, "Go you forth!"* Until he first aroused himself, this is not written. ... Mystery of the matter: *Lekh lekha*, for the blessed Holy One granted Abraham a spirit of wisdom, so he discovered and tested the conduits of the inhabited world, contemplating them, balancing them with the balance till he knew the powers appointed throughout the world. When he reached the central point of habitation, he balanced with the balance but failed. He gazed to discover the power appointed over it but could not attain his desire. After balancing several times, he saw that there the entire world was planted. He gazed, tested, and balanced to know; and he saw that the power over it is immeasurable, deep, and concealed—unlike the dimensions of inhabited rungs. He gazed, balanced, and knew that just as from the central point of habitation the entire world disseminated in all directions, so too from the power presiding over it issued all other powers appointed throughout the world, all linked to it. Then *they set out with them from Ur of the Chaldeans to go to the land of Canaan* (Gen 11:31). He again gazed, balanced, and tested to comprehend the clarity of that site, but he did not know, could not grasp. Seeing the power of this site, incapable of comprehending it, immediately, *they came as far as Haran and settled there* (ibid). What was Abraham's reason? He already knew and tested all those rulers conducting the entire inhabited world; he already balanced and tested those who ruled throughout the world, conducting stars and constellations—who overpowered whom. He had succeeded in balancing the entire inhabited world, but when he reached this site he saw an unbearable, impenetrable potency of depths. Once the blessed Holy One saw his arousal and desire, He immediately revealed Himself to him, saying: לך לך (*lekh lekha*), *Go to yourself*, to know yourself, to refine yourself. ... Come and see it is so, for they had already left Ur of the Chaldeans and were now in Haran. Why would He say *Go you forth from your land, from your birthplace*? Because the essence of the matter consists in what has been said. *To the land that I will show you*—I will show you what you could not comprehend and could not know: the power of that land, deep and concealed. (*Zohar*, 1:77a–78b)

The hermeneutical starting point of this homily lies in the well-known issue of Abraham's double departure from Ur. According to Genesis 12, Abraham set out for Canaan in obedience to a divine command: "Go you forth." In Genesis 11, however, we are told that Abraham had already departed with his father Terach, even though, for reasons not explained, they had not reached their destination. The *Zohar* regards this duplication as signifying a dual awakening—one from below (*itaruta de-letata*), one from above (*itaruta de-leela*). The first migration (Genesis 11) was initiated by Abraham, being followed by the divine call to go forth to the promised land.[2] In other words, the key point in Abraham's journey to Canaan was his own will and initiative. It was his self-arousal to go to mi-

---

[2] The clause "set out with *them*" leads the *Zohar* to maintains that "Terach and Lot set out with Abram and Sarai, who were the essential ones to leave the wicked" (1:77b). Cf. Nahmanides and Rashi on Gen 11:31.

grate that brought forth the divine call and God's assistance in fulfilling what he did not have the power to do on his own.

This passage is a prime example of the zoharic midrash. While other midrashim are compelled to artificially "fill in the gaps" in the biblical text, the *Zohar* deletes the very literary gap itself. Abraham's initial merit can be adduced from the sparse biblical account of his early life, the call to leave Ur being due to his own preceding decision to set out—noted explicitly in Genesis 11. The problem in effect providing its own solution, the *Zohar* could have concluded its exegetical discussion at the point. In a typical move, however, it transfers the context to the mystical sphere. This narrative, it asserts, is much more than the story of his physical wandering. It is also a search for the God of this land, so that he can find and cleave to Him.

The idea of the "God of the land" is derived from an ancient astrological notion that was also prevalent during the medieval period. According to this, every inhabited place on earth was ruled by the secondary powers of a metaphysical hierarchy—stars/constellations, angels, or princes—only the land of Israel lying under the direct rule of the Supreme God.³ In the words of Nahmanides:

> The glorious Name created everything and He placed the power of the lower creatures in the higher beings, giving each and every nation in their lands, after their nations some known star or constellation, as is known by means of astrological speculation. ... But the Land of Israel, which is the *axis mundi*, is the inheritance of the Eternal designated to His name. He has placed none of the angels as chief, observer, or ruler over it, since He gave it as a heritage to His people who declare the Unity of His name. (Chavel, 1971: 268–269 [on Lev 18:25])⁴

On the symbolic level, Abraham's migration to Canaan represents the zenith of a mystical desire that began long before. The "spirit of wisdom" he was granted by God gave him mastery over all the powers ruling the inhabited places of the world, only the "deep and concealed" power of the land of Israel, the *axis mundi*, lying beyond the reach of his knowledge and testing. This is the "power" of God in all His glory. Abraham's mystical skills can only bring him

---

3 Cf. Deut 32:8–9; *Jub.* 15:30–32, 17:17; 4QDeut.
4 See Garb (2004: 6–7). For the land of Israel in Nahmanides' thought, see Pedaya (2005: 255–284). For similar astrological views with respect to the land of Israel in the fourteenth century, see Schwartz (2004: 211–231). The *Zohar*'s conceptual affinities with Nahmanides are further evidenced by their common use of the phrase אמצעותא דישובא/הישוב אמצעות: see Liebes (2005: 190–208 and the bibliography cited therein). Liebes' in-depth analysis of the relation between the idea of sacred space as centre and the ancient view of God as centre is of particular relevance for our present purposes.

to a certain point—the symbolic juncture of "Haran." Henceforth, his path towards God is sealed. Here begins the mystical drama, God "awakening" above in parallel to the believer's awakening below. The Holy One, blessed be He, answers Abraham's longings to reach the mystical peak of the land of Israel, issuing a call to him, guiding him on his journey, and ultimately fulfilling his wish.

The *Zohar*'s exegetical path from the thorny hermeneutical question (alluded to at the beginning of the passage and elucidated at its end) to the religious-kabbalistic notion of the link between the "arousal from above" and the "arousal from below" demonstrates *par excellence* the distinctive qualities of the zoharic midrash, whose symbolic channels expand the homiletic horizon far beyond that to which the reader of classical midrash is accustomed.[5] Here, the merit on the basis of which Abraham reached the land—and primarily its God—is in fact his fierce yearning for them both.

The story of Abraham's origins in medieval Jewish literature

The *Zohar*'s medieval kabbalistic environs provide little help when we come to trace the background of this background of this zoharic story. Kabbalistic exegetes such as Nahmanides and Rabbeinu Bachya appear not to have had access to this tradition, turning rather to the ancient and well-known midrashic narratives when addressing these hermeneutical questions (see below). Only in regard to the story of Abraham's journeys in Canaan (Gen 12:8) does Rabbeinu Bachya offer a kabbalistic interpretation similar to that of the *Zohar*—articulated in ten-

---

[5] The roots of the tradition that perceives in a religious call in "Go forth" lie in Josh 24:2–3: "And Joshua said to all the people, 'Thus says the LORD, the God of Israel: Long ago your ancestors—Terah and his sons Abraham and Nahor—lived beyond the Euphrates and served other gods. Then I took your father Abraham from beyond the River ...'" While in this verse the focus lies on the fact that Abraham is delivered from idolatry to worship God, the *Zohar* speaks of a mystical journey. A closer concept to that found in the *Zohar* occurs in the pseudepigraphical *Apocalypse of Abraham* (Kulik, 2005). The *Zohar* adduces a double divine appearance: on the one hand, He reveals Himself to Abraham and guides him towards attaining his desire to know that deep power of the land; on the other, the power is the God of Abraham Himself. No reason existing to assume any sefiric splitting here, this literary device derives from the fact that, as its wont, the zoharic homily seeks to embed its distinctive story in the broader literary framework of Scripture and its ancient mythic character. The *Zohar*'s own language is sefiric rather than personal, however, The affinities between the various mythical languages is exemplified via God's dual revelation—once in His personal aspect and in close proximity in His kabbalistic-sefiric) garb. This feature is prevalent within the *Zohar*. Although it frequently convolutes and complicates the homily, it also enriches its form of expression.

tative terms. This absence is even more striking in Nahmanides (on Gen 11:28), the story he chooses to "fill in the gaps" being much closer to Maimonides' literary version than the *Zohar*.

R. Menachem Recanati also makes no reference to the issue of Abraham's origins. R. Joseph Gikatilla (1989: 51), however, tells us that Abraham entered into an "inquiry of the One," attaining the rung of love when "the mystery of His Oneness was revealed to him." This philosophical terminology and religious orientation betraying the influence of Maimonides, his statements cannot be taken as representative of any kabbalistic tradition (Liebes, 2005: 298 n. 72).[6] Polemicizing with Maimonides, R. Meir ibn Gabbai sets Abraham the founder of kabbalistic wisdom against the philosophic Abraham (1883: 2.21 [p. 83b]). In doing so, however, he retains the Maimonidean infrastructure, merely replacing the philosophical principles with kabbalistic ones. The zoharic homily thus has no parallels in any other kabbalistic texts. It therefore appears to constitute an authentic zoharic creation that reflects the *Zohar*'s ideational and phenomenological world.

The zoharic aggada must also be examined in light of another well-known narrative prevalent during this period that appears to have ancient roots—namely, that with which Maimonides chose to open the laws concerning idolatry in his *Book of Knowledge*:

> Once Abraham was weaned, he, as a child, began contemplating and thinking day and night, and wondered how a sphere could follow a fixed path without being directed. If so, who directed it? Surely it would be impossible for it to rotate on its own! Abraham did not have a mentor, but was immersed amongst the stupid idolaters of Ur Casdim, where everyone, including his mother and father, served idols, as did he. In his heart, however, he continued to contemplate, until he realised the way of truth and understood the ways of righteousness from nature, and knew that there is a God who directs the spheres, created the world, and besides whom there is none other. He also knew that the whole world was erring, and knew that what caused the mistake was that they [had] worshipped the stars and figures for so long that the truth had vanished. Abraham was forty years old when he recognised his Creator. (1.3)

According to Maimonides, Abraham succeeded in attaining religious truth of the One God by his own powers of reasoning, thus being chosen to disseminate and teach this faith to all human beings.[7] Maimonides fleshes this idea in his refer-

---

6 As is well known, Gikatilla wrote *Ginat egoz* in his youth, while still under influence of Abulafia's prophetic-kabbalistic thought and Maimonides' philosophic system.
7 In contrast to the *Zohar*, which interprets Abraham's journey to Canaan as a mystical path towards God, Maimonides regards it as a religious commission given to him after he had attained knowledge of the One God. In this context, it is important to note that in his detailed depiction

ences to Abraham elsewhere (*Guide*, 1.63, 3.29; Turner, 1996). Of particular significance for our present purposes is his explication of the nature of this knowledge:

> This was also the rank of the Patriarchs, the result of whose nearness to Him, may He be exalted, was that His name became known to the world through them ... Because of the union of their intellects through apprehension of Him, it came about that He made a lasting covenant with each of them. (*Guide*, 3.51)

Maimonides' Abraham was not only the Abraham known to the *Zohar*. Against this figure we may set Judah Halevi's Abraham as depicted in the *Kuzari*. Abraham's origins were of no relevance to Halevi's project: the patriarch having been consecrated from the womb, his election was hereditary and racial (*Kuzari*, 1.95, 2.14).[8] Representing the "essence of Eber, being his disciple" (1.65) and bearing within himself the superior human essence, his origins were thus immaterial to Halevi, whose interest lay solely in his spiritual development in light of the divine revelation and his own capacities (cf. 4.17).

Although the *Zohar* is undoubtedly closer to Maimonides than to Halevi, regarding Abraham as chosen by God due to his merit rather than his innate essence, it understands that merit in a different fashion to Maimonides. While the Maimonidean Abraham is a philosopher who became the father of the chosen nation due to his attainment of and cleaving to God—and in effect because of his becoming the father of the believers who know and recognize their Lord—in the *Zohar* he merits divine revelation on the grounds of his bold will and yearning to know and cleave to what his natural powers could *not* achieve.

If the figure of Abraham reflects the founding principle of the religious consciousness, the *Zohar* regards the supreme value as the awakening of the will rather than intellectual attainment. While Maimonides' faith is that of the intellect, the *Zohar*'s is that of the will.

---

of Abraham's life Maimonides skips over the call to "Go forth," representing Abraham's migration as the dissemination of the knowledge of the One God: "He went and gathered people together from cities and kingdoms, until he reached the land of Canaan, where he continued his proclamations" (ibid). Maimonides appears to understanding the divine call as an inner—perhaps even visionary—drive to go Canaan in order to declare God's name: see *Guide*, 2.39.

8 See Silman (2002: 134–137 and the bibliography cited on p. 135 n. 15).

The activist approach and its early roots

The divergence between the zoharic and Maimonidean treatment of Abraham may be examined from an additional perspective that sheds light onto the deep roots of the two traditions within the midrashic world. In addition to portraying Abraham an intellectual, the Maimonides also presents him as a radical activist. Through his power and knowledge, the father of the believers crosses the existential Sambatyon between man and God, effectively gaining his religious status and divine revelation through his "understanding, "gazing," and "attainment by knowledge." The Maimonidean Abraham reaches God and cleaves to him before God has even chosen him and revealed Himself to him.

This view flies in the face of the biblical narrative. Although Genesis frequently lauds and extols Abraham, it does so for keeping the covenant he made with God after his election rather than his actions prior to this event. While his response to the call to "Go forth" to Canaan, his faithfulness to the God who reveals Himself to him, his trust in Him (Gen 15:6), his keeping of His commandments, statutes, and ordinances (Gen 26:5), and his fear of God (as demonstrated by the test of the *aqeda* [Gen 22:1–18]) all stand to his merit for generations, they are not the basis of his election. As Liebes (2005:80–82) has demonstrated, all the biblical texts, early or late, confirm the literal reading of Genesis, according to which Abraham became a believer after his election and migration to Canaan and thus in response to the divine command rather than prior to it.[9] In his "praise of the fathers," for example, Sirach also only adduces the fact that "He kept the law of the Most High, and entered into a covenant with him; he certified the covenant in his flesh, and when he was tested he proved faithful" (Sir 44:20).

Abraham's representation as a religious activist thus runs directly counter to the biblical narrative, arising in the early texts and Maimonides not merely due to an exegetical problem but also as a response to a theological issue, his apparently arbitrary choice by God being inconsistent with the principle of reward and punishment. Having discovered God at some stage in his life, Abraham's primary mission and the grounds on which he attains the status of father of the chosen nation is that of disseminating this faith.[10] *Jubilees*, for example, explains the apparently redundant clause "in Ur of the Chaldaeans" as the fire Abraham set in order to burn all the idols, in which Haran died attempting to save them

---

9 See also Zakovitch and Shinan (2004: 129–137). For the existence and status of monotheism in Genesis, see Kaufmann (1960: 221–231)—countered by Liebes (ibid.).
10 For a comprehensive survey of early traditions about Abraham, see Sandmel (1971: 30–95 and the bibliography cited therein).

(12:12–14). Having reached Haran, he then sat vigil on the eve of the New Year in order to read the omens for the coming year, whereupon he received an insight: "And a word came into his heart and he said: All the signs of the stars, and the signs of the moon and of the sun are all in the hand of the Lord. Why do I search (them) out?" (v. 17). (Kister, 1994: 6–7). God answers his prayer for deliverance from idolatry (evil spirits), revealing Himself to him and commanding him to go to Canaan so that He might bless him and magnify his name and be his God: "And he made an end of speaking and praying, and behold the word of the Lord was sent to him through me, saying: 'Get thee up from thy country, and from thy kindred and from the house of thy father unto a land which I will show thee, and I shall make thee a great and numerous nation" (v. 22).

Josephus similarly depicts Abraham as devoting all his efforts to disseminating monotheism:

> He was a person of great sagacity, both for understanding all things and persuading his hearers, and not mistaken in his opinions; for which reason he began to have higher notions of virtue than others had, and he determined to renew and to change the opinion all men happened then to have concerning God; for he was the first that ventured to publish this notion, that there was but one God, the Creator of the universe ... For which doctrines, when the Chaldeans, and other people of Mesopotamia, raised a tumult against him. (*Ant.* 1.7.1)[11]

In Pseudo-Philo's *Biblical Antiquities*, Abraham is associated with the tower of Babel. The patriarch and his companions refusing to take part in its erection and rebel against God, they are seized and brought before the chieftains. Abraham and his twelve comrades declare: "We are not casting in bricks, nor are we joining in your scheme. We know the one LORD, and him we worship" (*LAB* 6:4).

These sources suggest that this early tradition attributed Abraham's merit to his loyalty to the One Supreme God at the risk of his physical safety rather than to his actual faith. This tradition is evident in the early Palestinian midrash (*Gen. Rab.* 38:13). From here, it spread to various other aggadic compositions (Ginzberg, 1976: 5:212–213 n. 34, 216–218 nn. 48–51). Thus, for example, we read in *Pirqe Rabbi Eliezer* that "After thirteen years he went forth from beneath the earth, speaking the holy language; and he despised idols and held in abomination the graven images, and he trusted in the shadow of the Creator, and said:

---

[11] Although Josephus refers to God's revelation of Himself (see below), this remains a marginal event in his hagiographical account of Abraham.

'Blessed is the man who trusts in Thee' (Ps 84:12)" (*Pirqe R. El.* 26). The same story is also found in the various *Acts of Abraham* midrashim.[12]

It is nonetheless difficult to ignore the changes that occurred within the midrash in relation to Abraham's activism. In *Genesis Rabbah*, we find for the first time an elaborate description of the polemic Abraham conducted against the customers who bought idols from Terach's shop and ultimately with Nimrod— i.e., the idolatrous religious establishment.[13] Abraham's religious revolutionarism also finds expression in his pedagogic activity, prompting common folk to question their conventional tenets. His dedication and defence of his principles in the face of the hegemonic establishment, leading to his being cast into the fiery furnace immediately recall Socrates. As a militant who fights God's battles, Abraham has hereby been transferred to the discursive plane, becoming a Jewish Socrates.

Alongside this tradition in *Genesis Rabbah* we find another that places his theological revelation at the centre of his activity—the very content of his faith —rather than his commission to save the soul of those lost in the darkness of idolatry.[14] Here, Abraham's religio-political activity is replaced with a spiritual search after God, his merit being increasingly attributed to the fact that he discovers and comes to know God:

> *Now the* LORD *said unto Abram: Get thee out of thy country*, etc. (12:1) ... Said R. Isaac: This may be compared to a man who was travelling from place to place when he saw a building in flames. Is it possible that the building lacks a person to look after it? he wondered. The owner of the building looked out and said, "I am the owner of the building." Similarly, because Abraham our father said, "Is it conceivable that the world is without a guide?" the Holy One, blessed be He, looked out and said to him, "I am the Guide, the Sovereign of the Universe." (*Gen. Rab.* 39:1)[15]

---

12 Cf. Jellenik (1967: 1: 25–34, 2:118–119, 5:40–41).
13 Although the text in *Gen. Rab.* is the oldest extant midrash that recounts the story of Abraham in idol temples, traces of this tradition can also be found in the apocrypha and pseudepigrapha: cf. Kulik (2005: 9–13). *y. Ber.* 9, 2, 13d transmits a similar account of Jonathan son of Gershon son of Manasseh, this possibly being the midrashic source: see *Minhat yehudah* on Genesis 1 in the Theodore-Albeck edition of *Gen. Rab.* (pp. 362–363); Ginzberg (2003: 218 n. 50).
14 Josephus also combines these two aspects (*Ant.* 1.7.1). In light of the specific agenda behind his historical writings, however, this example may not be of great use for our literary-midrashic purposes. Cf. also Kulik (2005: 9–16).
15 For later versions of this aggada, see the editors' comments there (Theodore-Albeck ed.); Ginzberg (2003: 2:210 n. 16); Lieberman (1991: 139–140). For an analysis of the text, see below.

The way in which these traditions have been inserted into the eclectic editing of *Genesis Rabbah* suggests that this second interpretation was that favoured by the editors.[16] The account of Abraham disseminating his faith is incorporated into the midrash in a relatively offhand fashion in order to explain the circumstances of Haran's death, the beginning of Genesis 12 ("Go forth")—the natural place to explicate Abraham's election—adducing the parable of the builder. If the background to the figure of Abraham as revealing and disseminating monotheism is in fact Greek (Liebes, 2005: 80–90), the inner transition within the "faith" tradition of Abraham from the political to the spiritual aspect may be identified as a shift from the Platonic ideal of the return to the cave towards the Aristotelian ideal of recognition and education. From our present perspective, this transformation within the early midrash appears to reflect a sublimation and spiritualization of the ancient religious activist tradition. As we shall see below, the parable of the building embodies an even more dramatic retreat from the activist model.

As a proponent of this activist tradition, Maimonides takes pains to paint a full picture of Abraham's pre-prophetic activities, portraying him in his younger years as discovering God and championing monotheistic faith. In tracing the midrashic source of influence reflected in the story of his recognition of God, we are taken back to the ancient tradition.[17] Although Maimonides could have relied on several later midrashim that state that Abraham "taught himself to know God," he preferred the early midrashic infrastructure of *Genesis Rabbah*. Even if not cited in the same language, this echoes in the background of Maimonides' text. According to the *Mishneh Torah*, Abraham learnt of God's existence from the natural order: he "began contemplating and thinking day and night, and wondered how a sphere could follow a fixed path without having a guide. If so, who directed it? Surely it would be impossible for it to rotate on its own!" The building's invisible guide is the person who directs the sphere and is responsible for the astronomical order. Although this interpretation of the midrash accords with Maimonides' portrait of Abraham as an activist, as we shall see below it may not be faithful to the original intention of the midrashic tradition.

---

[16] For the editing of *Gen. Rab.*, see Albeck's Introduction, 3: 111; Heinemann (1972); Meir (1987: 70–75; 1996 64–73); Goldberg (2005: 130–141).
[17] See Nickelsburg (1998: 155 n. 13); Urbach (1975: 1:320 and n. 13, who refers to *Pesiq. Rab.* 33.150 and *Num. Rab.* 14:2). These only appear to say, however, that Abraham found God without a teacher or guide in a hostile environment. If so, they do not directly relate to the relationship between intellect and revelation. Maimonides' attitude towards the early midrash is also evident in the fact that both sources call God "Guide/Leader.

The *Zohar*, Maimonides, and *Sefer Yetzira*

The figure of Abraham in the zoharic homily discussed in this chapter differs in all respects from the material reviewed above. Most strikingly, it focuses on mystical ascension rather than the public dissemination of monotheism. In a closely juxtaposed passage, the *Zohar* tells us that the "people of the God of Abraham" (Ps 47:9) gathered around him precisely he had experienced a miracle rather than because of his own deeds:

> On that day all the nations and tongues knew that none other than the blessed Holy One— the Only One of the world—had delivered Abraham. They brought their children to his abode and said to him: "We have seen that you trust in the blessed Holy One, the Lord of the world. Teach our children of the way you know. Of them it is said: "The princes of the peoples gather as the people of the God of Abraham" (*Zohar*, 1:77b)[18]

The most significant divergence between the *Zohar* and Maimonides lies in the nature of the spiritual process. The mystical experience Abraham undergoes in the *Zohar* is completely different to the way in which Abraham finds his way to God according to Maimonides. Beyond the self-evident disparity between the philosopher and mystic with respect to the theological view of the discovery and God and revelation, the dynamic relationship between the man who attains knowledge and the God who reveals Himself is fundamentally different. The Abraham of the *Zohar* wins supernal wisdom from God and comprehends the powers of the "entire inhabited world." Despite this, he cannot grasp the mystery of the "impenetrable potency of depths" of the land of Israel. All he is able to do through his wisdom and mystical powers is to acquire some important insights into this "deep and concealed" site. He already knows and understands that through this power all the world was "planted," controlling and sending out the rulers of the various inhabited places. At this point he is stymied, however. In the *Zohar*'s eyes, this represents the symbolic meaning of his unexpected sojourn in Haran on his way to Canaan. In contrast to the Aristotelian father of the believers we find in Maimonides, the *Zohar* focuses on the religious crossroads at Haran, where Abraham is helpless but full of yearnings and longings.[19] It is only

---

[18] This passage seems somewhat irrelevant to what precedes and follows after it, suggesting that it did not form a part of the original homily. In the Cremona edition, it is marked as part of the *Tosefta*. Haim Yosef David Azulai understanding as such in his *Netzotzei orot*. For a similar description of the gathering of the "people of the God of Abraham," see *Midrash de Abraham Avinu* (Jellenik, 1967: 5:41).

[19] For a striking example of this religious-existential position, cf. Eleazar ben Moshe Azikri's *piyyut* "Beloved of the Soul" ("Yedid Nefesh").

through God's mercy and His "awakening" to fulfil Abraham's aspirations—only through His guidance and self-revelation as the God of the land—that Abraham attains the desires of his soul.

The *Zohar* nonetheless does not form the extreme antithesis of the Maimonidean attitude. While the zoharic homily reflects a balanced religious view that holds human beings responsible for seeking God—and above all awakening to Him—it denies them the ability to reach Him on their own. That can only be attained via combined human effort and divine response—"arousal from below" and "arousal from above."

The idea that in order to awaken God one must first awaken oneself is not original to our homilist. The principle of "arousal from above" out of "arousal from below" forms a central pillar of zoharic thought, as the *Zohar* itself stresses in a proximate passage (1:77b).[20] Within the sefiric system itself, the relations of distance and closeness between the Holy One, blessed be He, and the Shekhina are derived from the power and repetition of the Shekhina's awakening in the face of her husband and his awakening towards her. The *Zohar* thus tells its mystics to "arouse the matron" via known means (Hellner-Eshed, 2009: 222–225). In other places, it makes use of the same method to describe the dynamic link between the mystic and the Torah: the former's awakening to know and desire to understand prompt the esoteric mystery in the Torah to reveal itself to him.[21] As is well known, the *Zohar* also regards physical erotic coupling as capable of influencing the upper realms. The significance of the text under discussion here thus lies in its application to the religious journey—the quest for God as exemplified by Abraham.

This religious orientation is also reflected in other homilies about Abraham as the religious archetype—as, for example, in one about the altars he set up in Canaan:

> He moved on from there ההרה (*ha-harah*), *to the mountain* (Gen 12:8). There he discovered הר ה׳ (*har he*), Mountain of *He*, and all those rungs planted there. ... Then he knew that the blessed Holy One rules over all, so he built an altar. There were two altars because here it was revealed to him that indeed the blessed Holy One rules over all, and he discovered supernal wisdom, which he had not known before. So he built two altars: one for the revealed rung, one for the concealed. Come see it is so! First it is written: *He built an altar there to*

---

20 For further parallels, see Hellner-Eshed (2009: 225 n. 50).
21 For this awakening as a characteristic of Torah-study in zoharic circles, see ibid: 204–251. The motif of mutuality in the arousal of love in this context is exemplified clearly and succinctly in the parable of the maiden in the palace in *saba de-mishpatim:* see Yisraeli (2005: 231–246, 263–266).

> YHVH *who had appeared to him* (ibid., 7), and afterwards simply: *He built an altar there to YHVH* (ibid., 8), without *who had appeared to him*. (Zohar, 1:80a)

Even when Abraham reaches Canaan and knows what he knows, he still faces the unknown divine dimension. Although he builds one altar to the God who appeared to him in Canaan, he also erects one for the "concealed rung"—i.e., to the God who has not revealed Himself to him. This dual standing before the known and unknown—the simultaneous experience of the visible and invisible—is one of the pillars of the *Zohar*'s religious thought. The dual religious phenomenon, which represents the sharp distinction between man's capacities and what lies beyond his powers, is understood within the fundamental kabbalistic framework in the tension between the Infinite and the *sefirot* and the dialectic and compartmentalized structure of the *sefirot* themselves (Tishby and Lachower, 1989: 1: 232–242).

It is difficult to ascertain whether the zoharic homily is intended as covert criticism of Maimonides and his philosophy. Maimonidean detractors were known in the fourteenth century, rather paradoxically primarily amongst other philosophers. His fiercest opponent, R. Hasdai Crescas, objected to his radically activist view in his *Light of the Lord*:

> How fitting this is to what our Sages said in the midrash: To what is this like? To a man who was journeying from place to place and saw a burning building. He said: "Will you say that it has no guide?" The owner of the building looked out at him and said: "I am the owner." Thus it was with our father Abraham. He said: "Will you say that this world is without a guide?" The owner looked out at him and said: "I am the owner of the wor[ld], etc." In other words, had he not had a proclivity towards the truth he would never have gotten past doubt until God shed His light upon him—namely, prophecy. (First essay, third rule, chap. 6, 19b)[22]

Even if this attitude is not directly Maimonidean, the *Zohar* undoubtedly alludes to several of his possible sources that embody this activist view. The most prominent of these appears to be *Sefer Yetzira*. This brief and enigmatic Hebrew work does not exhibit any profound biblical influence, the only biblical figure to

---

22 Although Crescas' approach resembles that of the *Zohar* it is not identical with it. In contrast to the *Zohar*, in which human ability is limited in accordance with the object to be attained (the accessible powers vs. the deep and concealed "power of all powers"), Crescas focuses on the *quality* of achievement. In other words, Abraham can reach the recognition of doubt but not that of certainty. Similarly, the element of the will that serves in the *Zohar* as the key for attaining the "arousal from above" is missing from Crescas. For this passage, see Shochat (2002: 194–195 n. 5).

which it refers being Abraham. Despite its concise and terse language here, the religious orientation of this passage is clear and sharp:

> And because Abraham our father, may he rest in peace, came and looked, saw, understood, probed, engraved and carved, he was successful [in creation], immediately there was revealed to him the Master of all, may His name be blessed forever. He placed him in His bosom, and kissed him on his head, and He called him "my beloved" (Isa 41:8) and made a covenant with him and with his children after him forever. (6.7)[23]

The Abraham of *Sefer Yetzira* seeks God through intense activity. Even if not all are clear, the plethora of verbs demonstrates Abraham's ceaseless, relentless pursuit of the desire of his soul. Gaining his goal, God reveals Himself to him and makes an everlasting covenant with him and his descendants. Our zoharic homily appears to allude to this passage: "He already *knew and tested* all those rulers conducting the entire inhabited world; he *gazed* at them and *balanced and knew* the powers who ruled throughout the world ... He *balanced and knew* ... After *balancing* several times, he *saw* ... He *gazed, tested, and balanced to know*; and he *saw* that the power over it is immeasurable ... He *gazed, balanced, and knew* ... He again *gazed, balanced, and tested to comprehend*."

In place of the multiple verbs in *Sefer Yetzira*, the *Zohar* suffices here with a more limited number. Those it does use, however, occur repeatedly. Its allusions to the *Sefer Yetzira* but restriction of its vocabulary suggest that the *Zohar* seeks to counter the earlier work.[24] While the Abraham of *Sefer Yetzira* achieves his varied and intrinsic plan, in the *Zohar* he exhibits "signs of distress," repeating the same actions over and over again. Although he makes modest gains, he does not attain his primary goal, his path to the power of all powers being blocked. The *Zohar* thus proclaims here that, *contra Sefer Yetzira*, Abraham did *not* in fact succeed—"could not comprehend/grasp" (a phrase that occurs thrice in this short passage). Despite the fact that in both cases he is given a revelation, in the *Zohar* this is not the result of his "success" but because of his incapacity to com-

---

[23] For this version, see Liebes (2005: 74–75, 290 n. 27).
[24] For the relation between the two compositions, see Liebes (2005: 74–75), who argues that *Sefer Yetzira* is one of the sources of this zoharic passage, the *Zohar* creating a synthesis between the midrash and *Sefer Yetzira*. In my opinion, the *Zohar* is tendentiously paraphrasing a midrashic text in order to voice its critique of it. For another example, see Yisraeli (2005: 255–256). In this sense, *Sefer Yetzira* differs from both the *Zohar* and the ancient midrash: see below.

prehend and as a response to his yearnings for the same power that reside in the land.²⁵

The various versions in the *Zohar*

Another midrashic tradition relating to Abraham's origins in the *Zohar* also pertains to the ideological position we are discussing here:

> R. Yehuda said, "Who aroused from the East"—Abraham, who absorbed arousal toward the blessed Holy One solely from the East. Since he saw the sun emerging in the morning from the East, his soul aroused to the awareness that it was the blessed Holy One. He said, "This is the King who created me!" He worshiped it the whole day. In the evening, seeing the sun shrivel and darkness advance, he said, "Certainly this rules over the one I worshiped all day, which darkened before it and shines no more!" So he worshiped the night. In the morning he saw that darkness disappear and the east brighten. He said, "Certainly over all these reigns a king, a ruler conducting them! He revealed Himself to him and spoke with him, as is written: *Righteousness calling him to follow him*—speaking with him, revealing himself to him. (*Zohar*, 1:86a)

Unlike the zoharic story that stands at the focus of our attention here and represents original, creative midrashic writing, this aggadic tradition belongs to the dominant zoharic trend of adapting prevalent traditional narratives as the basis for its message. Although the early midrashic sources do not contain this account of Abraham seeking God amongst the various celestial bodies, it does occur in the apocryphal *Apocalypse of Abraham* (Kulik, 2005: 14–15; Kister, 1994: 6, 24 n. 28), also being alluded to in an early *piyyut* (Mirsky, 1977: 141).²⁶ A version similar to that in the *Zohar* is widespread in later, in particular medieval,

---

25 Liebes (2005: 74) aptly calls this revelation in *Sefer Yetzira* an "unmediated bond of fatherly love," speaking of the "gazing" in the midrashic story in *Gen. Rab.* in the same terms. In my opinion, however, the revelation there is functional, serving to fulfil the desire of Abraham's soul: see below. At first glance, the *Zohar*'s criticism of *Sefer Yetzira* is rather surprising, the latter being one of the principal sources of influence upon the medieval Kabbalah. For another example, however, see Liebes (2005:193). This phenomenon requires further investigation, such a study being likely to shed more light on the *Sefer Yetzira*'s status in the medieval kabbalistic world. Reservations regarding it can also be found in Judah Halevi's *Kuzari*, who subtly criticizes its philosophical tendencies, attributing them to Abraham after he had already recognized God's unity but had not yet received any revelation: see *Kuzari*, 4.26–27.
26 Here, we find traces of an ancient extra-midrashic tradition according to which, before choosing to worship God, Abraham devoted himself to astronomy/astrology: see Kister (1994: 17); Nickelsburg (1998: 155 n. 13).

midrashim.²⁷ A relatively early and striking version also found its way into the Quran:

And thus did We show Abraham the realm of the heavens and the earth that he would be among the certain [in faith]. So when the night covered him [with darkness], he saw a star. He said, "This is my lord." But when it set, he said, "I like not those that disappear." And when he saw the moon rising, he said, "This is my lord." But when it set, he said, "Unless my Lord guides me, I will surely be among the people gone astray." And when he saw the sun rising, he said, "This is my lord; this is greater." But when it set, he said, "O my people, indeed I am free from what you associate with Allah. Indeed, I have turned my face toward He who created the heavens and the earth, inclining toward truth, and I am not of those who associate others with Allah." (Sura 7:75–79)

As we observed above, this tradition is found in medieval Jewish literature in diverse versions, each exhibiting minor changes. Despite the affinities between the various parallels, however, an essential difference exists between the Quranic version/some of the Hebrew formulations and the zoharic version and others that appear to be influenced by it. Thus while in the Islamic text Abraham reaches a decisive religious conclusion based on his contemplation of the celestial bodies, the zoharic story is much vaguer: "Certainly all these must have a king over them who rules and guides them." The continuation makes it clear that this insight is not what Abraham is seeking. The empirical "deduction" that the world must have a guide is only a midway point—Haran. Although Abraham recognizes God's existence, he is unable to know God Himself. He needs the Holy One, blessed be He, to see his yearning for Him and reveal Himself and speak to Him. The concluding and summarizing theological point of the earlier version becomes the starting point for mystical experience. This change is exemplified in the zoharic approach represented in the passage above that affirms it.

A comparison of the two zoharic passages is very instructive. Although they contain two separate aggadic traditions relating to Abraham's origins, each of which reflects a different religious orientation, they closely converge at their end. The concluding line, which in each denotes the height of the mystical drama, is virtually identical: "Once the blessed Holy One saw *his arousal and desire*, He immediately revealed Himself to him"; "Once the blessed Holy One *saw his desire*, He immediately revealed Himself to him …" This literary "fusion" indicates that the dramatic ending does not derive from a specific story but forms

---

27 See *Midrash Aseret Hadibrot*, 2.42; *Midrash Gadol*, p. 210; *Sefer Hayashar*, 4.68 l; Jellenik (1967: 2.26, 118). *Pirqe R. El.* 26 states that Abraham "was hidden under the earth for thirteen years without seeing sun or moon"—possibly alluding to the fact that when he emerged and saw them he came to a knowledge of the One God.

part of the *Zohar*'s world. The longing that is not realized in the attainment of God and cleaving to Him and the vitality of the divine response to this yearning are fundamentally exemplified in the *Zohar*'s "existentialism."

The *Zohar*, Philo, and *Genesis Rabbah*

Is this fundamental view, which blends the active with the passive, the assertive with the submissive and anticipatory, original to the *Zohar* or do its roots go back to early Jewish literature? We find it, in fact, in Philo's *De Abrahamo*. As Liebes has observed, "The activist, intellectual, and philosophical inquiries are followed by the passive mystical stage, in which, rather than man seeing God, God appears to him" (2005: 78).[28] In his allegorical interpretation of Abraham's journey from Ur of the Chaldeans, Philo presents the migration from Ur to Haran as his shift from Chaldaean astrology to the mystical revelation:

> For the Chaldaeans were, above all nations, addicted to the study of astronomy, and attributed all events to the motions of the stars, by which they fancied that all the things in the world were regulated, and accordingly they magnified the visible essence by the powers which numbers and the analogies of numbers contain, taking no account of the invisible essence appreciable only by the intellect. ... The man [Abraham] who had been bred up in this doctrine, and who for a long time had studied the philosophy of the Chaldaeans, as if suddenly awakening from a deep slumber and opening the eye of the soul, and beginning to perceive a pure ray of light instead of profound darkness, followed the light, and saw what he had never seen before, a certain governor and director of the world standing above it, and guiding his own work in a salutary manner, and exerting his care and power in behalf of all those parts of it which are worthy of divine superintendence. ... It is for this reason that Abraham is said to have made this first migration from the country of the Chaldaeans into the land of Charran. But Charran, in the Hebrew language, means "holes," which is a figurative emblem of the regions of our outward senses; by means of which, as by holes, each of those senses is able to look out so as to comprehend the objects which belong to it. ... But he, by reason of his love for mankind, did not reject the soul which came to him, but went forward to meet it, and showed to it his own nature as far as it was possible that he who was looking at it could see it. For which reason it is said, not that the wise man saw God but that God appeared to the wise man; for it was impossible for anyone to comprehend by his own unassisted power the true living God, unless he himself displayed and revealed himself to him. (*Abr.* 69–70, 72, 79–80).

---

28 For Philo's influence on the Jewish mystical tradition regarding Abraham, see ibid: 76–79. Liebes' primary stress lies on Philo's links with *Sefer Yetzira*. For our purposes here, however, the latter work belongs precisely to the activist tradition that runs counter to the spirit of Philo in this passage—as well as to that of the *Zohar*.

Like the *Zohar*'s, Philo's Abraham awakens to open his eyes and attend to the invisible. Shaking himself free from pure speculation, he follows the bright light and discerns the "governor and director of the world." He, too, is detained in Haran, on the edge of the "regions of the outward senses" where human beings can only look but cannot go any further by their own power.[29] At this point, God comes to meet the soul that yearns for Him, revealing Himself to it to the extent to which the soul is capable of bearing.

The nature of Abraham's faith and the revolution he instigates are thus not identical in Philo and the *Zohar*.[30] While Abraham bursts through the intellectual to the mystical in the former, in the latter this transition occurs up until the midpoint in the mystical space. The resemblance between the two views is nevertheless not coincidental. Philo's direct influence on the *Zohar* being very unlikely, however, we must look for another link in the chain.

This in fact is readily evident. If we engage in a close and sensitive reading of the short, succinct midrashic text in *Genesis Rabbah*, we discover that it itself presents us with this model:

> Said R. Isaac: This may be compared to a man who was travelling from place to place when he saw a building in flames. Is it possible that the building lacks a person to look after it? he wondered. The owner of the building looked out and said, "I am the owner of the building." Similarly, because Abraham our father said, "Is it conceivable that the world is without a guide?" the Holy One, blessed be He, looked out and said to him, "I am the Guide, the Sovereign of the Universe." (*Gen. Rab.* 39:1)

Although—unlike Philo and the *Zohar*—the theological questions relating to God's nature are of no interest to the midrashist here, he preserves the same religious paradigm. *Contra* the prevalent reading of this text, it does not portray Abraham as attaining knowledge of God through his own power.[31] If we look

---

29 According to Liebes (2005), Abraham's passivity in Philo represents the mystic's humility. In my opinion, however, the marking of the boundary of human achievement in terms of the "holes" of the human senses indicating the mystic's objective limitation. Philo's Abraham is thus also consistent with the zoharic Abraham in this respect.

30 Philo is closer here to another thirteenth-century Gerona kabbalist—R. Jacob bar Sheshet: "See what our Sages of blessed memory stated: Abraham knew his Creator when he was three. They did not say that God revealed Himself to Abraham but that Abraham knew his Creator. This knowledge was undoubtedly through wisdom and not through prophecy" (1968: 83).

31 The common reading is represented by Maimonides himself in the passage quoted above, which itself rests upon this midrashic source. In Maimonides' thought, the Archimedean point is also Abraham's perplexity: "[he] wondered how a sphere could follow a fixed path without being directed … Surely it would be impossible for it to rotate on its own!" Maimonides understands this as a rhetorical question, however, leading him to conclude that Abraham "real-

carefully at Abraham's response to the ownerless "burning building," it appears to reflect an initial, undeveloped stage of religious knowledge—a state of curiosity rather than an attempt to determine principles or draw theological conclusions: "Is it possible that the building lacks a person to look after it?" This wondering—which according to the literal meaning of the midrash is not yet revelation—expresses a deep will and longing for knowledge, these arousing their object to gaze out and identify Himself.[32] As in Philo and the *Zohar*, Abraham awakes on his own through self-inquiry—but only reaches half way, to the Philonic "Haran." The fruit of this arousal is the question, the wondering, and the request for a solution to the enigma of the burning building. Because Abraham can get no further than Haran in his own power, however, God responds to his "desire" and reveals Himself.[33]

This meaning of the question is also evident in an early *piyyut*, 'When All Was Not', published by Joseph Yahalom." The stanza relating to Abraham's origins appears to be an interpretation of the midrashic tradition in *Genesis Rabbah:* "He expounded the commandments: "Who made the moon? Is there a house that is laid out, built by itself? You gave balm to his heart, for You are Lord of all" (Yahalom, 1996: 115).[34] Here, God's revelation is a "balm" to the heart that seeks an answer to the enigma of the house owner. A later version

---

ised the way of truth and understood the ways of righteousness from nature." In other words, the divine revelation in the midrash is none other than Abraham's recognition of his Creator, as Maimonides states explicitly at the end of this text. Crescas (in the passage quoted above) adduces this midrash in fact *against* Maimonides, he too thus apparently understanding it in the traditional fashion. For the relation between Crescas' and the *Zohar*'s view, see above, n. 0.

32 According to the customary understanding of this parable, the building is burning rather than illuminated. In its later reworking (see below), however, this is not the case (see also Maimonides' account cited above). The question "Is it possible that the building lacks a person to look after it?" (according to the common reading) thus carries a much sharper connotation, which might even related to a wonderment about the first things. For the "building" in the real-life context, see Krauss (1914–1923: 1.2: 438–439); Mendel (1991).

33 For the fact that, *contra* the later midrash, *Gen. Rab.* depicts the knowledge of God as a consequence of revelation rather than human wisdom/intellect, see Urbach (1975: 319–319). A comparison of this midrashic source with Philo and the *Zohar*, however, demonstrates that the wondering signifies a strong desire to know. To this view in the *Zohar*, *Gen. Rab.*, and *Sefer Yetzira* must be added the account in *Apoc. Ab.* (Kulik, 2005: 16).

34 For the link between this *piyyut* and the early tradition relating to Abraham's origins, see Liebes (2005: 291 n, 31). Both Liebes and Yahalom (1996) note the parallelism between the phrase "lord of all" and *Sefer Yetzira* ("until the Lord of all was revealed to him"). In my opinion, the *piyyut* as a whole exhibits greater affinities with *Gen. Rab.*, even if the expression itself, in both the *piyyut* and midrash ("Sovereign of the Universe" אדון כל העולם) undoubtedly derives from *Sefer Yetzira*.

of the "building" midrash cited in *Midrash Hagadol* also suggests that Abraham's was an authentic rather than rhetorical wondering:

> A parable: To what does this compare? To a man who was journeying and saw a very large, tall building. He sought to enter it, going all around it, and found no entrance. He shouted out several times, but received no answer. He looked up and saw some red garments on the root. He then saw some white garments. He said to himself: Surely there is someone living here. If it were empty, why would these be here? Because the owner saw that he was sad, he said to him: Why are you sorrowful? I am the owner of the house. So Abraham our father, because he saw that these were sinking and these were rising, said: Had these not an owner they would not be such. It is not proper to worship these but only he who directs them. So he gave his mind to the truth of the matter. Because the Holy One, blessed be He, saw that he was sad, he said to him: "You love righteousness" (Ps 45:7). (pp. 204–205)[35]

Conclusion

Between the biblical story on the one hand and the activist tradition drawn from the apocryphal literature through *Sefer Yetzira* to Maimonides on the other another religious tradition can be clearly identified. This more moderate will-based tradition, that finds expression in the *Zohar*, has roots that lead through the early midrash to Philo. It asserts that the believer's awakening, his initiative to search for God, and his desire for Him are vital for stimulating the religious process. It can only be fulfilled, however, when God reveals Himself to those who pursue Him. Each of the links in this chain applies this tradition to its own spiritual and ideological environment. Philo regards Abraham as passing from the rational to the mystical. The ancient midrash regards him as moving from the physical to the metaphysical realm. The *Zohar* places his search within the mystic experience itself. Despite their variations, all these sources preserve the same paradigm as a foundational and existential framework.

The dual affinity—between the *Zohar* and the early midrash and between the latter and Philo—demonstrates the power of the zoharic spirit that, from a penetrating reading of the brief and succinct midrash, is able to resurrect the spirit embedded within it and give it life and an even fuller expression than the early

---

[35] For the link and parallelism between the midrash in *Gen. Rab.* and Philo's writings, see Albeck's introduction and indices to *Gen. Rab.* (3: 84–89); Niehoff (2008). For the affinities between rabbinic literature in general and Philo, see Niehoff (2008: 4 n. 10 and the bibliography cited therein). For the question of the association between *Sefer Yetzira* and Philo, see Belkin (1958); Baer (1985: 111–114); Werblowsky (1959); Scholem (1976a: 38 nn. 2, 3); Liebes (2005:11–126); Idel (2008: 235–239). For the renaissance spirit in the *Zohar* in general, see Liebes (2001: 511).

and freer Philonic version. Even if the link between the midrash in *Genesis Rabbah* and Philo's writings—not to speak of that between the Zohar and Philo—still requires elucidation, the zoharic homily we have discussed in this chapter may nonetheless be regarded to some extent as representing the renaissance of the pre-midrashic spirit, sprouting, blossoming, and shining here in a bright glow.

Chapter 8:
The *Aqeda:* From Test to Experience

The story of Isaac's binding as told in Genesis 22 is one of the foundational narratives of Judaism, exerting a huge influence upon the Jewish ethos of martyrdom and finding expression in the responsa literature, folklore, and liturgy through to modern Hebrew poetry. Although its imprint upon Jewish history has been extensively discussed, little attention has been paid to its treatment within kabbalistic thought and writings in general and the *Zohar* in particular.[1] While this circumstance may reflect the neglect of zoharic aggada in general, the role the narrative has played in shaping the Ashkenazi consciousness of martyrdom in the wake of the crusades also appears to have marginalized the way in which it was perceived in the spiritual world of medieval Jewish Spain, of whose literary creativity the *Zohar* is one of the most prominent examples.

In this chapter, I shall examine the distinctive fashion in which the *aqeda* is presented in the *Zohar*, the various ways in which it is treated, and the diverse understandings of it reflected in the zoharic texts.[2] The discussion centres upon the *Zohar*'s apprehension of the conclusion of the story, which causes its authors unease and even disappointment. The non-fulfilment of the divine command to sacrifice Isaac deeply disturbs them, appearing to constitute a failure to meet the lofty religious challenge—even when divinely sanctioned. This approach, which to us appears very strange, rests upon an interpretive premise that was prevalent not only during the Middle Ages but also in the talmudic and midrashic literature, only being rejected and suppressed in the later midrashic tradition. The first section of the chapter analyzes this principle and its roots and expressions in medieval exegetical and homiletical works up until the greatest medieval kabbalist, Nahmanides. The second section addresses the various ways in which the *Zohar* and its environs dealt with the problem of the narrative's "untimely ending." Investigating the varying faces of the *Zohar* in light of this biblical incident, I shall attempt to illuminate diverse aspects and changing trends within its spiritual world.

---

[1] Space constrains me from surveying all the literature. Some of the more important historical contributions are Spiegel (1969); Urbach (1975: 502–505); Blidstein (2007); Yuval (2006: 154–161); Brown (1982). For its literary tradition, see Yassif (1978); Elboim (1986); Efrati (1983); Shinan (2003a); Elizur (1997). For its treatment in modern Hebrew literature, see Levi (1991: 53–72); Weiss (2003).
[2] See Even Chen (2006: 57–88). For a discussion of the *aqeda* in the preface to the *Zohar*, see Lederberg (2005).

What did God really want?

In order to demonstrate the Zohar's attitude towards the way in which the biblical episode concludes, let me commence with a homily in *Parashat Shemot* that adduces the *aqeda* in passing. The homily deals with the framing story of Job, addressing the "64 million dollar question" of why Job was allowed to suffer. The answer it proposes very surprisingly adduces the *aqeda*:

> Come and see: When he [Satan] said *From roaming the land*, he was asking Him to execute judgment upon Israel. For he had a claim against Abraham to present to the blessed Holy One, because justice had not been rendered to Isaac when he was offered on the altar, since he should not have exchanged in any aspect a sacrifice that he had prepared on the altar for another, as is said: *he shall not exchange it* (Lev 27:10), Here Isaac was lying on the altar yet was not consummated as a sacrifice; justice was not rendered to him. This is what he sought from the blessed Holy One, just as he sought retribution for the selling of Joseph over many generations. Whatever he seeks, he seeks through justice. From the time when Isaac was saved, and exchanged as a sacrifice, the blessed Holy One prepared this one for the Accuser as his portion from all of Abraham's seed, so that he would not approach another side. (*Zohar*, 2:33a)

Here, the *aqeda* is joined to the framework of Job in order to "complete" the latter. In seeking to understand Job's suffering, the *Zohar* does not suffice with the biblical explanation, which presents it as a test, but rather endeavours to find another justification. Strikingly, it finds this in the *aqeda*, which it identifies as an indelible stain. The permission given to Satan to hurt Job is explicated as a tactical move designed to distract him from accusing Abraham for not having carried out the sacrifice of his son.[3] Here, the ending of Genesis 22 is perceived as possessing the gravest of implications, the homilist asserting that in failing to sacrifice Isaac Abraham forestalling the deed in just as it was about to be performed. In exchanging Isaac for the ram, he thus profaned the sacred —the sacrifice that had already been consecrated to God. Although the zoharic homilist is obviously aware that God commanded Abraham to release Isaac via the angel, he does not regard this formal approval as weighty enough to override the fatal flaw in the noble religious act and the fact that the sacrifice is not actually offered.[4]

---

3 For the links between Abraham and Job in the *Zohar*, see Liebes (1994: 84).
4 However strange they may sound to us, the perception of the *aqeda* as a serious *faux pas* and the idea that its non-fulfilment required atonement are also found in later kabbalistic homilies: see R. Natan Shapira, *Megalei amuqot*, 193, p. 262. The latter work forms the foundation of R. Bezalel b. Solomon of Kobryn's *Pelach ha-rimon* (Amsterdam, 1659), which clarifies its various aspects. My thanks go to Yehuda Liebes for bringing these sources to my attention.

Despite appearing in Satan's mouth, this perplexing criticism of the *aqeda* gives us some insight into the homilist's worldview. At its heart undoubtedly lies the belief that sacrificing one's son to God constitutes a religious and moral act.[5] Although Isaac is untied from the altar, this fact does not constitute any essential censure of child or human sacrifice. On the contrary, Abraham is held to account for not having fulfilled the high calling of carrying out the sacrifice. From a literary perspective, the homilist thus appears to believe that when God commanded Abraham to sacrifice Isaac, He intended and wished Abraham to carry out the act. This surprising fundamental religious understanding of the *aqeda* reflects the plot of the story and the outlines of its development in a different light to that to the prevalent view. This views the command given to Abraham at the beginning of the narrative as a fictitious request, lacking any real substance, the literary preface "After these things God tested Abraham" revealing to the reader that the sacrifice is merely a trial, God not truly seeking human sacrifices. His command is not meant to be carried out but to test Abraham's faithfulness to Him. Never intending Isaac to be sacrificed, the command was empty the moment it was issued, according to this understanding.

Is this the only possible interpretation of the passage, however? Can another one, no less true to the *pshat*, be offered? Precisely such an exegesis appears to lie behind the zoharic homily we are discussing here, one adopted by many others both in and outside Spain who were bothered by the theological problem entailed in God's rescinding of His initial command. Thus, for example, R. Joshua ibn Shuaib, one the disciples of Nahmanides disciples and a member of the zoharic generation, asserts:

> Many have asked how God commanded something and then revoked the order. Some say that He did not command but said: "Offer him" and this will be regarded as a sacrifice, Abraham misunderstanding, however, and taking fire and knife. Others say "Offer him" is like "offer them wine to drink" (Jer 35:2)—i.e., show him that you are offering him as a sacrifice in words but not acts. And some say "On one of the mountains that I shall show you"—i.e., אשר in the sense of "if" —as in אשר נשיא יחטא. Others interpret "Offer him" as relating to the ram who was made ready during the six days of creation. All these are forced explanations, however, Scripture removing all question and not being difficult. For God spoke only in the language of testing. (1992: 37)

---

[5] For the development and reinforcement of the view that Judaism sanctions or allows human sacrifice, see Levenson (1993). Although some of his conclusions are unnecessary, his study aids in elucidating the notion discussed here. For a similar understanding of the *aqeda*, see Liebes (2010). Even Yehezkel Kaufmann, who points to evidence of biblical objections to human sacrifice, observes that "According to the early story in Genesis 22, a man must offer even his only son to God if He asks for this sacrifice. In His compassion, however, God replaces it with a live animal" (1960a: 132).

This grave theological issue was not novel to ibn Shuaib's days, being raised centuries earlier by the lexicographer ibn Janah (1992: 6, p. 58) and Sa'adia Gaon (1970: 3.9, p. 140; 1984: 401–402). As previous scholars have already demonstrated, this discussion took place in a polemical context, being adduced in order to refute Christian and/or Muslim arguments regarding the abolishment of the commandments.[6] Following this, Ibn Ezra addressed it in his commentary on the Torah, like ibn Shuaib after him rejecting the formalistic-legal attempts to resolve the difficulty and similarly explaining that the command was given *a priori* without any expectation that Abraham would fulfil it, merely being a way to test his faith. God therefore did not retract or annul His words because He never intended Isaac to be sacrificed.

This answer, which to readers of another time and place might sound trivial, is not as straightforward as it appears at first glance. While ibn Shuaib accepts the notion of the divine "tactical ploy," his argument ("many have asked") indicates that the issue was broadly debated, the need for such forced explanations as adduced by ibn Shuaib and Ibn Ezra before him indicating that some groups read the biblical text in very different fashion, understanding the command "Offer him as a burnt offering" (Gen 22:2) as constituting God's true and essential intention. In other words, He truly expected Abraham to demonstrate his love and faithfulness by sacrificing his son and only beloved heir. According to this "essentialist" reading of the text, the angel's instruction to let Isaac go constitutes a comprises a dramatic turning point in the plot, which should have ended quite differently. This exegesis is also reflected in R. Menachem Recanati's explanation of the ram: "For when death was decreed upon Adam, he found an interceder above, and the indictment sealed by the angel could not be countered, for it cannot be rescinded until the Angel of Death has received his payment" (2003: 1: 129). Recanati regards God's command as an "indictment sealed by the angel" which cannot be removed until the Angel of Death has been paid his dues. The ram being provided in place of Isaac, God clearly intended Abraham to sacrifice Isaac.[7]

The medieval kabbalists' theological discussions and the *Zohar*'s own argument that Abraham failed to fulfil God's instructions thus contain an alternative reading of the *aqeda* that is no less faithful to the biblical text than the conventional one. The prefatory remark "After these things God tested Abraham" clarifying rather than dismissing God's *a priori* intention, the claim that He asked

---

[6] See Rippin (1986); Schlosberg (1990, 1994, 2002: 121–122 n. 24); Lasker (1995, 1997).
[7] For the idea of the ram as serving as an atonement/recompense in the early *piyyut*, see below.

Abraham to sacrifice his son as a test and thus meant him to perform the act does not fly in the face of the text.[8]

The essential view of the *aqeda* and its manifestations in midrash and *piyyut*

Does this surprising exegesis have roots earlier than the medieval period? As Spiegel (1969) has demonstrated, we find a tradition according to which Isaac is in fact sacrificed in amoraic midrashim. Thus, for example, *b. Ta'an.* 16a states: "And why does everyone else put ashes on his head?—With regard to this there is a difference of opinion between R. Levi b. Hama and R. Hanina. One says: [To signify thereby], We are merely like ashes before Thee; and the other says: That [God] may remember for our sake the ashes of Isaac." The fact that the "ashes of Isaac" are recalled elsewhere, suggests Spiegel, evinces that some Sages believed Isaac to have been actually sacrificed:

> There is no doubt about it. The haggadah about the ashes of Isaac who was consumed by fire like an animal sacrifice, and of whose remains nothing was left except the sacrificial ash, is ancient indeed, and its traces are already visible in the first generation of the Amoraim ... from the circle of R. Johanan's disciples, from the report of R. Isaac, that in their days they believed that Isaac's ashes were the foundation of the altar. (1969: 44)

According to Spiegel, this tradition represents the residues of ancient paganism:

> Possibly, too, "the blood of Isaac's Akeda" may be a fossil expression from the world of idolatry, some tiny stone fragment from pagan ruins sunk into the edifice of the Talmudic haggadah—and therefore we would have here, as occasionally also else in the Midrashim of early generations, some leftovers of belief before the beliefs of Israel. (1969: 57)

Spiegel's view is disputed by Urbach, who argues that the phrases "the blood of Isaac's *aqeda*" and "the ashes of Isaac" are equivalent to "the merit of Isaac."

---

[8] This approach is confirmed by intertextual biblical associations. Cf., for example, the affinities between "go to the land of Moriah, and offer him there as a burnt offering on one of the mountains that I shall show you" (Gen 22:2) and the indisputably real directive "Go from your country and your kindred and your father's house to the land that I will show you" (Gen 12:1). It may also adduced from the literary links between the *aqeda* and the story of Ishmael's expulsion in the preceding chapter—a similarity that suggests that just as Ishmael was delivered miraculously so Isaac was also rescued from a "clear and present danger": see Levenson (1993), who maintains that the motif of salvation in both passages is meant to highlight the new life granted to the son by the God who redeems him.

Intended merely to accentuate Isaac's greatness in being ready to sacrifice his life, they are thus irrelevant to the question of whether Isaac was actually sacrificed or not (1975: 502–505).[9]

While both scholars address the question of whether rabbinic literature contains the idea that Isaac was in fact sacrificed, however, neither deals with the preceding issue—namely, how the Sages understood God's initial command. Having discovered traces of the essentialist view in medieval writings, we must seek to discover whence it reached this period, how ancient it is, and whether residues of it can be discerned in the early talmudic and midrashic corpus.

The "tactical ploy" exegesis is unanimously accepted as occurring overtly and explicitly in the talmudic aggada. Jeremiah's criticism of those who "burn their children in the fire as burnt offerings to Baal, which I did not command or decree, nor did it enter my mind" (Jer 19:5), for example, is explicated in this fashion in several places: "Others say, 'Which I did not command' (Jer 19:5): concerning Jephthah. '… nor of which I spoke at all' (Jer 19:5): Concerning Mesha, king of Moab. '… neither did it come to mind' (Jer 19:5): that Abraham should actually offer up his son on the altar" (Neusner, 2006: 25 [*Sifre* 148]).[10] In another tannaitic version, this saying is explicated in such a way as to sharpen it in the broader context: "'Nor did it enter my mind'—that Abraham should sacrifice his son Isaac on the altar but it was merely a test" (*Mid. Tannaim* 17.3). Although the view that denies that God really intended Abraham to sacrifice Isaac is thus clearly deeply rooted in rabbinic thought, the polemical tone of these passages raises the question whether in and of itself this fact can serve as witness of an alternative, antithetical approach. While explicit expressions of this essentialist notion are difficult to find in the Talmud and midrashim, it is nonetheless reflected in several places. Thus, for example, a midrash in *Genesis Rabbah* is devoted entirely to this issue:

> R. Samuel b. Nahman commented thus: *God is not a man, that He should lie*, etc. (Num 23:18). Said R. Samuel b. Nahman: In this verse the beginning does not correspond to the end, nor the end to the beginning. Thus it commences, '*God is not a man that he should lie*,' etc., while it concludes, *When He hath said, He will not do it, and when He hath spoken, He will not make it good*. But the meaning is this: When the Holy One, blessed be He, decrees to bring good upon the world, then, '*God is not a man, that He should lie*'. But when he decrees to bring evil upon the world, then, '*When He hath said, "He will not do it*'. (*Gen. Rab.* 53:4)

---

9 See also Blidstein (2007).
10 Cf. *b. Ta'an.* 4a; *Gen. Rab.* 56:8.

Here, the angel's directive is understood as an annulling of the initial command to "Take your son ... and offer him there as a burnt offering," being adduced in order to demonstrate the principle that God can repent of His intent to bring evil upon the world after He has decreed it. The midrashist clearly views the *aqeda* as an example of just such a case as this.

Even clearer traces are visible in later midrashim. *Aggadat Bereshit*, for example (southern Italian in provenance and dating apparently from the ninth or tenth centuries), describes the climax of the story as follows:

> And why on the third day and not immediately? The Holy one said: Because the Nations of the World should not say: Out of fear did Abraham offer his son ... if he would have had one more hour, he would have changed his mind. Therefore the Holy One said: Let him suffer for three days, and search for the place, so that all will know that with his full consciousness and out of love he offered him and did not change his mind. This is what is written: *On the third day*. When he came to slaughter him, the Holy One immediately felt compassion, and cried: *Do not lay your hand on the boy* (Gen 22:12). (Teugels, 2001: 99 [Chap. 31])

Here, the midrashist explains the angel's appearance as due to God's compassion towards Abraham—an exegesis completely antithetical to the planned, deliberate, and orchestrated nature of the act when understood as a tactical ploy. Here, the command "Do not lay your hand on the boy" is represents Isaac's dramatic deliverance from death—a real rupture in the plot's natural progression towards the offering of the sacrifice. God changes His mind, Abraham's fear of offering up his son inducing Him to "move from the seat of judgment to the seat of mercy," as the Sages say in a different context. Implicit here is the essentialist view of the *aqeda*.[11]

The motif of the arousal of God's compassion at the story's dramatic turning point occurs in many *piyyutim* across the generations. In the *Aqeda piyyutim* in the various versions of the *Selichot* prayers, the angel's appearance is frequently described as a response, appeasement, or awakening of God's mercy. Thus, for example, in an anonymous *piyyut* we read: "In the morning Your mercy was awakened for your only son and You shone on him and the angel of God called to him: Do not lay your hand on the boy" (Goldschmidt, 1965: 39, p. 102). Others state: "You *answered* him from the heavens/ and it was twice sworn to him in

---

[11] Identification of this interpretive tradition in ancient rabbinic literature once again raises the question of the possible link between the Jewish motif of child sacrifice and Christian doctrine, a subject that lies beyond the brief of this discussion. See Levenson (1993); Swetnam (1982). In light of the early date of this tradition, however, we must reject the idea of medieval influence of the Ashkenazi martyrdom ethos prompted by the Crusades, although it is not impossible that this ancient exegesis found new expression under these circumstances.

Your name" (ibid: 58, p. 153, 84, p. 210). According to these texts, God "heeds" Abraham, answering and showing compassion. The same idea is also found in the *Seder Ha-avoda*, in its earliest versions no less, which regard the ram as being sacrificed in place of Isaac. Thus, for example, Yose b. Yose's "I will recall God's great deeds" refers to the "lamb [i.e. Isaac] was pardoned and ram was sacrificed as his ransom" (Mirsky, 1977: 143) and a contemporary *piyyut* to "You put in his place a ram and it was imputed to him as righteousness/ on this day we shall hear: 'I have found a ransom.'"[12] In forensic terms, a ransom is the redemption of a soul deserving of death.[13] The very use of this motif indicates that the *paytanim* believed that the bound Isaac would indeed have been sacrificed had the ram not appeared as his ransom. In a Byzantine *piyyut*, the angel encourages Isaac at the zenith of the drama: "Do not be afraid, boy, I am the redeemer/ who will redeem you" (Yahalom and Sokoloff: 130–131).[14] Here, the angel is represented as appearing in order to literally save Isaac from death.

Many of the *aqeda* and *Seder Avoda piyyutim* refer to the angels' lament. This motif, which has very early roots, is first found in *Genesis Rabbah*: "When the Patriarch Abraham stretched forth his hand to take the knife to slay his son, the angels wept, as it says, *Behold their valiants ones* [the angels] *cry without* ... (Isa 33:7)" (56:5).[15] Although most frequently adduced to heighten the story's tragic dimension, in some later midrashic sources this motif plays a more central role, constituting in and of itself the turning point in the plot. Thus, for example, *Pesiqta Rabbati* states: "As Abraham was about to put the knife to Isaac's throat, the angels came weeping and lamenting before the Holy One, blessed be He ... Thereupon, the Holy One, blessed be He, said to Michael: "Why doest thou stand still? Do not let Abraham go on!" (Braude, 1968: [40:6]). In a unique elaboration, a very moving version appears in later midrashic works:

> *And he laid him on the altar*. And there were Abraham's eyes on Isaac's and Isaac's eyes on the very heavens, and tears falling, pouring from Abraham's eyes until he stood virtually to his height in a pool of tears. He said to Isaac: "My son, since you have already begun to give

---

12 "You have established the world in Your mercy": see Goldschmidt (1984: 2: Yom Kippur, p. 469). For the identity of the author of this *piyyut*, see the editor's comments there; Mirsky (1977: 26 n. 53).
13 For the meaning of the term in the biblical context, see *Encyclopedia Biblica* 4:231–233. As we have already noted, R. Menachem Recanati later made use of the idea in his exegesis of the *aqeda*.
14 See also Shinan (2003a: 201 n. 16 and the bibliography cited therein).
15 For this motif in the Qumran scrolls, see Kister (1994: 20). For its parallels and evolution in later midrash, see the editor's comment in the Theodore-Albeck edition; Efrati (1983: 223–232).

up a quarter of your blood, may your Creator appoint some other victim in your place." At the same time, he opened his mouth widely and burst into tears, his eyes were shaking and observing the Shekina and he lifted his voice and said: "I lift up my eyes to the hills—from where will my help come? My help comes from the LORD, who made heaven and earth" (Ps 121: 1). At that time— *Behold their valiants ones cry*—the ministering angels stood in rows in the firmament and said to one another: "Come, see two unique ones in the world—one slaughters and one is slaughtered." They said: "Who will say before You: "This is my God, and I will praise him" at the sea [Exod 15:2], what will You do with Your oath "So shall your descendants be" [Gen 15:5]? Immediately [He said]: Do not lay your hand on the boy. (*Yal. Shim'oni*, Genesis 101 [p. 446]).[16]

As in other early versions, this homilist seeks to "fill in the gap" between Isaac's binding/Abraham's the taking of the knife and the angel's appearance. Here, however, he links the angels' weeping with Abraham's. In unparalleled fashion and in complete antithesis to the biblical narrative, Abraham arise and calls for salvation. The angels' groaning "at that time" echoes Abraham's agony, both breaking through the gates of heaven: "Immediately [He said]: 'Do not lay your hand on the boy.'" The conjunctive "immediately," which occurs in all the textual witnesses, points to a causal link: the averting of the sacrifice by the call "Do not lay your hand on the boy" is a response to the sighing and exclamations of Abraham and the ministering angels. This order of events undoubtedly reflects an essentialist view of the *aqeda*.[17] The representation of the incident as a real drama and reversal, not just from the father and son's perspective but also with respect to God's intention, is inconsistent with the "tactical ploy" approach, which regards the entire narrative as nothing more than a staged plot.

As we noted above, the literary witnesses to the causal link between the angels' weeping and the angelic directive "Do not lay your hand on the boy" only appear in late midrashim. The fact that motif occurs in sources from different places and periods, however, allows room for the cautious conjecture that the late midrashic texts reflect not only a late interpretation of the early midrashic motif of the weeping angels but also an authentic development of the biblical story itself. This premise strengthens my speculation regarding the early date of the essentialist version of the *aqeda*. This is further supported by the fact that this approach is also adduced by Philo:

---

16 Cf. also *Midrash Vayoshea* (Jellenik, 1878: 1:37–38); *Midrash Hagadol*, Genesis 354.
17 The fact that some of the midrashic sources place words in the angels' mouths that recall Moses' supplication after the sin of the Golden Calf and the spies reinforces this argument.

And so Isaac is saved, God supplying a gift instead of him, and honouring him who was willing to make the offering in return for the piety which he had exhibited. But the action of the father, even though it was not ultimately given effect to, is nevertheless recorded and engraved as a complete and perfect sacrifice, not only in the sacred scriptures, but also amongst those who read them. (*Abr.* 177)

According to Philo, God neither rejects nor forgoes Abraham's sacrifice, accepting Isaac as an offering but returning him to Abraham in recognition of his noble act. As early as the first century B.C.E./C.E., the *aqeda* was thus understood as a real sacrifice rather than Abraham's willingness to offer his son. Rather than representing a rejection of human sacrifice *per se*, Isaac's deliverance from death derives from God's pleasure in Abraham's intention. This is the only way in which Philo's tone of "apology" for the fact that the story fails to reach its natural climax can be understood. Although the act was not fully completed, because this itself constitutes the special reward given to Abraham it is as though it had taken place, thus being "recorded and engraved as a complete and perfect sacrifice."

Beyond embodying the essentialist view of the *aqeda*, Philo's "apology" also exhibits a direct link with our zoharic homily. Around 1,300 years earlier, Philo also viewed the sacrifice as not being completed as problematic. While he sought to reconcile the difficulty, the zoharic homilist rather criticizes Abraham for having violated the sacrifice ("he should not have exchanged in any aspect a sacrifice that he had prepared on the altar for another"). Missing an opportunity when he took him off the altar and replaced him with the ram, he was thus in need of atonement.

The essentialist approach in Nahmanides commentary on the Torah

Of the few the early Provençal kabbalists to address the questions we are discussing here, the most prominent is Nahmanides, who relates in his measured and enigmatic style to the "break" in the biblical story and the issue of why, if God had truly wished Abraham to sacrifice Isaac, He then repented? As we observed above, this issue drew the attention of medieval exegetes, some of whom suggested technical or legal solutions, others—like Ibn Ezra and ibn Shauib—rejecting the essentialist approach. In contrast to all of these, Nahmanides proposes another route: "The doctrine of this chapter which teaches that God is the One who tries Abraham and commands him about the binding of Isaac, and it is the angel of God who restrains and promises him, will be explained in the verse, *The angel who hath redeemed me* (Gen 48:16)" (Chavel, 1:279 [on Gen 22:12]).[18] The kabbalistic "tool box" at Nahmanides' disposal allows him to take an original approach, according to which a distinction must be made between the sefiric entity who commands and that which annuls the command. As he elucidates elsewhere (on Gen 48:15), the instruction to sacrifice Isaac comes from the "God of truth"—i.e., *Tiferet*, that abolishing it from the "redeeming angel" who "answers him in his time of need," identified with *Malkut*.[19] The contradiction between the command that opens the narrative and that which concludes it reflects the characteristic tension between various poles in the sefiric world—presumably *Din* and *Hesed*.[20] The dialectical worldview that stands at the foundation of medieval Kabbalah exempts the kabbalistic homilist from the need to seek a harmonistic solution to the break in the plot.

Nahmanides' understanding of the *aqeda*—which places him squarely within the essential camp—sharpens the distinction between the tactical-ploy and essentialist approaches. This is not solely literary or interpretive in nature but also reflects a fundamentally different perception of God. The first view paints Him in traditional garb as an immutable sophisticated calculator, the second as living, vibrant, sensitive, and ambivalent figure, both aggressive and compassionate, who changes in an instant from a royal, authoritative figure to a loving and affectionate father. It is also possible to assume that the two versions similarly represent opposite spiritual orientations, the tactical-ploy exegesis reflecting rationalistic tendencies or a type of rationalism and the essentialist seeking to preserve the ancient live and immanent biblical myth, even if in the later guise of the kabbalistic *sefirot*.[21]

Nahmanides' essentialist exegesis of the *aqeda* also transpires to lie behind the ostensibly perplexity of the medieval scholars who find the end of the narrative surprising. If, in reality, this sacrifice was an elevated expression of the idea of devotion and dedication to God, then the ideal was never attained. As

---

18 For an extensive treatment, see Rabbeinu Bachya (1998: 1:341[on Gen 22:13]).
19 Some of the interpreters of Nahmanides' supercommentors have shied away from the idea that the "Angel of the Lord" in Genesis 22 is not a divine figure. R. Shem Tov ibn Gaon states: "For the avoidance and the trust—all are from the attribute of *Ateret* [*Malkut*]" (2001: 17). R. Isaac of Acre makes a similar observation (Goldreich, 2010b: 2:51). This is a awkward and forced exegesis, however, Nahmanides' true intention being closer here in my opinion to R. Joshua ibn Shuaib in his commentary on Nahmanides' secrets (1875: 9:1), who regards אלוהים here as referring to God's might (the "fear of Isaac") in contrast to the "angel of the Lord" (*Malkut*).
20 See Rabbeinu Bachya (1998: 1:341 [on Gen 22:13]). This identification with *Din* and *Hesed* requires further investigation, *Tiferet* customarily being identified in Nahmanides' writing with Mercy and *Malkut* (the Angel of the Lord) with *Din*.
21 For the deep roots of this view in Jewish tradition, see Liebes (1993a, 2010).

noted above, while Philo proposed an almost forensic solution to this problem the zoharic homily levels fierce criticism at Abraham for not having completed the act and thus failed to demonstrate his absolute faithfulness to God. As we shall now see, other homilies in the *Zohar* evince still further ways of dealing with the difficulty of the "interrupted narrative" that are surprising and pregnant with meaning.

The zoharic aggada: The "completion" of the aqeda

The solutions the *Zohar* offers to the question of the *aqeda*'s "incompleteness" can be divided into two principal approaches—one that "completes" the story with a ritual or quasi-ritual act and one that makes the actual sacrifice redundant, regarding what happens as satisfactory despite being interrupted. Each of these views understands the significance of the sacrifice differently. While the first retains the essentialist starting point, not denouncing human sacrifice, the second—which regards the story's climax as lying elsewhere and does not require the cultic act itself—contains a note of cautious reservation towards the legitimacy (not to speak of the idealization) of Abraham's sacrifice of Isaac.

The roots of the conservative approach that is unwilling to "compromise" and forego the actual sacrifice are already evident in the pre-zoharic strata, appearing to be the way in which the talmudic statements regarding the "ashes of Isaac" and the "blood of Isaac's *aqeda*" discussed above should be read. Without determining the issue of whether these phrases indicate that Isaac was actually sacrificed, as Spiegel contends, or are merely figures of speech (as per Urbach), they undoubtedly exemplify a spiritual and ideational tendency towards "completing" the act and regarding it as though it was fulfilled. This approach is also evident in those traditions that refer to the quarter of Isaac's blood he gives, which also find expression in the halakhic-forensic link the midrash creates between Isaac and the ram as his substitute (Spiegel, 1998: 45–50, 60–64). Its first full manifestation, however, seems to be in *Pirqe R. Eliezer*, a work known to have heavily influenced the *Zohar*:

> R. Jehudah said: When the blade touched his neck, the soul of Isaac fled and departed; (but) when he heard His voice from between the two Cherubim, saying (to Abraham), "Lay not thine hand upon the lad" (Gen 22:12), his soul returned to his body, and (Abraham) set him free, and Isaac stood upon his feet. And Isaac knew that in this manner the dead in the future will be quickened. He opened (his mouth), and said: Blessed art thou, O Lord, who quickeneth the dead. (Chap. 31)

Although Isaac appears alive and well in the biblical text after the *aqeda*, this is only due to the fact that he was miraculously restored to life. This act recalling the resurrection of the dead—"in this manner the dead in the future will be quickened"—Isaac is clearly envisioned as dying here, only returning to life when he hears God rescinding the edict to sacrifice him. As Spiegel evinces, this version of the *aqeda* occurs frequently in the medieval period (1998: 28–37).[22] As in other cases, this tradition also finds expression in the zoharic homilies, where it is also further developed. A passage in the *Tosefta*, for example, demonstrates clear signs of a zoharic interpretation of *Pirqe R. Eliezer*:

> Why does the verse mention Noah's name twice—"These are the descendants of Noah. Noah was a righteous man" (Gen 6:9). Every righteous person (*tzaddik*) in this world has two spirits, one in this world, and one in the world to come. Thus you find with all the righteous: "Moses Moses," "Jacob Jacob," "Abraham Abraham," "Samuel Samuel," "Shem Shem"—all except Isaac, whose name is not mentioned [twice successively] in Scripture as theirs is, because when Isaac was offered as a sacrifice on the altar the soul that belonged to this world departed from him and because it is written of Abraham "Blessed art thou, O Lord, who quickeneth the dead" his soul belonging to the next world returned to him. For that reason you find that the blessed Holy One only singled out Isaac's name, because he was considered dead. (*Zohar*, 1:59b, *Tosefta*)

The principle behind this statement is that of the pre-existential double soul—i.e., that each person possesses two souls, one that descends to this world and the other predestined for the world to come (Tishby and Lachower, 1989: 2:698–703).[23] Hereby, the *Zohar* considerably expands the horizons of the passage in *Pirqe R. Eliezer*. Henceforth, there is no longer any need to say that Isaac's soul departed and returned. He was actually sacrificed and his soul departed eternally, the soul that returned to him being his second soul, given to all who are worthy of the next world after the resurrection of the dead. [24] The resurrec-

---

22 This tradition closely recalls Philo's exegesis discussed above, according to which Abraham gave Isaac to God, who returned him to his father, Philo albeit not suggesting that Isaac actually died.
23 This idea requires further investigation, primarily in relation to its affinities with other concepts, such as the image or garb: see Scholem (1976a: 361–367).
24 The perception of Isaac's sacrifice as complete is also reflected in the phrase "the perfect sacrifice" (קרבנא שלים) the *Zohar* attributes to Isaac on several occasions: see *Zohar*, 1:39a: Cf. also *Zohar hadash*, *tiqqunim* 122b. It appears to be an translation into Aramaic of the Hebrew עולה תמימה, referred to already in an ancient midrash in relation to the edict forbidding Isaac to go down to Egypt: see *Gen. Rab.* 64:3. It may also represent an early tendency towards regarding Isaac as an actual sacrifice. It is striking that in his homilies the Admor of Piaseczno, Kalonymus Kalman Shapira, makes use of the idea that the martyrs of all generations complete the *aqeda* in their self-sacrifice: see Piekarz (1990: 395–397).

tion becoming an essential, historical, and mental watershed in the medieval kabbalistic world, Isaac's status and his life following the *aqeda* are imprinted with the nature of the world to come. Henceforth, according to this view, Isaac in fact existed in the world to come despite being mired in the swamp of this life. He was thus the only person to whom God attached His name while he was still alive.[25]

The zoharic aggada: The *aqeda* as an incense offering

In contrast to the *Tosefta* chapters of the *Zohar*, its central section (the "body of the *Zohar*") contains few manifestations of this understanding of Isaac's fate. Other, no less surprising, methods of "completing" the plot do exist herein, however. The most extensive discussion of this issue, at the end of *Parashat Vayera*, which we shall analyze below, includes an elusive but significant comment:

> Rabbi El'azar said, "Isaac was sifted, ascending favorably in the presence of the blessed Holy One—like the fragrance of burning incense offered before Him by the priests twice a day—and the sacrifice was consummated. For Abraham agonized when he was told, "*Do not lay your hand on the boy, do not do anything to him!*" (Gen 22:12), thinking that his offering was incomplete, that he had built an altar and arranged everything in vain. Immediately, *Abraham raised his eyes and saw: here, a ram ...* (Gen 22:13). (*Zohar*, 1:120b)

According to this text, Isaac was purified and refined and ascended favourably before God, thereby fulfilling the sacrificial act. The homilist does not regard the sacrifice as being dependent upon the slaughter, sprinkling of blood, or taking of life, the incense offering offered by the priests in the Temple not containing any of these elements but still being considered a sacrifice. The *aqeda* can thus be completed by an act that does not entail Isaac's death. The most important element is the intention to offer a real sacrifice before God. The ram accordingly did not play a real role in the *aqeda*, only appearing in order to reassure Abraham, who was remorseful, thinking he had offered an imperfect sacrifice.[26]

---

25 In other words, God only calls Himself the "God of x" after that person has died. Isaac is the exception to this rule, God telling Jacob while Isaac was still alive "I am the LORD, the God of Abraham your father and the God of Isaac" (Gen 28:13): see *Tanh.* Toldot 7; Rashi on Gen 28:13. For a homily close in spirit to that under discussion here, see *Zohar*, 3:55b, *Tosefta*.
26 This motif can be traced back to *Gen. Rab.* 56:7, which depicts Abraham's supplications after the angel's appearance that he be allowed to injure or blemish Isaac in some form. For its surprising occurrence in the eighteenth century, see Liebes (2007).

The first printed editions of the *Zohar*—the Mantoba and Cremona editions—and several reliable manuscripts cite a version that sharpens this motif even further.[27] In place of אתבריר יצחק ואסתליק ברעותא קמיה קב"ה, these read: – אתבריר יצחק ואסתליק רעותא קמיה קב"ה, i.e., "Isaac was sifted, the aspiration arising before the blessed Holy One." Here, the subject of the sentence is the aspiration, rather than Isaac, this constituting the incense offering, its aroma arising and pleasing God.

This idea, which highlights the motif of intention, is consistent with the *Zohar*'s view of sacrifice. Several well-known homilies indicate that the primary element of the offerings, including animal sacrifices, lies in the expression of intent, the blood and flesh simply serving to appease the *sitra achra* or distract its attention: "Similarly with an offering: aspiration ascends to one site, flesh to another" (*Zohar*, 1:65b).[28] In other words, the principal aspect of sacrifice is aspiration and intention—whether to unite the *sefirot* or in the commitment of the soul. Not containing any flesh, the incense offering is thus the paradigmatic sacrifice, the question of whether the object of the sacrifice—here Isaac—was in fact slaughtered being irrelevant for the completion of the act. Abraham's readiness and full dedication to sacrificing Isaac is the focal point and fulfillment of the sacrifice.[29]

In tying the *aqeda* together with the incense offering, the *Zohar* may make use of an early midrash according to which the name of the "land of Moriah" is said to derive from *mor*—one of the ingredients of the incense offered there: "To the place where incense would be offered, as you read, *I will get me to the mountain of myrrh—Mor*" (*Gen. Rab.* 55:7). In this case, however, we have a double entendre. As we noted above, the *Zohar* seeks here to present the *aqeda* as the spiritual offering of the aspiration/intention, thus identifying it with the bloodless sacrifice that involves no slaughter or death. The incense offering also serves in the biblical context—which the *Zohar* heavily stresses—as a form of appeasing God and deliverance from death, however.[30] The sacrifice of

---

27 E.g., Vitkin ms.; Neofiti 22; Modena Astanza 12; Prima Fero 15; BM 762.
28 Cf. *Zohar*, 2:265b–269a. For an elaboration of this view, see Tishby and Lachower (1989: 2:891–892).
29 The notion of intent is also evident in the kabbalistic belief that everyone who recites the *Shema* and is willing to deliver his soul is regarded as though he had in fact done so: see Liebes (2010). To the references he adduces must be added an earlier source in the *Midrash Hane'elam* in the *Zohar* (1:124b). Abraham is also associated with the high priest in the zoharic symbolism, the *sefira* of *Hesed* being identified with both Abraham and the symbol of the priest or (on occasion) the high priest: see Brody (1991: 641–651).
30 Cf. Num 17:12–13; *Zohar*, 2:218b–219a. See also the language of the author of the *Tiqunnim* in the additions to *Tiquna tanina:* "There is no sacrifice that annuls the plague as the *aqeda*"

the aspiration/intention thereby operates on two levels, functioning both as a substitute for Isaac and as an annulment of his death sentence.

A fine line divides the tendency towards viewing Abraham's will and devotion as a type of sacrifice and the more radical approaches that *a priori* strip the element of sacrifice in the *aqeda* of all relevance. This shift is also of immense exegetical significance. The willing to forego self-sacrifice as a goal potentially alters the very nature of the act, transferring it to another plane. In addressing this issue, I shall seek to examine the character of this watershed and its hermeneutical and phenomenological significance.

The *aqeda* as the "binding of *Din*" in early kabbalistic writings and the *Zohar*

Several of the prominent thirteen- and fourteenth-century kabbalists, both within and without the zoharic circle, characteristically shift the arena of events from the real-this worldly to the Infinite-sefiric realm. Thus, for example, R. Joseph Gikatilla—one of those close to the zoharic circle and perhaps even one of its authors—expounds the *aqeda* in his *Sha'arei ora* thus:

> After you know this, I must tell you that if Isaac was not bound upon the altar, and Abraham did not take the fire and the knife in his hand, no one from Israel could exist before the judgment of Isaac ... And when the attribute of compassion which is the attribute of *EL*, which is the attribute of Abraham, saw that if Israel's judgement will be fulfilled in exile, everyone would be finished and destroyed, Not one from the city or two from a family would escape, so the attribute *EL* took the fire and the knife in his hand so that Israel would not be destroyed in exile. (1998: 204 [Gate 5])[31]

According to R. Joseph, the focal point of the *aqeda* is Isaac's binding, Abraham the man representing and symbolizing the attribute of *Hesed*, which restrains the attribute of *Din* from destroying Israel in the exile. In his *Sha'arei tzedek*, this concept is placed in a more universal context: "If Isaac had not been bound, no human being would have been able to fulfill his wishes because of the meticulousness of *Din* in that place" (2007: 25b). Here, the drama takes place within the godhead itself rather than between the horns of the altar, in the titanic— and slightly absurd—struggle between *Din*, which seeks to expand, and *Hesed*,

---

(see below). Thence derives the great significance attached in kabbalistic circles to the daily recitation of the *aqeda* section, in similar fashion to that relating to the incense.
[31] For Joseph Gikatilla's relation to the zoharic authors, see Liebes (1993a: 99–119).

which restrains and binds it.³² The act performed by Abraham the man symbolizes that of *Hesed*, this being the epitome and purpose of the *aqeda*. The story thus has nothing to do with Isaac's sacrifice, the goal being the very struggle —the binding—rather than the slaughter.

The idea of the binding of *Din* also occurs in the writings of another "zoharic" kabbalist, R. Joseph Angelet. In his *Sefer livnat ha-sapir*, composed in 1325, he provides an explanation of the command to bind Isaac in a style similar to that of the *Zohar*: "*Et binkha* [your son]—the *et* includes all those who come from his side and all those with harsh judgments, who will all be subject to Abraham's right hand. *Et yechidkha* [your only]—Where it not for this one, the world would not be able to endure the harshness of its judgments" (1913: 27a).³³

As with the other passages in *Livnat ha-sapir* that follow this pattern, it is difficult to determine whether Angelet is citing an early zoharic source or the idea originates with him.³⁴ It is nonetheless clear that the notion adduced here is based on the same tradition referred to by R. Joseph Gikatilla.³⁵ We find a similar thought from the same period in R. Menachem Recanati: "Had Abraham not bound Isaac, the world would not exist through Isaac's fear and might" (2003: 1:178). Despite their difference in time and spirit from the *Zohar*, both *Sefer ha-pli'yah* and *Sefer ha-qana* also regard the *aqeda* as representing Abraham's binding of *Din* (1997: 101) in order to weaken Isaac's power (1998: 224). The same idea appears in *Tiqunnei zohar* as well:

> A voice issued and said: From the six days of creation, on which the *aqeda* was created, because there is no sacrifice that annuls a plague as the *aqeda*, as it is written: And he bound Isaac his son—the attribute of *Din* was bound and fettered above and had no license to approach the Great Court, which is *Gevura*, to make an indictment. (*Tiqqunei zohar*, 139a)

---

32 The early source of this idea may be traced to *Gen. Rab.* 56:5: "R. Hanina b. Isaac said: Even as Abraham bound his son Isaac below, so the Holy One, blessed be He, bound the Princes of the heathens above." Apart from the divergent theosophic language, however, the early midrash deals with the consequences and reward given to Abraham and his descendants rather than with the nature and purpose of the *aqeda* itself. My thanks go to Daniel Lasker for bringing my attention to the fact that the stress laid on the suffering entailed in the *aqeda* may reflect Christian influence.

33 For the date and provenance of *Sefer livnat ha-sapir*, see Felix (1991: 2–6).

34 For Angelet's relationship to the *Zohar*, see Liebes (1993c: 224 n. 298); Felix (1991: 15–17).

35 Angelet's links with Gikatilla are also exemplified by the fact that one of the near-contemporaneous commentaries on the *Sha'arei ora* appears to have been written by Angelet: see Felix (1991: 8–11). For R. Joseph's influence on Angelet in general, see ibid: 11.

When we trace its evolution in the *Zohar* itself, we find that here, too, the *aqeda* is said to infuse *Din* with *Hesed*. On several occasions, however, significant differences exist. Thus, for example, we read:

> Here we should contemplate: *Elohim tested Abraham.* The verse should read: *tested Isaac,* since Isaac was already thirty-seven years old and his father was no longer responsible for him. If Isaac had said, 'I refuse,' his father would not have been punished. So why is it written: *Elohim tested Abraham,* and not *Elohim tested Isaac?* But *Abraham,* precisely! For he had to be encompassed by judgment, since previously Abraham had contained no judgment at all. Now water was embraced by fire. Abraham had been incomplete until now, when he was crowned to execute judgment, arraying it in its realm. His whole life long he had been incomplete until now, when water was completed by fire, fire by water. So, *Elohim tested Abraham*—not *Isaac*—calling him to be embraced by judgment. When he did so, fire entered water, becoming complete. One was judged, one executed judgment—encompassing one another. Therefore the evil impulse came to accuse Abraham, who was incomplete until he executed judgment upon Isaac. For the evil impulse appears *after devarim*, coming to accuse. (*Zohar,* 1:119b)

Like the kabbalists discussed above, the *Zohar* regards the *aqeda* as an act designed to balance *Hesed* and *Din*. While all the previous sources, without exception, stress the repair, inhibition, and restraint of *Din*, however, the *Zohar* posits that the primary purpose of the *aqeda* is to correct the refining *Hesed* and mix it with a small measure of *Din*. It is Abraham who must form part of *Din*, having no part of it before the *aqeda* but now mixing water and fire. In other words, it is precisely *Hesed* that requires moderating and blending.

While the first version is common amongst the kabbalists of the generation of the *Zohar* and later, the formulations in the latter are distinctive and without outside parallel. A combination of the two can nonetheless be found both within its pages and without. Thus, for example, we read: "When Abraham bound Isaac, in order to bring some *Din* into himself and in order that the left be found in the right and the right over the left" (*Zohar,* 2:257a; cf. also 1:133b). The mystical-theosophical nature of the *aqeda* operates in two directions here, subjecting *Din* to *Hesed* on the one hand and blending *Hesed* with *Din* on the other. This interesting version also appears in R. Moses de Léon:

> Let me introduce you to a mystery with regard to Abraham's binding of his son, what these are about. The proper essential is that the [purpose of the *aqeda* is to ensure that the] attributes below should be a true example of the divine, each forming part of the other because at that hour this was mixed that and that in this. Abraham, was on the side of *Hesed* without any *Din*, became harsh *Din* and cruel and true *Din* to his son. And Isaac, who was harsh *Din* then became white and as though part of the mystery of *Hesed*, to give himself to the will of his master and his desire and this was mixed with that and that in this. And so the attributes were mixed together. (Scholem, 1976b: 372)

Here, too, the two traditions are combined to create one complex entity. The fact that the element of *Hesed*'s oppression of *Din* is softened and moderated, *Din* becoming "white and as though part of the mystery of *Hesed*," may suggest signs of editing. Here, Moses de Léon's thought is closer to the spirit of the zoharic homily in *Parashat Vayera* than its textual parallels.

To complete the picture, we must note that the *Zohar* also seeks to balance the account on the margins of this *Parasha* by drawing Isaac into the centre of the plot. The way in which it does so gives us some insight into the history of the tradition we are discussing:

> Although we have said that *Abraham* is written, not *Isaac*, Isaac is encompassed by this verse through the mysterious wording: *Elohim tested* את (*et*) *Abraham*. It is not written: *tested* לאברהם (*le-Avraham*), *Abraham*, but rather *tested et Abraham*—*et* precisely! This is Isaac, for at that hour he dwelled in low power. As soon as he was bound on the altar, initiated into judgment fittingly by Abraham, he was crowned in his realm alongside Abraham—fire and water encompassing one another, ascending. (*Zohar*, 1:119b).

The attempt to integrate Isaac not only interrupts the logic of the homily but also impinges on its purpose—namely, an elucidation of why Abraham was tested rather than Isaac. Similarly, despite the ostensible "return" to the ancient motif of the binding of Isaac/*Din*, the familiar classical formulation is not adduced, the homilist to a certain degree proposing a completely different explanation. In contrast to the kabbalistic homilies discussed above, according to which Abraham's act was designed to bind the "fear of Isaac"—the smiting and destroying attribute of *Din*—here the violence is meant to increase Isaac's attribute and raise it from the lower *Din* (*Malkut*) to the place destined for it in the upper *Din* (*Gevura*). This addition appears to represent an attempt to preserve a (rather reserved) link with an older tradition—i.e., the complex interpretive tradition. In other words, we must surmise that the *Zohar* took the tradition known to it, according to which the encompassing took place in both foci at once, in *Hesed* and *Din*, and delicately poured it into the thematic paradigm of the homily in *Parashat Vayera* in service of its own exegetic purposes.

If this theory is correct, the unique version in *Parashat Vayera* is later than the complex version, possessing a dual focus in which *Hesed* and *Din* are both repaired in Isaac's binding—in the simultaneous blending of *Din* into *Hesed* and *Hesed* into *Din*. This final version appears to form a transitional link between the classical—"Isaacian"—kabbalistic tradition and the later "Abrahamic" one in *Parashat Vayera*.[36]

The heart of the innovation in the zoharic version, however, lies not in transferring the focus of repair from divine judgment to divine mercy but in the shifting of the homily to a completely different plane. A close reading of the homily reveals that although the text before us is also replete with theosophical connotations, in essence the "repair" is of Abraham as a personalistic figure rather than of the theosophic *Hesed*. The stress on Abraham as imperfect all his life until this point, thus being accused by Satan, evinces beyond a shadow of doubt that the homily deals with Abraham the man. The drama represented by the *aqeda* takes place within his soul rather than in the upper sphere of the *sefirot*. It is Abraham the son of Terach who has not been perfect up until now and thus in need of the *aqeda*, which will bring him to dialectical perfection.[37] Abraham is called upon here to perform a cruel act (in the language of the *Zohar* itself) in order to blend within his soul an attribute that is completely antithetical to his character and temperament, thereby creating a better balance between them within himself.[38] According to this version, too, the question of the incompleteness of the *aqeda* is clearly no longer relevant, the point of the test not being to slay Isaac but the existential status of the one tested. The Abraham who raises the knife to slaughter his son has in fact already passed through the refining fire of cruel *Din* that has stamped its imprint on him, making the sacrifice superfluous.

The *aqeda* in the *Zohar*: From theosophic to a personal-existential midrash

The suggestion that the *Zohar* shifts the focus of the plot from the world of the *sefirot* to Abraham's soul in the homily under discussion in this chapter is further confirmed by the continuation, which bears a clearly psychological-existential

---

[36] For the significance of this midrashic "genealogy," which regards the *Vayera* homily as a later chain in the kabbalistic tradition of the *aqeda*, see below.

[37] The theosophical allusions at the end of the homiletic passage (ואתתקנו ... באתרייהו ולאתעטרא עלאי ותתאי) do not affect its clear general import and should be perceived as part of the *Zohar*'s literary tendency towards concluding with a poetic flourish whereby the human and concrete is elevated to the theosophical and abstract.

[38] Rather than achieving perfect balance, Abraham is asked here to moderate *Hesed* with a measure of *Din*. As is well known, the *Zohar* reserves the full and complete balance between the two for Jacob, who in his personality combines Abraham's *Hesed* with Isaac's fear, thus constituting the "perfect man" (cf. *Zohar*, 1:139b).

nature. A close reading of the text and sensitivity to what occurs in the human soul leads the homilist to a masterful description of the dramatic changes that occur in the father's soul—the purpose of the *aqeda*. One of these is linked to the brief dialogue between the father and son as they go up the mountain: "Isaac said to his father Abraham, 'Father!' And he said, 'Here I am, my son'" (Gen 22:7). What in the eyes of the readers of the biblical text may seem as a prefatory remark opening the body of the discourse regarding the fire, wood, lamb, and offering in actual fact constitutes the essential element:

> *Isaac said to Abraham his father, "My father"* (Gen 22:7) ... but why didn't he answer him at all? Because he had withdrawn from a father's compassion for his son, so it is written: '*Here I am, my son.*' Here I am—compassion had vanished, transformed into judgment. *Abraham said* (ibid., 8), and it is not written: *His father said*, for he did not appear as a father but rather as his adversary. (*Zohar*, 1:120a)

The repetition "and he said ...and he said" is interpreted here as Isaac's double call to Abraham, the delay in the latter's response exemplifying in the homilist's view the change in Abraham's mental state at this juncture—from loving father to harsh judge. The metamorphosis of love into judgment also finds expression in Abraham's reply, the homilist understanding the fact that he is referred to as Abraham rather "his father" as indicating that Abraham has become a stranger or even adversary to Isaac. A father's sacrifice of his son being beyond imagination, Abraham cannot be a father here. He must thus have shed this role and become a stranger—this transformation being the purpose of the test.

A parallel but reverse psychological drama occurs within the *Zohar*'s midrashic perspective with the angel's appearance and annulment of the command: "*Abraham, Abraham!* Rabbi Hiyya said: "To arouse him with another spirit, another act, another heart" (ibid: 120b). The formal rescinding of the decree is insufficient: the only way Abraham can escape from carrying out this cruel slaughter is by transforming his spirit and his heart and turning back into a loving father. The double call thus relates to the need to re-awaken his spirit of love and compassion (at this moment more balanced and mixed with *Din*) so that he will not carry out the sacrifice he was on the point of performing.

The focus on Abraham the man leads the homilist to devote his attention to the *aqeda*'s psychological aspects. Here, the shifting from the theosophical-symbolical to the earthly arena does not revolve solely around the meaning of the test or the degree to which it is passed but is also exemplified in other parts of the biblical text. Thus, for example, the *Zohar* accompanies Abraham on his way to the event, seeking to discover the profound religious dilemma with which the call to sacrifice his son faced him:

> *On the third day, Abraham raised his eyes and saw the place from afar* (Gen 22:4) ... why: *On the third day ... he saw the place from afar?*: Because it is written: *Through Isaac, seed will be named for you* (Gen 21:12), namely Jacob, who issued from him; this is *the third day* ... Abraham gazed at *the third day*—third rung—and saw Jacob, destined to issue from him ... *From afar*, not soon. Rabbi El'azar asked him, "What is so admirable about Abraham if he gazed and saw that Jacob was destined to issue from him? For look, as he was about to bind Isaac, this is not very laudable!" He replied, "He certainly did see Jacob, for previously Abraham had discovered wisdom, and now he gazed at *the third day* – third rung – consummating. Then he saw Jacob, as is written: *He saw the place* – but now existing for him *from afar*, because he was going to bind Isaac and did not want to harbor suspicions against the blessed Holy One. (*Zohar*, 1:120a)

As is well known, the biblical text fails to tell us how Abraham felt as he made his way to the place where the *aqeda* was destined to take place. The rabbinic Sages also pass over this aspect of the text, generally addressing it indirectly and on the basis of remote needs (Elboim, 1986: 346). This literary gap allows later exegetes and thinkers to seek to fill it in, primarily with respect to the "measure" of Abraham's faith." How did Abraham deal with the fact that God was requiring him to sacrifice the son through whom his descendants were to become like the sand of the sea and the stars in the heavens? Did Abraham still believe in this promise? On the one hand, abandoning his faith in the future assured to his family damages Abraham's image as the father of all the believers. On the other, if he still trusted that God would keep His word, does he not necessarily know that the sacrifice will not be carried out—and if so, what sort of test is the *aqeda*?

The zoharic discourse in the homily we are discussing here sharpens this aporia: "What is so admirable about Abraham if he gazed and saw that Jacob was destined to issue from him? For look, as he was about to bind Isaac, this is not very laudable!" (ibid). The solution it proposes reflects a profound psychological insight founded upon an undermining of the believer/non-believer dichotomy and a recognition of the rich and varied mental space between these two poles. Adding another dimension to Abraham's mental faculties, the *Zohar* brings us to a point at which we can speak of Abraham as being able simultaneously to "see" and "not see." The father of the believers sees his seed Isaac—i.e., Jacob—but only from "afar," through a "darkened mirror." In order to allow room for the test of the *aqeda* and the religious capacities it demands, the promise is pushed back to a remote cognitive-mystical horizon, whence it appears even vaguer. Although Abraham's trust and faith in it do not fail, its absolute religious certainty and significance fade. As the *Zohar* states in a nearby passage: "Abraham said: The blessed Holy One assuredly knows another way of seeing things" (ibid). Although Abraham clove to the belief that "it is through

Isaac that offspring shall be named for you" (Gen 21:12), the import and realization of this promise become vaguer and remoter.

The *Zohar* was not the first to raise the question of the contradiction between the promise and the command, this issue already being addressed by the early Sages. For the ancient, classic midrash, however, it formed a way of elevating and ennobling Abraham's faith and his merit in obeying the divine commandment in the face of the sharp religious dilemma (cf. *y Ta'an.* 2, 4, 64d; *Lev. Rab.* 29:9).[39] The zoharic homily, in contrast, takes the bold step of confronting the existential question, wondering not only how Abraham could have been faced with such a challenge but also how he dealt with it, sketching his mental state in fine, complex, and subtle lines.

The homily we are discussing here may form part of a broader homiletic treatment of Abraham's life, stretching intermittently from the beginning of *Parashat Lekh lekha* up until this point (*Zohar*, 1:76b–120b).[40] If so, the description of Abraham's personal-psychological state during the *aqeda* may be surmised to constitute the peak of the zoharic depiction of Abraham's arrival in Canaan, his journeys throughout the land, his descent into Egypt, and the various trials he encountered along his mystical path—the drawing near and cleaving to God (or "crowning" in the *Zohar*'s language) of Abraham's attribute, i.e., *Hesed*. We cannot rule out the possibility, however, that it may in fact be a disguised autobiographical passage, the treatment of Abraham's mystical and religious longings and desires representing the homilist's own. As is well known, the zoharic authors generally sought to avoid indulging in overt autobiographical content.

The various versions of the *aqeda* in the *Zohar* and their interrelations, together with the existence of a distinctively psychological-existential homiletical stratum, must be examined in the light of the recent studies of the book's history and structure.[41] If it was in fact compiled by numerous authors, we may endeavour to identify figures or schools within the zoharic "community" and discern early and late stages within its corpus. Great importance attaches in this regard to our present focus, since, as demonstrated above, the version that posits the blending of Abraham the man's attribute represents a later development with respect to zoharic and extra-zoharic kabbalistic traditions.

Even more significant is the fact that this broad homily at the end of *Parashat Vayera* has no parallel amongst the zoharic collections of the thirteenth century and first half of the fourteenth—the works of R. Menachem Recanati, R. Jo-

---

39 See also the editor's notes to the latter in the Theodore-Albeck edition. For this discussion in a different context, see *Gen. Rab.* 56:10.
40 For Abraham's origins in the *Zohar*, see above, chapter 7.
41 See above, chapter 1.

seph Angelet, or R. Menachem Zioni. These three figures, whose writings are organized according to the weekly Torah portion and appear to reflect the zoharic inventory at their disposal, adduce some of the zoharic homilies on the *aqeda* at the end of *Parashat Vayera* but appear to pass over the broad homiletic spectrum representing the psychological-mystical trend discussed in this chapter. Despite the difficulty of arguing from silence, the fact that Recanati and Angelet cite the motif of the blending of *Din* with *Hesed* in its early form suggests that the personal-existential version in the *Zohar* here was not available to them. At the same time, however, this homily forms an integral part of the "body of the *Zohar*" in the extant fifth-century manuscripts onwards and the zoharic exegetes of the generation of the Expulsion and all the printed editions. We thus seem to be dealing here with a relatively late zoharic stratum, parallel to the *tiqqunim* literature or even later in date.

This late layer may attest to a surprising midrashic turn. If the innovation made by the kabbalistic exegetes and medieval midrash lay in transferring the biblical signifier beyond the signified in the lofty and elevated theosophic space in which the true drama takes place, our homily reflects a reverse direction—a return to the real and the human. Rather than biographical, political, or national, however, this human reality is that of the mysterious soul in its simplest psychological sense. The shift from the theosophic to the psychological—attributed most commonly to the late Hasidism—thus occurs centuries earlier in an inner-zoharic development.[42]

Furthermore, if we examine the homily's evolution within Hasidic literature, we discover that no traces of it exist at all. Thus, for example, R. Menachem Nachum of Chernobyl writes:

> And for this mystery, it is Abraham's binding of Isaac, for Abraham our father, of blessed memory, passed on the attribute of Hesed from above to his generation, as it is written: Abraham my beloved—who drew the attribute of *Hesed* and love to the world but to the measure of the manifestation of the light of *Hesed* was an annulment of reality of the act. For that there was the drawing of *Gevura* which is the fear of Isaac, the upper fear, drawn by Isaac into the world so that the act of *Hesed* might exist that Abraham had already begun to pass on, that through the fear of Isaac reduced *Hesed* so that the receivers could receive it. But this requires mixture, the mixing of *Gevuras* and *Heseds*. So Abraham our father, of blessed memory, was commanded to bind Isaac—from the language of tying—so that by arousing in himself the attribute of cruelty from the attribute of the fear of Isaac

---

[42] For another profound and equally surprising mystical expression, in relation to Esau, see below, chapter 9. It is noteworthy that this midrashic sources, the *saba de-Mishpatim*, also appears to represent a later stratum of the zoharic creation: see Yisraeli (2005: 270).

for his love of the Creator, blessed be He, the attribute of Isaac might also be mixed in Abraham.[43]

The affinities between this passage and the zoharic *Vayera* homily are clear and undisputed, no doubt existing that it represents an exegesis of the zoharic text by one of the fathers of the Hasidic movement. In contrast to the personal-psychological nature of the idea in the *Zohar*, however, R. Menachem Nachum "returns" us, in his own fashion, to the cosmic realm. Abraham's attribute of *Hesed* is not just a human quality but a tool for drawing the divine light into the world, the notion of the restriction of his light—the light of *Hesed* that floods the world —being identified here with the Lurianic concept of *tzimtzum*. The Hasidic midrash thus appears not to have assimilated the psychological exegesis of the *aqeda* as exemplified within the *Zohar* itself, as in other cases the zoharic spirit finding a way to reach literary heights and peaks unparalleled before or after it.[44]

Conclusion

The account of the *aqeda* presents several thorny theological and moral issues. In this type of text, every exegetical and homiletic saying reflects aspects of its author's spiritual world. Despite the *Zohar*'s complex and eclectic nature, its homilies thus give expression to some of the key features of the circles in and from which it sprang. Firstly, we may note that on the hermeneutical level these—as other thirteenth-century kabbalistic groups—favour the essentialist understanding of the *aqeda*. Herein, the command to sacrifice Isaac is regarded as a "real" instruction rather than a "ploy," even if ultimately being rescinded. The angel's interruption of the act thus leaves it imperfect and blemished. Secondly, here, too, the *Zohar* reflects the later midrashic tradition transmitted in *Pirqe R. Eliezer*, as well as presenting us with a clear and sharp expression of the *Zohar*'s unique approach to the cultus. This spiritualizing tendency stresses intention over "flesh and blood," thus finding no difficulty in foregoing the actual sacrifice and accepting the idea of a bloodless offering—on a par with the incense offering. Finally, the way in which the *Zohar* perceives the significance of *aqeda* in its positing of the mixing of *Hesed* with *Din* demonstrates its kabbalistic spirit.

Not only the spirit that pervades the book but also the direction this takes is of great significance. It is precisely the *Zohar*'s eclectic nature and complex and

---

43 *Ma'or einayim*, Toldot, 16b; Lekh lekha, 8b.
44 For a further example, see Yisraeli (2005: 231–239).

layered structure that makes it important to address the ideological and religious changes—or more precisely movements—that occurred in the zoharic circle over the years and centuries of its activity. As I have demonstrated in this chapter, if the early days of the Kabbalah and the *Zohar* itself are characterized by the classical tendency towards transferring the focus from the biblical plot or law to the theosophic realm, the *Vayera* homily on the *aqeda* exhibits the reverse trend, shifting from the theosophic to the psychological, the theoretical to the existential. Here, the blending of *Din* and *Hesed* is necessary to repair man rather than the godhead, balancing and perfecting his soul. The reshaping of an old theme relating to the mixture of *Din* and *Hesed* in a psychological context appears to signify a return to the human, the attention paid to the existential situations the believer finds himself facing in his most difficult moments undoubtedly exemplifying a variant spiritual orientation that displays more interest in the roots of the religious experience within the human soul than in the upper realms.

This is not to claim that the spirit of existentialism in the *Zohar* only awoke in its later strata. On the contrary, the place given to religious experience and the nature of the mystic soul in virtually all its layers and sections is well known. The *Zohar* does not deal solely with the faith of its theoretical subjects but also with the believer and his inner world. The way in which it shapes the early tradition relating to the blending of *Hesed* and *Din* in the *aqeda*, however, clearly reveals a process of formation and development. The outlines of the flow of the midrashic idea discussed here and the transformation it undergoes during the process of transmission within the zoharic circle reflect the transition from the pre-zoharic mystical world, whose focus lies on the upper realms and the dramas that take place therein, to a mystical spirituality that is increasingly self-aware and displays a growing interest in the mystical experience, the "dark night of the soul," its spiritual longings and yearnings, and its indecisions and oscillation between nearness to and distance from God. Although the Lurianic kabbalah was pushed aside and relegated in favour of the sophisticated and complex Lurianic concept of the godhead, it eventually burst forth with the rise of Hasidism, becoming one of the latter movement's key features. If in recent years the Jewish world has witnessed a renewal of Hasidism, this is due in large part to this spiritual aspect, whose buds, as we have seen in this chapter, can already be seen to sprout and blossom in the *Zohar*.

Chapter 9:
The Birthright and the Blessing: Esau's Suppressed Cry

The figure of Esau in kabbalistic literature in general and the *Zohar* in particular plays a key role in the myth of evil and its origins and manifestations. Either expressly or via other names—Seir and Edom—Esau is repeatedly represented as the dark side of the theosophic experience—cosmic evil, the *sitra achra*. In this chapter, I shall attempt to trace the midrashic roots of this kabbalistic signifier and its history within the zoharic literature. I shall begin by endeavouring to identify its footprints in the ancient midrashic tradition, examining how the symbol arose. I shall then present and discuss the later zoharic position, which contains a very surprising response to its radical incarnation. As we shall discover, the zoharic spirit does not merely create or use the signifier but is aware of itself, reacting fiercely and daringly to its radical midrashic expressions.

'That wicked one': Esau as archetype

The starting point for our discussion of Esau's status in the aggadic midrash is, of course, the story of the twins in Genesis, according to which Esau is cheated out of his birthright and election and pushed to the margins of the Hebrew family tree. Already in the biblical text, Esau is painted as the rejected brother who has no part or inheritance in the God of Israel.[1] Herein, he is identified with the father of Amalek and the Edomites, so thoroughly denounced in the prophetic literature (see below). The biblical antagonism towards Esau/Edom reaches down into the midrash, passing from there like a scarlet thread through to medieval thinkers, commentators, and kabbalists. The post-biblical tradition further blackened his name and figure, linking him with the troublers of Israel throughout the generations. Henceforth, the Edomites were regarded as the forefathers of the Romans who destroyed the Temple—in the Middle Ages then coming to be identified with Christianity.

Where, why, and how did this identification arise? Many scholars have addressed this question, all noting that the first occasions on which Edom and

---

1 Cf. Mal 1:2 – 3: "I have loved you, says the Lord. But you say, 'How have you loved us?' Is not Esau Jacob's brother? says the Lord. Yet I have loved Jacob but I have hated Esau."

Rome are associated occur in the context of the political crisis of the Bar Kokhba revolt. The most striking ancient extant source in this regard is indeed a dictum attributed to R. Judah bar Ilai in *y. Ta'an.* 4, 5, 68d: "It was taught: R. Judah bar Ilai son of R. Ilai said: My blessed master used to expound 'the voice is the voice of Jacob but the hands are the hands of Esau'—Jacob's voice cries out over what the hands of Esau did at Beitar." From here onward, it appears to have spread and become a self-evident tenet in the talmudic and midrashic tradition.[2]

Numerous proposals have been made with regard to the nature and meaning of the identification between Edom and Rome.[3] Graetz and Ginzberg (2003: 1:314 n. 19) maintain that they were linked via Herod's Edomite kingdom, which the Roman Caesars supported. Others adduce note that the midrashic statements exhibit close affinities with the prophetic denunciations of Edom. Gerson Cohen (1967) argues that the tendency to identify allusions to the destruction of the Second Temple in Lamentations led the Sages to view the Edom referred to therein as Rome. He also suggests that Roman self-consciousness clashed in many respects with the Israelites' belief that they were the chosen nation, giving birth to a tension between the two peoples that put the midrashists immediately in mind of Jacob and Esau's struggle for the birthright/election. Israel Yuval (2006: 15–20) refutes this contention, alleging that the move was rather a polemical response to the Christian identification of Jacob with the Church and Esau with historical Israel that led Jewish homilists to inversely identify Israel with Jacob and Esau with the "evil kingdom" of the time—Rome.

In my view, this argument is also untenable. While the ancient identification of the Jewish people with Jacob is found in the biblical text itself, it also being universally acknowledged that they were the "Israel of the flesh"—thus requiring no homiletic apologetic—the association between *Rome* and Esau appears to lack any meaning in the context of the polemic with *Christianity* over "Verus Israel." Even in the latter aggadic literature from the Byzantine period Edom is not

---

2 Amongst the examples of the identification of Rome with Edom we must note the witness of one of the Amoraim in *y. Ta'an.* 1, 1, 64a, according to which an exegesis was found in R. Meir's book on Isa 21:11—"The oracle concerning Dumah. One is calling to me from Seir"—that identifies the "oracle concerning Dumah" with Rome (an interpretation confirmed by context of the *sugiya*). Cf. also *Lam. Rab.* 4.20–22, §24: "'Rejoice and be glad, O daughter of Edom' (Lam. 4:24): i.e., Caesarea and Rome." Cf. also *Sifre Deut.* 343: "*and arise from Seir unto them* ... this refers to the Roman language" (Hammer, 1987: 351). *Pirke R. El.* 38 similarly states: "As a reward because he [Esau] removed all his belongings on account of Jacob his brother, He gave him one hundred provinces from Seir unto Magdiel, and Magdiel is Rome." *Trg. Ps.-Jon.* to Num 24:18–19 and Isa 34:9 also transmits a tradition according to which the kingdom of Greater Rome was built by Zepho son of Eliphaz son of Esau.
3 For a comprehensive review, see Aminoff (1981: 169–181).

yet identified with Christianity, clear evidence of this step only emerging in the late Middle Ages.⁴ Moreover, none of the talmudic texts that regards *Rome* as Edom deals with the Jewish-Christian polemic, the majority rather focusing on the cruel nature of the Roman troops.⁵

It thus appears necessary to understand Esau's figure and status in rabbinic literature in literary rather than historical terms. As early as the sixteenth century, R. Isaac Abrabanel suggested that the names Esau, Edom, and Seir serve as a midrashic archetypes of human evil. Addressing the issue of the identification between Edom and Christianity in his commentary on Isaiah, he engaged in an extensive discussion of the matter. While not appearing to compromise his firm assertion of the Edomit-Christian identification, and proving the reliability of the tradition with signs and wonders, he then offers an alternative explanation:

> On the basis of our religion and faith, the Christians should be called Edomites and the seed of Esau, just as the prophets called people on the basis of their deeds. Did not Isaiah call his generation "chieftains of Sodom and Gomorrah [1:10] and Ezekiel say to Israel "your sister Sodom" [i.e., Samaria]. Israel was the brother of Sodom in their family only because of her deeds and we already find images relating Rome and Israel, just as between Esau and Jacob ... The great commentator Nichola[s of Lyra] has already written in his books sacred to the Christians, in his exegesis of Obadiah's prophecies, that because Esau always hated Jacob all the haters of Israel were called by the name of Esau and Edom, which is true. (1954: 172 [on Isaiah 35])⁶

According to Abrabanel, the Roman Empire—called in these sources the "evil" or "wicked" kingdom (מלכות הרשע/מלכותא חייבתא)—was regarded by the generations of the revolt and destruction as the embodiment of evil and wickedness, thus being identified with Esau and Edom. The same idea is also evident in the well-known aggada on the giving of the Torah, which reveals the rabbinic Sages' view of the "sons of Esau" who represent "the very essence of these people and that their forefather was a murderer" (*Sifre Deut.* 343]).

Abrabanel's archetypal explanation not only provides a solution to the midrashic riddle but goes back to the biblical text itself, as he himself notes. The

---

4 For the identification of Edom and Rome/Christianity in a Byzantine *piyyut*, see below.
5 Even the parable of the tenants in *Sifre Deut.*, cited by Yuval (2006: 17), is not necessarily linked to this religious polemic—despite the affinities it demonstrates with the Parable of the Vineyard in the Gospels (Matt 21:33–44; Luke 19:9–10).
6 Nicholas of Lyra's (fourteenth century) commentaries on the Bible were already published and well known in the fifteenth century.

wrath and anger expressed towards Edom in political prophecies in the prophetic literature clearly exceed the criticism levelled at other nations, however, no support existing in the biblical historiography for such denunciation. To the best of our historical knowledge of that period, while Israelite/Edomite relations were sometimes strained and hostile, this antagonism did not exceed what was regarded as accepted behaviour at the time.

Nowhere does the biblical text provide us with the concrete geo-political background to the harsh prophecies of calamity against Edom.[7] Nor is it clear from the contexts in which they appear that they do not in fact relate to Israel's enemies, whoever they may be. Thus, for example, immediately after condemning all the nations—"For the LORD is enraged against all the nations, and furious against all their hordes; he has doomed them, has given them over for slaughter" (34:2)—Isaiah singles out Edom: "When my sword has drunk its fill in the heavens, lo, it will descend upon Edom, upon the people I have doomed to judgment" (v. 5). Similarly, while God announces His intention to pour out His vengeance on Edom—"Who is this that comes from Edom, from Bozrah in garments stained crimson? Who is this so splendidly robed, marching in his great might? It is I, announcing vindication, mighty to save"—He includes all the nations in His wrath: "I have trodden the wine press alone, and from the peoples no one was with me; I trod them in my anger and trampled them in my wrath; their juice spattered on my garments, and stained all my robes. For the day of vengeance was in my heart, and the year for my redeeming work had come ... I trampled down peoples in my anger, I crushed them in my wrath, and I poured out their lifeblood on the earth" (Isa 63:1–6). This is also the sense in which the opening of Deborah's war song should be understood: "LORD, when you went out from Seir, when you marched from the region of Edom, the earth trembled, and the heavens poured, the clouds indeed poured water" (Judg 5:4)—especially in light of the fact that the Seirites took no part in the battle against Barak.[8] The same appears to apply to the passages that assert that the Edomites were involved in the destruction of the First Temple—a claim that finds no support in the biblical historiography.[9]

---

[7] This does not refute the fact, of course, that sometimes (though rarely), the literary context reveals that the prophecies against Edom were directed towards the actual people: cf. Amos 1:11 and Ps 83:6.

[8] Cf. also Deut 33:2; Hab 3:3. For Edom as a typological signifier, see Weinberg (1984: 5–10).

[9] Cf. Obad 1, 11; Ps 137:7; Lam 4:21–22. 1 Esd 4:45 similarly states: "You also vowed to build the temple, which the Edomites burned when Judea was laid waste by the Chaldeans." References to Edom during the period of the destruction and/or restoration, during which the country was certainly no longer a significant political factor, also occur in Jer 49:7–22; Ezek 25:12–14,

The symbolic meaning of the identification of Rome and Edom also arises from its later evolutions, the same arrows being directed in the Middle Ages, as we have already seen, against Christianity, whose adherents were thenceforth regarded as Esau's descendants. Even if it is reasonable to assume that the Christianization of the Roman Empire played a key role in this development, the transfer of the stereotype from the national to the religious realm confirms the argument that it does not constitute a truly genealogical idea, the names Edom and Esau always bearing a symbolic meaning.[10] Henceforth, all those representing evil on earth and the troublers of Israel were necessarily identified as "Esau's descendants."[11]

35; Joel 4:19; Amos 9:12; Obad 1; Mal 1:2–5; Sir 50:26. See also Liver (1964: 202–203). A similar archetypal exegesis also appears in *Gen. Rab.* 16:4: "R. Huna said in R. Aha's name: All kingdoms [which] are designated after the name of Asshur [are so called] because they enrich themselves (*mith-'ashroth*) at the expense of Israel. R. Jose b. R. Judah said: All the kingdoms [which] are designated after the name of Nineveh are so called because they adorn themselves (*mith-na'oth*) at the expense of Israel. R. Jose b. R. Halafta said: All the kingdoms [which] are designated after the name of Mizrayim (Egypt) are so called because they persecute (*meziroth*) Israel."

10 Although the Byzantine *piyyut* tradition strongly denounces Edom, it contains scarcely any explicit objection to Christianity or its followers: see Rosensohn (2002: 62–63). Likewise, the few *piyyutim* in which anti-Christian allusions can be found—such as Yanai's "Those Who Call a Knave Noble" (Rabinovitz, 1985: 221, together with the preface and notes) or the Purim *piyutim* collected by Sokoloff and Yahalom (1985) and Swartz and Yahalom (2005), in which the recurrent motif of Haman's crucifixion may suggest that of Jesus—make no reference to Edom. The use of this name to designate Christians is primarily prevalent in Ashkenaz in the centuries after the crusades (cf. the well-known thirteen-century "Ma'oz Tzur," in which the author pleads: "O thrust the red one [i.e., Edom] into the shadows of death [דחה אדמון בצל צלמון]). It thus reasonable to argue that the identification of Edom with Christianity was finally made due to the crusaders, who legitimately merited the stereotype.

11 Opposition arose as early as the medieval period, in fact, to the fundamentalist view of the direct association between Edom and Rome. In his response to Hiwi al-Balkhi, Sa'adia Gaon observed: "Did you not know that Mount Seir in the Glorious Land and the Romans are not from Esau?" (Wertheimer, 1931: 49). Ibn Ezra also fiercely criticized the identification: "And there are some who have not woken up from their stupor and think that we are the in exile of Edom. This is not the case ... The nation that exiled us [the Romans] is from the seed of the Kittim ... and is the kingdom of Greece itself" (commentary on Gen 27:40). Nahmanides proposed a rather surprising—and forced—solution in his *Book of Redemption:* "We, who rely on the opinion of our Rabbis of blessed memory, believe that today we are presently in the exile of Edom ... However, the main intent of this verse is as follows: The Edomites were the first to mistakenly follow after the man who claimed that he was the Messiah. They also ascribed godliness [i.e., divinity] to him. When they came to the land of Edom, their error spread to the nearby city of Rome. There in the days of Constantine who ruled over Rome, the Edomite [nation] ... established it [as the religion of the empire]. This, above all else, is the main cause and reason that Rome

If my thesis is correct, the question regarding the meaning of the identification must be reformulated, now relating to the literary framework in which the archetype of "Esau the Wicked" arose rather than to the historical context in which Esau/Edom and Rome were connected. Here, it becomes even sharper, requiring an explanation of why the people whom the law of Israel prohibits hating ("You shall not abhor an Edomite for he is your brother" [Deut 23:8]) serves in the midrashic literature as the archetype of human evil and wickedness. I suggest that a close and sensitive reading of the midrashic traditions and talmudic passages concerning Esau can aid in answering this question.

---

and Edom are considered as one kingdom although they are different nations. In spite of that [difference], they are related because of their uniformity of belief which makes then one people and one nation" (Chavel, 1978: 2:619–620). According to this view, Christianity forms the chain that links Edom, whence sprang the "cause and root" of the new religion, and the Roman Empire that accepted it. The association of Edom with the pre-Christian Roman Empire is thus retroactive, being merely symbolic or typological. Cf. also Radak's commentary on Obad 1:1. There is also no doubt that during the Middle Ages the Christians were in no way thought to be actual Edomites. Such a genealogical identification would have caused a severe halakhic problem. According to the halakhic tradition that relies on Deuteronomy, the Edomite resident alien was regarded as disqualified from marrying an Israelite "up until the third generation." We never hear of Christians who converted being prohibited from entering the community, however. Maimonides had in fact already ruled on this matter: "When Sennacherib, king of Assyria, arose, he mixed up all the nations, intermingling them one with the other, and exiled them from their homelands; the result was that the people who now dwell in Egypt are not the original Egyptians, nor are the Edomites now in the plains of Edom the original ones. Therefore, once these four forbidden nations have become commingled with all the other permitted nations, they all became permitted. ... when nowadays a person becomes a proselyte anywhere, whether he is an Edomite, and Egyptian ... he is permitted to enter the congregation at once" (Maimonides, 1965: 86 [*Book of Holiness*, Forbidden Intercourse 12:25]). This fundamental halakhic view not only refutes the link between Edom and the twelfth-century Christian world but in effect completely repudiates the early identification between Edom and Rome, Sennacherib's act long preceding the rise of the Roman Empire. Maimonides thus also appears to deny any historical and halakhic validity to the midrashic association. In eighteenth-century Ashkenaz, R. Jacob Emden was asked about the "alien who comes from Italy ... if he is allowed [to marry] an Israelite woman." In his rather surprising response, Emden fears violating a biblical prohibition, recommending: "It is better not to be in doubt with respect to the Torah and avoid marrying an Israelite woman, courting a convert one instead" (1884: 1:46). The fact that is only worried about an alien who is a "suspected Edomite"—being Italian in orgin—indicates that regarded the Christians amongst whom he dwelt as being clear of any such suspicion.

The literary roots of the archetypal image

When we examine the context in which the midrashic figure of Esau emerged, all the threads lead us to the charged discussion of Isaac's blessings. Thus, for example, when we closely analyze the midrashic methods employed in such works as *Genesis Rabbah*, which devotes great space to this issue (primarily in sections 65–67), we can clearly perceive its "nerve centre." The motivation behind it appears to lie in the ethical considerations associated with this complex narrative, which hang over it like a dark cloud. From every step and virtually every homiletical avenue arises the same troublesome thought, the status of Esau the man also being derived here from the way in which the Sages chose to illuminate and deal with this difficult story.

The difficulty is, of course, the central question of the Jacob and Esau account—the ethics of Jacob's cheating Esau out of the birthright.[12] Does the act represent a serious flaw in the character of the forefather of the nation—or can it be explained and justified? The Sages' approach to this question is ambivalent, on occasion even contradictory, the medieval commentators being equally preoccupied with the same issue.

The biblical text itself raises the question, offering various solutions. In general terms, three biblical-midrashic trends can be discerned: denunciation of the act, reducing Jacob's responsibility for it or absolving him from it, and justification as part of and in opposition to the negative image of Esau.

The first view can be found in the biblical account of Jacob's life and history. As is well known, on several occasions the vicissitudes he experienced are suggested as being linked to other events.[13] Jacob's request from God to be given "bread to eat and clothes to wear" reflects his destitute state, alluding to the two narrative sections in which the brother's relations are established—that in which Jacob gains the birthright in exchange for a pot of stew (food) and that in which he wins the blessing by placing hairy skin over his arms (clothing). During his subsequent wanderings in Haran, Jacob himself falls victim to Laban's deception, the latter justifying with the claim that "This is not done in our country—giving the younger before the firstborn" (Gen 29:26). The midrashist also regards the parallelism between the two sections as reflecting the principle of "measure for measure." Thus, in answer to Jacob's criticism of Leah for collaborating in her father's scheme ("What, you are a deceiver and the daughter of

---

[12] I am not concerned here with the issue of the religious or metaphysical validity of blessings gained by deception, despite the fact that the Sages also addressed this question.
[13] For an extensive survey of the implicit criticism of Jacob in the biblical text, see Garsiel (1983: 63–79).

a deceiver") it contends that she retorted: "Is there a teacher without pupils? Did not your father call you 'Esau, and you answered him!'" (*Gen. Rab.* 70:19).

The Sages unquestionably regarded Leah's pretending to be Rachel as a form of "measure for measure" for his ruse of disguising himself as Esau. Laban's use of Jacob's "instruments of deception" is also meant to arouse associations with his appearing before Isaac: "So Jacob went up to his father Isaac, who felt him ... [but] did not recognize him" (Gen 27:22)—the goat hair that signals to Jacob (again through deception!) that "Joseph has been torn to pieces" also being a retribution for his covering his hands with goat's skin in order to make Isaac think he was Esau.[14]

The same is true with respect to Jacob's charged meeting with Esau on his return to Canaan, when, in stark contrast to the blessing "may your mother's sons bow down to you" (Gen 27:29), Jacob is forced to humble himself before Esau (Gen 33:3–15). In our section here, Rebecca, the instigator of the plot, is parted from her beloved son forever in recompense for having ruptured the brothers' relations with their father.

Above all, however, the biblical text itself conveys a sense of profound empathy towards the two who are deceived—Isaac and Esau: "Then Isaac trembled violently" (Gen 27:33); "When Esau heard his father's words, he cried out with an exceedingly great and bitter cry" (v. 34). Esau's wounded cry is picked up by the midrashist's sharp senses, leading him to conclude the episode bluntly and forcefully: "Jacob made Esau break out into a cry but once, and where was he punished for it? In Shushan, the castle, as it says, *And he cried out with a loud and bitter cry*, etc. (Est 4:1)" (*Gen. Rab.* 67:4).

The second approach seeks to diminish Jacob's part and responsibility in the deception. This also has ancient roots in the biblical text itself. The biblical account places Rebecca, the twins' mother, centre stage, pulling the strings, Jacob merely being a passive partner. Even in the chapter in which he is required to act, his mother's image and spirit overshadow him.[15] Just as Esau is devoted to his father, so Jacob acts in accordance with his mother's wishes. Here, too, the midrash seeks to sharpen the events, penetrating into the depths of Jacob's soul and

---

[14] In this context, cf. Jacob's confession: "Is it possible that the trembling which I caused my father when he said: *Who then* (efo) *is he* (Gen 27:33) has now come home to me!" (*Gen. Rab.* 91:11).

[15] According to *Jubilees*, Abraham is also enlisted on Jacob's behalf: "He said to her, 'My daughter, guard my son Jacob because he will be in place of me upon the earth and for a blessing in the midst of the sons of men and a glory to all the seed of Shem because I know that the LORD will choose him for himself as a people who will rise up from all the nations which are upon the earth" (19:17–19).

depicting the internal turmoil he endures as he obeys his mother, "under constraint, bowed down, and weeping" (*Gen. Rab.* 65:15). In the Sages' eyes, Jacob remains pure and upright, rightfully owning the name Yeshurun.[16]

The more sophisticated versions of this approach stress that it was not only Rebecca who pulled the strings but also God Himself:

> When Isaac said to Jacob, *Come near, I pray thee, that I may feel thee, my son* (Gen 27:21), perspiration poured over his legs and his heart melted like wax. But the Holy One, blessed be He, sent two angels, one at his right side and one at his left, who supported him by his elbows so that he should not fall. (*Gen. Rab.* 65:19)[17]

In a nearby passage, the midrash also reveals the imprint of God's hands in the very first stages of the scheme: "Thus, why did Isaac's eyes grow dim? So that Jacob might come and receive the blessings" (*Gen. Rab.* 65:8). Here, too, the biblical text serves as inspiration, even before the twins' birth Rebecca being forewarned that "Two nations are in your womb, and two peoples born of you shall be divided ... the elder shall serve the younger" (Gen 25:23). On this reading, Jacob's act being the fulfillment of divine prophecy, it does not interfere with family history but rather brings it to its rightful and proper fruition.

These two views are overshadowed, however, by the far more striking and dominant assertion of Jacob's merit as linked to Esau's wickedness—which must be countered by cunning and deceit. Right from the outset, the two adult men are contrasted with one another: "Esau was a skillful hunter, a man of the field, while Jacob was a quiet man, living in tents" (Gen 25:27). Whatever the meaning of the phrase כי ציד בפיו, Esau clearly comes out badly.[18]

---

16 For Yeshurun, see *Encyclopedia Biblica* 3:937–938. The name Israel may also reflect the same meaning. Many translators thus refused to accept Isaac's assertion that "Your brother came deceitfully" at face value, choosing to render the verse "in wisdom" or "in the wisdom of the Torah" (see Onqelos and the Palestinian targums). The midrash on Jacob's words at the height of the drama—"I am Esau your firstborn"— also belongs to this trend, signifying: "I am to receive the Ten Commandments. But *Esau* [is] *thy firstborn*" (*Gen. Rab.* 65:18). Cf., with slight variations, Rashi ad loc. (Gen 27:35) and Ibn Ezra's fierce criticism there.
17 A midrash in *Tanh.* Toldot 11 similarly states that an angel of the Lord delayed Esau in the fields in order to give Jacob time to carry out the deception. This tendency is even more pronounced in *Jubilees:* "And he [Isaac] did not know him because the change was from heaven in order to distract his mind" (26:18). Cf. *Jub.* 19:26–29, 22:10–30.
18 The question is whether the subject here is Esau or Isaac. *Trg. Onq.* (ad loc.)—followed by Rashi and Rashbam—understands the latter: "And Itzhak loved Esau, *because he ate of his hunting."* This exegesis, however, acknowledges that the expression is elliptical, requiring to be read: "because he put hunting into his mouth." The midrash in fact appears to have properly comprehended the meaning of the biblical text, which seeks to convey that Esau hunted his father with

The account of the selling of the birthright further sharpens the contours of Esau's character, portraying him as a rude, hedonistic figure wholly given over to his needs and drives: "Then Jacob gave Esau bread and lentil stew, and he ate and drank, and rose and went his way. Thus Esau despised his birthright" (Gen 25:34). His wicked nature is also exemplified in relation to his Hittite wives, who made his parents' "life bitter" (Gen 26:35). He then adds insult to injury—literally—by marrying an Ishmaelite.[19]

The talmudic-midrashic literature thus developed a thorough-going hatred and resentment towards Esau, turning him into the incarnation of cunning. He is depicted as someone who hunted his father with his words while pretending to be righteous, "trapping at home [by asking]: 'How do tithe salt?', in the field [by asking] 'How do you tithe straw?'" (*Gen. Rab.* 63:10).[20] If he is thus a schemer, capturing his father's heart deceitfully, Jacob's cunning is must be understood as right and proper behaviour, intended to correct what Esau has deformed. This quality in Jacob is also alluded to in a talmudic aggada that reports Jacob and Rachel's discussion of the morality of deception:

> He said to her, Will you marry me? She replied, Yes, but my father is a trickster, and he will outwit you. He replied, I am his brother in trickery. She said to him, Is it permitted to the righteous to indulge in trickery? He replied. Yes: with the pure thou dost show thyself pure and with the crooked thou dost show thyself subtle. (*b. Meg.* 13b)[21]

Esau's chicanery and craftiness are also reflected in the following sections, which depict the complex and unresolved relationship between the two brothers. Some even see deception and cunning concealed in the moving displays of sib-

---

his mouth. Cf. Prov 6:26: "For a prostitute's fee is only a loaf of bread, but the wife of another stalks a man's very life." See also Ibn Ezra's commentary on איש יודע ציד: "He will always be full of deceit, for most animals are caught by cunning" (Gen 25:27). This makes the contrast between איש תם and איש ידע ציד clear and explicit, hunting being in essence deception. *Jubilees* portrays a similar antithesis: "Jacob was smooth and upright, but Esau was a fierce man and rustic and hairy ... And the youths grew up and Jacob learned writing, but Esau did not learn because he was a rustic man and a hunter. And he learned war, and all of his deeds were fierce" (19:13). Interestingly, Josephus (*Ant.* 18.1) says nothing on this matter, not presenting Esau in a negative light.

19 Rashi appears to allude to this fact: "He added evil to evil." According to Genesis' view of election, in allying himself with the house of Ishmael he thus drove himself further out of the national camp.

20 Cf. a slightly different parallel in *Pes. Rab Kah.* 1.

21 The motif of deceiving the deceiver occurs in early Greek literature: cf. Aristotle, *Poetics* 1356a; Halevi (1973: 141–142). See also *Tanh*. Toldot 11: "You went to hunt and have been hunted."

ling affection in their meeting: "And thine enemies shall dwindle away (*we-yik-kahasu*) before thee (Deut 33:29). When Israel is prosperous, the nations of the world flatter (*mekahasim*) them and act as if they were brothers. Thus Esau said to Jacob, *I have enough, my brother, let that which thou hast be thine* (Gen 33:9)" (*Sifre Deut.* 356). Esau's kiss was also suspected, to the point of being interpreted as a bite (נשך vs. נשק) (cf. *Gen. Rab.* 78:9), his hypocrisy being regarded as lasting until the eschaton: "In the future, Esau the wicked will cover himself with a *tallit* and sit with the righteous in the Garden of Eden, and God will drag him out and remove him" (*y. Ned.* 3, 8, 38a).

Henceforth, the aggada sought to sharpen his cunning nature, attributing to him the malicious character of Ben Beliyaal, appealing to various scriptural verses—in particular the chapters relating to the birthright and blessing in *Toldot* (Gen 25:1–28:9).[22] His ruddiness (from birth) was easily associated with his tendency towards blood-shedding: "*Ruddy* [ויצא הראשון אדמוני כלו] (Gen 25:25). R. Abba b. Kahanna said: Altogether a shedder of blood" (*Gen. Rab.* 63:8). Isaac's blessing "by your sword you shall live" (Gen 27:40) is similarly understood as signifying Esau's military prowess (cf. *Mekh.* Beshall. 2).[23] He is also accused of additional crimes that have no scriptural base. Thus, for example, the amora R. Johanan stated: "That wicked [Esau] committed five sins on that day. He dishonoured a betrothed maiden, he committed a murder, he denied God, he denied the resurrection of the dead, and he spurned the birthright" (*b. B. Bat.* 16b).[24] According to *Gen. Rab.* 65:1, for forty years he "used to ensnare married women and violate them." Ascribing them to the "product of incestuous relations," Scripture is said to mention them "only to disclose their degeneracy" (*Tanh.* Vayeshev 1 [Berman, 1996: 222]). Ultimately, Esau is accused of committing the three cardinal sins:

> Said the Holy One, blessed be He: "I made a promise to Abraham, assuring him, *But thou shalt go to thy fathers in peace; thou shalt be buried in a good old age* (Gen 15:15)": is this a good old age when he sees his grandson practicing idolatry, immorality, and murder! Better that he quit this world in peace! (*Gen. Rab.* 63:12)[25]

---

22 Particularly harsh statements concerning Esau occur in the Byzantine Palestinian *piyyut* tradition: see Rosensohn (2002).
23 In Arabic, חרב = war.
24 For his denial of the world to come, cf. *Gen. Rab.* 63:14; *Trg. Ps.-Jon.* on Gen 24:29. The New Testament also paints Esau as an adulterer who profanes God's name (cf. Heb 12:16–17).
25 For Esau as an idolator, cf. *Lev. Rab.* 4:6: "Esau worshiped many deities." The Sages thus compared Jacob and Esau to the myrtle and wild rose-bush respectively, one yielding fragrance, the other thorns when they mature. After their thirteen birthday, one thus "went to the house of study and the other to idolatrous shrines" (*Gen. Rab.* 63:9). According to the midrash, Esau is

The disgust and revulsion the Sages felt in regard to Esau finds its expression in the epithet "Esau the Wicked (עשו הרשע)" frequently given him.²⁶ The "kingdom"—i.e., Rome—gained a similar designation, appearing most prevalently in the expression the "evil kingdom" (מלכות הרשע or מלכות חייב/חייבתא).²⁷

Esau and Edom in the zoharic myth

The *Zohar* exhibits a similar diversity in its treatment of Jacob's deception.²⁸ Here, however, his demonized figure takes on completely different proportions, assuming cosmic and mythic dimensions. Henceforth, he no longer only symbolizes the kingdom of evil and wickedness in anthropological-cultural terms but embodies the *sitra achra* itself.²⁹ As we observed above, Esau—as Edom and in particular Seir—constitutes one of the most prevalent designations of the *sitra achra* in the *Zohar*.³⁰ The *Zohar* exploits the diverse contexts in which these ref-

---

accustomed to frequenting such places even from birth. For the far-reaching implications of this view, see below.
26 It occurs over two hundred times in talmudic and early midrashic literature. עשו רשיעא also appears on numerous occasions.
27 For these usages and their various occurrences, see Herr (1970: 132–135). In this context, the Sages also stress Esau's merit on numerous occasions, primarily his honouring of his father: see Heineman (1974: 33); Aminoff, (1981: 93–97); Rosensohn (2002: 71–73).
28 The *Zohar* also clearly shapes the traditional solutions surveyed above in its own unique way, of course, at times even infusing them with a radical meaning. Thus, for example, where the ancient midrash adduces a link between Esau and Mordechai's cries, in the homily that concludes *parashat Toldot* (1:146b), at the end of the discussion of the problem of the disparity between the blessings Jacob obtained and his historical fate, R. Yeisa Saba ascribes the exile as a whole and the historical bondage to the Edomites in particular to Esau's merits and tears: "Similarly with Esau, the honor he rendered his father prolonged his domination so persistently in this world." In other words, through judgment and merit, Esau delays the fulfillment of the blessing, ensuring, moreover, that it will be not realized until Israel have also returned to God in weeping and tears. The same idea is expressed in 2:12b: "The deliverance of Israel depends only upon weeping—when the tears of weeping shed by Esau before his father will completely end, as is written: *Esau raised his voice and wept* (Genesis 27:38). Once those tears cease through the weeping of Israel, they will come out of his [sic] exile, as is written: *With weeping they will come, and with consolations I will guide them ...* [Jer 31:8]."
29 In addition to its broad and varied expression in the *Zohar*, this symbolic usage also occurs in pre-zoharic kabbalistic works: see, for example, Nahmanides' commentary on Lev 16:8; R. Isaac Hacohen's Essay on the Left-Hand Emanation (Scholem, 1927: 91).
30 For *sitra de-Esau*, *hulqa de-Esau*, and *darga de-Esau*, cf. 1:144b, 146b, 160a, 166a, 171a, 172c, 177a–b; 3:64a, 185a; *Zohar hadash*, 54a, 78a, 87a–b. This *sitra* is explicitly identified with Esau in 1:138b: "Since Esau, being an aspect (*sitra*) of that serpent." For Edom in this con-

erences appear in order to exhaust all that it has to say about the question of evil. Thus, for example, it understand "Edom" as an allusion to the colour red and Mars, both striking symbols of Samael, "Seir" recalling the scapegoat sent away on the Day of Atonement (cf. 1:65a, 138b) and the goats offered on *Rosh Hodesh*, the first of the month—which also form part of the symbolic field of evil. From here, the symbol made its way naturally into Lurianic kabbalah, Sabbatean literature, and Hasidic homiletics. The *Zohar* thus preserves the symbolic usage of the Sages, imbuing it, however, with a metaphysical content drawn from its own unique world.

The transition from the symbolic to the mythic is reflected in the parallel evolution and status of the figure of Samael. While in the *hekhalot* and *merkava* literature—the cradle of his birth—Samael is always referred to as "Esau's prince" and distinguished from Satan himself, in the talmudic and early midrashic literature, in addition to his title as Esau's or Rome's prince Samael also appears in the guise of an ordinary wicked angel, with no connection to Esau.[31] In a later midrash, he is already given the epithet "head of all the satans" (*Deut. Rab.* 11:10), being held responsible in *Pirqe R. Eliezer* 44, 45 for introducing evil into the world. From here, it is a short jump to Samael's mythical incarnation within kabbalistic literature as the *sitra achra*. Here he is depicted for the first time as bringing destruction and ruin, his power being

> the cause of the stars of the sword, wars, quarrels, wounds, plagues, division and destruction. In short, it is the spirit of the sphere of Mars, and its portion among the nations is Esau, the people that inherited the sword and the wars, and among animals [its portion consists of] the *se'irim* (demons) and the goats. Also in its portion are the devils called "destroyers" in the language of our Rabbis, and in the language of Scripture: *se'irim* (satyrs, demons), for thus he [Esau] and his nations were called *sa'ir*. (Nahmanides, commentary on Lev 16:8)[32]

In other words, Esau's demonization also led to a changes in his second-in-command, who came to be identified with Satan himself, serving in the kabbalistic literature as the root and cause of all evil.

---

text, cf. 1:177b; *Zohar hadash*, 40a. For "Seir" and *sitra de-Esau*, cf. 1:172b; 3:192b: "He shone forth to them from Seir" (Deut 33:2)—Seir being a name of Samael." On several occasions, the impression is created that "Seir" is the standard and obvious symbol, adduced freely without any need of explanation in contrast to "Esau" and "Edom" that sometimes require a clarificatory note.

31 Chavel (1978: 3:219–220). Cf. *b. Sotah* 10b; *Gen. Rab.* 56:4. In *Abot R. Nat.* A addendum 2, chap. 4, Samael is identified with the Angel of Death.

32 For the history of the figure of Samael, see Dan (1998).

All this notwithstanding, the polished linear evolution from the biblical protagonist to a mythic symbolic-archetype appears to be too simple. Even though Esau's demonic status only emerges in medieval kabbalistic literature, its roots can be traced back to rabbinic midrashic corpus. A clear echo can be found, for example in a midrash on the creation: "*And God called the light day* (Gen 1:5) symbolizes Jacob; *And the darkness He called night*, Esau" (*Gen. Rab.* 2:3).[33] Elsewhere, evil forms an essential element of Esau's character. Thus, for example, the midrashic treatment of the story of the brothers' birth bears a strongly deterministic character: the sons are distinguished already in the womb by their congenital antithetical personalities: Jacob is accustomed to spending his time in the synagogue and study hall, Esau in idolatrous shrines (*Gen. Rab.* 63:6). According to *Pesiq. Rab Kah.* 3, "At his going forth from his mother's belly he ripped her womb so that she bore no more children." We have already referred to the midrash describing the boys' adolescence:

> *And the boys grew* (Gen 25:27). R. Phinehas said in R. Levi's name: They were like a myrtle and a wild rose-bush growing side by side; when they attained to maturity, one yielded its fragrance and the other its thorns. So for thirteen years both went to school and came home from school. After this age, one went to the house of study, the other to idolatrous shrines. (*Gen. Rab.* 63:10)

Here, the midrashist clearly seeks to identify the dichotomy between them as reaching back to before they were born. Another nearby homily similarly regards the twins' "struggling together" referred to in the verse as occurring in the womb. In one passage, the name "Esau" is interpreted to signify "It is for naught (*shaw*) that I created him in My universe" (*Gen. Rab.* 63:8), another close by bestowing upon him the epithet "demonic" (*Gen. Rab.* 65:15).[34]

Generally speaking, according to this midrashic approach, Esau's wickedness—like Jacob's righteousness—and no less than these the rivalry, resentment, and hostility between them—are not portrayed as a result of their education or environmental factors but as congenital traits—in just the same way as a myrtle gives off a fragrance and the rose-bush develops thorns. In light of this, we should not wonder at the "halakhah" transmitted in R. Shimon bar Johai's name: "Halakhah, as it is known that Esau hates Jacob" (*Sifre Num.* 69). Al-

---

[33] This midrash appears to relate to the historical figures of Jacob and Esau, the following homily exegeting the same verse in relation to the nations of the world.

[34] Esau's demonic character may also be alluded to in *Est. Rab.* Proem 5: "*And a serpent bit him* (Amos 5:19)—this refers to Edom, of which it says, *The sound thereof shall go like the serpent's* (Jer 56:22). Occurring in the context of a homily on the animals in the verse as standing for historical empires, this meaning is uncertain, however.

though this relates to the antagonism between Jacob and his brother, it shifts their rivalry from the historical-biographical to the metaphysical realm.³⁵

Esau's demonic nature is also reflected in his national incarnation as Edom:

> R. Isaac also said: What is meant by the verse, *Grant not, O Lord, the desires of the wicked, draw not out his bit, so that they exalt themselves, selah?* [Ps 140:9] Jacob said before the Holy One, blessed be He: Sovereign of the Universe, grant not to Esau the wicked the desire of his heart, draw not out his bit [i.e., further not his evil device]: this refers to Germamia of Edom, for should they but go forth they would destroy the whole world. (*b. Meg.* 6a)³⁶

Germamia's role in the Roman Empire was to exhaust its power and resources, thereby reducing its destructive capabilities and the catastrophic eruption of evil. It is thus reasonable to assume that the roots of "Edomite myth" found in the *Zohar* lie intuitively deep within the classical midrashic corpus.

The symbolic use of "Esau" fits the idea of evil propounded in the *Zohar* and kabbalah in general, easily being assimilated into it. Esau's antecedence of Jacob at birth well reflects the place evil holds in the process of emanation, the winnowing out of the evil waste from the good being a prerequisite for the emanation of the worlds: "Come and see: the head of the beginning of faith within the thought struck the strong spark, ascending within the thought and emitting sparks ... and winnowed the waste from out of the thought and it was sifted" (*Zohar*, 2:254b).³⁷

---

35 For the various versions of this dictum, see Shochetman (1997) and in response Rosensohn (1998). According to these scholars, the original text may have been: "Does Esau not hate Jacob?," the "halakhah" perhaps first being introduced by Rashi in his commentary on Gen 33:4.

36 Cf. *Gen. Rab.* 75:9. In this context, we must also note the metaphysical "version" cited in *b.Meg.* 6a: "Caesarea and Jerusalem [are rivals]. If one says to you that both are destroyed, do not believe him; if he says that both are flourishing, do not believe him; if he says that Caesarea is waste and Jerusalem is flourishing, or that Jerusalem is waste and Caesarea is flourishing, you may believe him, as it says, *I shall be filled, she is laid waste* [Ezek 26:2]: if this one is filled, that one is laid waste, and if that one is filled, this one is laid waste." R. Nahman's statement—and his "prooftext"—are of great interest for our present purposes: "R. Nahman b. Isaac derived the same lesson from here: and the one people shall be stronger than the other people [Gen 25:23]." For the political background of this homily and the rivalry between Caesarea and Jerusalem, see Avi-Yonah (1984: 112, 193).

37 On occasion, the *Zohar* describes the antecedence of evil as the shell vis-à-vis the kernel: cf. 2:108b. For the theological significance of this view, see Tishby and Lachower (1989: 1:566–569); Idel (1979/1980) and the references in the latter to the Zurvan myth of the birth of Hormiz and Ahriman, which he suggests lies behind the zoharic doctrine of the root of evil. Several thick strands link this story with that of Jacob and Esau here. For the messianic significance of the idea, see Liebes (1993d: 65–67).

This fundamental concept is reflected in the zoharic homiletic in the motif of the rejection of the firstborn in the Genesis account, also lying behind the homily on the death of the Edomite kings. As is well known, the cathartic antecedence of evil in the process of emanation also stands at the centre of the Lurianic kabbalistic notion of evil (Tishby, 2002: 41–49; Har-Shefi, 2007).

Esau's cry: The wronging of evil and its vengeance

A shift in the *Zohar*'s attitude towards Esau the biblical figure and the evil his figure represents occurs in *Saba de-Mishpatim*, one of the preeminent poetic works within the zoharic corpus. This composition is incorporated as an independent unit, representing a later literary strata than the central section of the *Zohar* (Yisraeli, 2005). At its heart lies the story of the encounter between two members of the zoharic circle—R. Hiya and R. Jose—and an elderly eccentric figure, ultimately revealed to be R. Yeiva Saba, who delivers lengthy homilies on various theological and kabbalistic subjects. In one of his key expositions on the phrase "tears of the oppressed," he expresses his profound identification with their woes.[38]

Who are these men? In concrete terms, the Saba laments the death of innocent infants who have not sinned. This is merely the launching pad, however, for a thread addressing oppression in general: "Again I saw *all* the oppressions." The homily raises here the issue of fate and its bitterness in diverse circumstances of life, the lack of understanding of how the world operates, and the natural demand for justice that remains unfulfilled. Amongst the things against which he rails are the classic dilemmas of the doctrine of reward and punishment, the sin of the fathers visited on their descendants to the third generation, and the fate of the bastard—together with inner-kabbalistic problems linked to the soul's pre-existential descent into the world, such as its capture by the *sitra achra* before its descent and the arbitrary mechanism of the *tiqla* or scales of deceit that determine its destiny.[39]

At one of the peaks of the work, the Saba lets out a cry that has yet to be heard in any Jewish homiletic or hermeneutic text, claiming no less than that evil has been wronged, itself being numbered amongst the oppressed. His ethical sensitivity to the injustice from which the oppressed suffer does not preclude

---

38 Qoh 4:1: "Again I saw all the oppressions that are practiced under the sun. Look, the tears of the oppressed—with no one to comfort them! On the side of their oppressors there was power—with no one to comfort them."
39 Yisraeli (2005: 143–144). For the *tiqla*, see Liebes (1977: 327–335).

him from thinking that a harsh sentence has been passed on the *sitra achra*. Here, he makes a quantum leap. Up until now, he has lamented the fact that evil has been given permission to oppress the human soul prior to its descent into the world. Now he claims that evil itself has been unfairly treated. Its vengeance—which thus possesses a measure of justice—in effect serves as the source of its power, thereby meriting the right to "oppress" holiness in the world—Israel, the talmud scholars, and the spirit of prophecy.

What, then, is this mythological oppressed entity onto whose hooves evil clings in this world in such a way as to make it invincible? In picking its way back to the roots of this figure, the *Zohar* returns us to the ancient biblical trauma. In the homily "God's controversy with Esau," it does not flinch from "a mountain [i.e., forefathers] dispute," reproving Jacob with rare courage for his behaviour towards his brother:

> *Hear, O mountains, the grievance of YHVH, and you firm ones, foundations of the earth!* (Mic 6:2) ... *For YHVH has a grievance against His people* (ibid). Who can endure the grievance of the blessed Holy One? ... All those disputes with Israel and all those reprimands are entirely like a father toward his son, as they have established. Concerning Jacob, when He sought to quarrel with him, what is written? *For YHVH has a genuine grievance against Jacob* (Hos 12:3). What is the grievance? As is written: *In the womb he seized his brother by the heel* (ibid., 4). For this matter came reprimand and all those grievances. (*Zohar*, 1:110b)

Following a brief apology for the critical nature of his words, the Saba opens with a contention against the people of Israel—Israel (Jacob) the person. He begins by objecting to Jacob's distancing himself from his brother in his hour of need: "... at this sound the blessed Holy One shook the heavens and their array. For his prince did not demand *blessing* or *birthright* nor say anything about this; he could have demanded *blessing* but did not. However, brotherhood he surely did demand: *Do not hide yourself from your own flesh and blood*'(Isaiah 58:7), yet Jacob did not want to give him anything to eat before he took his birthright from him" (ibid, 111a). It quickly becomes clear, however, that his focus lies not on the historical plane, with the relationship between the brothers, but on something entirely different:

> Is this not a weighty matter: In the womb he seized his brother by the heel, and in his strength he strove with God? This is no small matter, what he did in the womb. Now, is there deception in the womb? Surely, he practiced deception in the womb; but Jacob thrust away his brother entirely so that he would have no share at all. And Esau complained only about one that is two, as it is written: *He deceived me* זה (*zeh*), *this, two times* (Gen 27:36). The verse should read אלה (*elleh*), *these, two times*; why *zeh, this?* Well, once comparable to two, one emerging as two. And what is that? ברכתי (*bekhorati*), *my birthright*—letters reversed, becoming ברכתי (*birkhati*), *my blessing* ... Esau did not know what he did to him

in the womb, but his appointed prince knew, and at this sound the blessed Holy One shook the heavens and their array. For his prince did not demand *blessing* and *birthright* nor say anything about this; he could have demanded *blessing* but did not. ... *So, he seized his brother by the heel* (Hos 12:4), precisely—deceiving him, casting him behind. What is 'behind'? He made him emerge first into this world. Jacob said to Esau, 'You take this world first, and I will follow.' Come and see what is written: *Afterward his brother came out, his hand gripping Esau's heel* (Gen 25:36). Now, do you imagine that his hand was grasping the other's foot? Not so. Rather, what did his hand grasp? The one who was a *heel*. And who is that? Esau. For Esau was called *heel* from the moment that [Jacob] deceived his brother; yet since the day the world was created, the blessed Holy One called him *heel*, as is written: *He will strike you at the head, and you will strike him at the heel* (Gen 3:15)—you, called *heel*, will strike him first, and finally he will strike your head right off you. Who is that? Samael, head of the serpent, who strikes in this world. So, *in the womb he seized his brother by the heel*—making him a heel—and Esau acquired this world first. (ibid)

What is the crime for which Jacob is condemned here? The Saba immediately rejects the conventional answer—the sale/stealing of the birthright—as merely the outward manifestation of the true, essential breach Jacob brought upon Esau, of which even the historical Esau is unaware, only his prince understanding it. The injustice Jacob committed against Esau was primarily the struggle prior to their birth—*So, he seized his brother by the heel*. The hand with which Jacob grasps Esau's heel as they are born is that which makes Esau into a heel—the latter being the early symbol of the *sitra achra:* "since the day the world was created."[40]

In a typically zoharic shift from the biblical-historical to the symbolic-mythic plane, the Saba challenges the predestination that attributes a negative connotation to the "heel," laying the blame on Jacob, as we have seen, who in the very formation of his identity conquered the holy. Thereby driving Esau out of its realm, he turned him into a "heel," inheriting the world to come in his place. The injury Jacob inflicts on Esau thus does not lie in his taking of the birthright or the blessing but possesses a much deeper existential dimension: he robs him of his original identity, leaving him only with the *sitra achra*. Total, mythical evil requires its day in court for being just that—evil.

The evil that is oppressed, the Saba proceeds to explain, does not accept the judgment, struggling tirelessly to capture pieces of this world and regain control of them. His partial success derives from the compensation he receives due to his —largely rightful—claim of injustice. The Saba highlights the tragic aspects of this struggle and its implications. Thus, for example, the *sitra achra* woos the

---

40 In light of the verse "He will he will strike your head, and you will strike his heel" (Gen 3:15): see *Zohar*, 2:111a.

woman's womb but is not given permission to govern it. Instead, and in recompense, he is given control of the womb of the *sotah*, of whom it is thus stated: "her womb shall discharge, her uterus drop" (Num 5:27). It is also given authority over the "thigh of holiness"—the power of prophecy that proceeds from the *sefira* of *Netzach*—after Esau's prince touched the hollow of Jacob's thigh (Gen 32:25). This injustice has already been corrected by Samuel the prophet, however, who "took that thigh and lifted it from that place, snatching it from him. Since that time it has been withheld from him, and he has no share in holiness at all" (*Zohar*, 2:111b). Even the "fatigue in the knees" of the talmud scholars, the wearing out of their clothes, and the bruising of their feet is to be attributed to the arousal of evil, whose tortured longings for holiness (even after his realm was delimited) leave their "mark" in this space, primarily amongst those who "dwell in tents"—i.e., those who engage in Torah-study, the members of the "congregation of Jacob."[41] Finally, the injury done to the *sitra achra* means that "no human can speak—even words of Torah are tiresome!" (*Zohar*, 2:111b). In other words, even the stopping up of the wellsprings of creativity are due to this historical-mythic guilt.

Evil takes its vengeance on the "Achilles' heel"—the *sotah*, the spirit of prophecy, and the knees and feet of the Talmud scholars—with the concurrence of God Himself: "for this is the belly upon which he wreaks vengeance as he wishes; this belly is his, given to him so that he not be utterly thrust away" (ibid). In other words, God Himself gives him control over the thigh in order to confine him within his borders, thereby purifying the heart of the sacred space:

> The blessed Holy One did not rob or reject him totally, through Samael taking his thigh; rather, he provided him with one portion. What is that? He gave him that thigh of the straying wife, in exchange for the thigh that he confiscated from him, and the belly of the straying wife, in exchange for the belly that he confiscated from him. Thus both of them the blessed Holy One gave him, so that it would be a place of holiness ... like someone throwing a bone to a dog, saying, 'Take this for your portion.' ... So the blessed Holy One casts him this bone of a straying wife, and with this he is satiated and delighted. ... Everything returns

---

41 *Zohar*, 2:111b, 112a. The source of this idea is a *baraita* in *b. Ber.* 6a: "Abba Benjamin says, If the eye had the power to see them, no creature could endure the demons. Abaye says: They are more numerous than we are and they surround us like the ridge round a field. R. Huna says: Every one among us has a thousand on his left hand and ten thousand on his right hand. Raba says: The crushing in the Kallah lectures comes from them. Fatigue in the knees comes from them. The wearing out of the clothes of the scholars is due to their rubbing against them. The bruising of the feet comes from them. If one wants to discover them, let him take sifted ashes and sprinkle around his bed, and in the morning he will see something like the footprints of a cock."

to its place, and the blessed Holy One does not omit anything necessary at all; He wants only His people and share, His portion and inheritance, to approach holiness.

The turning point in *Saba de-Mishpatim*'s attitude towards the *sitra achra* is illuminated by the link between the motif of recompense given to Samael and the zoharic interpretation of the scapegoat.[42] According to the Zohar's exegesis of the commandment to send the scapegoat away on the Day of Atonement, the goat serves as a bribe to persuade him not to indict Israel. Nahmanides had already noted the ostensible redundancy lying at the heart of the ordinance to offer a sacrifice to Samael, devoting a lengthy passage in his commentary on Lev 16:8 to a discussion of the problem (Chavel, 2005: 218).[43] As we have remarked above, the idea of the appeasement of the *sitra achra* also occurs explicitly in numerous other places in the *Zohar*, standing, in effect, at the heart of the zoharic doctrine of sacrifices (Tishby and Lachower, 1989: 1:453–454). The denial of the necessity of allocating the *sitra achra* its portion constitutes, in zoharic eyes, a recipe for disaster.[44]

Here, too, the *Saba de-Mishpatim* marks a watershed in the history of the *Zohar*'s attitude towards Samael. Even if we are not deal with a sacrifice or a goat, the theological foundation is clearly the recognition of the fixed and indisputable status of evil and its unassailable hold over the realms of holiness. If Samael forms a cruel adversary in the central section of the *Zohar*, the extent of his power paralleling the depth of the damage he inflicts on holiness, in *Saba de-Mishpatim* he acts as a litigant who files his suit and takes his vengeance—righteously. Here, we find another myth, according to which evil does not fully play the part of the "anti-hero." In the hierarchy of power in the world, evil is injured not by its own fault, pushed out of the womb and thigh to the margins of mystical dominance, his principal asset having been expropriated—the purity of its identity.

The Saba's ambivalence towards evil finds expression not only in a theological tenet but also and primarily in a tortured mental stance. The recognition of

---

[42] This connection is also exemplified in the *Zohar*'s use of the very same parable in the two very different contexts, the goat that was sent away (3:63a–b) also being understood via the parable of the dog and bone—despite the difference in nuance in the two places in accord with their theological tendencies.

[43] For Nahmanides' contribution herein to the kabbalistic doctrine of evil, see Dan (1994).

[44] The *Zohar* views Job's error and sin in a similar fashion, "turning away from evil" and not giving the *sitra achra* its portion—and thereby leading to its eruption and dominance over holiness: see *Zohar*, 2:181b–182a. For this and the *Zohar*'s complex attitude towards evil in general, see Tishby and Lachower (1989: 1:453–454); Liebes (1993d: 16–19; 1994: 83–85).

its inalienable reality derives principally from the Saba's deep desire for justice—as an ethical footprint in the face of the ruling of evil and the appropriation of its "poor man's lamb"—from the *sotah*'s womb and anywhere else it places its hooves at any time. He touches here, of course, on a fundamental problem within zoharic theology. While the process of emanation, in which all the antithetical elements within the godhead are separated out, refines holiness it also identifies and determines the other, rejected, component as total evil. The sober realization of evil's firm establishment in the world illuminates in the Saba's eyes the profoundly tragic dimension inherent in the complex relationship between good and evil. The mythic Samael also being the biblical Esau and historical Edom identified with Rome, however, herein also lies the explanation for the historical hatred of Israel as a whole: "All nursing of hatred of Israel is based on this" (*Zohar*, 2:112a). God's "mountain dispute" with the father of the nation thus takes the form of an irrevocable historical decree: "Hear, you mountains, the controversy of the LORD, and you enduring foundations of the earth; for the LORD has a controversy with his people, and he will contend with Israel" (Mic 6:2). The Saba's sensitivity to the fairness of fate and reward/punishment leads him to find himself occupying the paradoxical position of defending evil in the world.[45] It is thus not surprising that this forms the root of his pessimistic outlook, which foresees evil's continued existence not only because it is impossible to overcome but also—no matter how strange this may sound—because it is unethical.

The shift from the mythic drama to the realm of historical existence is, of course, characteristic of the new zoharic spirit, which jumps back and forth between the various spheres of the universe, in its penetration into mythic realms never neglecting real events or its commitment to the biblical narrative. The Saba's cry thus relates first and foremost to the drama of the sibling rivalry, the painful suffering being above all that of Esau the man. While, as we have noted above, this finds a place in the ancient midrash, the cause of the wrong here differs completely to that with which we are familiar in the talmudic literature. The Saba knows the approach that justifies Jacob's act by adducing Esau's contemptible character and his evil traits. He is also aware of his demonic aspect —the fact that he is evil in his very creation, from birth, thus being the very personification of wickedness. It is precisely because of and to this view, however, that he objects. He emits the cry of "Esau's prince"—the charge that Esau's evil

---

[45] The tendency towards literary identification with the mythological anti-hero, primarily in the figure of Esau, is worthy of investigation in its own right: cf. Shalev (1994).

nature was imposed on him against his will from the womb, when Jacob "seized him by the heel."

From a broad literary perspective, Esau's radical midrashic demonization over the course of many years appears to be the fruit of the challenge laid down in *Saba de-Mishpatim*'s homily on the "tears of the oppressed." Paradoxically, the "stretching" of Esau's figure into mythic proportions constitutes the launching pad of the midrashic activity described above. Whereas the ancient midrash asked whether Jacob's deception could be justified, however, the zoharic homilist wonders why and how Esau came to serve as the symbol of evil in the world. This question has no answer, not even in *Saba de-Mishpatim*.

The cry regarding the fate and tortured and oppressed figure of Esau that erupts in *Saba de-Mishpatim* and the exceptional courage and openness with which the Saba demands retribution for the rejected brother thus expresses a strikingly non-conformist stance. The complex attitude the early midrashic tradition exhibits towards Esau indicates that the wonder and moral weight stretched from the biblical account never diminished. Indeed, the revealing and daring nature of the *Saba de-Mishpatim* homily are intimately associated with the work's general trends, the composition not turning its face away from any of the lofty secrets. Here, however, it becomes clear that the zoharic authors' esoteric orientation also possesses a rather surprising midrashic aspect. In addition to daring to open and disclose, with all due caution, the treasures concealed in the Torah, the book also reveals the hearts and minds of its midrashists. The light shed onto the homily's incubation and the inner workings and bold spirit of its instigators clearly manifests the creative powers and motives that drove it over the generations—the homiletic unconscious or subconscious.

Conclusion

The Saba's cry remains as a voice crying in the wilderness. A faint trace of this reading echoes several centuries later, not surprisingly, in the writings of Jacob Frank, who deeply identified with Esau's suffering. Rachel Elior suggests that "Jacob Frank identified with Esau's bitter fate, with the injustice done to him, with his insult and banishment to the margins, and with the theft and deception that were his lot, as also with the change and powerful threat and danger his figure underwent in Jewish tradition" (2001: 496). Although it is difficult to assess to what extent if any the Saba influenced Frank's view, there can unfortunately be no doubt that this depiction suited and expressed the anarchist position. The empathy in modern Hebrew literature towards his figure also reflects the status and critical weight of the humanistic-moralistic approach that makes itself heard even at the cost of shattering traditional myths.[46]

Even if it is not easy to link all these expressions into a coherent worldview, they all appear to derive from a single source—the ineradicable dissonance between the *qere* and *ktiv*, the plain meaning of the literary biblical text and the way in which its reading according to the midrashic tradition developed. We should nonetheless note that while the Saba takes pain to preserve his cry within the dogmatic theological framework—"God's laws are true and they lead to truth"—in its later evolution it bursts beyond these fragile bounds, as in so many other instances in the history of religious thought only a hairsbreadth separating wonder from defiance and revolt.

---

46 For Esau's figure in modern literature, see Kam (2001).

Chapter 10:
The Exodus and the Liberation of the Kabbalistic Spirit

The unique status the Exodus possesses in Scripture is exemplified in the detailed account given of it and the numerous laws and ordinances associated with it, first and foremost the direct command: "Remember this day on which you came out of Egypt, out of the house of slavery, because the LORD brought you out from there by strength of hand" (Exod 13:3). This remembrance is intimately linked with the Passover festival, all of which is "in memory of the Exodus from Egypt," the first night being the night on which the Seder is held and the haggada commemorating the event recited. The place the memory of the Exodus holds as an integral part of Jewish life is clearly indicated by Maimonides : " … it is a duty to recall [the Exodus] by day and night, as it is said, "that thou mayest remember the day of thy going forth from the land of Egypt all the days of thy life (Deut 16:3)."[1] What is the precise and nature and purpose of this formative event, however, and what religious consciousness does it seek?

A number of answers to these questions are found in the biblical text itself, which illuminates the subject from various angles. An analysis of the biblical references to the Exodus evinces that in addition to a national-historical consciousness of freedom, remembrance of the event is intended to shape an ethical consciousness: "You shall not oppress a resident alien; you know the heart of an alien, for you were aliens in the land of Egypt" (Exod 23:9). It also plays a role in the vision of the messianic era, which serves as a prototype of sorts for the future redemption, as indicated in the words of Micah: "As in the days when you came out of the land of Egypt, show us marvelous things" (Mic 7:15). Above all, it establishes a concrete religious commitment, forming the basis upon which the people of Israel worship their God: "I am the LORD your God, who brought you out of the land of Egypt, out of the house of slavery" (Exod 20:2)—or even more explicitly: "I am the LORD your God, who brought you out of the land of Egypt, to be your God: I am the LORD your God" (Num 15:41).[2] The Israelites were thus freed from slavery under Pharaoh in order become God's servants.

---

[1] *Mishneh Torah*, Book of Adoration, Laws of Reading the Shema 1:3.
[2] This aspect was addressed in twelfth-century Spain on the eve of the appearance of the Kabbalah by R. Judah Halevi in his *Kuzari* (1.11–25).

All these trends also find expression in rabbinic literature, which emphasizes and develops diverse aspects of it in line with its needs and purposes. The kabbalistic corpus, however, paints the Exodus in a very different light, attributing a completely new meaning to it. In this chapter, I shall examine the significance the Exodus carries in kabbalistic literature in general and the *Zohar* in particular, also addressing the nature of kabbalistic memory.

From the deliverance of the people to the deliverance of the spirit

The meaning of the Exodus is discussed directly and explicitly in a zoharic midrash dealing with the status attributed to it by the Torah:

> *I am the Lord your God.* Regarding this verse R. Issa the Little, one of the Companions, asked Shimon bar Johai: I have one question to ask you, but I am afraid to ask it. I said: If I ask, I am afraid lest I will be punished; if I do not ask, I will have a distorted view. Shimon bar Johai said to him: Ask. He said: Why does the blessed Holy One remind Israel time and again 'I am the Lord your God who brought you out of the land of Egypt,' 'I am the Lord your God, who brought you out of the land of Egypt'—what great thing did He teach here? It was a surety that he told Abraham: 'Know this for certain, that your offspring shall be aliens in a land that is not theirs, and shall be slaves there, and they shall be oppressed for four hundred years; but I will bring judgment on the nation that they serve, and afterward they shall come out with great possessions' [Gen 15:13–14]. If so, why does He refer to it time and again? R. Shimon said to him: Come and see my son: the blessed Holy One only assured Abraham that He would bring Israel out of exile in Egypt. He did not promise to deliver them from bondage to other service. For when they were in Egypt they defiled and polluted themselves with every type of uncleanness until they became subject to the forty-nine powers of impurity. But the blessed Holy One delivered them from serving all the other powers until He brought them unto the parallel forty-nine gates of wisdom. He only pledged to bring them out of Egypt to Abraham, dealing graciously and mercifully with them. So you find that the Torah refers to the Exodus fifty times in order to demonstrate to the peoples of the world the compassion He showed to the people of Israel, bringing them out from under these impure powers and bringing them into the powers of purity—i.e., the fifty gates of purity. And we count them from the Passover, counting days and weeks. And the Companions awoke [to say]: It is a commandment to count days and a commandment to count weeks, because every day He brought them out from the power of impurity and brought them into the power of purity. (*Zohar hadash*, Jethro 31a)

The question R. Issa reverently raises here relates to the Torah's dramatization of the story of the Exodus: why does it make it such a 'big deal' of referring to it when it was predetermined? Is it not merely the payment of a debit note given to Abraham, the father of the nation, who was informed about the redemption when he told the edict? The response R. Shimon bar Johai, the great teacher of the *Zohar*, gives is that the deliverance from physical bondage was not the primary purpose of the Exodus, the Torah not relating to this on the numerous other occasions it refers to the event. Nor was it national redemption. Its real meaning is rather spiritual liberation—or more precisely, the deliverance of religious life. According to this view, the Israelites in Egypt were not only compelled to perform forced physical labour but also to serve the forty-nine gates of impurity, being subject to the authority of the powers ascribed to Egypt. The Exodus freed and liberated them from this spiritual bondage, as a result of which they gained a higher status and purification in the forty-nine gates of wisdom.[3] The real drama therefore occurs on the spiritual plane, the Exodus transforming the Israelites' religious world, taking them out of the world mired in the depths of the abyss of the *sitra achra* and bringing them into the forty-nine gates of wisdom. Abraham was thus not in fact made privy to all the promise, God only acting on the basis of compassion in bringing his descendants out of Egypt.

This is a revolutionary understanding of the Exodus, which replaces its national aspect with a spiritual meaning. It nonetheless has ancient roots. Egypt is identified with impurity in the Torah itself, which calls Egyptian culture an "abomination." Thus, for example, the section dealing with forbidden relations, which opens with the statement: "You shall not do as they do in the land of Egypt" (Lev 18:3), repeatedly stresses the "impurity" and "abomination" of this act.[4] Scripture very rarely alludes, to the deliverance from this culture as constituting the essence of the Exodus, however, always referring to it in fact as "from the house of bondage."[5] According to an ancient tradition—whose roots can be traced back to Ezekiel, who accuses the Israelites of worshiping the "idols of Egypt"—the people's purification from their idolatry is thus a prerequisite for their deliverance rather than the liberation itself:

---

[3] While talmudic tradition states that there are fifty gates of wisdom, the fiftieth—the highest of all—does not lie within human power (even that of Moses, master of all the prophets): see *b. Roš. Haš.* 21b. This tradition was adopted by several of the kabbalists, first and foremost Nahmanides, who discusses it extensively in the introduction to his commentary: see Pedaya (2003: 135–142).

[4] Cf. Lev 18:6–26. The "abomination of Egypt" in Exod 8:22 refers to the gods of Egypt, however.

[5] Cf. Exod 13:3, 14, 20:20; Deut 5:6; et al. The spiritual aspect of the Exodus may perhaps be hinted at in the Haggada: "In the beginning our fathers served idols; but now the Omnipresent One has brought us close to His service." This version, which also appears in *b. Pes.* 116a in the name of the amora Rav, is merely meant to broaden the story's scope, transferring its beginnings to ancient history, before Abraham's election, however—not seeking to change the actual meaning of the Exodus: see Safrai (1998: 125).

> On that day I swore to them that I would bring them out of the land of Egypt into a land that I had searched out for them, a land flowing with milk and honey, the most glorious of all lands. And I said to them, Cast away the detestable things your eyes feast on, every one of you, and do not defile yourselves with the idols of Egypt; I am the LORD your God. But they rebelled against me and would not listen to me; not one of them cast away the detestable things their eyes feasted on, nor did they forsake the idols of Egypt. (Ezek 20:7)

In the tannaitic midrash, this issue is linked to the people's turning their back on the deliverance:

> R. Judah the son of Bathyra says: Behold it says: "But they hearkened not unto Moses for impatience of spirit," etc. (Exod 6:9). Can you imagine a man receiving good tidings and not rejoicing; being told, "a male child is born unto thee," and not rejoicing; being told, "your master sets you free," and not rejoicing? What, then, does Scripture mean by saying: "But they hearkened not unto Moses"? Merely that it was hard for them to part with their idols. And so it is also said: "And I said unto them: Cast ye away every man the detestable things of his eyes, and defile not yourselves with the idols of Egypt" (Ezek 20:7); and it says further: "But they rebelled against Me and would not hearken, etc. ... But I wrought for My name's sake" (ibid, 20:8–9). This is what is meant by the passage: "And the LORD spoke unto Moses and unto Aaron, and gave them a charge unto the children of Israel" (Exod 6:13)—charging them to give up idol worship. (*Mek*. Pisha 5)

According to this tradition, the national deliverance was delayed because the Israelites were reluctant to shake themselves free of their involvement in idolatrous Egyptian practices. As we noted above, however, this step is a condition for being set free rather than the deliverance itself. The Exodus's spiritual nature must thus be regarded as a zoharic innovation.

From national enterprise to mythical struggle

The formation and development of this idea can nonetheless be identified in the early midrashic tradition, resting on a very ancient foundation that embodies the reworking of an early biblical motif. On more than one occasion, Scripture alludes to the fact that the Israelites' struggle for deliverance from the bondage in Egypt was a religious-mythical one conducted by the God of Israel against the gods of Egypt rather than merely a national one. Thus, for example, we learn that the plagues were meant *a priori* not only for the Egyptians but also their gods: "For I will pass through the land of Egypt that night, and I will strike down every firstborn in the land of Egypt, both human beings and animals; on all the gods of Egypt I will execute judgments" (Exod 12:12). This view is also reflected in a later memory: "... the Egyptians were burying all their firstborn, whom the LORD had struck down among them. The LORD executed judgments even against their gods" (Num 33:4). In light of these verses, Jethro's astonishment takes on a new meaning: "Now I know that the LORD is greater than all gods, because he delivered the people from the Egyptians, when they dealt arrogantly with them" (Exod 18:11). In the Exodus, the God of Israel revealed his superiority over the gods of all the other nations through His mighty hand and outstretched arm.

What is the meaning and nature of the divine struggle against other gods? Does this representation of the events contain a recognition that the gods of Egypt possess some power? Not necessarily. The verses may be understood ironically, presenting the pagan-festishist worship of wood and stone as foolishness and wickedness. Thus, for example, the *Mekilta* uses this notion to interpret God's "judgments" on the gods of Egypt: "*And against all the gods of Egypt I will execute judgments: I am the LORD* [Exod 12:12]. Judgments differing one from the other. The stone idols melted, the wooden ones rotted away, the metal ones corroded" (Pisha 7). In this context, the ancient midrash also understands the commandment to sacrifice a lamb on the night of the Exodus as being in order to "teach them that their gods are really nothing at all" (*Exod. Rab.* 16:3). The same approach appears to be taken in *Jub.* 48:5: "and upon all of their gods the LORD took vengeance and be burned them with fire." The majority of the medieval commentators also adopted this exegesis.⁶

While Nahmanides, one of the earliest Spanish kabbalists of the thirteenth century, cites the *Mekilta* on this verse (Exod 12:12), as his wont he also adds a very significant comment that sheds a very different light on the matter:

> In my opinion, Scripture alludes to here to the lords on high, the gods of Egypt, something like the verse *The Eternal will punish the host of the high heavens on high, and the kings of the earth upon the earth* [Isa 24:21]. Thus He subdued the power of the Egyptians and that of the lords over them. But Scripture hints and deals briefly with hidden matters. (Chavel, 1971: 2:129–130)

Despite their esoteric tone, Nahmanides' words are clear and direct. God's "judgments" against the gods of Egypt constituted an attack on the "lords on high"—unquestionably a reference to the "prince of Egypt" as he is known in the midrash. God's blows were thus directed at Pharaoh's power, his star/constellation, and the latter's prince.⁷

---

6 Cf. Rashi, Ibn Ezra, and Hezquni on Exod 12:12. For another view, see Sforno *ad loc.*
7 The picture Nahmanides paints here must be understood in light of the ancient astrological notion of powers, princes, and deities ruling over specific territories and nations, all being subject to the "high above the high"—the king of the king of kings, the Holy One, blessed be He: see Loewenstamm (1986; 1992: 115–117).

The meaning of this combat is elucidated by some of the kabbalists of the following generation. The thirteenth-century Joseph Gikatilla, for example, says of the first *sefira—Malkut—*in his detailed discussion of the *sefirot* in the *Sha'arei tzedek*:

> This attribute is called Yam Suf (the Red Sea), being thus called in order to accept his children and deliver them from their enemies ... For God placed Egypt's prince in the second chariot. He was thus compelled to work signs and wonders in the land of Egypt as he was the supreme prince over all the princes, so that Egypt would become Israel ... He thus gave signs and wonders to the great prince of Egypt so that no one would say that there is a supreme prince whom the Holy One, blessed be He, cannot defeat ... Therefore the Torah says: "so that all the days of your life you may remember the day of your departure from the land of Egypt" [Deut 16:3]—so that we shall be sure that there is no prince or ruler in all the nations whom the Holy One, blessed be He, the omnipotent, cannot overcome. (5b)

We find a similar thought in the writings of other kabbalists from the end of the thirteenth century.[8] R. Joseph Gikatilla himself in his *Sha'arei ora* reveals the place of Israel's deliverance in this mythic context:

> Know that it has already been said that the land of Egypt is second to the land of Israel and the "celestial prince" of Egypt was the greatest of all the other nations of the world ... Because Pharaoh was preoccupied with his celestial prince and cleaved to him, he didn't have a portion in the name YHVH, and because his celestial prince was only his, God had to send Moses to tell him that there is a master and governor of all the princes and all the forces of the world; and that master is the blessed YHVH. Israel are his portion and his endowment. When Moses cautioned Pharaoh to send them out, it was to tell him that Israel is not part of a guardian planet, or a celestial body, but she is part of the blessed YHVH. (1998: 41)[9]

Gikatilla understands the demand that Pharaoh let Israel go as part of the struggle between God and the greatest of the princes of the world, the prince of Egypt, this confrontation being necessary in order to establish God's sovereignty over all the princes and gods. Pharaoh is not yet presented here as a demonic figure or the representative of the *sitra achra*, even his prince not embodying mythical evil in the form of Samael.[10] The latter forms part of the hierarchical structure of

---

8 Cf. Recanati on Genesis, p. 309; Exodus, p. 26: see also Zioni (1882: 27a).

9 In his earlier *Nut Garden*, no intimation of this mythic view is yet visible, Gikatilla focusing herein on God's efforts to demonstrate His sovereignty over all flesh in response to Pharaoh's arrogance and boast "I do not know the LORD" (Exod 5:2).

10 This claim is confirmed by another passage in the *Sha'arei ora*, in which Gikatilla expounds Exod 14:7 —"he took six hundred picked chariots and all the other chariots of Egypt with officers over all of them"—as alluding to the fact that the "prince of Egypt joined forces with Sa-

the meta-astrological world of the princes of the nations of the world, each of which possess his own designated territory. His status at the head of this hierarchy, however, means that he can potentially pose a threat to the one over him, the king of the king of kings, the Holy One, blessed be He.

From mythic struggle to personal-spiritual freedom

Like the writings of other kabbalists in its environs and field of influence, the *Zohar* itself also contains the view discussed above.[11] Here, however, it is sometimes clothed in a very different garb:

> It has been taught: Israel did not leave Egypt until all those rulers above were severed from their links and Israel left their dominion, entering the holy supernal dominion of the blessed Holy One and becoming bound to Him, as is written: For *Mine are the Children of Israel as servants, they are My servants* (Leviticus 25:55). Why are they *My servants*? Because: *whom I brought out of the land of Egypt* (ibid.)—for I took them out of another domain and brought them into Mine. (*Zohar*, 2:40a)

As in Nahmanides and Joseph Gikatilla, the victory here is the subjugation of the upper rulers—i.e., the prince of the world, headed by the prince of Egypt. As in the *Sha'arei ora*, this finds expression in the determination of Israel's status as God's lot and inheritance. The focus of the battle has altered, however. Although God's right and authority over His people is highlighted, the Exodus not only transfers them from the prince of Egypt's realm into God's but also "binds" them to Him. This term forms part of the distinctive mystical vocabulary, signifying a dramatic change in the nature of Israelite spirituality, now being bound to the "holy supernal dominion." Here, the early mythical kabbalistic interpretation takes on a religious-mystical dimension, God's subjugation of the gods of Egypt

---

mael." In other words, the prince of Egypt is not Samael himself. In early, pre-zoharic kabbalistic literature, Samael and the *sitra achra* are represented by Esau's prince. In contrast to all this, Pharaoh's demonic nature appears in a parallel contemporaneous source (found in several manuscripts) dealing with the mystery of the war between Israel and Egypt: "This is the mystery of the lower war which is drawn against the upper forces and intention stands against intention and matter against matter. From all this you understand that Pharaoh's power was drawn from the power of Ashmadai and Israel's power from the Active Intellect" (MS Munich 22, pp. 227–229): see Scholem (2004: 9–10 and n. 6). According to Scholem, "The style and content of this manuscript conclusively indicates that its author was Joseph Gikatilla." Our comments here, together with other factors we cannot discuss at present, cast doubt on this claim, however.

11 A link even exists in the *Zohar* between the "gods of Egypt" and Duma, the prince of Gehinnom: see *Zohar*, 2:18.

being transferred to the religious-personal realm, the Israelites being lifting out of the sphere of the rule of the lesser divine powers (rulers) and bound to Supreme and Only God.

If we return at this point to the zoharic homily with which we opened, we find that it, too, implicitly contains a mystical interpretation of the battle against the gods of Egypt. According to the personal-mystical exegesis, the deliverance from the forty-nine gates of impurity and binding to the forty-nine gates of wisdom embodies the mythical victory of the God of Israel over the gods of Egypt. The homiletic move that is sharpened most forcefully here in relation to the early evolution of this notion lies in the fact that henceforth Egypt is perceived not only as a sovereign adversarial entity within the supernal hierarchy but as the root and source of impurity.[12] Israel's defilement in Egypt is their immersion in the forty-nine gates of impurity: "When they were in Egypt, Israel defiled and profaned themselves with every type of uncleanness until they became subject to the forty-nine powers of impurity." The Exodus was thus a purification from uncleanness and a cleaving to the forty-nine gates of wisdom and purity. The struggle between the God of Israel and the gods of Egypt is itself that between the world of holiness and the *sitra achra*. The war over the Israelites' spiritual and religious nature and the purity of their mystical status took place on the field of battle between these two poles.

The Exodus thus appears in classical kabbalistic sources in spiritual-mystical garb, the goal of their deliverance no longer being the demonstration of God's sovereignty over all other gods but human salvation. The return to the human is not necessarily a reversion to the plain meaning of the biblical text, however. Henceforth, salvation no longer refers to the deliverance of Israel from the hands of the Egyptians but their liberation from the depths of Egyptian impurity and abomination.

In several zoharic homilies, this view of the Exodus is linked to the biblical text's mystifying preoccupation with the food the Israelites ate after they left Egypt—primarily the bread, which changed its nature from time to time. Why, for example, do we find such a strict prohibition, even while the Israelites were still in Egypt, against eating leaven and the commandment to eat matza? These ordinances, which have been meticulously obeyed throughout the generations, piqued the interest of the zoharic authors—and many others. The *Zohar* sought to explain them by enlarging its perspective. As is well known, the Israelites only ate matza at the time of the Exodus, the biblical account stating that in

---

[12] The midrashic roots of this idea may possibly be discernible in the identification between Egypt and Ashmadai: see Scholem (2004: 10 and n. 6).

the future they would be given a new form of bread during their long wanderings through the desert. This is the manna, of course, called "bread from heaven" (Exod 16:4). Under the influence of a rabbinic dictum stating that "a child does not know how to call 'father' and 'mother' until it has had a taste of corn" (*b. Ber.* 40a). The replacement of leaven with matza and matza with the manna was understood as an expression of the people's progression in their knowledge of God and spiritual-mystical binding to Him:

> He further said, "When a person issues into the world, he knows nothing until he tastes bread. Upon tasting bread, he is stimulated to know and perceive. Similarly, when Israel left Egypt, they knew nothing until the blessed Holy One gave them a taste of the bread of this *earth*, as is written: *Earth, from which bread emerges* [Job 28:5]. Then Israel entered into knowing and perceiving the blessed Holy One. ... The blessed Holy One wanted Israel to know more of the realm befitting this *earth*, but they were unable until they tasted bread from that realm. What is that? Heaven, as is written: *I am going to rain bread from heaven for you* (Exodus 16:4). Then they knew and contemplated that realm. Before eating bread from these sites, they knew and perceived nothing. (*Zohar*, 1:157b–158a)

The "change in menu" reflects in distinctively biblical fashion the internal transformation that occurred within the souls of the Israelites who were delivered from Egypt in the Exodus. Those who ate leaven knew nothing about God because they had no part in Him, the most they could achieve being to make contact with the "sides" by which they were held—i.e., the gods of Egypt.[13] Only when they ate matza, whose origin lies in the "supernal earth," in the sefira of *Malkut*, were they able to cling to and know that *sefira*. When God determined to lift them to an even higher place, He then gave them the manna, the bread from heaven that comes from *Tiferet*, which is called "heaven."

Here, the Exodus is perceived on the one hand as a process of spiritual-mystical maturation and on the—no less important—other as the story of the birth of the doctrine of Jewish mysticism and a formative event in the history of the Kabbalah. According to the *Zohar*, the Exodus narrative is thus the founding charter for the Israelites' liberation from superficiality and religious ignorance and the foundation and establishment of kabbalistic faith within its spiritual world.

The existential meaning the Exodus holds for the zoharic authors is exemplified in another homily which also deals with the changing forms of bread given to the Israelites when they left Egypt. This attributes to the process reflected in the culinary plot and spiritual-mystical saga a psychosomatic aspect that relates to the oscillating balance between body and soul:

---

13 Cf. *Zohar*, 2:50a, where the bread of Egypt is referred to as the "bread of the evil eye."

> Come and see: When Israel entered and cleaved to the King by revealing the holy insignia, they became worthy of eating other bread—higher than at first, when they went out of Egypt, entering the bread called *matzah*. Now they entered and proved worthy of eating other, higher bread from a high place, as is written: *Look, I am about to rain down bread for you from heaven* (Exodus 16:4)—*from heaven*, really! At that time it appeared to Israel from this place. Companions engaging in Torah are nourished from another, higher place. What is it? As is written: *Wisdom gives life to its possessors* (Ecclesiastes 7:12)—a higher place. ... Come and see: All foods of the inhabitants of the world derive from above. The food that comes from heaven and earth is food that comes in Judgment, from a place where Judgment prevails; it is finer food. The food that appeared for Israel at that time—from a high place called *heaven*—is finer food, entering the soul most deeply, dissociated ever more from the body, called *ethereal bread* (Numbers 21:5). Highest food of all is food of the Companions, those engaging in Torah, who eat food of spirit and soul-breath—not eating food of the body at all—namely, from a high place, precious beyond all, called Wisdom. Therefore the body of the Companions is weaker than inhabitants of the world, for they do not eat food of the body at all. They eat food of spirit and soul-breath, from a distant, supernal place, most precious of all. So that food is refined of the refined, finest of all. Happy is their portion, as it written: *Wisdom gives life to its possessors* (Ecclesiastes 7:12)! Happy is the share of the body that can be nourished by food of the soul! (*Zohar*, 2:61b–62a)

The tradition of the manna as bread that is "absorbed into the organs" or the food of the ministering angels is ancient, occurring in tannaitic sources and being extensively discussed by Nahmanides:

> Now the manna was a product of that Higher Light which became tangible by the will of its Creator, blessed be He, and thus [according to R. Akiba], both the people who ate the manna and the ministering angels were sustained by the same substance. (commentary on Exod 16:5 [Chavel, 1971: 2: 227])[14]

Here, Nahmanides proceeds to note the link between the status of those who ate the manna and that of the inhabitants of the world to come. In contrast to this exclusive focus on the manna, the *Zohar* in the homily cited above describes a lengthy and complex process of release from the biological needs of eating and drinking. In the Exodus itself, the Israelites were commanded to exchange the ordinary, regular form of bread for matza, which emanates from *Malkut*. They then were given to eat of the manna, which emanates "from heaven"—*Ti*-

---

14 See also ibid, 223–229. For the tannaitic source, see *b. Yoma* 65b. For its history and versions, see Zakovitch and Shinan (2004: 50–56), who argue that a counter tradition exists in Scripture that holds that the manna is the bread of the angels on high—i.e., the "bread of the mighty ones" (Ps 78:25) according to R. Akiba there: "The bread that the ministering angels eat." If this is correct, the zoharic exegesis with which we are dealing here that posits that the manna is the spiritual food that nourishes and enlarges the soul may in a certain sense represent a resurrection of this ancient tradition. This subject requires further investigation.

feret—whose finer nature nourishes the soul more than the body. The manna, the bread from heaven, also called the "bread of the mighty ones" (angels), was consistent with the Israelites' spiritual status at that time—when they were only minimally mired in the material. The most elevated food of all, however, is that eaten by those who engage in Torah-study—i.e., the kabbalists, who only eat the "refined of the refined," the "finest of all" food that feeds the soul, originating from the most exalted and elevated of all the *sefirot*— *Hokhma* (Wisdom).

This status attributed to the Companions reflects, of course, the high self-image of the zoharic kabbalists, also undoubtedly being associated with the biblical figure of Moses, unparalleled in Israel, of whom it is said that when he attained the height of his prophetic achievements in ascending Mount Sinai "neither ate bread nor drank water" (Exod 34:28), having no need of physical sustenance at that moment.

Conclusion

A direct thread thus links the Exodus, the eating of the manna, and the emergence of the group of kabbalists responsible for the *Zohar*. The Exodus is a liberation from the impurity of Egypt governed by the unclean forces of the gods of Egypt and the launching pad for the ascent to the supernal sefiric spheres. The gradual process of transcendence is reflected in the gradual transformation of human existence, which increasingly divests itself of its physical aspect, eventually taking on the form of a spiritual corporality in those who preoccupy themselves with the mysteries of the Torah. The Exodus thus reveals itself as constituting the liberation of the kabbalistic spirit into its historical emergence and establishment within the medieval band of kabbalists. We may not be far wrong if we say that this homily views the Exodus from Egypt as the festival of the release of the historical Kabbalah.

Chapter 11:
The War Against Amalek: Human vs. Divine Needs

Israel's war and first victory over Amalek shortly after having left Egypt was a matter of great interest to exegetes and homilists, from a variety of perspectives. Firstly, the circumstances of the conflict itself are very obscure: who was Amalek and why did he attack the Israelites? Secondly, the abstruse oath that concludes the narrative—"A hand upon the banner of the LORD! The LORD will have war with Amalek from generation to generation" (Exod 17:16) and the stringent commandment linked with the incident in Deuteronomy ("You shall blot out the remembrance of Amalek from under heaven; do not forget" 25:19]) are unparalleled in Scripture. How does this war differ from all the others to which the biblical text refers and why is this enemy so harshly denounced? Rabbinic literature, medieval exegetical works, and the *Zohar* all address these questions extensively, the insights arising from their efforts in many cases contributing to the way the myth has been shaped in Jewish memory.

This chapter examines the *Zohar*'s discussion of another question—also not new in its day— however, namely the "tactics" through which the Israelites defeated Amalek: "Whenever Moses held up his hand, Israel prevailed; and whenever he lowered his hand, Amalek prevailed" (Exod 17:11). What did Moses' hands do and was it a form of magic? This issue obviously garnered attention from an early stage, beginning with the Mishna and *Tosefta* and through to the *Zohar* and medieval kabbalistic works. In this context, numerous diverse opinions are expressed with respect to magic in general and the extent to which it may be considered legitimate in particular. As we shall see below, the *Zohar* combines traditional views with very different contemporary kabbalistic doctrines, its integration of these divergent approaches opening up another window on its vigorous and lively, complex nature.

"Did Moses' hands wage war?": The *Zohar* and *Roš. Haš.* 3:7

While the circumstances of the war are obscure—"Then Amalek came and fought with Israel at Rephidim" (Exod 17:8)—the text describes the tactics in detail:

> Moses said to Joshua, "Choose some men for us and go out, fight with Amalek. Tomorrow I will stand on the top of the hill with the staff of God in my hand." So Joshua did as Moses told him, and fought with Amalek, while Moses, Aaron, and Hur went up to the top of the

hill. Whenever Moses held up his hand, Israel prevailed; and whenever he lowered his hand, Amalek prevailed. But Moses' hands grew weary; so they took a stone and put it under him, and he sat on it. Aaron and Hur held up his hands, one on one side, and the other on the other side; so his hands were steady until the sun set. And Joshua defeated Amalek and his people with the sword. (Exod 17:8–13)

This passage is discussed directly and extensively already in the tannaitic layer of the rabbinic corpus. The questions raised regarding the nature of this act and the unusual form of victory are exemplified in the well-known mishnaic formulation in Roš. Haš. 3:7: "Now did the hands of Moses wage war or crush the enemy? Not so; only the text signifies that so long as Israel turned their thought above and subjected their hearts to their Father in Heaven they prevailed, but otherwise they fell." The query, "Now did the hands of Moses wage war or crush the enemy?" reflects a fundamental reservation regarding the plain meaning of the text and its magical overtones.[1] The wonder-working staff, the raising of Moses' hands, the victory's direct dependence on the latter, and the fact that God is not referred to at any stage as bringing about the victory all represent prime examples of thaumaturgical techniques regarding which Scripture elsewhere expresses severe reservations.[2]

The mishna asserts that Moses' hands were not directly responsible for the miracle, the act rather being a pedagogical attempt to draw the Israelites' attention, prompting them to lift their eyes and voices to their Father in heaven. The

---

[1] For our present purposes, magic is defined as a "manipulative action directed upwards; the performance of technical procedures, far removed from love or awe, in order to compel God or His angels to do a person's will" (Liebes, 2004: 4). Idel defines theurgy, on the other hand, as "An action designed to influence the godhead, primarily in relation to its inner state or internal dynamics" (1990a: 157). For the Sages' attitude towards magic and sorcery in general, see Urbach (1975: 97–123); Harari (1998: 68–90).

[2] Some scholars suggest that the mishna reflects an anti-Christian polemic against the identification of Moses' raised hand with Christian ritual: see Ginzberg (2003: 3:61 n. 145); Hirshman (1992: 49–53); Zimmer (1996: 79–80); Wieder (1998: 2:733–736). Contra this view, see Rokeach (2002: 36–40). See also Ehrlich (2004: 115–119); Walfish (2001: 118 n. 58). It is difficult to get around the anti-magical tone of this dictum, however, whatever its motive. The lack of any allusion to God's active involvement in the war—with the exception of the divine response that concludes the episode—is particularly striking in light of the previous unit—Masa and Meriba. Portraying Moses as helpless—"What shall I do with this people? They are almost ready to stone me?" [Exod 17:4]—it portrays (in language very reminiscent of our text here) God as coming to his aid: "The LORD said to Moses, 'Go on ahead of the people, and take some of the elders of Israel with you; take in your hand the staff with which you struck the Nile, and go. I will be standing there in front of you on the rock at Horeb. Strike the rock, and water will come out of it, so that the people may drink'" (ibid, vv. 5–6).

intention of the heart towards God via what might be described as a meditative technique on Moses' part was what turned the tide of the battle and ultimately brought about the Israelites' great victory.

Two tannaitic parallels exist to this mishna, in the two *Mekiltot*. While this is not the place to discuss the divergences and nuances between the two traditions, neither asserts that the goal of Moses' act was to induce the Israelites to pray, employing more concrete and intentional expressions to describe the mental processes of the fighters instead. *Mekilta de-Rabbi Ishmael* states that "When Moses did so, the Israelites would look at him and believe in Him who commanded Moses to do so" (Amalek, 1). The *Mekilta de-R. Shimon bar Johai* goes even further, declaring that the Israelites "did God's will and believed in what He had commanded Moses to do" (Kahana, 1999: 166–167). The deliverance here being dependent upon total religious commitment, it reinforces the tannaitic trend toward de-thaumaturgizing the biblical text.[3]

Reservations of this type are evident as early as Philo. In *Mos.* 1.39, he alleges that, "having purified himself with the customary purification, he [Moses] rode up with speed to a neighbouring hill, and there he besought God to hold his shield over the Hebrews and to give them the victory and the mastery, as he had delivered them before from more formidable dangers and from other evils" (216). According to Philo, as in previous instances the victory over Amalek was due to Moses' intercession, his raised hands constituting a sign from heaven of the miraculous nature of the victory:

> And just as the two armies were about to engage in battle, a most marvellous miracle took place with respect to his hands; for they became by turns lighter and heavier. Then, whenever they were lighter, so that he could hold them up on high, the alliance between God and his people was strengthened, and waxed mighty, and became more glorious. But whenever his hands sank down the enemy prevailed, God showing thus by a figure that the earth and all the extremities of it were the appropriate inheritance of the one party, and the most sacred air the inheritance of the other. And as the heaven is in every respect supreme to and superior over the earth, so also shall the nation which has heaven for its inheritance be superior to their enemies. For some time, then, his hands, like the balances in a scale, were by turns light, and by turns descended as being heavy; and, during this period, the battle was undecided. But, on a sudden, they became quite devoid of weight, using their fingers as if they were wings, and so they were raised to a lofty height, like winged birds who traverse the heaven, and they continued at this height until the Hebrews had gained an unquestionable victory ... (ibid, 217–218 [Yonge])

---

3 According to Walfish (2001: 121), the mishna expresses serious reservations regarding the supernatural in general, the term מתגברים being perceived as a heightened psychological religiosity—"the intention of their hearts to their Father in Heaven enabling Israel to draw power and overcome Amalek." In my opinion, this case has yet to be well established .

The author of *Pirqe R. Eliezer* (ca. eighth century) adopts a similar view, understanding the story as a whole as depicting an event of mass public prayer, Moses standing on the top of the hill and acting as the prayer leader in the synagogue:

> All the Israelites (were standing) outside (their tents); they had gone forth from their tents, and saw Moses kneeling on his knees, and they were kneeling on their knees. He fell on his face to the ground, and they fell on their faces to the ground. He spread out the palms of his hands towards the heavens, and they spread out their hands to heaven. Just as the precentor officiates, in like manner all the people answer after him. (Chap. 44).[4]

Most medieval exegetes also followed this trend, citing or paraphrasing the mishna in *Roš Haš* 3:7.[5] The first turning point in the treatment of this incident occurred with the emergence of the Kabbalah in the sixteenth century, exemplified first of all in *Sefer Habahir*. This homiletic work, which introduces the theory of the *sefirot* for the first time, regards Moses' ten fingers as alluding to the ten sefirot:

> "And it was when Moses would raise his hands, Israel would prevail." This teaches us that the Attribute that is called Israel has in it a "Torah of Truth." What is the meaning of a "Torah of Truth"? It is that which teaches (*Moreh*) the Truth of [all] worlds, as well as His deeds in thought. He erected Ten Sayings, and with them the world stands. It is one of them. In man He created ten fingers, paralleling these Ten Sayings. Moses raised his hands and concentrated to some degree on the Attribute that is called Israel, which contains the Torah of Truth. With his ten fingers, he alluded that he was upholding the Ten. For if [God] would not help Israel, then the Ten Sayings would not endure every day. It was for this reason that "Israel prevailed." [The verse continues], "And when he lowered his hands, Amalek prevailed." Would Moses then do anything that would cause Amalek to prevail? But [this teaches us] that it is forbidden for a person to stand for [more than] three hours with his hands spread out to heaven. (1989: 51 [Part 1, §138])[6]

Turning its back on the talmudic approach, *Sefer Habahir* resurrects the magical interpretation, affirming that Moses' hands *did* wage war and crush the enemy. Moses "sets" all the *sefirot* around "Israel"—*Tiferet*—thereby charging it with the

---

[4] Cf. Tg. Ps.-Jon. on Exod 17:11: "And the hands of Moses were raised in prayer." An echo of this interpretative view can also be heard in several places in the *Zohar*: cf. 2:57b.

[5] Cf. the references in Rashi's and Ibn Ezra's commentaries on Exod 17:11. Of note is Samuel ben Meir's (Rashbam) realistic approach, according to which the victory was due to the fact that "This is the way of those who wage war: as long as they see banners ... they prevail." See Ibn Ezra's criticism of this stance (ibid). For Nahmanides' understanding, see below.

[6] The link between the ten fingers of the hand and the ineffable *sefirot* is already manifest in *Sefer Yetzira*. Here, however, the ineffable *sefirot* are not identical with the kabbalistic notion of the *sefirot*.

energy it needs.⁷ The precise nature of the act—magic or theurgic—remains unclear in the *Bahir*. The early kabbalistic exegesis that follows in its wake, however (which we shall discuss below), however, regarded Moses' raised hands as exerting a direct impact on the outcome of the war—i.e., as a form of magic.

As the "official" kabbalistic interpretation of Moses' act, *Sefer Habahir*'s understanding of it as a form of magic circulated broadly, also appearing amongst Nahmanides' disciples and the zoharic circle. In the writings of the former, we find it in R. Shem Tov ibn Gaon (2001: 32b–33a), Ibn Shuaib's homilies (1992: 135)), *Sefer Habahir*'s "hidden light" (Perush Or ganuz [Margolioth] 138), R. Isaac of Acre in the name of Saportan kabbalah (Goldreich, 2010b: 99–100), and *Ma'arekhet Ha'elohut* (1558: Chap. 13, 193b). In the zoharic circle and its field of influence, it occurs in the writings of Rabbeinu Bachya (on Exod 17:12), Recanati (2003: 68–69), and *Sefer Zioni* (1882: 34a).⁸

The *Zohar*, however, adopts a very different approach, representing a significant development in the history of the idea:

> *Amalek came.* R. Shim'on said, "Mystery of wisdom: He came from a decree of severe Judgment, and a single war took place above and below. You cannot find a word in Torah that does not contain supernal secrets of wisdom linked to the Holy Name. The blessed Holy One said, as it were, "When Israel are virtuous below, My power gains strength over all; and when they are not virtuous, they weaken—as it were—the power above and the power of severe Judgment is strengthened."
>
> Come and see: When Israel sinned below, what is written? *Amalek came and fought with Israel*—coming to provoke Judgment against Compassion, all appearing above and below. ברפידים (*biriphidim*), *At Rephidim*—ברפוי ידיים (*be-rippui yadayim*), with slackening of hands, for they slackened their hands from Torah, which is the blessed Holy One, as we have established.
>
> Rabbi Yehuda said, "Twice Amalek waged war against Israel: once here, and once as is written: *The Amalekite and the Canaanite who dwelled on that mountain came down and struck them and crushed them as far as Hormah* (Numbers 14:45).
>
> Rabbi Shim'on said, "Above and below, assailing the blessed Holy One. Above, as has been said. Below, against the blessed Holy One, for they seized men and cut them on the sign of holy engraving, and they took these and threw them upward, saying, 'Take what You wanted!' So in any case, all pertained to the blessed Holy One.
>
> Now what did Moses see to make him withdraw from this first battle of the blessed Holy One? Why did he remove himself? Well, happy is the share of Moses, for he gazed

---

7 The precise nature of Moses' act—magic or theurgy—nevertheless remains unclear.
8 For another magic tradition, cf. *Sefer Hatemuna:* "'And when Moses raised his hands'—from the semantic field of weaponry, because it is an armed weapon ready for victory. Moses raised his hands in the shape of a *zayin* and its attribute" (1.7.2b). The letter *zayin* alludes to the sefira of *Netzach* (Victory)—the attribute ascribed to it according to this tradition. When brought into play, this gave Israel the victory.

and knew the essence of the matter! Moses said, "I will prepare myself for the battle above, and you, Joshua, prepare yourself for the battle below." This corresponds to what is written: *When Moses would raise his hand, Israel prevailed* (Exodus 17:11)—Israel above. Therefore, Moses removed himself from the battle below, in order to gird himself for the battle above, which would be won through him.

Rabbi Shim'on said, "Now, is this battle of Amalek insignificant in your eyes? Come and see: From the day that the world was created until that time, and from that time until King Messiah comes—even God and Magog—nothing like it exists. Not because of numerous fierce warriors, but rather because on all flanks it affected the blessed Holy One.

Moses said to Joshua (Exodus 17:9): Why *to Joshua* and not someone else? At that time, he was young, as is written: *Joshua son of Nun, a youth* (Exodus 33:11), and there were many in Israel mightier than he. However, Moses gazed in wisdom and knew. What did he see? He saw Samael descending from the aspect above to assist Amalek below. Moses said, "Surely the battle is fittingly so!"

Joshua at the time occupied a very high rung. Now, if you say that he was situation in *Shekhinah* at that time—not so, for She was married and joined to Moses; consequently, Joshua was joined beneath him. How? Rabbi Shim'on said, "By that place called Youth."

This corresponds to what Rabbi Yehudah said: "What is the meaning of the verse *Your eyes will see Jerusalem a tranquil abode, a tent not to be packed up* (Isaiah 33:20)—no longer going into exile." This is the mystery written: *Joshua son of Nun, a youth—a youth*, surely! *Would not depart from within the Tent* (Exodus 33:11)—the one called *a tent not to be packed up*. This teaches that every single day he would suckle from *Shekhinah*, like that Youth above, suckling from her continually.

So, when Moses saw Samael descending to assist Amalek, he said, "Surely, this *youth* will confront him, overpowering and defeating him." Immediately, *Moses said to Joshua, "Choose men for us and go out, battle against Amalek* (Exodus 17:9)—"this battle below is yours, and I will gird myself for the battle above." *Choose men for us*—"righteous sons of righteous ones, worthy of accompanying you."

Rabbi Shim'on said, "When Joshua the youth set out, Youth above aroused and was arrayed plentifully, with numerous weapons prepared for him by his Mother for this battle, in order to avenge with vengeances of the Covenant, corresponding to *a sword avenging with vengeance of the covenant* (Leviticus 26:25). This is the mystery written: *Joshua disabled Amalek and his people by the edge of the sword* (Exodus 17:13)—*by the edge of the sword*, precisely! Not by the edge of spears and weapons, but by the one called *avenging sword*. And Moses arrayed himself for the battle above.

Moses' hands were כבדים (*kevedim*), *heavy* (Exodus 17:12)—really *kevedim, glorious*, venerable, holy, never defiled! Venerable—worthy of waging war above.

They took a stone and placed it beneath him (ibid)—for Israel was in distress and he would share their distress.

Aaron and Hur supported his hands, one from this side and one from that side, and his hands were אמונה (*emunah*), *steadfast* (ibid)—*emunah, faith*, surely! Now, was it simply because Aaron and Hur supported his hands that these were *faith*? Rather, Moses acted totally in wisdom: Aaron and Hur, each from his own side, and his hands in the middle; therefore, *his hands were faith*. Aaron, to arouse his side; and Hur, to arouse his side; they grasped his hands from her and from there, so that assistance would appear above.

When Moses would raise his hand (Exodus 17:11). *When he would raise*—raising right above left, intending so while spreading his hands. *Israel prevailed*—Israel above.

> *When he would let down his hand, Amalek prevailed* (ibid)—when Israel below waned from prayer, Moses' hands could not stand erect and *Amalek prevailed*. From here we learn: Although the priest needs the sacrifice in order to array himself totally, Israel must accompany him with their prayers.
> It has been taught: In this battle of Amalek, above and below appeared. Therefore, his hands were אמונה (*emunah*), *faith*, fittingly. ויהיה ידיו (*vayhi yadav*), *his hands was*—the verse should read ויהיו (*va-yihyu*) [*His hands*] *were*. However, since all depends on the right, as is written *vayhi*, [*His hands*] *was*; and it is written ידו (*yado*), *his hand*, since this is the essence of all—as is written: *Your right hand, O YHVH, glorious in power* (Exodus 15:6). (*Zohar*, 2:65b–66a)

What is the relationship between this zoharic passage and the talmudic tradition on the one hand and the kabbalistic thought represented by *Sefer Habahir* on the other? Does it possess its own distinctive voice and if so, what is it? At first glance, like other contemporary kabbalists its author appears to have accepted the thaumaturgical interpretation: "*When he would raise*—raising right above left, intending so while spreading his hands. *Israel prevailed*—Israel above." In other words, Moses' raised hands continually charged and empowered "Israel above"—*Tiferet*—thereby ensuring their victory. When his hands fell, on the other hand, room was given to the demon represented by Amalek, unleashing the potential for disaster.

At this point, however, the *Zohar* introduces a further clarification whereby this interpretation is virtually turned on its head: "When Israel below waned from prayer, Moses' hands could not stand erect and *Amalek prevailed*." Here, traces of the talmudic tradition according to which Israel's victory is a function of their faith and prayers are rather surprisingly still evident. This view is adopted cautiously, however, and with great deliberation, taking care not to engage in any confrontation with the prevalent kabbalistic interpretation or directly and blatantly rejecting it. While the homily thus appears to cleave closely to contemporaneous kabbalistic thought, according to which Moses' raised hands constituted a thaumaturgical technique, it does not relinquish the talmudic tradition that attributes the victory to prayer. Moses' raised hands were therefore a necessary but not sufficient factor in the victory, the defeat of Amalek being primarily due to Israel's prayers. In contrast to *Roš Hašana*, which holds that the prayer was dependent upon Moses' hands, the *Zohar* thus asserts that Moses' hands were dependent on prayer.

Another attempt to blend the mishnaic and kabalistic approaches was made in a slightly earlier generation by R. Todros Abulafia. In his *Otzar Hakavod*—a commentary on the talmudic aggada—Abulafia seeks the prevalent kabbalistic exegesis within the mishna itself:

This dictum comes to teach us the mystery of the raising of Moses' hands and his intention. He raised his hands for Israel as a whole because he was the mediator between them and God and a man's agent is like himself. And Moses would look upwards and direct his heart in order to draw the power and unite the emanations Ten fingers towards faith—Israel prevailed. (1987: 47b)

In his efforts to eradicate the disparity between the mishna and the accepted kabbalistic understanding, Abulafia forces the former out of its literal sense, arguing that "Israel" here refers solely to Moses—so called because he stands between the people and the divine world ("a man's agent is like himself"). Israel's intention is thus in fact their leader Moses'—being the kabbalistic intention that seeks to "draw the power and unite the emanations Ten fingers towards faith—Israel prevailed."

The *Zohar* chooses a completely different exegetical approach to Abulafia. While it harmonizes the talmudic and kabbalistic traditions, its assertion that Moses' hands were dependent upon Israel's prayers virtually divests them of any magical dimension, the act therefore being no different to any other conditional upon prayer and divine grace. This comparison between Abulafia and the *Zohar* sharpens the latter's unique view. Not only does it harmonize two fundamentally antithetical worldviews but it also subverts the thaumaturgical exegesis characteristic of kabbalistic thought. In this sense, it reflects the spirit of the anti-magical attitudes that resonate within the *Zohar* alongside those that reject them.

The war against Amalek: A double and triple war

The *Zohar*'s anti-thaumaturgical tendency in this homily also finds expression in the way in which it shapes other elements of this story that are distinctively magical in character—i.e., not only the source whence Moses' hands drew their power but also the nature and essence of the act. What exactly did Moses do? Within what space did he act and what kind of influence did he seek? In seeking to answer these questions, we must examine the zoharic homily in the light of contemporaneous kabbalistic writings, primarily thirteenth-century kabbalistic biblical exegesis.

Before turning to the parallels, however, we must first note that the zoharic homily in effect "deconstructs" the biblical narrative into two distinct but analogous sections, the relationship between which is far from self-evident. Two centres of struggle are identified, echoing the two loci in the biblical narrative—the battle field and the hill. In parallel to the earthly military battle fought by Joshua another plot unfolds above—led by Moses, who is ultimately responsible for the victory. Moses' war "above," however, is not to be simplistically identified with the mystical root of the earthly battle as the practiced *Zohar* reader might assume but forms an integral part of the mandate given to Joshua:

> He saw Samael descending from the aspect above to assist Amalek below. Moses said, "Surely the battle is fittingly so!" Joshua at the time occupied a very high rung. ... So, when Moses saw Samael descending to assist Amalek, he said, "Surely, this *youth* will confront him, overpowering and defeating him." Immediately, *Moses said to Joshua, "Choose men for us and go out, battle against Amalek* (Exodus 17:9)—"this battle below is yours, and I will gird myself for the battle above." (*Zohar*, 2:194b–195a)

Joshua's selection, in other words, possesses a mystical significance, even being linked in the zoharic homilist's eyes with his designation as a נער: "... Joshua son of Nun, a youth, would not leave the tent" (Exod 33:11). The *Zohar* regards this status as "a very high rung," equal to that of Metatron, who is also said to be a "youth." For this reason, Joshua was chosen to go out and contend with the forces of Samael, Amalek's prince.[9] The war "above," over which Moses is appointed, thus refers to another battle. What is this? The answer to this question, so it appears, is already found in the opening section of the homily we are discussing, which presents the ideational-theurgical foundation lying at his base: "The blessed Holy One said, as it were, 'When Israel are virtuous below, My power gains strength over all; and when they are not virtuous, they weaken—as it were—the power above and the power of severe Judgment is strengthened.'" Moses is thus called to the fight "above" in order to settle the world of the *sefirot* and restore the status quo.[10]

The footprints of this idea of a "dual war" can be found as early as a tradition cited in the name of one of the founding fathers of medieval Kabbalah, R. Isaac Sagi-Nahor:

> This is the intention of the saying, that neither the name nor the throne are full until that moment, because that power that was their prince takes from the Fear of Isaac who blessed him: "You shall live by the sword" [Gen 27:40] ceased because he fought Israel and did not

---

[9] This motif of defeating an enemy by destroying his upper roots occurs already in rabbinic midrashim: "God does not cast down a nation before He destroys their guardian angel first" (*Exod. Rab.* 21:5): see Pedaya (2005: 107 n. 26).

[10] For the phrase the "theurgy of the status quo," see Idel (1990a: 181–199).

fear the great חייר ... Moses had to lift up his hand because he fought with the prince to cast his influence down from there.[11]

Although the *Zohar* and this passage share a common thematic foundation, they also differ in significant respects. While R. Isaac Sagi-Nahor regards the upper war—that between Moses and Amalek's prince—as a sort of "retaliation" intended to cut off the root of the prince's power in the "Fear of Isaac" (i.e., the *sefira* of *Gevura*), thereby allowing Israel to win the battle below, the *Zohar* adduces no causal link between the two wars. Rather than constituting a response to Amalek's act, the upper struggle is an end in its own right. As we have noted, the lower battle, in both its military and mystical aspects, makes way for another war, that relates to different issue. The association between the two in the *Zohar* is exemplified most clearly in another text:

> Well, surely the battle against Amalek was on all fronts: above and below; for at that time the evil serpent was empowered above and empowered below. Just as a serpents lurks on the crossroads, so here too Amalek was an evil serpent for Israel, lurking for them on the crossroads, as is written: *that he set against him on the way when he was coming up from Egypt* (1 Samuel 15:2). He was lurking above to defile the Sanctuary, and lurking below to defile Israel. (*Zohar*, 2:194b–195a)

According to this passage, the biblical episode relates to the various manifestations of the serpent's demonic powers as representative of the *sitra achra*, below and above. Here, we see that in order to defeat the *sitra achra* and destroy its influence two battles must be fought: one to preserve Israel and its purity, the other to purify the upper "Sanctuary"—the divine space—from the impurity of the *sitra achra*. Although they are both intended to repel Amalek's diverse machinations, they neither serve nor are related to one another. This appears to be the meaning of the assertion "one battle was above and one below." This "mother of all wars," which dwarfs all the historical, apocalyptic ("even God and Magog"), and mythical battles that have or will be fought in the world, may also be elucidated here. This differs from every other war because "on all flanks it affected the blessed Holy One."[12] The emphasis upon *"Israel prevailed—*Israel above" is

---

[11] Ibn Shuaib, Commentary on Nahmanides, 17a. The passage is cited in the name of the Rav ha-hasid, the designation for R. Isaac Sagi-Nahor conventionally employed by the early kabbalists: see Pedaya (2005: 105–109).

[12] This may also represent an exegetical polemic against Nahmanides, who also employs the model of the dual wars against Amalek, although in an entirely different context. In his commentary on Exod 18:9, he states: ""Now whatever Moses and Joshua did with them [the Amalekites] at first, Elijah and Mashiach ben Yoseph will do with their descendants. This was why

similarly intended to highlight the fact that the reference is not to the earthly Israel but only to the "Israel above"—i.e., the theosophic entity. We may sum up the matter thus: if the *Zohar* regards Joshua's war, in its military and mystical aspects, as a מלחמה צורך הדיוט; Moses' waged by the raising of his hands is not a human but a divine war.

Moses' hands and Amalek's defeat

The *Zohar*'s attempt to avoid any magical dimensions in the story of the war against Amalek—the virtually "official" medieval kabbalistic interpretation of the text—is reflected in its understanding of the technique Moses used to win the battle, which deviates from the exegesis found in *Sefer Habahir*. As we observed above, whether citing it explicitly or not the thirteenth-century kabbalists generally adopted a thaumaturgical approach to the "Bahiran" homily that holds that Moses' ten fingers united the ten *sefirot*, drawing their influence over Israel and thus giving them the victory. Thus, for example, we find the following account in Rabbeinu Bachya's commentary on Exod 17:12

> A kabbalistic approach: Moses' raising of his hands was a matter of his concentrating on his ten fingers being pointed at what is called רום השמים, "the heights of the Heavens" … He did something similar to what the priests do when they raise their hands in the priestly blessing. By concentrating on the number ten, they also concentrate on the ten emanations and the source of blessing that flows from that region to disembodied spirits. At such a time the power of any force opposing such prayers is checked and its influence halted (at least temporarily). At such moments the Israelite soldiers would be victorious. The words וגבר ישראל, "Israel had the 'upper' hand," was therefore something closely linked to Moses' continued ability or willingness to raise his fingers and concentrate on the number ten. Whenever Moses' concentration flagged, the accusing finger of the celestial representative of Amalek made itself felt and the Israelites retreated. (1998: 3:1015)

Moses strained himself in this manner" (Chavel, 1971: 2:244). This suggests that the war against Amalek serves as a paradigm for another historical combat, namely that of the future redemption. The *Zohar* categorically rejects the allusion to any future historical war because that Moses waged is the "mother of all wars," thus superceding even what "Elijah and Mashiach ben Yoseph will do with their descendants"—i.e., the war of Gog and Magog. Nahmanides' exegesis reflects his well-known hermeneutical principle "The deeds of the fathers are a sign for the sons." While he builds his interpretation—which is not "by way of the truth"!—upon a "horizontal," historical paradigm, however, the *Zohar* adopts a vertical-theosophic paradigm. A similar link between Nahmanides and the *Zohar* is evident in other exegetical passages—a phenomenon that has yet to be thoroughly studied.

Bachya understands Moses' raised hands as drawing power and bringing down the upper forces in order to strengthen Israel in the war against Amalek. We find a similar thought in other kabbalists belonging to the "zoharic circle" or influenced by it, as well as other kabbalistic groups.[13] Like Rabbeinu Bachya, these suggest a link between Moses' raised hands and the priestly blessing. Discussing this issue at length, Pedaya (2005: 116–120) has drawn attention to its diverse implications in kabbalistic works, beginning with *Sefer Habahir* itself.[14]

The zoharic homily offers a very different tradition, asserting that the war took place in the upper realms between "Israel above" and "severe Judgment"—i.e., the *sefira* of *Gevura*. The power of Judgment increasing because of Israel's sins, the fragile balance within the sefiric realm is upset, threatening its unity. Moses' raised hands are thus meant to restore sefiric harmony by reinforcing the attribute of *Hesed* over that of *Din*, his higher right hand seeking to make—*Hesed*—prevail over the left-hand side of the godhead (i.e., *Gevura*). This technique differs significantly from that depicted in *Sefer Habahir*. The *Zohar* also associates Moses' action with the priestly raising of hands, adducing the biblical description of Aaron's blessing in several places: "Aaron lifted his hands toward the people and blessed them; and he came down after sacrificing the sin offering, the burnt offering, and the offering of well-being" (Lev 9:22).[15] As in the case of other kabbalists, it appears to rely here on the deficient spelling ידו, arguing from the singular that Aaron raised one hand over the other—i.e., his right over his left.[16]

Rather than seeking to purify the divine holy space, removing all traces of the *sitra achra*, the struggle depicted here is clearly intended to redistribute the disproportionate weight of the divine attribute of Judgment within the upper realms of the *sefirot*. This repair is not meant to "draw" influence from the upper world into the lower battlefield at Rephidim but to augment the

---

13 Cf. also later writings: Recanati (2003: 68–69); Zioni (1882: 34a). For this tradition and its various parallels, see Gottlieb (1970: 217–218); Matt (2003–2007: 4:301 n. 363).
14 For the use of the hands and fingers in the priestly blessing, see Brody (1993: 152–153).
15 וישא אהרן את־ [ידו כ] (ידיו ק) אל־העם ויברכם וירד מעשת החטאת והעלה והשלמים.
16 Cf. *Zohar*, 2:66a, 3:92b, 146a. For other kabbalistic parallels, see Matt (2003–2007: 4:301 n. 363). This tradition may rest, *inter alia*, upon *Mekilta de-Rabbi Ishmael* on Exod 15:6: "Thy Right Hand, O Lord, Glorious in Power. When the Israelites do the will of God, they make His left hand, as it were, to be like a right hand, as it is said: 'Thy right hand, O Lord ... Thy right hand O Lord'—two times. And when the Israelites fail to do the will of God, they make His right hand to be like a left hand, as it is said: 'He hath drawn back His right hand" (Lam 2:3)'" (Shirata 5). Cf. the ruling that the priests should raise their right hand slightly higher than their left: see *Zohar*, 3:145a, 146a, *Raya Mehemna*, etc. For the evolution and halakhic expressions of this ruling, see Ta-Shma (1995: 29, 119–120 n. 45).

power of the right hand, raising it over that of the left and restoring the balance of power within the divine sphere to its proper "*status quo.*"

To demonstrate even more sharply the way in which the *Zohar* deviates from the conventional kabbalistic thought of the thirteenth century, we may compare the zoharic idea with a striking parallel in R. Moses de Léon's *The Book of the Pomegranate*. Wolfson (1988a: 69 n. 1 et al.) has already discussed this issue in the notes to his edition of this work. Here, I would like to draw attention to the instructive divergences:

> In the mystery of the spreading of the <priest's> hands they must be raised and lifted up. The mystery of the right over the left as is written *Aaron lifted his hand*—that the right hand must be raised over the left because the right is everything, the left being contained within it. A person is indeed composed of all the spiritual things above, being adorned with ten fingers on his hands and feet and all this is in the true mystery. Thus when the priest who awakes who comes from the right side, the mystery of the right is over the left, as we have said—the blessings awake and are drawn from the essence of their being and Israel are blessed from the source of life. When the essence of their foundation is blessed above, the essence of their foundation is blessed below. And you may know the mystery contained in the verse *When Moses raised his hand—Israel prevailed*—ordinary Israel, when the essence of the root above is blessed at the beginning from the source of life. And afterwards the blessings continue and Israel below is blessed. (ibid: 254–255)

Although the link between this passage and the zoharic homily we are discussing is self-evident, we cannot ignore the different context. R. Moses de Léon describes Moses not as someone working to repair the divine world but as practicing an isomorphic technique of virtualizing the sefiric world in order to win the real battle. The right hand must be raised over the left because even in the upper realm "the right is everything, the left being contained within it."[17]

This picture of the world of the godhead is also reflected in a text attributed to R. Isaac Sagi-Nahor: "The lifting of the right hand—heavenwards above the head as a sort of raising of the hands. The lifting of the left hand—hung below, as is written *his hands were faith* and *Aaron lifted his hands toward the people. His hand* ידו is written—and the person who understands understands."[18] The natural place of the left hand in the upper realm being below the right hand,

---

[17] This practice is based on the anthropomorphic depiction of the godhead in the form of a human body, of course. For this tradition in the kabbalistic context, see Scholem (1976a: 153–186); Idel (1986, 2009); Liebes (1993a); Wolfson (1989a, 1993b). For the anthropomorphic image of God in angelic guise, see Abrams (1996).

[18] Cited in R. Abraham Ardutiel's *Avnei Zikaron*, Jerusalem MS 8°404, p. 108b. For this passage, see Scholem (1929: 271–272); Idel (1982: 258 n. 97); Pedaya (2005: 120–121). For the discrepancy between this text and the masora, see Pedaya (2005: 122–123 n. 80).

the priests' and Moses' imitation of the godhead must correspond to this positioning.[19]

R. Moses de Léon's view also finds expression in another passage in this work. There, too, he links the mystery of the priestly blessing with Moses' raised hands:

> The mystery of Moses' raised hands lies in the overcoming of his attribute and giving it power from below to above. At any rate, it repairs the fault as is proper above in an example that must be copied—as is written: *When Moses raised his hands—Israel prevailed*. The mystery lies in the matter of his attribute, as we have said: when he prevailed in the matter of demonstrating an example. This is the mystery and Aaron and Hur supported his hands, one on this side and one on the other. (Wolfson, 1988a: 57)

Although this text does not refer to the elevation of the right hand over the left, Moses' act is clearly understood as an effort to empower his attribute—*Tiferet*—by imagining it as the trunk of the body standing between the right and left hands. Elsewhere, R. Moses completely divests Moses' action of its military dimension:

> You should know that the war against Amalek was a great matter. You thus find that it required Moses and Joshua. Moses stood in the upper war, preparing to stand in the upper mystery, preparaing his knowledge and understanding *and strengthen his hands for him*. And the meaning is to prepare his place and live. *And be a help against his adversaries* (Deut 33:7). (ibid: 68–69)

Here, Moses is not engaged in any battle, merely repairing his place in the upper spheres—i.e., *Tiferet*—by enlarging his knowledge and understanding, only by the way also gaining "help against his adversaries." We should thus not be surprised to find that R. Moses de Léon's starting point here is the Bahiran orientation that stresses the analogy between the ten fingers of the hand and the ten *sefirot* ("being adorned with ten fingers on his hands and ten fingers on his feet and all this is in the true mystery"). The view of the "right hand above

---

[19] Here, I diverge from Pedaya (ibid), who regards the picture reflected here as the image of the distorted godhead, whose left hand drops after having been displaced by Amalek's sin. In my view, the depiction of the left hand under the right represents the proper, complete, and repaired image of God. This idea also occurs in the interpretation given to the *aqeda* by the early kabbalists and their perception of the latter as the binding of the "Fear of Isaac" by "Hesed Abraham" in order to bring the former under the latter's control: see Gikatilla (1988: 121, 133). Addressing this issue from another perspective, Wolfson (1986: 45–46) regards the left hand's inferior position as an expression of a broader tendency within the *Zohar* to correct the demonic left-hand side of the *sitra achra* by containing it within the right hand.

the left" here in effect constitutes a development of the Bahiran notion of virtualization that was prevalent in the writings of contemporaneous kabbalists.

In contrast, the zoharic homily depicts a militaristic war. Moses seeks to correct the catastrophe that has occurred in the world of the godhead due to the fact that the divine right hand—whose power has been diminished by Israel's sins—has lost its hegemony. This idea also occurs elsewhere in *Parashat Beshallach*:

> Come and see: When a person raises his hand in prayer, he directs his fingers above, as has been said, for it is written, *When Moses would raise his hand* (Exodus 17:11), since all depends on the right. And it is written: *Aaron raised* יָדָיו (*yadav*), *his hands* (Leviticus 9:22) —ידו (*ydv*), deficiently …When the right hand is present, the left is there with it. But if the right is withdrawn, the left is poised; then judgments arouse in the world, and Judgment prevails over all. When Rabbi Shim'on reached this verse, he wept, for it is written: *He has withdrawn His right hand in the face of the enemy* (Lamentations 2:3). Well, *He has withdrawn His right hand*, for the left hastened to descend into the world, and the right remained in another place. (*Zohar*, 2:57b–57b)

The repaired world is one in which everything is dependent upon the right hand —"everything" being first and foremost the left hand. The system was disturbed when the right hand moved from its place, thereby giving more power to the left and allowing it to become dominant. Under such circumstances, the role of the man of God is to restore the power of the right hand by raising his own right hand over his left, thus returning the divine world to its proper state. In contrast to the interpretation of Moses' raised hands in *Sefer Habahir* and the works that follow it, as well as to the idea propounded in *The Book of the Pomegranate*, this is not a virtualization of the *sefirot* and their augmentation in order to draw influence down to the battlefield but a virtualization of the repaired image in order to change and restore the world of the godhead itself after its disruption by Israel's sins. Moses intervenes in the upper titanic struggle between the left and right hands, ensuring that the latter becomes stronger than the former.[20]

Despite its close semantic and symbolic affinities with the zoharic idea, this exegesis does not appear in *The Book of the Pomegranate*. It does, however, occur in another work, apparently composed by R. Joseph b. Shalom Ashkenazi, whom Liebes (1988: 12–15) suggests was a member of the "zoharic circle."[21] He writes thus in his commentary on *Sefer Yetzira*, a work attributed to R. Abraham b. David: "It is a great wonder why it is said *his hand* instead of *his hands*. Is it

---

[20] For the sources of the idea of impaired godhead and its restoration in the early Kabbalah, see Pedaya (2005: 103–147).
[21] For R. Joseph b. Shalom Ashkenazi and his kabbalistic sources, see Hallamish (1969–1970, 1984: 11–27).

not written *his hands were steady until the sun set* [Exod 17:12]? For this reason he raised his right hand in order to diminish the power of the left hand of Esau who came from Isaac. But this I cannot elucidate."²²

Here, it is clear that Moses raised his right hand in order to diminish the power of the left hand in the sefiric world. Although the nature of the link between our homily and R. Joseph b. Shalom Ashkenazi's words is not obvious, all the extant parallels indicate that our homily was not composed by the author of *The Book of the Pomegranate*, in which a very different spirit prevails.²³

From a general perspective, the *Zohar*'s reservations regarding the thaumaturgic interpretation of the war against Amalek evidently derives from its antipathy towards magic as a whole. Although virtually all the kabbalists tended to adopt the "Bahiran" understanding of Moses' raised hands (and in effect also of the priestly blessing), this fact does not necessarily indicate the relatively late date of the zoharic homily, which takes a more complex and balanced view. This exegetical option may well have been rejected for polemical reasons, the stress laid on the raising of one hand arousing, so it appears, a sense of discomfort in Jews living in a Christian environment. This contention finds support in Rabbeinu Bachya's commentary on Lev 9:22:

> The commentators who disagree with us and dress themselves up in fancy garments to lend weight to their words, are wrong when they say that the meaning of these words is that Aaron lifted his hand in order to indicate to the people that they should raise their right hand as affirmation. These commentators [Christian theologians] quote (glossaries of Maymoniut on Maimonides' Hilchot Tefillah 14.3) that the word ידי with the vowels of the plural, is spelled without the letter י indicating that it is really a singular, i.e., "his hand." Our answer to them is simply that traditionally we read the word as if it had been spelled with the letter י, i.e., that Aaron raised both his hands. Their argument that Aaron only raised his right hand is null and void. The reason that we encounter this unusual spelling is to indicate that the right hand is more important than the left hand concerning mystical matters which are revealed only to select individuals. (1998: 5:1584)²⁴

Here, Bachya alludes to the mystery of the superiority of the right hand over the left, possibly referring to the zoharic tradition with respect to the priestly blessing and Moses' victory in the war against Amalek. Irrespective of this issue, the

---

22 Abraham b. David, commentary on *Sefer Yetzira* 1, mishna 3, 22a. For the identification of R. Joseph b. Shalom Ashkenazi as the author of this work, see Scholem (1928).
23 The note of reservation derives from the fact that echoes of the *Bahir*'s interpretive approach can be heard in the broader context of R. Joseph Ashkenazi's words. For the ways in which the sources in "R. Abraham b. David's commentary on Sefer Yetzira" are reworked, see Hallamish (1969).
24 For another expression of this polemic, see *Sefer Joseph Hameqane*, §31, p. 51.

historical-polemical context evident here may help to explain why this tradition was downplayed—by Rabbeinu Bachya and other kabbalists—in favour of the "Bahiran" interpretation, according to which Moses' raised hands signifies the drawing of influence by the virtualization of the ten *sefirot*.

Despite this and in light of the discussion above, we cannot but wonder about the reservations the author of our homily exhibits regarding the magical connotations of the biblical texts. Why does he prefer a theurgic explanation over a thaumaturgical one? What lies behind his reluctance to adopt the conventional line? Although no clear answers to these questions can be given, we may offer some conjectures. It is precisely in the exegetical context with which we are dealing that we sense a degree of unease regarding the involvement of magic in other kabbalists as well. As *Sefer Habahir* notes: "Would Moses then do anything that would cause Amalek to prevail? But [this teaches us] that it is forbidden for a person to stand for [more than] three hours with his hands spread out to heaven."

Commentators have struggled with this obscure statement, adduced in order to explain that Moses' lowered hands was not as a sign of physical weakness but a metaphysical limitation. Why is a person forbidden to raise his hands and draw down the upper influence for a long period of time? Here, we discover that all the kabbalists who follow in the *Bahir*'s footsteps prophesy in the same manner. Thus, for example, Rabbeinu Bachya observes on Exod 17:12:

> Moses was compelled to lower his hands from time to time as it is not admissible to interfere with opposing spiritual forces to such an extent that one neutralises them altogether. God has not created forces in the universe in order for them to be totally ineffective. This is what the prophet Isaiah also had in mind when he spoke of God creating כי לו תוהו בראה לשבת יצרה, "He did nor create it a waste but formed it for habitation" (45:18). (1998: 3:1015–1016)[25]

Very surprisingly, Bachya adduces an 'ecological'-mystical rationale. Drawing down the influence and opposing spiritual forces for any length of time is likely to disturb the "ecological balance" of the divine world, thereby leading to its collapse. Thus even when human beings are given (magical) powers, when they come to employ these upper resources they must do so wisely and responsibly —and primarily in the right measure—in order not to wreak havoc and ruin. This exegesis, which is found amongst many thirteenth-century kabbalists, being founded on *Sefer Habahir*, reflects recognition of the unlimited powers inherent in the magical act on the one hand and concerns over this and the

---

25 Cf. also *Or Haganuz* on *Sefer Habahir* (Margolioth), §138; Ibn Shuaib (1992: 135), et al.

scorched earth it may leave in its wake on the other. In my view, it is very plausible that this is also the reason for the *Zohar*'s reservations regarding the thaumaturgical explanation in our homily. In raising his right hand over his left and virtualizing the divinity, the kabbalist repairs what has been broken, averting the catastrophe and restoring the sefiric world to its proper state. The covert argument that *Zohar* conducts with its fellow kabbalists conjures up modern 'ecological' approaches that exemplify the conflict between the controlled exploitation of the world's natural resources and their preservation.[26]

Conclusion

Within the diverse voices of the members of the "zoharic circle" of the thirteenth century—the band of kabbalists from whose ranks the zoharic artifact appears to have emerged—this homily on the war against Amalek sounds a unique note. As in other cases, we find that its statements have no parallel in R. Moses de Léon, R. Joseph Gikatilla, R. Joseph Angelet, R. Menachem Recanati, or their colleagues. Despite the exegetical and homiletical foundation the *Zohar* shares with other kabbalists and the faithfulness they all demonstrate to the midrashic-talmudic literature, while the dominant kabbalistic spirit blows in the direction of the Bahiran anti-magical interpretation the zoharic homilist identifies more with the anti-thaumaturgical spirit of the mishna and tannaitic midrashim. At the same time, however, he seeks to create a bridge between these two views that are essentially antithetical. The tension within which this zoharic homily is woven clearly reflects the spiritual context in which the zoharic kabbalists worked and their complex consciousness as bearers of the kabbalistic tradition within a traditional world founded upon the ancient talmudic ethos.

---

[26] The idea of the preservation of the divine world in all its parts also occurs in other contexts—in the treatment of evil, for example. As Wolfson (1986) has demonstrated, the theosophic consciousness of redemption in the *Zohar* seeks to contain evil within the right hand—the *sitra de-qedusha*—rather than eradicate it. For the zoharic attitude towards evil in general, see Liebes (1994: 83–85) and above, chapter 9.

Chapter 12:
Nadab and Abihu's Sin as a "Holy Revolt"

The story of Nadab and Abihu's sin is one of the most abstruse and enigmatic episodes in the Hebrew Bible, its mysterious nature being compounded by the diverse accounts given of it. The dramatic circumstances in which it took place —on the dedication of the tabernacle—being regarded as highly significant by many commentators and homilists, they have been compelled to deal with the difficulties the text poses. The narrative has thus been extensively addressed both by ancient midrashists and medieval commentators. This chapter deals with the zoharic aggada relating to this episode. Reviewing and analyzing the roots of the zoharic story and its evolution, I shall endeavour to reveal the tendencies and views of the *Zohar*'s authors with respect to existential questions relating to authority and hegemony.

Early and earlier traditions

The first time the story is recounted is in Lev 10:1–2: "Now Aaron's sons, Nadab and Abihu, each took his censer, put fire in it, and laid incense on it; and they offered strange fire before the LORD, such as he had not commanded them." Many details of this description are obscure. What is the אש זרה? If, as the context suggests, it is a halakhic term, it has no parallel in the entire biblical text. Who did not obey God's command and in what way? How is this edict related to the "strange fire"? These difficulties are exacerbated by the divergences between this passage and the second account of the event: "The LORD spoke to Moses after the death of the two sons of Aaron, when they drew near before the LORD and died" (Lev 16:1). Here, Aaron's sons are said to have died because they "drew near before the LORD." The same may also be inferred from the following command: "Tell your brother Aaron not to come just at any time into the sanctuary inside the curtain before the mercy seat that is upon the ark, or he will die; for I appear in the cloud upon the mercy seat" (v. 2). What then was the precise nature of Nadab and Abihu's sin? Did they engage in a forbidden ritual or did they seek to approach God too closely?[1]

---

[1] For a discussion of these exegetical issues in their biblical context, see Gelander (1985/87); Greenstein (1989).

The Targums tend to focus on the offering of "unholy fire," as does Josephus (*Ant.* 3.8.7).[2] Rabbinic literature, on the other hand, takes a more surprising direction, although a close inspection reveals its roots to lie in the biblical text. Generally speaking, the ancient midrash offers a broad range of understandings. *Leviticus Rabbah*, for example—dated to the fifth or sixth century—refers to both the ideas of offering and approaching together with additional homiletic directions that diverge more radically from the literal sense. According to one of these, Nadab and Abihu entered the sanctuary intoxicated with wine or naked or without having washed their hands or feet. Another suggests that they had not married women or begotten children.[3] This midrashic collection thus regards the sin as arrogance with regard to Moses and Aaron, and the uneducated masses (refusing to marry women on the grounds that they did not know which women were fit for them), and God Himself ("they fed their eyes on the Shekhina").

If we arrange the reasons offered chronologically, however, we discover that the earliest stratum—the tannaitic midrashim and Talmuds—focuses primarily on a single explanation that takes various guises. The early literary sources relevant for our purposes here are principally *Sifra* (*Aharei mot*) and the appended tannaitic *Mekilta de-miluim*.[4] The latter work is itself not a unified whole, rather comprising two different layers of exposition (Epstein, 1957).[5] The *Sifra* thus in fact includes no less than three separate sources that relate to our story. While in other contexts this bibliographic phenomenon might constitute a hindrance, it serves our current purposes very well. Rather than presenting us with one tex-

---

2 Onqelos translates Lev 16:1 as אישתא נוכריתא as in 10:2. Trg. Ps.-Jon., on the other hand, renders 10:1 as "strange fire taken from (under) the hearth-pots," the slightly different renderings of Lev 16:1 and Num 3:4 also pointing in the same direction: see Shinan (1979b; 207). For the LXX and Vulgate versions, see Gelander (1985/87: 73).
3 As we shall see, while the tannaim discuss this issue in *Sifra de-bei Rabbi*, it only being adduced infrequently as a tannaitic tradition in the Talmuds, the early amoraic literature addresses it at length: cf. *Lev. Rab.* 20:6–10; *Pes. Rab. Kah.*, Aharei mot 26. For a comprehensive summary of the various rabbinic views, see Shinan (1979b: 210–214).
4 Although the *Mekilta de-miluim* appears as an indivisible part of the *Sifra* in some printed versions of the appears, as scholars have demonstrated it is in fact an independent work: see *Sifra de-bei Rab*, introduction, v; Hoffman (1928); Epstein (1957: 641).
5 As Epstein himself observes, R. Abraham b. David was the first to note this fact, identifying the second part as *Panim Acherim* and "more complete" than the first: see his commentary on *Sipra de-bei Rab*, 45a. Epstein similarly remarks that this midrash is closer to the *Mekilta de R. Ishmael* and earlier. For the relationship between the various strata in the printed *Sifra* relating to the Nadab and Abihu account, see Goldberg (1981).

tual witness we thus have two or three independent tannaitic sources, all of which assert that Nadab and Abihu sinned because they had not consulted Moses and Aaron. Thus, for example, we read in the original "sifraic" homily on *Aharei mot*:

> *The LORD spoke to Moses after the death of the two sons of Aaron:* Why is this written? As it is written: "Aaron's sons, Nadab and Abihu, each took his censer"—the *sons of Aaron* did not take counsel from Aaron, *Nadab and Abihu*—did not take counsel from Moses, *each took his censor*—each did according to his own understanding, not taking counsel from one another. (1, 79b)[6]

The author of the *Panim Acherim* section of *Mekilta de-miluim* also regarded them as having sinned by not taking counsel from Moses, sharpening this claim even further:

> But in their joy, because they saw a new fire they thought to add love upon love ... Why is it written *Aaron's sons?*—they did not respect him. *Nadab and Abihu*—they did not take counsel from Moses. *Each took his censer*—each acted on his own initiative and did not take counsel from the other. (Shemini, 32, 45b)

In other words, although the motive behind the act was pure and lofty, arising from an authentic religious love for God, Aaron's sons were severely punished because they did not respect their father or take counsel from Moses. The author of the first homily in the *Mekilta de-miluim* similarly attributes the sin to Nadab and Abihu's attitude towards Moses and Aaron. Here, however, the midrashic background is slightly different:

> When they saw that Moses and Aaron went first, Nadab and Abihu walked behind them, and all Israel followed, and Nadab and Abihu were saying: "When will these two old men die and we assume authority over the community?" The Holy One, blessed be He, said: "Let us see who buries whom. They will bury you and serve as the leaders over all the people." (ibid, 21, 44b)

A third view, adduced in the *Panim Acherim* section of *Mekilta de-miluim*, is transmitted in the name of R. Eliezer, being echoed in various places in the Talmuds:

---

[6] Cf. also Shemini 2, 47a: "If so, when does it say *his remaining sons?* He said to them: 'You should not have looked at those who performed an act without taking counsel and were destroyed.'"

> R. Eliezer learned: The sons of Aaron only died on account of their having given a religious ruling in the name of Moses their master and anyone who does so merits death. An incident is related of a certain disciple who gave a religious ruling in his presence. He said to Imma Shalom: "Alas for the wife of this man! He will not live the week". After the Sabbath, the Sages came in to him and said to him: "Are you a prophet?" Said he to them: *I am no prophet, nor am a I prophet's son* (Amos 7:14), but I have the following tradition: Whose gives a legal decision in the presence of his master incurs the penalty of death. (ibid, 32, 45b)[7]

Despite the divergences between these sources, they all share a common trend. Nadab and Abihu's wish to replace Moses and Aaron, their religio-mystical desire to love God even more, and their desire to give religious rulings all impugn Moses' and Aaron's authority and status.

This change may derive from the transition from a temple religion to a rabbinic-halakhic religion, which altered Jewish views regarding ecstatic impulses—reflected in R. Eliezer's view that it is a sin to give a religious ruling in the presence of one's master.[8]

This exegesis, which does not flow directly or straightforwardly from the biblical text, introduces a dramatic shift in the understanding of Nadab and Abihu's sin, even appearing to diminish its severity by diverting it from the religio-ritual into the social-procedural context. The textual peg on which it appears to lie derives from the juxtaposition of the explanation of the sin as offering אש זרה and the phrase "such as he had not commanded them." This led the midrashist to conclude that the "strangeness" of the fire consisted of the fact that it was not commanded or affirmed by Moses or Aaron, who sanctioned all the service performed in the sanctuary. This view is substantiated by the fact that the term זר in the ritual context generally refers in Scripture to a person unauthorized to serve in the sanctuary.[9]

As Greenstein (1989) has demonstrated, this exegesis already occurs in an inner-biblical midrash in 2 Chronicles 26, which recounts the consequences of Uzziah's hubris:

> But when he had become strong he grew proud, to his destruction. For he was false to the LORD his God, and entered the temple of the LORD to make offering on the altar of incense. But the priest Azariah went in after him, with eighty priests of the LORD who were men of

---

7 For early parallels, cf. *b. ʿErub.* 63a; *y. Šebu.* 6, 1, 36c; and the parallels in *Lev. Rab.* and *Pes. Rab. Kah.* cited above.
8 Yisraeli (2001: 275–277 and the bibliography cited therein).
9 Cf. Exod 30:9, 33; Lev 22:10, 12–13; Num 1:51, 3:10, 38, 17:5, 18:7. Many English translations in these places render זר as a "lay person." R. Eliezer's statement cannot be dissociated from his overall worldview, however, according to which it is not permitted to transmit anything not received from one's master, anyone doing so causing the Shekhina to depart from Israel.

valor; they withstood King Uzziah, and said to him, "It is not for you, Uzziah, to make offering to the LORD, but for the priests the descendants of Aaron, who are consecrated to make offering. Go out of the sanctuary; for you have done wrong, and it will bring you no honor from the LORD God." Then Uzziah was angry. Now he had a censer in his hand to make offering, and when he became angry with the priests a leprous disease broke out on his forehead, in the presence of the priests in the house of the LORD, by the altar of incense. (vv. 17–19)

The close affinities between the two episodes are striking. The problematic act is precisely the same—offering incense. The warning given by the priests adduces the fact that Aaron's descendants were "consecrated" to make the offerings and the statement that his act would thus bring him no "honor/respect" from God recall and even appear to interpret Moses' words to Aaron after Nadab and Abihu's death: "Through those who are near me I will show myself holy, and before all the people I will be glorified (בקרובי אקדש ועל פני העם אכבד)" (Lev 10:3). Just as Nadab and Abihu are punished by fire coming out from before the Lord, so Uzziah is punished "in the presence of the priests in the house of the LORD." Finally, the removal by Aaron's kinsmen of Aaron's son "by their tunics out of the camp" (Lev 10:5) is echoed in 2 Chr 26:20: "They hurried him out, and he himself hurried to get out" (Greenstein, 1989).

2 Chronicles 26 thus clearly constitutes a mirror story of the account of Nadab and Abihu. Although the story of Uzziah is not our concern here, the inner-biblical exegesis indicates that the Chronicler understood Aaron's sons as having trespassed against the priests' authority over the sanctuary. In other words, while they may have engaged in a legitimate and ritually-proper act, it was one they were unauthorized to perform. The tannaitic tradition in *Sifra* and the Talmuds thus finds support in the biblical text itself. It therefore appears to be the earliest exegesis of the pericope with which we are dealing.[10]

The emergence of this interpretation may also be a function of historical circumstances, however. As suggested above, the stress laid on obedience, compliance, and the acceptance of authority corresponds well with the tendencies exhibited by the Yavneh generation of Sages, who made great efforts to transfer the traditional restriction on temple service to the world of Torah-study after the destruction (Alon, 1980–1984: 119–131).

---

10 Shinan's argument (1979b: 214) that this homiletic direction reflects a pedagogic trend in which the biblical story "serves as the peg on which to hang worldviews that have no basis in the text" rather than belonging to a group of sources that do not derive from an interpretive orientation or desire to understand the story is thus untenable in my view. I rather contend that precisely this exegesis embodies an early, authentic tradition—despite not readily fitting the literal text.

As we remarked above, speculative interpretations began to abound in subsequent generations, the sins attributed to Nadab and Abihu growing and expanding. When these drain into the kabbalistic furrow represented by the *Zohar*, however, the midrashic tendency again focuses upon a narrow channel relating to defiance of authority or even subversive ambition. The way in which the *Zohar* chooses to express this view nonetheless differs significantly from the early tannaitic tradition, reflecting the new orientations that arose with the emergence of the new kabbalistic environs of its authors.

Nadab and Abihu's sin in the *Zohar*

Apparently familiar with the various aspects of the tradition relating to the circumstances and reasons for Aaron's sons deaths, the *Zohar* makes its own contribution to them.[11] As its wont, however, it pays particular attention to those in which it has a special interest. In several places, it thus refers to the sin of drinking wine, interpreting this as a dangerous mystical experience in the vineyard of the Strange Woman.[12] Elsewhere, it cites the sin of the unmarried women—reflecting its worldview regarding the values of married life.[13] Without doubt, however, the explanation that takes pride of place in the *Zohar* is that of rebellion against authority. As we noted above, while this midrashic tendency resumes the early tannaitic tradition, the way in which the *Zohar* treats this sin indicates the change in attitude it exhibits towards and—we shall see below—a significant ideational development. In order to demonstrate and sharpen this conceptual and spiritual watershed, I shall examine three midrashic-zoharic examples that address it from various perspectives via diverse literary expressions and levels of clarity.

In one of these, subtle expressions "soften" the denunciation of Aaron's sons' sin. Thus, for example, we find the following passage in *Aharei mot*:

> *After the death of Aaron's two sons.* Rabbi Yose said, "The verse should read *after the death of Nadab and Abihu.* Why *Aaron's two sons?* Don't we know they were his sons? Well, it has been taught as follows: Until now, they were not under their own authority, but rather

---

[11] Cf. *Zohar*, 3:33b, which, *inter alia*, adduces the sin of offering the incense offering at a time when the candles were not being lit in the sanctuary. Elsewhere (2:37b), the *Zohar* cites the theurgical transgression of connecting the impure rather than the *sefirot*, understanding the term קטורת as deriving from the root קט"ר (i.e., to link)—i.e., the instrument with which to bind.
[12] Cf. Zohar 1:73a–b, 192a; Zohar Hadash, 22b (Midrash Ne'elam).
[13] Cf. *Zohar*, 3:5b, 33b, 37b. See Tishby and Lachower (1989: 3:1355–1356). This sin later came to occupy a central place in the Lurianic kabbalah: see Liebes (1992: 160–164).

under the authority of their father. Thus, *when they encroached upon the presence of YHVH and died* (Leviticus 16:1)—for they forced the hour in their father's lifetime." (*Zohar*, 3:56b)

According to this homily, the reference to the "sons of Aaron" is not coincidental, alluding to their sin of demonstrating their independence in offering the incense despite still being under their father's authority. The basis of this understanding is clearly the early midrashic tradition discussed above, which perceives Nadab and Abihu's sin to have been their refusal to accept their father's authority or respect him—and above all their wish for Moses and Aaron to die so that they could take their place. Here, however, the indictment is formulated slightly differently, being attributed to the fact that they "forced the hour." If the midrashic question "When will these two old men die and we assume authority over the community?" paints Nadab and Abihu in a despicable light, their pursuit of honour and status prompting them to wish for the death of their father and uncle, the zoharic homily displays a far more sympathetic attitude towards them. Rather than seeking to take their elders' place, here they are merely impatient to act before the time was right. In other words, the incense was simply offered earlier than it should have been. This formulation makes it difficult to determine whether the *Zohar* regards the act as a truly religio-ethical sin or merely a tragic error—an unfortunate choice of timing not transgressive in and of itself. The fact that this indictment is cited verbatim in various places suggests that it represents a new view of the sin and its evaluation.[14]

Several of the other zoharic passages that relate to Nadab and Abihu's sin interpret it in a kabbalistic vein. As early as Nahmanides, we find an explicit tradition that holds that Aaron's sons' sin lay in the fact that the offering was linked to the אש זרה—i.e., to *Malkut* alone without reference to the "special Name," the supernal *Tiferet*. In other words, the fire they offered was not אִשֶּׁה לה' ("by fire") as required by Nahmanides' kabbalistic thought. Hereby, they impinged upon and separated things that cleave together—"cutting down the shoots," in kabbalistic terminology.[15] Other kabbalists of the period cited the same explanation—

---

14 Cf. *Zohar*, 3:33b, 37b, 60a, et al. This focus on timing appears to been linked associatively with the beginning of *Aharei mot:* "Tell your brother Aaron not to come *just at any time* into the sanctuary inside the curtain before the mercy seat that is upon the ark, or he will die" (Lev 16:1–2). עת is also charged with kabbalistic symbolism, however, representing in various places and context the sefira *Malkut*. The very fact that this term does not occur here explicitly, together with the general context, nonetheless makes it clear the sin is to be understood in a real-life social rather than a kabbalistic sense.
15 Nahmanides, commentary on Lev 10:12.

the author of *Ma'arekhet Ha'elohut* (126a), R. Todros Abulafia (1987: 26a; 1989: 136), and R. Isaac of Acre (Goldreich, 2010b: 2:151), for example.

The sin of cutting down the shoots—i.e., relating cognitively and ritually to the lower *sefira* of *Malkut* alone and ignoring the higher sefiric world—lay at the centre of the medieval kabbalistic world, Nahmanides himself making use of it to explain Adam's sin, that of the generation of the dispersion, the Golden Calf, etc.[16] On most of these occasions, the *Zohar* follows the early kabbalistic tradition, adding its own comments. In this particular case, however, it chooses another, unusual route that runs largely and rather surprisingly in precisely the opposite direction. This is exemplified in a homily that appears to have been omitted in the extant printed versions but which is cited as from the *Zohar* by R. Menachem Recanati and other kabbalists from the fourteenth century onwards.[17] In adducing it, Recanati himself counters the zoharic explanation with Nahmanides'. While the latter identified Nadab and Abihu's sin as "cutting down the shoots" by focusing on the lower *sefirot*, the *Zohar* asserts that Aaron's sons did precisely the opposite, neglecting *Malkut* in seeking to directly approach the supernal *sefirot* of *Tiferet*:

> *And fire came out from the presence of the* LORD (Lev 10:2). Come and see: At the beginning, they joyfully sought to bind all together on the left-hand side, as is written: *O that his left hand were under my head* (Cant 32:6). But when the offerer approached to bind a bond, a fire went to take hold of him, and when the fire—which is the left—took hold of him, the right came near him on the other side, as is written *his right hand embraced me* (ibid)—until everything was bound together and stood in the spirit. And this spirit is what contains everything and holds everything in water and fire. And the supernal spirit rests on them in peace (במנוחה), as is written *a pleasing aroma to the Lord* (ריח נחוח)—rest and peace as is proper. Come and see: When Aaron's sons offered a sacrifice of incense, a fire went out and met the place that the fire entered it to bind its body, as is written: *Then Isaac brought her into his mother Sarah's tent* (Gen 24:67). When it went out to take hold of him, finding nothing in their hands it took hold of them and burnt them up. [To what can this be compared?] To a man who was walking along and met a lion. He raised his eyes and saw it and took a piece of meat he had with him and threw it to him, saving himself. Were not for that piece of meat he would have been eaten. Said R. Shim'on: Not so; this matter is very ob-

---

[16] A collection of all the kabbalistic interpretations of Nahmanides' use of this concept can be found in *Ma'arekhet Ha'elohut*, chap. 9.

[17] According to Scholem (1992: 3:38b), this homily belongs to 4:38b, where a *vacat* is signified. Cf. Rubin (1992: 89). The source of this *vacat* appears to be the Lurianic kabbalistic school, appearing already in the annotations to the Zohar attributed to Luria published by R. Moses Zakut in his *Derekh Emet* (Lev 6:1). The identification has no support within the text itself, however. The cited homily lies on its own, manifesting no links with the printed material in that place. For this reason, and the fact that the *vacat* is not rare in the printed versions of the Zohar, this conjecture must remain speculative.

scure. It is written: *For the LORD your God is a devouring fire* (Deut 4:24)—a fire that consumes fire. But there is no fire that takes the supernal fire and tolerates it and gathers it in except that [fire]. And when this fire went out and found nothing in Aaron's sons' hands, that same fire that tolerates fire burnt them up. And some say אש זרה—fire that cannot tolerate the supernal fire and is consumed, and they were burnt up. Come and see: if they were burnt, why is death written of them? Because of Aaron's status.

In the opening lines of this passage, the *Zohar* describes how the incense offering creates harmony in the sefiric world by serving as a "pleasing aroma"—ensuring right and proper peace and joy. The success of this act is dependent, however, upon its initial procedure—i.e., the raising of the fire and the awakening of the attribute of Judgment (*Din*), represented by the left-hand side ("his left hand were under my head") to be held by this fire. Raising the improper fire entails catastrophic risks because if opposite the attribute of Judgment that descends from heaven no legitimate lower fire goes forth that may be absorbed by it, it burns and consumes everything in its path.

In order to elucidate this concept, the *Zohar* adds another explanation—or more precisely two alternative ones. The first views the offering of the incense as a tactical ploy—a bribing, as it were, of Judgment or attempt to distract it so that it will not injure the offerers. A mythical notion of this type exists in relation to the "goat that is sent away" on the Day of Atonement, which the *Zohar* also regards as a way of mitigating the force of the *sitra achra* or distracting its attention.[18] This is an ancient idea, appearing already in *Pirqe R. Eliezer* (Chap. 46). Nahmanides also adduces it in his commentary on the Torah, engaging in an extensive discussion of the problem of the dualism that appears to lie at its base.[19] Despite this, the *Zohar* appears here to exhibit reservations towards this explanation, preferring another—which it attributes to R. Shimon bar Johai himself—according to which the issue is purely technical or naturalistic. In other words, only the legitimate fire—not that which is illegitimate—possesses the power to contain and "tolerate" the consuming supernal fire. The priest who goes to sacrifice without this fire is thus condemned to come to harm at the hands of the upper Judgment, represented by the upper fire.[20]

---

[18] For this idea in connection with Esau and the status of evil in the world, see above, chapter 9. For its history and various occurrences in the *Zohar*, see Tishby and Lachower (1989: 1:453–454); Yisraeli (2005: 156–159 and the bibliography cited therein [pp. 266–270]).

[19] For Nahmanides' distinctive approach to this issue and his contribution to the kabbalistic doctrine of evil, see Dan (1994).

[20] The shift from the mythical to the mechanical perspective is of great significance for the study of the zoharic myth. This trend towards the softening of myth and its reworking into technical or even mechanical modes is characteristic of the *Zohar*, ripening and coming to maturity

The homilist's primary interest, however, lies in the lethal power of the upper Judgment, represented here by Isaac, due to the fact that the necessary step to restrain, distract, or contain it has not been taken by employing the proper form of fire. What is this "fire" that is consumed and not offered and what is the meaning of this offence in the kabbalistic context? The answers to these questions are provided in the continuation of the homily:

> Come and see: It is written *this one shall be called Woman* (Gen 2:23)—this one and not another one, because of the ה in אשה. ה is the one held in אש but אחרת is not called ה. And when this fire awakes, this is the other because the ה is not held in אש and is thus called אש זרה. It is not written אשה, for the ה does not occur there. *This one shall be called Woman*—in fullness for her and not another. (Recanati, 2003: 43)

Aaron's sons thus ignored the entity symbolized by the letter *he*, which represents *Malkut*. Only with the addition of this *he* does the consuming אש become the 'אשה לה' and thus legitimate. Recanati summarizes this view as follows:

> Aaron's sons offered אש זרה with the ה omitted—not אשה זרה and didn't pay attention to זאת which is called אשה and the *he* is missing from the אשה so that they entered without the Shekhina. When they illuminated the upper forces, the upper Judgment which its desire and sought is to cleave to its daughter, as is written: *Then Isaac brought her into his mother Sarah's tent*, it wasn't in the hand of Aaron's sons because they made it strange by the their intention, *then Isaac trembled violently* (Gen 27:33)—and Judgment fell upon them. According to both explanations, their punishment was due to the fact that they did not relate to the Shekhina in this matter and forgot and *You shall not omit from your grain offerings the salt of the covenant with your God; with all your offerings you shall offer salt* (Lev 2:13) as is interpreted. And the great allusion to this interpretation is intimated in *Aharei mot*: **Thus only shall Aaron enter** בזאת יבוא אהרון (Lev 16:3) demonstrates that their punishment came because they entered without זאת.

The "Shekhina," "salt," and *zot* are all symbols of *Malkut*. In this passage, Recanati alludes to the fact that at, immediately following the account of Nadab and Abihu's sin at the beginning of Leviticus 16, Moses is instructed to warn Aaron to enter the shrine בזאת. In his eyes, the juxtaposition of the two incidents confirms the zoharic exegesis that Aaron's sons sinned by not entering with *zot*—i.e., by means of *Malkut*. *Contra* Nahmanides' understanding that their sin reflected the religious danger of sufficing with the lowest and most concrete levels of the godhead, the *Zohar* identifies it as the skipping over of the lower *sefirot* to reach the highest divine *sefira*.

---

in Lurianic kabbalah. This subject not yet having been sufficiently studied, I hope to remedy this situation at a later date.

Why does the *Zohar* deviate here from the common kabbalistic view of Nadab and Abihu's sin, understanding it as a "cutting down of the shoots?" From a hermeneutical perspective, its interpretation is more faithful to Leviticus 16 and the statement that Aaron's sons died "when they drew near before the LORD"—i.e., when they entered too far into the sanctuary rather than remaining too far away from and ignoring it. It is nonetheless difficult to assume that the *Zohar* chose to reject the kabbalistic tradition and subvert it on purely exegetical grounds. It seems far more likely that it sought to follow in the footsteps of the ancient midrashic tradition discussed above, according to which Nadab and Abihu rebelled against Moses and Aaron's authority. In this sense, the sin of ignoring the *zot*—i.e., *Malkut*—and the mystical hubris of cleaving to holiness (*Tiferet*) without the mediation of *Malkut*—constitute a form of circumventing authority and sweeping mystical eruption that pays no attention to procedure and regulations. While the early midrash identifies Nadab and Abihu's sin as an affront to the social order, however, the *Zohar* shifts it to the metaphysical sphere, understanding it as a "sefiric subversion" and defiance against the upper mediator and moderator, *Malkut*.

What is the significance of this transfer from the earthly to the metaphysical sefiric realm? Although the nature of the shift is preserved, the weight given to what occurs in the metaphysical world reflects a watershed in the social context. Whoever removes the sin from the Establishment context unwittingly or wittingly thereby neutralizes the early midrashic call for the centralization of power and the acceptance of tribal authority and the political legislator. As in other zoharic midrashim, the opening up and expanding of horizons to include the metaphysical provides literary tools of expression and a critique of the ancient midrash by transposing the latter into new fields and dissociating it from conformist elements that may, in their original form, no longer correspond to the spirit of the *Zohar*.

Nadab, Abihu, and Phinehas

As we have seen, the way in which the *Zohar* makes use of ancient material reflects its reservations towards the ancient tradition and a new orientation. Let us now look at another prominent example of this trend. On several occasions, the *Zohar* suggests that Nadab and Abihu's souls were reincarnated in Phinehas:

> R. Abba said, "Why is it written *Nadab and Abihu died before YHVH when they offered alien fire before YHVH in the Desert of Sinai, and they had no children, and Eleazar and Ithamar served as priests* (Numbers 3:4). What does one have to do with the other: *they had no chil-*

dren, and Eleazar and Ithamar served as priests? Well, mystery of the matter is as I have said: *and they died*—because they had no children. Certainly so, but not like other inhabitants of the world, and even though they were not married; for these died only a bodily death, not a death of their souls. How do we know? As is written: *Eleazar son of Aaron took himself one of the daughters of Putiel as a wife, and she bore him Phinehas. These are the heads of the fathers of the Levites according to their clans* (Exodus 6:25). *These?* But Phinehas was alone! And it is written: *These are the heads of [the fathers of the Levites].* Thus, they died a bodily death, not a death of their souls."

Rabbi El'azar said, "Certainly, as implied by *these* and by *the heads.* Consequently it is written: *Phinehas son of Aaron the priest* (Numbers 25:7), and similarly: *Phinehas son of Eleazar the priest was the priest in those days* (Judges 20:28). The verses should read *Phinehas son of Eleazar the priest.* But wherever Phinehas appears, it is written *son of Aaron the priest*, whereas regarding Eleazar, it is only written *Eleazar the priest*, as is written: *Before Eleazar the priest he shall stand* (Number 27:21); *Eleazar the priest said ...* (ibid, 31:21). Thus, they died a bodily death, not a death of their souls. We have earned in the mystery of our Mishnah: "Two, a pair: פן חס (*pan, ḥas*)." As has been said, a small י (*yod*) among the letters of פינחס (*Pinhas*), Phinehas, for *yod* combines two as one. This is the mystery of the matter, as has been established. (*Zohar,* 3:57a–b)[21]

According to this homily, the dual account of Nadab and Abihu's death alludes to a double tragedy: not only were they condemned to death but they also died childless.[22] As the homilist takes pains to make clear, however, their death did not destroy the family line because while their bodies were destroyed their souls lived on.

As explicitly indicated in other zoharic passages, the homilist alludes here to the doctrine of reincarnation or transmigration.[23] This fact, he posits, explains the use of the plural in a genealogical list that only contains one person—Phinehas. In other words, Phinehas is not merely a single individual but several, because Nadab and Abihu (his uncles) are reincarnated in his soul. In the second part of this homily, the notion of transmigration is also supported by a textual phenomenon—namely, the fact that in every reference to Phinehas' lineage he is identified as *Aaron*'s descendant (grandson): "Phinehas the son of Eleazar the son of Aaron the priest." This contrasts with the common biblical custom of adducing a person by his own name and his *father*'s name. This fact leads the *Zohar* to conclude that Phinehas was not only Eleazar's son but also Aaron's because he was the reincarnation of his two uncles.

---

21 For this homily and its evolution in the works of R. Joseph del Castillo, Luria, and R. Jacob Joseph of Polonne, see Liebes (1977: 278).
22 This issue is stressed primarily in a passage previous to that cited here: see the *Zohar* there.
23 Cf. *Zohar,* 2:26b, 3:215b, 217a.

Although the doctrine of reincarnation forms part of the *Zohar*'s spiritual and conceptual world, it appears most commonly as a theoretical principle associated with the doctrine of reward and punishment.[24] Only on rare occasions does the *Zohar* make exegetical or homiletical use of it in concrete contexts, also only appearing in isolated instances in the *Zohar*'s close environment.[25] Even if the idea of the transmigration of Nadab and Abihu's souls into that of their uncle is anchored in the law of levirate marriage, as maintained by medieval kabbalists—this allowing the soul of a person who died without issue to be reincarnated in his nephew through the act of *yibbum*—the connection the *Zohar* creates between the various figures and Torah sections carries profound religious and ethical significance.

A close examination reveals that it draws rather surprising affinities between Phinehas' praiseworthy act and Nadab and Abihu's sin, in particular in light of the way in which the deeds of these figures were understand in the early talmudic midrash. Perhaps more than anyone else, Phinehas is identified in the biblical text with a lethal form of zealotry devoid of any legal-procedural judgment and execution.

The problematic aspect of acting as a vigilante as exemplified in Phinehas' deed is extensively discussed in the Talmud. On the one hand, in line with the biblical text it praises and lauds Phinehas, the amoraim taking pains to demonstrate the halakhic validity of his act and thus legitimize it. Thus, for example, we read in *b. Sanh.* 82a:

> Samuel said: *Phinehas the son of Eleazar saw.* What did he see? He saw that *There is no wisdom nor understanding nor counsel against the* LORD (Prov 21:30). Whenever the Divine Name is being profaned, honour must not be paid to one's teacher [i.e., seeing the profanation of God's name, Phinehas did not wait for Moses' ruling].

On the other, it displays a measure of ambivalence towards his deed, exemplified in the well-known ruling: "If one ... cohabits with a heathen [lit.: Syrian] woman, he is punished by zealots" (*b. Sanh.* 81b).[26] Here, silence or retrospective legitimization (although given as an a priori ruling) justify a radical act that violates all rules and legal definitions. Significantly, Rashi, with whose commentary on

---

24 For the idea of reincarnation/transmigration in the *Zohar* and thirteenth-century kabbalah, see Scholem (1945; 1976a: 308–322); Oron (1989b).
25 See Bachya b. Asher, commentary on Num 3:1. In may thus be understood as heralding the emergence of the reincarnated souls and dynasties in post-zoharic and Saphedian kabbalah (Scholem, 1976a: 322–325).
26 Cf. also the critical rabbinic texts relating to Elijah, whom an ancient tradition identifies with Phinehas: see below, chapter 15.

the Talmud the *Zohar* was undoubtedly familiar, remarks concerning this statement: "Phinehas thus gave a ruling in the presence of his master" (on *b. Sanh.* 82a). As we observed above, giving a legal decision in the presence of one's master is one of the sins the tannaim attributed to Nadab and Abihu. When the *Zohar* merges Aaron's sons with the figure of Phinehas it thus appears to seek to present the other side of the coin of rebellion against authority, the fanatic religious fervor that led the brothers to break the rules and carry out an act they were unauthorized to perform coming from the same place in the soul and from a similar drive to that which prompted Phinehas' zealotry.

Despite its threat to law and order, the impulse to defy authority is frequently based on a positive need, even ultimately meriting divine favour. The above discussion demonstrates that the zoharic doctrine of the reincarnation/transmigration of Nadab and Abihu's souls into that of Phinehas if not legitimizing Aaron's sons problematic act at least moderates and softens its severity according to the plain meaning of the text.[27] The *Zohar*'s examination of the deed through a double prism—Nadab and Abihu's act and that of Phinehas—paints a broader picture, portraying the full extent of its complexity.[28]

The meaning of the homily in its historical context

How are we to understand this trend towards softening and mitigating Nadab and Abihu's sin? Can its roots be traced to contemporaneous exegesis or do they lie in earlier sources? Although attempts to exonerate Aaron's sons can be discerned here and there, they never reach the status of the full-blown idea represented in the zoharic homily. It may be associated with Philo's view that Nadab and Abihu did not sin at all, their death not being a punishment but rather an ecstatic elevation achieved by those who transcend human limits and, coming close to God, inherit eternal life.[29] Although in other places rather surprising connections can be adduced between Philo's interpretation of the *Zohar*'s

---

[27] The zoharic sources that attribute the sin to an offering made at the wrong time, due to impatience, may also allude to the fact that Phinehas' act being performed at the right time was right and proper.

[28] The conceptual and ideological significance of the identification between Nadab and Abihu and Phinehas well illustrates the exegetical and homiletical potential this doctrine carries, creating as it does an extensive system of ties and affinities between figures and passages that are frequently far removed from one another. The study of the early doctrine of transmigration has yet to fully examine this fascinating aspect.

[29] *Somn.* 2.67; *Leg.* 2.5758; *Migr.* 169. See Flusser (1985).

midrash, here such a link seems highly implausible. Precisely here it seems that the zoharic approach must be understood in the light of its historical and geographical context. A homily illustrating how Nadab and Abihu "forced the time" supports this claim:

> Rabbi Shim'on said to Rabbi El'azar, his son: "El'azar, stand erect and say a new word in the presence of Rabbi Pinhas and the other Companions!" Rabbi El'azar rose. He opened, saying, *YHVH spoke to Moses after the death of Aaron's two sons, when they encroached upon the presence of YHVH and died* (Leviticus 16:1). This verse should be investigated ... when the blessed Holy One presented aromatic incense to Aaron, He wanted no one but him to use it in his lifetime. Why? Because Aaron increased peace in the world. The blessed Holy One said to him, "You wish to increase peace in the world, and by your hand peace will increase above. Surely, aromatic incense will be delivered to your hand from now on, and during your lifetime no other person will use it." In their father's lifetime, Nadab and Abihu offered prematurely what was not entrusted to them, and this is what caused them to err.
>
> It has been taught: Moses wondered what caused this error, and he was sad. What is written? *YHVH spoke to Moses after the death of Aaron's two sons*. What did He say to him? בקרבתם (*be-qorvatam*), *When they encroached upon, the presence of YHVH and died*. It is not written בהקיבתם (*be-haqrivam*), but rather *be-qorvatam, when they encroached upon*. The blessed Holy One said: "Moses, this was the cause, for they forced the hour in their father's lifetime, and they erred"—corresponding to what is written: *when He had not commanded them* (Leviticus 10:1)—*them* he had not commanded. Now if Aaron's two sons brought all this upon themselves by forcing the hour in their father's lifetime, then I—in the presence of my father and Rabbi Pinhas and the other Companions—how much more so!" Rabbi Pinhas came and kissed him and blessed him. (*Zohar*, 3:60a)

Here, as R. Eleazar seeks to make Torah innovations in the presence of his father and the other companions he recalls the fate of Aaron's sons. Homiletics and innovations taking the place of sacrifices and incense offerings in the world of the *Zohar*, the caution to be taken in the sanctuary against exhibiting a religious fervor that might subvert the priests' authority is thus also required in the kabbalistic study halls. The authority of the scholars and elders of the generation—in particular that of Rashi, the "high priest" of the zoharic band—forming the foundation and even the prerequisite for the creativity of the generation as a whole, it cannot be defied by independent homilies, even if these are approved by Rashi himself or his companions. At the same time, however, the empathic attitude reflected in moderate formulation represents the yearning of the zoharic band to engage in their own expositions articulating their own religious creativity.[30]

The moderate and tolerant tone we find in the *Zohar* in comparison with the early midrash may thus reflect the medieval kabbalists' relation with other rab-

---

[30] For the tensions in the zoharic narrative regarding Rashi's prominence, see Meroz (2002a).

binic circles. *Contra* Scholem, who argues that the original band of kabbalists emerged from exclusivist separatist groups, ascetics, and pietists in Provence and Spain, Idel argues that they developed from two kabbalist elites working side by side during this period. The first of these—the "primary elite"—was comprised of a group of kabbalists who were also known as halakhists, such as Nahmanides, R. Jonah Geronidi, and R. Shlomo ben Aderet. These did not produce kabbalistic works, their esoteric contribution being transmitted by word of mouth. The "secondary elite," on the other hand, consisted of scholars completely dedicated to mystical thought and its articulation—the Gerona kabbalists (with the exception of Nahmanides), R. Ezra, R. Azriel, R. Jacob ben Sheshet, and Castilian kabbalists such as R. Isaac ben Samuel of Acre and the zoharic authors. While the latter regarded themselves as championing kabbalah, the halakhic authority of the former ensure their spiritual-kabbalistic hegemony.

Our homily thus appears to substantiate and strengthen Idel's argument, which sheds light on the zoharic views we have discussed above. The empathy for Nadab and Abihu we find amongst these kabbalists, who resist the religious authority held by Moses and Aaron and seek to find ways to expression their personal religious bents, appears to be linked to their desire not to stand in the shadow of those in authority or confine their spirit to the religious realms dictated by others.

Conclusion

Although the zoharic authors do not seek to revolt, they make use of the literary figures of Nadab and Abihu to raise the hope that even if they cannot presently "force the hour," a more auspicious time will arrive when Aaron's sons will arise in another incarnation and enter the temple to offer their own personal incense—this time authorized and sanctioned by religious authority.[31]

---

[31] For the various attitudes towards Nadab and Abihu's act as reflected in the new homiletics—Hasidic and non-Hasidic—see Blidstein (2006).

Chapter 13:
"But Amongst the Nations of the World There Did Arise One Like Moses": Moses and Balaam

Rabbinic literature displays a great antipathy towards Balaam son of Beor who, according to the biblical tradition, sought to curse Israel but ultimately found himself blessing them.¹ The Sages attributed to him an "evil eye, a haughty spirit and a gross soul" (*m. ʾAbot* 5:19), regarding him as practicing bestiality (*b. Sanh.* 105a) and inciting fornication, thus going "to receive his reward for the twenty-four thousand Israelites whose destruction he had encompassed" (ibid, 106a). Claiming him to one of Pharaoh's advisors, they even held him responsible for the harsh Egyptian decree that "Every boy that is born to the Hebrews you shall throw into the Nile" (Exod 1:22) (*b. Sotah* 11a).

The clear biblical implication that he was a prophet being in direct contradiction of this view, the Sages sought ways to reconcile his wickedness with the prophecies he delivered. Although the book of Joshua speaks of him as "practicing divination" (Josh 13:22), Balaam is never explicitly referred to as a prophet, God clearly revealed Himself to him and gave him words to speak: "God came to Balaam and said ..." (Num 22:9, 12) and "met" him" (Num 23:4; cf. v. 16). The clearest indication of all is the notation that "Then the spirit of God came upon him" (Num 24:2)—which unambiguously refers to prophecy in the biblical text.² Doubts concerning the nature and status of Balaam's prophecy is evident from the ancient midrash through to the Middle Ages, the early kabbalists also discussing this issue. This chapter examines the way in which the medieval Spanish kabbalists in general and the *Zohar* in particular dealt with the exegetical dilemma in the light of age-old traditions.

---

1 For the changes in attitude towards Balaam within biblical literature itself, see Rofé (1979: 45–49).
2 The story in Numbers itself already alludes to divination via the obscure phrase וקסמים בידם (Num 22:7): see Hurowitz (1993). The nature of this technique and its relationship to the נחש do not lie within our present purview.

Prophet or diviner: From the ancient aggadah to the early Kabbalah

The attitudes displayed towards Balaam's status in the Talmud and midrash clearly indicate that the fact that he prophesied is nowhere denied. He is even numbered amongst the seven prophets who prophesied to the nations of the world (*b. B. Bat.* 15b).[3] This acknowledgement heightening the contradiction between his personality and prophetic ability, however, the Sages sought to reconcile the difficulty in various ways. According to the Palestinian amora R. Johanan, for example, "At first he was a prophet, but subsequently a soothsayer" (*b. Sanh.* 106a; cf. *Tanh.* Balak 12). In other words, although he started out as a prophet, when he sinned he lost this status. Other views distinguish between the stature of the prophets of Israel and his inferior position or (in some versions) all that of all the prophets of the nations. Thus, for example, noting the unusual form ויקר employed in relation to Balaam, a midrash in *Leviticus Rabbah* holds that "*wayyikkar* is an expression denoting uncleanness ... but [with regard to divine speech to] the prophets of Israel, the expression used is one of holiness, an expression of purity, a clear expression, an expression used by the ministering angels in praise of the Holy One, blessed be He" (*Lev. Rab.* 1:13). Another states that: "You find that the Holy One, blessed be He, appears to the heathen nations of the world only as one who comes from a distant land ... but to the prophets of Israel He either appeared or called directly [i.e., without first 'coming']. R. Jose said: The Holy One, blessed be He, appears to the heathen nations of the world only at night, at a time when men are separated from one another" (ibid). Generally speaking, they thus recognized Balaam as a prophet of an inferior status to those of Israel.

Philo took a very different approach:

> Now there was a man at that time very celebrated for his skill in divination, dwelling in Mesopotamia, who was initiated in every branch of the soothsayers' art. And he was celebrated and renowned above all men for his experience as a diviner and prophet, as he had in many instances foretold to many people incredible and most important events; for, on one occasion, he had predicted heavy rain to one nation at the height of summer; to another he had foretold a drought and burning heat in the middle of winter. ... From all which he had obtained a name of wide celebrity, as he was believed to have foreseen them all, and so he had attained to great renown and his glory had spread everywhere and was continually increasing. (*Mos.* 1.264–265)

---

[3] Cf. *Tanh. B.*, Balak 5: "In the beginning he was an interpreter of dreams. He turned to being a diviner. Then he turned to the Holy Spirit."

Balaam only being a diviner who gained his reputation on the basis of his soothsaying skills, he was not a true prophet, it only "being believed" that he had foreseen all the things he claimed to have prophesied. Although Philo does not precisely define the difference between a prophet and diviner, he is evidently reluctant to bestow prophetic status on Balaam, whom he regards as unworthy of such stature. He thus maintains that when Balaam prophesied,

> he became inspired, the prophetic spirit having entered into him, which drove all his artificial system of divination and cunning out of his soul; for it was not possible that holy inspiration should dwell in the same abode with magic ... he became like the interpreter of some other being who was prompting his words, and spoke in prophetic strain. (ibid, 277–278)

In other words, he became a prophet for a short while only due to an external force that took over his body and organs. Josephus takes a similar approach: "Thus did Balaam speak by inspiration, as not being in his own power, but moved to say what he did by the Divine Spirit ... 'canst thou suppose that it is in our power to be silent, or to say anything, when the Spirit of God seizes upon us?—for he puts such words as he pleases in our mouths, and such discourses as we are not ourselves conscious of'" (*Ant.* 4.6.5).

Although traces of this view can be found in rabbinic literature, in general it was not adopted by the Sages.[4] The majority of the rabbinic dicta relating to Balaam remain faithful to the plain meaning of the biblical text, refraining from attributing to him any spirit of prophecy even if in somewhat reserved and delimited terms. This trend can also be discerned in the Middle Ages in Maimonides' philosophical environment, in which Balaam's prophecy was considered to be one of the lowest ranks possible.[5]

A distinctive expression of the recognition of Balaam's words as prophecy occurs in the writings of the early Geronian kabbalists. Here for the first time in kabbalistic literature we find Balaam's status being addressed. A well-known passage that occurs, with minor variations, in both R. Ezra's commentary on the aggadot and R. Azriel's writings, contains a phenomenological descrip-

---

4 Cf. *b. Sanh.* 106b, which interprets the verse "The LORD put a word in Balaam's mouth" (Num 23:5) in similar fashion—either God placing in his mouth an angel or a hook (i.e., moving his lips involuntarily).
5 For Maimonides' opinion in this matter, see Klein-Braslavi (1994: 65 n. 29). Cf. also Gersonides' commentary on Num 25 (התועלת השניה), p. 136; Levi ben Abraham (2004: 153 and the editor's note 48, 161–167). In a later period, we find other approaches within this circle: see Crescas (1980: Chap. 20); Nissim of Marseilles (2000: 463).

tion of prophecy.⁶ In contending that prophecy is involuntary, the two kabbalists rely on the detailed biblical account of Balaam's prophecy. According to R. Azriel's version:

> The prophets possessed varying statuses in rank, knowledge, and cleaving and said things as though they had received them from above and as though their speech were taken hold of—like fish hooked by the mouth. You already know how much Balaam hated Israel and wished to curse them but could not speak anything but the words the Holy Spirit planted on his lips and tongue, as is written: *Must I not take care to say what the LORD puts into my mouth?* (Num 23:12). And thus spoke the prophets of Israel: *If I say, "I will not mention him, or speak any more in his name," then within me there is something like a burning fire shut up in my bones*, etc. (Jer 20:9). So there is nothing lacking or added in all their words and all is said involuntarily. (1945: 40–41)⁷

The appeal to Balaam's prophecy in the midst of a discussion regarding the nature of prophecy in general and its use as a model for understanding the prophets of Israel indicate that both R. Azriel and R. Ezra perceived a phenomenological affinity—if not identity—between Balaam's prophecy and that of the prophets of Israel. It is thus clear that they regarded Balaam as an actual prophet.

This view is fiercely countered by another contemporaneous Catalonian kabbalist—Nahmanides.⁸ Although it is difficult to determine whether his statements in this regard are directed towards R. Ezra and R. Azriel or other Jewish exegetical and/or philosophical approaches of his day, he clearly polemicizes against the opinion reflected in the kabbalistic commentaries on the aggadah that places Balaam's prophecy on a par with that of the prophets of Israel. In his commentary on Numbers 22–25, he adopts a firm if complex line. Closely analyzing the verse "Then the LORD opened the eyes of Balaam" (Num 22:31), he maintains: "From this verse we learn that Balaam was not a prophet [who habitually received Divine messages], because had he been a prophet, how could it be that he required 'opening of the eyes' to see the angel, which is the term used by Scripture about someone who has *not* reached the degree of prophecy …" The biblical text explicitly stating that "the spirit of God came upon him," however, he is forced to resort to distinguishing between prophets who prophesy by virtue

---

6 For the numerous parallels between these two commentaries, see Tishby (1945: 4–11).
7 For R. Ezra's parallel passage, see *Liqutei shikhecha u-pe'ah* 8a. For a discussion of this text, see Pedaya (2002: 140–162); Afterman (2011: 253–265 and the bibliography cited therein [p. 254 n. 118]). For Balaam's prophecy, see Pedaya (2002: 151 n. 30).
8 For the relationship between Nahmanides and the Geronian kabbalists, see Scholem (1948: 146–161). For a different view, see Idel (1995).

of their own personality and religious stature and those who are sent by God *ad hoc* in response to specific circumstances.[9] Balaam belongs to the latter, not being a prophet in and of his own right, Nahmanides appeals to the same phrase ויקר we noted above to substantiate this claim: "*And God happened to meet' Balaam*. Because this man had not reached the status of prophecy, therefore Scripture speaks of him in this way, [meaning to say] that now the [Divine] communication came to him by way of change, and in honor of Israel" (Chavel 2005: 3:265 [on Num 23:4]).[10] He sums up his position with the statement: "… he was a diviner, and thus future [events which would befall the people of Israel] would come into his heart [through divination]; but now on account of Israel he also heard the [Divine] utterance about them" (ibid, 277 [on Num 24:1]).

Despite this reductive distinction, however, Nahmanides refrains from explicitly acknowledging that Balaam attained—by right—the same status as the prophets of Israel, regarding even this incidental prophecy as divination and soothsaying and thus the complete antithesis of biblical prophecy. This fact is of great significance in light of the criteria Nahmanides employs elsewhere to argue that divination is specious and false. Thus, for example, he determines in his well-known dictum on the matter in his commentary on Deut 18:9:

> To know the future it will be unnecessary for you to resort to a diviner or soothsayers who receives [the knowledge] from the stars or from the lower powers among the lords above, whose words are not all true and who do not provide all necessary information. But prophecy informs us of God's desire and not one of its words will fall to the earth.[11] (Chavel, 2005: 229)

If Balaam's powers derived from divination and soothsaying, the "spirit of God" that rested upon him could thus not be that of true prophecy.

Although the complex and intricate exegetical structure Nahmanides erects for interpreting Balaam's words is important and instructive, the premises upon which it is built are more significant for our present purposes, these covert axioms establishing the inferiority of Balaam's prophecy and the huge gulf between it and classical biblical prophecy. The same approach had already been adopted by Ibn Ezra who, rejecting the idea that Balaam prophesied or even possessed magical powers, asserted that he was merely an astrologer whose wisdom derived from observing the stars (commentary on Num 22:28). These presupposi-

---

9 Nahmanides, commentary on Num 24:1.
10 This explicit statement is at variance with his remarks regarding Balaam in the *Book of Redemption:* "It is known from Scripture that he was a great prophet" (Chavel, 2010: 1:566). This being an aside, however, it must be regarded as secondary to his more detailed discussion here.
11 Cf. his commentary on the *teraphim* in Gen 31:19 and the false prophet in Deut 13:2.

tions appear to rest on an exclusivist view of prophecy whose roots can be traced back to rabbinic literature, also being influenced by R. Judah Halevi.[12] This in turn is based on the belief that prophecy is a divine gift rather than a philosophical or mystical skill—the latter being a more universal (human) phenomenon.[13]

The controversy amongst medieval kabbalists regarding this issue reflects the exegetical tension between faithfulness to the biblical text and loyalty to traditional dogmatic conventions. While the rabbinic aggada—and later the philosophical approach and that taken by the Geronian kabbalists—sought to preserve the spirit of the biblical account and thus insisted that Balaam must be a prophet in some sense, Nahmanides (and Josephus and Philo before him) preferred to defend the traditional notion that prophecy is an exclusively Israelite phenomenon. In the following sections, I shall endeavour to present a mediating view that "holds both ends of the string" at the same time—i.e., one that puts the biblical text to the test without relinquishing its authority. This unique interpretive method arose in the *Zohar* and the generation of kabbalists after Nahmanides. Before we turn our attention to this approach, however, let us first look at a striking early tradition that not only acknowledges Balaam to have prophesied but even makes him equal in stature to Moses.

Moses and Balaam: An aggadic tradition and its meaning

Although the Sages customarily regarded Balaam as a prophet, they usually accorded him a lesser status than those upon whom the divine spirit rested. One of the exceptions to this rule is a tradition found in several tannaitic sources that places him on a par with Moses himself:

> *And there hath not arisen a prophet since in Israel like unto Moses* (34:10): None has arisen in Israel, but one has arisen among the nations. Who was he? Balaam son of Beor. Yet there is a difference between the prophecy of Moses and that of Balaam: Moses did not knew who was speaking to him (out of the burning bush), whereas Balaam did know who was speaking to him, as it is said: *The saying of him who heareth the words of God* (Num 24:16). Moses did not know when God would speak with him, whereas Balaam did know, as it is said, *And*

---

12 Cf. *b. Ber.* 7a: "R. Johanan further said in the name of R. Jose: Three things did Moses ask of the Holy One, blessed be He, and they were granted to him. He asked that the Divine Presence should rest upon Israel, and it was granted to him. For it is said: *Is it not in that Thou goest with us [so that we are distinguished, I and Thy people, from all the people that are upon the face of the earth]* (Exod 33:16)." For this tendency in the biblical text, see Rofé (1979: 47–49).
13 For Nahmanides' view of prophecy in general and its visual aspect in particular, see Halbertal (2006: 198–211).

knoweth the knowledge of the Most High (Num 24:16). Moses was spoken to by God only while he was standing, as it is said, *But as for thee, stand thou here by Me (and I will speak unto thee)* (5:28), whereas Balaam was spoken to when he was fallen down, as it is said, *Who seeth the vision of the Almighty, fallen down, yet with open eyes* (Num 24:4). To what may this be likened? To the parable of the king's butcher who knows what the king's expenses are for supplying his table. (*Sifre Deut.* 357)[14]

As we have noted, this dictum is opposed first and foremost to the stance that refuses to accept Balaam as a prophet. Although in the *Book of Redemption* Nahmanides rejects the tannaitic tradition as "a great exaggeration," in his commentary on the Torah and direct discussion of the matter he seeks to reconcile it with his own position.[15] The weight of gravity in his opinion lies in the second half of the midrash, which defines and distinguishes between Balaam's prophecy and Moses', demonstrating the inferiority of the former even while acknowledging it to represent the height of his mystical powers. In his opinion, the "parable of the butcher" stresses and sharpens precisely the magical foundations upon which Balaam's prophecy rested, these being the complete antithesis of those undergirding biblical prophecy.

Whether or not Nahmanides' tortuous explanations are accepted, the difficulties the midrash poses must be acknowledged. Balaam's comparison with no less than Moses himself cannot be passed over without comment. Why did the midrashist bestow such a status upon Balaam and on what basis? According to Urbach, he seeks to justifies why prophecy belonged to the Israelites alone: "This tannaitic homily comes … to highlight the fact that the gentile nations were given precisely the same opportunity as that given to Israel and that Israel were not arbitrarily given precedence and uniqueness" (1956: 277–278). This understanding rests upon another tradition that appears in a number of versions:

> The Holy One, blessed be He, did not give the idolaters an opportunity of saying in the time to come: "It is Thou that hast estranged us!" What did the Holy One, Blessed be He, do? In the same way as He raised up kings, sages, and prophets for Israel, so He raised them up for the idolaters. … He raised up Moses for Israel and Balaam for the idolaters. See what a difference there is between the prophets of Israel and those of the idolaters! The prophets of Israel caution Israel against transgressions … The prophet who arose from among the nations, however, made a breach in the moral order so as to destroy men from the world. Nay, more; all the prophets retained a compassionate attitude towards both Israel and the idolaters … But this cruel man rose to uproot a whole nation for no crime! The reason why the

---

14 Cf. *Sifre Zuta*, p. 254; *Mid. Tann.* on 34:10 (pp. 227–228). Despite minor stylistic variations, these parallels are identical in content.
15 Chavel (2010: 2:566) translates this sentence as "His great distinction is traditionally related for the purpose of elevating his prophecy."

section dealing with Balaam was recorded is thus to make it known why the Holy One, blessed be He, removed the Holy Spirit from the idolaters, for this man rose from their midst, and see what he did! (*Num. Rab.* 20:1)

Although this midrash is clear polemical, it is very difficult to draw a straight line between it and the view that "There arose not in Israel a prophet like Moses—but among the nations one did arise" given that the polemical tone only appears in other later midrashim—such as *Numbers Rabbah*, *Tanhuma*, *Ecclesiastes Rabbah*, and *Seder Eliyahu*.[16] The use of such a late idea to explain the tannaitic sources is very dubious. In order to offer an alternative explanation, let us look at some of the insights within the *Zohar* and the kabbalistic literature in its environs. As with other subjects discussed in this volume, here too we see that on occasion the zoharic homily seeks to elucidate the literal meaning of the ancient midrashic tradition upon which it rests even while doing so in a very different theological language. The zoharic interpretation of the early aggada also reveals its unique and original stance with respect to the general question of Balaam's prophecy, its nature, and status.

Balaam's and Moses' prophecies in the *Zohar* and R. Moses de Léon's Writings

As is the case with numerous other issues, the *Zohar*'s attitude towards Balaam's prophetic status is varied and multifaceted. In general terms, it exhibits a tendency towards diminishing Balaam's stature. In several places it interprets the biblical description of him as one "whose eye is clear (שתום העין)" (Num 24:3) as a negative attribute indicative of the inferiority of his prophecy.[17] Elsewhere (1:110b), it stresses that it was not God but His envoy who revealed himself to Balaam (Cohen-Eloro, 1989: 142–143). On other occasions (cf. 3:210b, 211b–212a), it almost completely denies Balaam any prophetic status, regarding him as a passive vehicle through whose mouth the Shekhina itself speaks in line with Josephus and Philo. As a whole, he is depicted as a soothsayer and diviner.[18]

---

16 See Ginzberg (2003: 3:347 n. 355).
17 See Liebes (1977: 291–293 and the references cited therein). Cf. in particular the homily in 2:69a–b, which the adduces the distinction between Balaam's and Moses' prophecy as part of a clearly-delineated phenomenological description.
18 Cf. 1:125b–126b, 2:69b, 3:112a–113a, 184b–185a, 192a, 2–7a, 210a; *Zohar hadash*, 54a–c. The zoharic midrash takes a particular interest in Balaam's evil eye as a source of magical power: cf. 1:68b, 3:206b, etc.

Although these homilies rest in large part on early talmudic and midrashic traditions, the *Zohar* paints these in much stronger and bolder colours, providing detailed descriptions of the techniques Balaam used—doing nothing for his reputation to say the least. In this regard, the *Zohar* follows in Nahmanides' footsteps, denying all prophetic stature to Balaam and perceiving his powers to derive solely from his divination and soothsaying skills. It introduces a new idea, however, that has no precedent in any other Jewish literature. Interpreting the view that places Balaam on a par with Moses, this asserts that the difference between the two men's prophecies lay not in their ability to foresee the future but in the source of their inspiration. While Moses prophesied on the basis of his proximity to theosophic sacred vistas Balaam did so by virtue of his mystical attachment to the impure forces of the *sitra achra*. One of the zoharic homilies in which this idea is adduced is that which concludes *Parashat Shemot* in the printed editions, which appears to belong to one of the earliest strata of the book:

> Said R. Johanan: [Moses] attained ten degrees, as is written: *he is faithful in all my house* (Num 12:7). Is it not written *my house?* Happy is the portion of that man whose master testifies to him in this manner. Said R. Dimi: Indeed it is written *There arose not in Israel a prophet like Moses.* Said R. Joshua: No one arose in Israel but one did arise in the nations of the world. Who is that? Balaam. He said to him: You have said well. He did not reply. When R. Shimon came, they asked him about this matter. He said: Drops of resin do not mingle with the good persimmon, God forbid. But it is certainly so with the nations of the world, wherein a prophet like Moses arose. Who was it? Balaam. Moses' works are above, Balaam's below. Moses used the holy crown of the king above, Balaam the unholy lower crowns below. Both used them in precisely the same way, however. So it is written: *and they also killed Balaam son of Beor with the sword* (Num 31:8). If you think more, go and ask his ass. R. Jose came and kissed his hand. Said he: This wine in my heart came out, for this indicates that there are upper and lower realms, right and left, Judgment and Compassion, Israel and the nations of the world. Israel use the upper holy crowns, the nations of the world the unholy lower crowns. The former belong to the right, the latter to the left. At any rate, the upper prophets are distinguished from the lower one, the prophets of the Holy Spirit from the prophets that are not of the Holy Spirit. Said R. Judah: As Moses was distinguished from all the prophets in his supernal holy prophecy so Balaam was distinguished from the rest of the prophets and soothsays in unholy, lower prophecy. In any event, Moses is above and Balaam is below and many rungs separate them. (*Zohar*, 1:21b–22a)[19]

---

[19] For the text and structure and character of the homily/*parasha*, see Meroz (forthcoming). My thanks go to her for kindly sharing the fruit of her research. Due to its exceptional nature, which differs from the body of the *Zohar*, and its early date, this homily does not appear in the Pritzker edition. Its early provenance is reflected in an internal reference elsewhere within the *Zohar* to the opinion held by R. Shimon here (3:207b).

Discussing Moses' preeminent stature, the *Zohar* here asks how this can be so if Balaam possesses equal status. The debate coming to a dead end, it appears to be dissatisfied with the well-known explanations, thus prompting an appeal to R. Shimon himself. His answer in effect sets up a new system of coordinates: "Moses used the holy crown of the king above, Balaam the unholy lower crowns, below. Both used them in precisely the same way, however." The latter phrase is undoubtedly meant to stress that the early midrash is intended to be understand literally—i.e., that Balaam attained the same prophetic status as Moses, being capable of seeing precisely the same things. The only difference between them lay in the fact that Moses used the "holy crown"—i.e., the upper source of holiness—whereas Balaam achieved what he did only through the "lower crowns" belonging to the realm of impurity of the *sitra achra*.[20] The companions being surprised and excited by R. Shimon's explanation, the homilist appears to have regarded it as novel and original.

Although the frank and unmitigated "dualist" claim that Balaam possessed the same prophetic status as Moses has virtually no precedent during the period during which the "zoharic circle" was active, it found a firm foothold in the *Zohar*'s environs, clear traces of it being evident in the *Zohar* itself in several places.[21] In the works of the one of the most important members of the zoharic circle, R. Moses de Léon, it occurs on two occasions, demonstrating the development in R. Moses' thought regarding the question of Balaam's prophecy. While in his early writings he still holds to the quintessential midrashic position denying any analogy between Moses and Balaam, in his later texts the dualistic approach becomes more prominent. Thus, for example, in his very early and brief work *Balaam's Mystery*, printed as appendix to *The Wise Soul*, he states:

> The Holy One, blessed be He, wished the nations of the world to have a prophet without giving them the opportunity to say anything in the future, and the one who attained this in the hour when he blessed Israel above is greater than glory, since as our Sages of blessed memory have said: "*There arose not in Israel a prophet like Moses*—in Israel no one has arisen; but in the nations of the world, one has arisen." And precisely at the time of the bless-

---

[20] In this homily the *Zohar* thus seeks to reinterpret rather than dispute the early midrash ("but one did arise in the nations of the world"). For a different reading, see Cohen-Eloro (1989: 142).
[21] Cf. 1:125b, 126a, 2:69a–b, 3:113a, 192a, 193b–194a, 200a–b, 206b–210b. In his *Treatise on the Left Emanation*, R. Isaac ben Jacob Hacohen had already alluded to the possibility that the forces of the *sitra achra* can "foretell the future to men when they appear to them in human form ... and the person who asks who they are, his question will be asked as he wishes if he is worthy of being answered." See Scholem (1927: 95). The fact that this idea is not associated with Balaam here, however, as might have been expected, suggests that the exegetical usage of this context was still unfamiliar.

ing, because without it the glory would not exist in the drawing of everything, because it is the attribute of Compassion. But after the blessing was taken away from him and he became like before, he had need of divination like the other diviners and is thus called "Balaam the diviner."

R. Moses manifests two divergent exegetical opinions here that he combines into one—the (later) midrashic view according to which Balaam's prophecy was a test and a trial for the nations of the world and that which resembles Nahmanides' position, according to which Balaam only temporarily attained the same status as Moses in order to bless Israel. The conclusion "But in the nations of the world one like Moses did arise" is not yet found here.

In contrast, the "dualistic" approach is found in his later writings in fullyfledged form—in precisely the same fashion as the zoharic homily discussed above, Balaam being said to derive his power from the lower crowns:

> For Moses our master, of blessed memory, achieved a prophetic degree attained by no other prophet. And should you say that the Sages said that *There arose not in Israel a prophet like Moses*—but in the nations of the world one did arise, Balaam—the Sages have already explicated this matter, asserting that Balaam was not like Moses because, God forbid, holiness is not defiled by impurity. Does not a man purify himself with several purifications and consecrate himself with several consecrations and may it be God's will that the Spirit may rest upon him. But Balaam the diviner, who defiled himself with several defilements and soiled his body and his ass will prove that he was an evil man—how can the holiness that is above awake and rest upon this wicked defiled man whose sins corrupted and defiled him? But assuredly the degree of Moses our master of blessed memory was from above, placing him above all the other prophets, allowing him to prophesy through a clear mirror and see what the rest of the prophets could not see. And because his status was above them all, there was nobody who could say: Stand and I will tell you what God has commanded you. Balaam was his counterpart amongst the nations of the world, being of the other side—the spirit of impurity and its rungs—and proficient in its divination and omens. And just as Moses immediately received everything he asked for from the side of holiness, so Balaam immediately received everything he asked for from the side of impurity. (Tishby, 1993: 174–75)

Here, Balaam is clearly compared with Moses with respect to the horizons of his vision—and perhaps also the degree of his prophetic experience. The difference between them lies in the metaphysical source of their inspiration. While Moses foresaw through the *sitra de-qedusha*, Balaam sought through the spirit of impurity of the *sitra achra*.

In *Sheqel ha-qodesh*, composed in 1292 and thus apparently the latest of all R. Moses de Léon's works, R. Moses writes as follows:

> And should you say: If so, why were the Sages so precise in asserting that *"There arose not in Israel a prophet like Moses—but in the nations of the world one did arise, Balaam the*

wicked"? His comparison with Moses is a great and lofty matter. We have already indicated in what is written ויקר—from the language of impurity. So how did he merit the Holy Spirit resting upon him and how did the Holy Spirit rest upon a place of impurity? Did not God order His servants, His holy people, *Do not defile yourselves in any of these ways* (Lev 18:24)?

Some interpret this thus: They said that he was blessed with the Holy Spirit and all his works and devices were fire and it made no difference to him because the fire lacked nothing and was not defiled by impurity and despite the holiness that is fire, as it is written *For the LORD your God is a devouring fire* (Deut 4:24), he lacks nothing of its holiness. The Torah itself teaches that it was given from the side of fire, as it is written: *lightning flashing out from His right* (Deut 33:2) and *Is not my word like fire, says the LORD* (Jer 23:29). As fire is not defiled by impurity, so the words of the Torah are not defiled by impurity.

I do not think this explanation is correct because I do not say whether or not it is defiled by impurity because this matter is well known to the wise. But it is an obscure matter, how he who is impure and defiles himself can prophesy through the Holy Spirit. We have already said *Your dwelling is not with the evil*, because the Holy One, blessed be He, does not dwell with impurity.

The truth is that it is already known to all that have eyes that the one who comes to defile is defiled, and the person who defiles himself draws upon the spirit and impurity and defiles himself further. And when a man denies himself through good deeds and follows after holiness, they sanctify him from above and he draws upon himself the Holy Spirit and the supernal holiness rests upon him. And observe that in defiling himself the wicked person draws the spirit of impurity upon himself and they defile all of him. And he slept with his ass, and this is the law of diviners and soothsayers who do not attain sight until they have defiled themselves, as in the matter of the degree of the holy prophets, the servants of the Most High, who seek the degree of the spirit of prophecy and in order to gain pleasing things consecrated themselves and immersed themselves in holiness in order to find and attain their achievement. And this is the matter of those diviners and soothsayers, that they defile themselves with known impurity so that the spirit of impurity rests upon them. Because as their deeds so the spirit rests upon them, whether from the side of holiness or the side of defilement. And with respect to this matter, Balaam the wicked was a diviner and soothsayer and could not attain his wishes until he defiled himself with his ass, and then he drew upon himself the spirit of impurity. For the mystery of the matter of the degree of his prophecy is that it was none other than from the side of impurity and with that spirit he attained his wish to know, just as Moses did from the side of purity. Moses was above in the degree of holiness, and Balaam was underneath in the degree of impurity. And this matter is taken from the Sages and they answered as we have alluded to. (1996: 14–15)[22]

Here R. Moses directly addressed the issue of how the Holy Spirit could rest on Balaam in light of his impurity. The explanation with which he is familiar— namely, that the words of the Torah are not defiled—does not suffice him because his interest lies not in the theological-metaphysical but in the tradition-

---

22 See Cohen-Eloro (1989: 135–136); Goetschel (1989: 235–236).

al-religious aspect of the question.²³ In his view, it is inconceivable that immersion in the forces of impurity can enable a person to attain the same prophetic rank as the greatest of all the prophets. As in the zoharic homily and *Elijah's Mystery*, here too a dualistic resolution to the problem is offered: while Balaam's prophecy was equal to Moses' in its efficacy in foreseeing the future, it was different and far inferior to it in its source.²⁴

Examining this version closely, however, we discover that it bears an even more radical character than at first glance. If in his early writings, R. Moses contrasts the divergent metaphysical source of the prophecies of Moses and Balaam, here he addresses the question of the mystical techniques themselves. According to this text, just as conventional Mosaic prophecy is conditional upon the prophet's consecrated life, so prophecy based on the spirit of impurity is predicated upon the practice of impure ritual acts—"Because as their deeds so the spirit rests upon them, whether from the side of holiness or the side of defilement." ²⁵ In other words, Balaam attained his parity with Moses only by virtue of his impure acts. "Balaamic" magic is thus conditional upon the living of an abject, abominable, abhorrent lifestyle. Here, R. Moses pushes the new idea towards bold and daring vistas.²⁶

This Léonid view of prophecy, which acknowledges the value of mysticism and magic, was unquestionably anchored not only in popular custom but also in ancient rabbinic tradition. Although belief in the powers of sorcerers and magicians was prevalent during the rabbinic period, a huge gap lies between the knowledge of the "scientific" period of magical practices and its identification as prophecy—let alone its parity with the greatest prophecy of all.²⁷

---

23 As Goetschel (1989), notes, this interpretation may have circulated amongst the Geronian kabbalists.

24 The support appealed to here—"And this matter is taken from the Sages and they answered as we have alluded to"—may indicate the relatively late date of this text, R. Moses apparently referring to one of the zoharic sources, at the least the earliest of them in which the statements are transmitted in the name of R. Shimon bar Johai. This may be the subject of the discussion in 2:21b. But see Tishby (1993: 74–75 n. 14); Mopsik in Léon (1996: 15 n. 131).

25 The magical use of the spirit of impurity is also well known in the Talmud: cf. *b. Sanh.* 65b. See Harari (1998: 209, 326–327). For sorcery in the rabbinic world, see ibid, 68–90 and the broad summary and extensive references cited therein; Urbach (1975: 97–123); Bohak (2008: 70–226);.

26 For the notion that black magic in general and that practiced by Balaam in particular is bound up with moral corruption and the adoption of unlawful ritual norms, cf. 1:125b–126a. Here, however, the prophetic context does not appear, no claim being made at all that through his art the magician can achieve the same prophetic status as Moses.

27 Traces of this idea in relation to the Torah and prophecy can already be found in R. Isaac Hacohen's *Treatise on the Left Emanation:* see above, n. 21.

Where could such an idea have sprung from? I suggest that it derives from a close and sensitive reading of the midrashic source we have been discussing in this chapter, the *Zohar* thus properly understanding—and developing—the original intention of the early tannaitic midrash.

As Nahmanides had already pointed out, alongside the comparison between Moses and Balaam herein the qualitative disparity between the status of the two men is also stressed: "To what may this be likened? To the parable of the king's butcher who knows what the king's expenses are for supplying his table." If Balaam is the king's butcher, Moses must be regarded as his crown prince. It is clear to all, however, that even if the two—the butcher and the crown prince—govern the palace secrets, he who knows the king's banquet from the kitchen is not on a par with he who is invited to the feast. The midrashist thus contends that in contrast to Balaam, who gained his knowledge manipulatively behind the curtains, Moses was made privy to the king's secrets because of God's revelation to him face to face. Moses therefore not only knew God's secrets but was also a partner to them because he was His confident and "faithful in all His house." While this perspective, which measures the prophet not only according to the extent of the revelation and scope of the knowledge of the future he is granted but also on the basis of his closeness and intimacy with the revealer, forms the foundation of R. Moses' interpretation, he takes it several steps further. While the "parable of the butcher" presents Balaam's prophecy as a manipulative practice devoid of any spiritual-mystical value, the zoharic aggada maintains that it draws its power from the illegitimate mystical resources that lie in the demonic depths of the *sitra achra*.

As in the early aggada, the difference between Moses and Balaam in the *Zohar* thus lies in the nature of the faces that reveal themselves to the prophet. While the tannaitic texts deal with the varied expressions these carry, however, the *Zohar* already distinguishes between the *sitra de-qedusha* and the *sitra achra*. Despite the variant spiritual language, R. Moses de Léon and the *Zohar* therefore both draw on and develop the spirit of the ancient midrash.

Criticism of the dualist view of prophecy

The innovative nature of the *Zohar*'s interpretation of Balaam's prophecy is perhaps most clearly demonstrated by the criticism levelled against within the book itself, echoes of which exist in the very homily itself. As we have seen, the text concludes with a comment by R. Judah that expresses significant reservations regarding R. Shimon bar Johai's novel exegesis: "As Moses was distinguished from all the prophets in his supernal holy prophecy so Balaam was distinguished from the rest of the prophets and soothsays in unholy, lower prophecy. In any event, in Moses this was above and in this below, several rungs separating them." Despite the associative affinity between them, these sharp words cannot be perceived as a continuation of R. Shimon's homily. On the contrary, they represent a completely different and even contradictory approach to the previous comment regarding the equivalence between Moses' and Balaam's prophecies. If R. Moses de Léon acknowledges that the biblical text places the two men on a par ("Both used them in precisely the same way"), R. Judah shatters the analogy completely. We never meant to say, he asserts, that Balaam should be compared with Moses —and anyone who does so merely means that just as Moses was the head of the prophets of holiness so Balaam was the head of the diviners and false, dark prophets. In relation to Moses' prophecy, Balaam's prophecy moreover was infinitely inferior in quality and status.[28] The terms כתרים דלתתא (lower crowns) and דרגין תתאין (lower rungs), which in kabbalistic terminology refer to the secondary entities of the *sitra achra*, are here interpreted as marking their place at the bottom of the theosophic system—or even below it. In other words, they form the lowest level not only with respect to their demonic nature but also in regard to their hierarchical rank in the theosophic system.[29] *Contra* the position taken by R. Shimon, R. Judah alleges that diviners and soothsayers such as Balaam can never truly achieve the same status as the prophets of holiness, for "Moses is above and Balaam is below and many rungs separate them." Although this interpretation of the aggadic statement that "but in the nations of the world one like Moses did arise" is constructed on a dualist basis and makes use of the parallelism between the upper and lower rungs, it strips the ancient tradition of all its radical significance, turning the comparison of Moses and Balaam into a mere outward affinity.

The new dualistic approach was thus not accepted by all even in the *Zohar*'s surroundings.[30] The homily also exemplifies what we learn from numerous other

---

28 A similar view may be reflected in the zoharic homily in *Parashat Jethro* (2:69a–b), which states that Balaam obtained a "little tenuous glow" (נהירה דקיק זעיר) from the *sitra achra* while Moses attained an "immense supernal radiance" (נהירו עלאה רב וסגי) from the *sitra de-qedusha*.
29 For the term כתרים תתאים in the *Zohar* and its association with the doctrine of the left emanation in the Cohen brothers' kabbalistic thought, see Scholem (1927: 33).
30 This fact also indicates that in the early strata of the *Zohar* R. Shimon bar Johai's status was (still?) disputed and reservations regarding his stance could legitimately be expressed. The subtle way in which R. Judah does so here is instructive. While he accepts the fundamental premise that Balaam's prophecy derived its power from the lowest rung and Moses' from the highest rung, he constructs the theosophical balance of powers in very different fashion, thereby in fact divesting R Shimon's view of all its radical implications. This form of reservation, which mitigates the dispute between the two men, evinces a measured caution towards impinging on R.

places in the book—namely, that it contains varied voices that can be readily discerned when though the tendency of a particular author/editor of the homily is clearly evident. If the "Shimonite" outlook of the homily is identified with R. Moses de Léon's thought—in which it appears for the first time and in several passages—the view represented in it by R. Judah also occurs in contemporaneous Hebrew writings in the *Zohar*'s environs. R. Moses' colleague R. Joseph Gikatilla, for example, observes:

> Know that just as Moses was the head of all the prophets and obtained superior to any other the attribute of *Tiferet* as he was in purity, so Balaam the wicked was the head of the diviners and soothsayers and was superior to all of them out on his arm as he was in extreme impurity. And the one countered the other, Moses inside for purity and asceticism and Balaam for impurity and defilement, as the Sages said in the midrash: There arose not in Israel a prophet like Moses—but among the nations of the world one did arise. (1998: 3)

The dictum cited at the end of this text parallels R. Judah's exegesis in the zoharic homily. In contrast to the essentialist comparison highlighted in R. Moses' writings and R Shimon bar Johai's remark in the zoharic homily—"Both used them in precisely the same way"—the analogy here is merely external. If in *Elijah's Mystery* R. Moses definitively declares that "Just as Moses immediately received everything he asked for from the side of holiness, so Balaam immediately received everything he asked for from the side of impurity," in Gikatilla's *Mystery of the Serpent* Moses is "superior to all in glory for purity," Balaam merely being "out on his arm"—undoubtedly a reference to the impotence of Balaam's prophecy as well as its abhorrent nature.

It thus transpires that the discourse manifest in the zoharic homily and the divergence in worldview between R. Shimon and R. Judah reflect the disparities between two of the most prominent zoharic kabbalists—R. Moses de Léon and R. Joseph Gikatilla—with respect to the dualistic concept of prophecy. While it is difficult to determine whether the criticism levelled at R. Shimon in this regard forms an authentic part of the homily or whether it was added at a later stage, R. Shimon's statement clearly carries the greater weight, perhaps representing within the zoharic context the hegemonic stance revealed to be that adopted by R. Moses.

In the framework of the study of the *Zohar* and the process of its formation, this link between the literary figures and historical personages is of great impor-

---

Shimon's status. For the tensions within the zoharic band over R. Shimon bar Johai's leadership, see Meroz (2002a).

tance for understanding the historical background against which the zoharic homily developed. If further traces of it can be found, this may shed much light on the relations between key figures within the thirteenth-century kabbalistic community—as well as on the way in which the zoharic homily took shape.[31]

The dualistic view of prophecy: Exegetical and ideological aspects

The Léonid-zoharic interpretation of the dictum "There arose not in Israel a prophet like Moses—but among the nations of the world one did arise" also reflects a new and original approach to the more general question discussed above of the status of Balaam's prophecy. The *Zohar* proposes a novel solution here to the tension between the literal sense of the biblical text and the tenet that prophecy was confined to Israel. According to this view, Balaam was one of the greatest prophets of all generations, thus being on a par with Moses himself. The superiority of the prophets of Israel, headed by Moses, is based solely on their intimacy with the *sitra de-qedusha* in the godhead—which prophets of the likes of Balaam can never attain. This posits an unbreachable gap between Balaam's and Moses' and the prophets of Israel's prophecy without accepting Nahmanides' rejection of Balaam's prophetic status, which requires a harmonization of the biblical texts.

This unique approach to magic must be perceived not only as the fruit of midrashic analysis but also as an expression of a clearly-delineated ideology whose traces are evident in other passages in the *Zohar*. The most well known of these is the story of the "wisdom of the children of the East." Found in the printed editions in *Parashat Vayera*, this lore—in effect magical praxis—is both greatly admired and harshly criticized:

> R. Abba said: "One day I happened upon a certain town formerly inhabited by children of the East, and they told me some of the wisdom they knew from ancient days. They had found their books of wisdom, and they brought me one, in which was written: 'As one's aspiration is directed in this world, so he draws upon himself a spirit from above, corresponding to the aspiration to which he cleaves. If his aspiration focuses on a supernal entity, he draws that from above to himself below.' They said the essence of the matter depends on words, action, and the aspiration to cleave, whereby the side to which one cleave is drawn from above to below. I found in it all the ritual acts of star-worship, requisites, and how to focus the will upon the, drawing them down. ... I said to them, 'My chil-

---

[31] For the historical approach to the study of the *Zohar* see above chapter 3.

dren, this is close to words of Torah, but you should shun these books, so that your hearts will not stray after these rites, toward all those sides mentioned here, less—Heaven forbid— you stray from the rite of the blessed Holy One!' For all these books deceive human beings, since the children of the East were wise—having inherited a legacy of wisdom from Abraham, who bestowed it upon the sons of the concubines, as is written: *To the son of his concubines Abraham gave gifts, while he was still alive, and he sent them away from his son Isaac eastward, to the land of the East* (Genesis 25:6). Afterward they were drawn by that wisdom in various directions. Not so with the seed of Isaac and the share of Jacob, for it is written: *Abraham gave all that he had to Isaac* (ibid, 5)—holy heritage of faith to which Abraham cleaved. From that share, from that side issued Jacob. (*Zohar*, 1:99b–100b)

R. Abba unquestionably recognizes their validity and efficacy of this wisdom, having no qualms about declaring them to be "close to words of Torah" or having been bequeathed by Abraham to his offspring via his concubines whom he sent "eastward, to the land of the East."[32] He nevertheless cautions his disciples not to stray after it because it will take them into the paths of idolatry, the fact that its techniques work and are based on sanctioned principles not being sufficient to legitimize it.[33]

As in the homily on Balaam, this story also reflects a complex and balanced attitude towards its mystical-magical environment. Within the prophetic context of the "Balaam homilies," however, it bears a far more radical character, the recognition of magical practices not being equivalent to acknowledging the possibility that their use can lead to attainment of the same prophetic status as Moses. Not only is Moses the father of the prophets set against Balaam the diviner in the mysterious prophetic system embodied in R. Moses de Léon's writings and the parallel *Zohar* dicta but the "diviners and soothsayers" also stand against "the holy prophets, the servants of the Most High" and the holy commandments against the unhallowed arts as two equally efficacious ways of achieving knowledge of the future.

---

[32] The tradition relating to the gifts Abraham gave to his concubines is found already in *b. Sanh.* 91a, where he is said to have "imparted to them [the secrets of] the unhallowed arts."
[33] In Nahmanides' comments on the various forms of divination and soothsaying referred to in Deut 18:10–11, he similarly asserts that they are forbidden not because they are not valid or efficacious but despite this fact. In his polemic against those who "dispose themselves to be liberal with regard to these enchantments"—directed against Maimonides and his followers (cf.)— he insists that "We cannot deny matters publicly demonstrated before the eyes of witnesses" (commentary on Deut 189 [Chavel: 4:219]) (cf. *The Law of the Eternal is Perfect* 1:147 [Chavel, 2010: 1:49–50]; Maimonides, *Mishneh Torah*, Hilchot Avoda Zarah 11, 16). Nahmanides' opposition to magic differs essentially from that reflected in the zoharic homily. For his complex attitude towards magic, see Halbertal (2006: 268–272 and the bibliography cited therein).

In this light, it is easier to understand the internal reservations expressed in the *Zohar* itself (based, as we have seen, on the approach taken by R. Joseph Gikatilla) towards the Léonid view, which recognizes the power of the thaumaturgical potential embodied in the *sitra achra* to a degree unprecedented in any other Jewish writings. Whoever recognizes these practices, which draw their power from the "lower crowns," in effect places them on "on the shelf" even at the same time as warning that they are not completely "kosher." Acknowledgement of the efficacy of a contingent prophetic possibility opens a door that a warning of the kind found here is unlikely to prevent entrance through. On the level of theology, the blurring of the hierarchical scale between the upper and lower crowns and the attribution of equal magical power to each also raises difficult questions regarding the monotheistic nature of this kabbalistic view.[34]

At the same time, however, the placement of prophetic praxis within the new channel of the use of "lower crowns" paradoxically mitigates and softens their magical use. The claim that the praxes founded on demonic consecrated theosophic systems alike constitute efficacious models is likely to transfer the focus of choice between them elsewhere. Henceforth, the practical test of the two "tracks" and the preference of one over the other will not be based on their efficacy—a now obsolete factor—alone but upon a broader religious principle. This worldview may well establish a new system of coordinates in which the value of the magical act will be (primarily) determined by virtue of the links the act of foreseeing exhibits with the metaphysical space and the ethical nature of these associations.

Conclusion

R. Moses de Léon's unique approach to Balaam's prophetic status reflects a dramatic development in a centuries-old exegetical problem on the one hand and a growing mystical-magical tendency on the other. If in the ancient world, the discussion of prophecy revolved around the question of its reliability and basis, in the zoharic homilies influenced by R. Moses de Léon's thought another form of judgment is required. Here, rather than being measured in terms of truth and falsity, prophecy has become a matter of holiness and impurity, kosher and non-ko-

---

[34] The dispute over Balaam's prophecy and its features should also perhaps be understood in the historical context of the attitude towards magical-mystical phenomena in the *Zohar*'s non-Jewish environment in Christian Spain. This issue lies beyond my present brief, however.

sher—indices that derive, as we have noted, from an approach that accepts the comparison between Moses and Balaam literally and without question. When we come to examine the spiritual image reflected in R. Moses' various dicta and the zoharic homilies discussed in this chapter, the fundamental issue of preoccupation with magic—the question of the scientific validity of divination and soothsaying—has long faded into the background. At this mystical watershed, in which a straight line is drawn between Balaam's and Moses' prophecies, the two men's practices being equally potent, the issue of efficacy is no longer relevant. It is precisely at this point that the matter of the normative ethical contexts of magical practice is likely to arise again, the world of the mystics—in which magic has already prevailed—being, paradoxically, likely to resemble that in which it never appears to have existed.

Chapter 14:
"Then Moses, the Servant of the Lord, Died There": Did Moses Really Die?

The account of Moses' death that appears at the end of Deuteronomy leaves the event shrouded in mystery: "Then Moses, the servant of the Lord, died there in the land of Moab, at the Lord's command. He was buried in a valley in the land of Moab, opposite Beth-peor, but no one knows his burial place to this day" (Deut 34:5–6).[1] What is the meaning of the phrase "at the Lord's command" and why was his burial place not marked? Although these and other questions have preoccupied many biblical commentators and midrashic scholars over the generations, few have doubted that Moses die indeed die. Unlike Elijah and Enoch, the end of his life is definitively noted—"Moses died there." As with other cases, however, this text is not as plain and clear as it appears at first glance. Rabbinic literature contains numerous disputes regarding Moses' death according to the way of all flesh. This chapter deals with the sources of this surprising view, the way in which it made its way into the *Zohar*, and its treatment therein.

The *Zohar* links the question of Moses' death with his status in general, thereby shedding light on the latter. Much has been written on the subject of the figure and role of Moses in the book. Liebes (1993d) has devoted a lengthy study to the relationship adduced between Moses and R. Shimon bar Johai, Huss also addressing the same theme (1999, 2008). The latter demonstrates that the similarities between the two figures derive from an integrated reading of the early talmudic sources. Noting that the *Zohar* even asserts that R. Shimon was greater than Moses in several places, he also suggests that the zoharic Moses reflects the kabbalistic personality of another Moses—R. Moses b. Nahman—thereby affirming its superiority over that of the humble and conservative scholar. Goldreich (1994) has also examined the references to Moses in the later zoharic strata—the *Tiqunei Zohar* and *Raya Mehemna*. Analyzing and elucidating his messianic role in destroying the ערב רב ("mixed crowd") and lifting up the "Torah of the Tree of Life," he shows that several of the dicta present the Raya Mehmna ("faithful shepherd")—i.e., Moses—as a real, living person who may well be the author of the *Raya Mehmna* itself.[2] Liebes (2007b) has also dis-

---

[1] For the exegetical problems attendant upon this verse, see Loewenstamm (1972).
[2] As Goldreich notes (1994: 482 n. 88), this proposal had already been made by Tishby and Lachower (1989: 2:1107 n. 193). See also Liebes (1977: 202; 2007b: 251–301).

cussed Moses' status in the later zoharic strata, evincing that, in contrast to the *Zohar* itself, the author of the *Raya Mehemna* and *Tiqunei Zohar* place Moses on a higher plane than R. Shimon bar Johai, favouring Moses, the humblest of all who is unaware of his mystic stature, over R. Shimon and his consciousness knowledge that "his face shone." This chapter hopes to add and illuminate the question of Moses' status from the perspective of the tradition that holds him to be immortal, carefully analysing some of the premises and conclusions.

Moses' death in the pre-zoharic literature

Our first task herein is to distinguish between the various versions of the ancient tradition. Despite their outward resemblance, these are neither identical nor consistent. According to the prevalent minimalist view, unlike other human beings who fall into the hands of the Angel of Death Moses escaped this fate. In *b. B. Bat.* 17a, for example, Moses is said to be one of six men not governed by the Angel of Death:

> Our Rabbis taught: Six there were over whom the Angel of Death had no dominion, namely, Abraham, Isaac and Jacob, Moses, Aaron and Miriam. Abraham, Isaac and Jacob we know because it is written in connection with them, in all, of all, all; Moses, Aaron and Miriam because it is written in connection with them [that they died] *By the mouth of the Lord* (Num 33:38; Deut 35:5).

This tradition finds broad expression in both early and late aggadot, the parallels indicating that it discusses the way in which Moses died rather seeks to deny that he did so:

> And Moses died there—Moses said to the Holy One, blessed be He: "Master of the Universe, because you have decreed death upon me, deliver me into the hands of the Angel of Death." The Holy One, blessed be He, said to him: "By your life, I shall take care of you and conceal you ..." The Holy One, blessed be He, said to the Angel of Death: "Go and bring Moses' soul." He went and searched throughout the earth and did not find it ... He went to human beings and said to them: "Have you seen Moses?" They said to him: "God knew his way and his place; He has stored him for life in the world to come." (*Mid. Tann.* 34:5; cf. *Sifre Deut.* 205)

This aggadic tradition regarding Moses' victory over the Angel of Death appears in a richer and more developed form in later midrashim, from *Deuteronomy Rabbah* through to medieval aggadot.[3] Despite the divergences between the early

---

[3] For the former, see *Deut. Rab.* Vezot habracha (Lieberman, p. 129); *Deut. Rab.* 11:10; *Tanh.* Zot

and late sources, however, none questions his death—a fact that also arises from Moses' request in one of the early texts: " Because you have decreed death upon me." Moses not being bold enough to question the decree, he wishes merely not to be delivered into the hand of the Angel of Death. A person being able to depart the world without delivering his soul to the Angel of Death, we must distinguish between the inevitability of his fate—bound up with the end of his life on earth—and the way in which he took his leave of the living.

This view of death without the intervention of the Angel of Death is also found in other talmudic sources—as, for example, in the well-known story of R. Joshua b. Levi who cunningly disarmed the Angel of Death of his weapon and tricked him by jumping into paradise (*b. Ket.* 77b).[4] Even the tradition to which we referred to above regarding the six who were not governed by the Angel of Death does not dispute their death, for they include figures whose burial place is well known.[5] The realistic clarification in *Sifre Deut.* 357 in relation to the Angel of Death is also relevant here: "When God takes the soul of the righteous, He takes it with gentleness, but when He takes the souls of the wicked, He does so through merciless and cruel angels, so that they would drag their souls along" (Hammer, 1987: 381). Here, the homilist appears to hold that death not via the Angel of Death is the regular form of death, merely without suffering.

In contrast to and alongside this tradition we find another, slightly more clandestine, in rabbinic literature that holds that Moses did not in fact die at all. The buds of this view are already evident in the early midrashic elucidation of the notation that at his death לא נס לחה ("his vigor had not abated") (Deut 34:7): "R. Eliezer ben Jacob says: Read not *nor his natural force abated* but 'even now his natural force is still not abated,' for if anyone should touch the flesh of Moses, its natural force would spring out in all directions" (Hammer, 1987: 382).[6] It finds even more explicit and unambiguous form in a *baraita* in *b. Sotah.* 13b:

---

habracha 3; for the latter, see the two versions of the midrash on Moses' death in *Beit Hamidrash*—*Midrash petirat mosheh rabbeinu* (Jellenik, 1:115–129 and 6:71–78); *Drash liftirat mosheh rabbeinu* (Eisenstein, *Otzar Midrashim*, 2:372–383). For a comprehensive survey and analysis of the evolution of this tradition, see Kushelevsky (1995, 2004–2013). Although an earlier version occurs in an appendix to *Pesiqta Rab Kahana* (Mandelbaum, Appendix 1: 444 448), as the editor himself observes (444 n. 1), this was added to the work at a later stage.

4 The traumatic notion of the encounter with the Angel of Death appears to be associated with the amoraic identification of the latter with Satan.

5 Jacob is the exception to this rule, of course, of whom it is explicitly said that "Jacob our patriarch is not dead" (*b. Ta'an.* 5b).

6 Cf. also Rashi's comment on Deut 34:7.

It has been taught: R. Eliezer the Elder said: Over an area of twelve *mil* square, corresponding to that of the camp of Israel, a *Bath Kol* made the proclamation, "So Moses died there," the great Sage of Israel. Others declare that Moses never died; it is written here, "So Moses died there," and elsewhere it is written: *And he was there with the Lord* (Exod 34:28). As in the latter passage it means standing and ministering, so also in the former it means standing and ministering.[7]

The definitive nature of this statement suggests a polemical background. Despite the pathos of the pronouncement, a counterview is immediately adduced that maintains that Moses did not die. Here, it is not only the special circumstances under which Moses' soul departs that are under discussion but the nature of life after death. In other words, Moses is presented as immortal. We find a similar stance in an anonymous *piyyut* published by Brodie, in which the author seeks to console Moses as he laments over his approaching death, revealing to him that, in contrast to other mortals, he will not be brought down to the grave:

> The man who dies, the splendour of his face changes / But your radiance will not change
> The man who dies, the Angel of Death terrifies him / But the Angel of Death will not terrify you
> The man who dies goes to his grave / But you will ascend to the Garden of Eden, so why do you mourn? (1936: 18)

Philo, who discusses Moses' life at length, makes no reference to the idea that he did not die at all, it also being absent from Pseudo-Philo (*LAB* 19.14–16), suggesting that it held no place in these authors' hellenistic spirituality. It is also possible, however, that the claim that Moses died arose in a polemical context, as part of attempts to counter the christological strains linked to the notion of the dead-alive prophet.[8] While this view has scriptural backing, however, the denial that Moses died both contradicts an explicit biblical verse and R. Eliezer the Elder's opinion. What prompted such an unusual and contentious assertion?

Part of the answer may lie in the fact that Moses' stature was conducive to the view that he could not have suffered the same fate as ordinary mortals. Thus, for example, the medieval kabbalist-exegete Bachya b. Asher asserts: "Many people ask the question how it was possible that someone of the stature of Moses who became the instrument of giving the Torah to the people of Israel died, whereas Elijah and Enoch, both people of less stature, did not die?" (Munk,

---

[7] Cf. the parallels in *Sifre Deut.* 357; *Midrash Hagadol* to Deut 34:5 (p. 763); *Midrash Leqach Tov* 67b. The latter contains the elucidation: "This teaches that the righteous do not die." See Loewenstamm (1972: 200).
[8] For Josephus' view, see below.

1998: 2863 [on Deut 34:5]).⁹ A late medieval midrash similarly describes Moses as being transformed into an angel on high in precisely in the same fashion as Enoch and Elijah's ascent was perceived in the early *hekhalot* literature: "And afterwards [Metatron] stood up and changed his flesh into flames of fire and his eyes into the wheels of the chariot, and his power into the power of the angels, and his tongue into a tongue of fire and he lifted Moses up to heaven."¹⁰ Is this in fact what the Sages intended in alleging that "Moses did not die"? In the following, I shall analyse this tradition in the *Zohar* and suggest another solution to the problem.

"Death by a kiss"

In a number of passages in rabbinic corpus we find Moses' death depicted as "by a kiss" (Fishbane (1994: 16–19). Derived from the biblical specification that he died 'על פי ה (lit.: by God's mouth), this idea first appear in *Midrash Tannaim* on Deuteronomy (34:5) and *b. B. Bat.* 17a (cf. also *b. Mo'ed Qat.* 28a). The number of midrashic/talmudic references to this notion suggest that it relates to a form of death rather than a type of after-death existence. *Midrash Tannaim*, for example, understands the phrase "by God's mouth" to mean that he did not die by the mouth of the Angel of Death.¹¹ Other allusions to the idea, unassociated with Moses' death, substantiate this supposition. On one occasion, it appears as the easiest form of death in a list of various types (*b. Ber.* 8a). Elsewhere, the one who reaches old age is said to die by a kiss (*b. Mo'ed Qat.* 28a). It is thus a well-known and common occurrence rather than an unusual and exceptional fate.

Although R. Levi b. Abraham, a thirteenth-century Provençal rationalist commentator, maintains "death by a kiss" signifies a death "without sickness

---

9 *Midrash ke-tapuach be'etzei baya'ar* (Wertheimer, *Batei Midrashot* 1: 277). For the relationship between this description and that of Enoch's ascent in the *hekhalot* literature, see the editor's note there (ג). Wertheimer (p. 274) dates this midrash to the end of the fourteenth or beginning of the fifteenth century. Haberman (1947: 96), on the other hand, believes it to belong to ca. the eleventh century. For Enoch's ascension in the *hekhalot* literature, see above, chapter 6.
10 A midrashic tradition according to which Moses was an angel, his name before being taken out of the Nile being Malachia, can be traced back to the Qumran scrolls: see Kister (2012: 84–88). For Moses' divine stature, see ibid (88 n. 81).
11 The context in *b. B. Bat.* 17a also indicates that the "death by a kiss" is a form of death that does not involve the Angel of Death.

or expiration ... only a natural death after the essential vigor fades away" (2004: 110), the greatest of all the medieval rationalists, Maimonides, regards it as the transfer to another form of spiritual existence.[12] He finds support for this view in that "Moses did not die": "This was his death thus in relation to us, being taken from us, but his life in transcending it, as Moses our master said, that he did not die but ascended and ministers in the heavens" (*Commentary on the Mishna*, Preface 3). He further explicates the idea in one of the final chapters of the *Guide for the Perplexed*:

> [The Sages], *may their memory be blessed*, mention the occurrence of this type of death, which in true reality is salvation from death, only with respect to *Moses, Aaron,* and *Miriam*. The other prophets and men of excellence are beneath this degree; but it holds good for all of them that the apprehension of their intellects becomes stronger at the separation, just as it is said: *And they righteousness shall go before thee; the glory of the LORD shall be at thy rear* (Isa 58: 8). After having reached this condition of enduring permanence that intellect remains in one and the same state, the impediment that sometimes veiled it having been removed. (3:51).

In typical fashion, Maimonides understands the dictum that Moses did not die to signify the Aristotelian idea of the existence of the soul after death and the cleaving to the Active Intellect.[13] Gersonides follows the same path, perceiving the fact that Moses' burial place is unknown to allude to his attainment of "eternal life—after separation from the body—that cannot be obtained by men" (1967 [on Deut 34:5]).

This view of the "death by a kiss" as mystical union with the godhead also occurs in the *Zohar*, philosophy and Kabbalah herein finding common ground.[14] Thus, for example, it states that everyone who engages in Torah-study dies by a kiss: "This is the kiss that is the soul's cleaving to the Root" (1:168a).[15] This also appears to be the death experienced by some of the Companions according to the Idra stories in the *Zohar*, which mark the peak of the zoharic framing plot that concludes with the "cleaving of the soul" and ecstatic transcendence. With respect to Moses' death, however, the traditional explanation of this idea

---

12 In the continuation (p. 327), R. Levi relates to the tradition according to which Moses did not die, remarking that: "So people say of their soul that it is 'bound in the bundle of life'" (cf. 1 Sam 25:29).
13 See Schwartz's comments on this passage and its sources (2002: 665–666 nn. 91, 87–101).
14 For the mystical character of the death by a kiss in the *Guide*, see Liebes (1993d: 51 n. 146)
15 Cf. R. Azriel (1945: 40). Recanati (2003: 37d) repeats R. Azriel's statement, adding: "And that's [the term of] 'death by a kiss'... because his soul then cleaves to the Shekhina." For death by a kiss in the *Zohar*, see Liebes (1993d: 51–53).

does not suffice the *Zohar*, which offers its own unique understanding of this notion, virtually unparalleled in other medieval texts.

Moses' death in the *Zohar*

Like the classical midrash, the *Zohar* generally gives expression to diverse and varied views and approaches. We thus find in it the notion that Moses did in fact die, merely being delivered from the impurity of the Angel of Death.[16] In most of the sources in the *Zohar*, and the later strata—*Raya Mehemna* and *Tiqunei Zohar*—in particular, however, contain the view that Moses did not die at all. Thus, for example, 1:53a states that death came into the world by virtue of the serpent's grasping of the moon. The damage thereby caused to the latter brought death upon all human beings under its jurisdiction—with the exception of Moses who, being patterned on the sun, governed the moon and was not subject to death: "His death was on another, upper side." This abstruse statement is elucidated by another passage:

> ... at the moment when the blessed Holy One desired to raise him to the supernal holy academy and to conceal him from humanity ... R. Shim'on aid, "Moses did not die." Now, you might say, "But look at what is written: *Moses died there* (Deuteronomy 34:5)! Well, the righteous are always referred to as dying, but what is death? From our perspective it is called so. For it has been taught: Rabbi Shim'on said that one who has attained perfection, upon whom holy faith depends, is independent of death and does not die. (*Zohar*, 2:174a)

Moses' fate can only nominally be called "death," in fact being something completely different. Although in human eyes, he appeared to have died in reality he did not. Not only are the affinities between this passage and Maimonides' perception of Moses' death readily discernible but the way in which the *Zohar* interprets the verse "And Moses died there"—"From our perspective it is called so"—also recalls the Rambam's statement in his commentary on the Mishna: "This was his death thus in relation to us, being taken from us; but it was his life in transcending it, as Moses our master said, that he did not die but ascended and ministers in the heavens." Here, the *Zohar* appears to have been influenced by Maimonides' philosophical-mystical approach.

Elsewhere, Moses' death is given another, far sharper, interpretation that suggests that the eternal existence of his soul is of significant practical import. In this context, the assertion that "Moses did not die" denotes the fact that he is

---

16 Cf. *Zohar*, 1:131b. For a slightly different direction, cf. 2:157a.

actively involved in human affairs, thus playing a central role in human existence. Explicating Gen 6:3 ("My spirit shall not abide in mortals forever"), this passage runs as follows:

> R. El'azar said, בשגם (*be-shaggam*) *Since too*—this is משה (*Mosheh*), Moses, who illumines the moon, by whose energy humanity endures for many days in the world. *Let his days be a hundred and twenty years* (Genesis 6:3), alluding to Moses, through whom Torah was given and who thereby poured life lavishly for humanity from that Tree of Life. So it would have been, had Israel not sinned, as is written: חרות *harut*, *engraved, on the tablets* (Exodus 32:16)—חרות (*herut*), freedom, from the Angel of Death, for the Tree of Life extended to those below. So, בשגם (*be-shaggam*), *since* [*he,*] *too, is flesh*, the event transpires: the spirit of life is lavishly poured. בשגם (*be-shaggam*), *Since, too*—embraced below and above. So we have learned: "Moses did not die, but was rather gathered from the world and illumines the moon." For even when the sun is gathered from the world, it does not die but illumines the moon. So too, Moses. (*Zohar*, 1:37b–38a)

According to a prevalent early exegetical tradition (supported by *gematriya*), the obscure term בשגם alludes to Moses.[17] In the kabbalistic symbolic system, Moses represent *Tiferet*, this explaining the adducing of the sun, the Tree of Life, and the (Written) Torah here, all of which are also prominent symbols of this *sefira*. Within the historical drama of the giving of the Torah on Mount Sinai, the homilist gives Moses the role of giving life and Torah to human beings. Although when Israel sinned—presumably with the Golden Calf—they lost the right to complete freedom from the Angel of Death and eternal life, the Tree of Life, of whose lower branches they had already taken hold, continued to imprint its stamp on their lengthy lifespan. According to this homily, even before he became immortal Moses was the father of immortality on earth because he gave the "upper" Tree of Life its grasp of the "lower." This life allowing the world to exist, his death is inconceivable. He thus did not actually die but was merely gathered from the world—in precisely the same way as the sun sets on the horizon but does not cease to exist, continuing to shed its rays indirectly via the moon.[18] The determination that Moses did not die is therefore derived here

---

[17] Cf. *b. Hul.* 139b; *Gen. Rab.* 26:6; et al.
[18] Elsewhere, the *Zohar* addresses the subject of Moses' death via Deut 31:16: "This is the mystery of *Soon you will lie down with your ancestors*—even though you will be gathered you will continue to illumine the moon" (3:181b). This truncated verse had already been explicated by the Sages, who found in it an allusion to the resurrection of the dead: see *b. Sanh.* 90b.

from the recognition that his mythical role has not ceased and will not do so until the end of time.[19]

The fact that the sun sets only to return the next day suggests that the *Zohar* may be attributing a future messianic role to Moses here. This conjecture is not easy to substantiate. On the one hand, as Maimonides pointed out in the introduction to the *Guide* (p. 14), caution must be taken with "stretching" a parable beyond its primary meaning. On the other, the idea that Moses will play a role in the future redemption is not surprising in light of the allusion to this idea in various places in the *Zohar*, medieval kabbalistic writings, and rabbinic literature (Goldreich, 1994: 460–467; Green, 1979: 124–125). This function is in fact explicitly and emphatically adduced in the later zoharic strata, wherein his immortality is of great import. Thus, for example, a passage printed within the book but identified as *Tiqunei Zohar* states:

> He again opened and said: *God made the wild animals of the earth of every kind, and the cattle of every kind, and everything that creeps upon the ground of every kind* (Gen 1:25). Woe to mankind, who are always be hardhearted and unseeing, unable to see or know the secrets of the Torah. For the beasts of the field and the birds of the air are *amei ha-aretz* and even though they had living breath in them none was a fit helpmate for the Shekhina. The Shekhina was in exile, but not for Moses who was with them, for every time the Shekhina was exiled he went with it ... for this reason Moses did not die and is called a "man." And because of him it is said that in the final exile *there was not found a helper as his partner* (Gen 2:20). But all were כנגדו (*ke-negdo*), *as against him*. Thus it is said of the middle pillar: *for the man there was not found a helper*—who will bring his Shekhina out of exile.

Here, it is clear that Moses did not die because his role is to serve as the Shekhina's "helpmeet" throughout its exile and deliver it from exile into the time of its deliverance. The homilist also alludes to *Tiferet*, of whom Moses is the most prominent symbol in the kabbalistic system. As per its wont, however, the *Zohar* (whether in its early or late strata) makes no distinction between the symbolic and the real are intertwined, Moses—the "middle pillar"—thus being decreed to be immortal so that he could deliver the Shekhina from its eschatological exile.

When we examine the parable of the sun from a messianic perspective, it reveals itself to contain an even more radical statement in relation to Moses' messianic role: he lavishly pours out not only life but Torah itself. Can we under-

---

[19] The link between Moses' life and death as a human being and his mythical role, together with the attribution of his immortality to his sefiric status, are prominent examples of the features of Jewish myth (Liebes, 1995).

stand Moses' messianic flourishing as the renewed emanation of the Torah? The answer to this question appears to lie in the text itself, which belongs to the central of section of the *Zohar* and discusses Joshua's appointment on the eve of Moses' departure:

> Then Moses summoned Joshua (Deut 31:7) ... But the verse says: *you will lie down with your ancestors* (ibid, 16). The blessed Holy One said to Moses: Although you will lie down with your ancestors, you will always illumine the moon, just as the sun, although it sets, does so only to illumine the moon, and then illumines the moon when it sets. So *you will lie down*—to illumine, and that's *I will commission him* (ibid, 14). Then Joshua attached himself to illumine. For this reason it is written: *You will lie down with your ancestors* and *charge Joshua* (Deut 3:28)—to illumine. (*Zohar*, 3:284a)

Here, we encounter some of the more obscure aspects of the parable of the sun and moon. The moon, which receives light from sun, is none other than Joshua bin Nun.[20] According to the homilist, the instruction to "charge Joshua" relates not to his testament on his deathbed but to the period after it—i.e., Moses' perpetual illumination to his successor and the impartation of his power to him. Hereby, the identification of the "illumination"—which is also the "charge"—with the Torah becomes virtually self-evident.[21]

This dictum is elaborated in the *Raya Mehemna* in a homily that pushes the parable to radical lengths with respect to the status of the Torah after Moses' death and the world to come. As per its *Raya Mehemna*'s literary wont, the reference to Moses is formulated in the second person and put into the mouth of R. Shimon bar Johai, the "holy lamp":

> And this is *and by his bruises we are healed* (Isa 53:5)—in his joining with us in the exile are we healed, for you are like the sun that illumines even though it sets at night, illumining by all the stars and constellations. Thus you illumine through all the halakhists and kabbalists and they draw from you in secret as from a spring that waters the trees under their roots in secret until its waters burst out in the open, as is written: *Should your springs be scattered abroad* (Prov 5:16). You are just like that, as the sun that travels through the winter under springs and when the redemption arrives you will be like the sun that rises in the summer from springs that are cool with Compassion, and when you are under them they are warm with Judgment. (*Zohar*, 208a [*Raya Mehemna*])

---

20 This identification is also indicated in several other places in the *Zohar:* cf. 3:156b–157a.
21 The novelty of this idea is indicated by Isaiah Horowitz who rejects (!) the zoharic exegesis on the grounds that: "We only accept the literal meaning" (2000: 5, vavei ha-amudim 24, p. 174).

Here, the *Zohar* mixes the parable of the sun and moon with other images. After his death, Moses resembles the setting sun that illumines by night via the moon, a spring that secretly waters the trees, and the sun that warms the spring under the ground.[22] This passage makes the nature of the influence very clear: Moses sheds abroad the light of his Torah. As Liebes (2007b: 275) has demonstrated, the moon and stars in this parable are the "halakhists and kabbalists" (including R. Shimon bar Johai himself, who appears to be the moon), all of whom illumine through their teaching on the strength of Moses' secret illumination of them. This view of Moses' perpetual illumination and inspiration of the Torah scholars is exemplified in others passages in the *Raya Mehemna* and *Tiqunei Zohar*.[23] Some of these even evince traces of the parable of the sun and moon—such as R. Shimon's comment about Moses hiding in the rock: "Something of him spread over sixty myriads of Israel and he illumines them with his Torah like the sun which is covered at night and illumines all the stars and constellations—and night is none other than exile" (*Zohar*, 3:238b [*Raya Mehemna*]).[24]

On occasion, the author of *Raya Mehemna* chooses to convey the idea and its meaning more directly. Thus, for example, in 3:256a, R. Shimon bar Johai hears supernal voices revealing to him that the Raya Mehemna illumines through him, so that he, via the Companions, illumines all the scholars of the generation. A similar statement also occurs—in more depth and detail—in R. Moses de León's responsa:

> Likewise Moses is the praise, who died outside the land and comes to illumine the moon, because the sun in setting illumines by it. And this is the secret of Moses' face as the face of the sun and Joshua's face as the face of the moon ... If so, according to this the last sages and elders who lived in the days of Joshua, like the value of those who lived in the days of Moses, were minor in their prophecy and teaching and compared to the rest of the minor stars in their light and activity less than the seven constellations. Just so the last of the last, our generation now, are less in their knowledge and prophecy because prophecy

---

22 The *Zohar* frequently associates light and water, apparently on the basis of the root נה"ר common to both semantic fields.

23 Cf. *Zohar*, 3:232a (*Raya Mehemna*), which says of Moses that "The blessed Holy One and Shekhina speak through his mouth and write by his hand these secrets, the like of which have not been heard since the giving of the Torah on Sinai until today." Cf. also *Zohar*, 3:256a (*Raya Mehemna*), in which it is said to R. Shimon and of him that "The faithful shepherd illumines through you." Elsewhere (*Zohar*, 3:153b [*Raya Mehemna*]), the author states that Moses is the source of all secrets, his humility ("more so than anyone else on the face of the earth," as the Torah informs us [Num 12:3]), precluding him from holding the good for himself, however, so that he delivers and reveals all the secrets through R. Shimon and other tannaim and amoraim.

24 Cf. *Zohar*, 3216a–b [*Raya Mehemna*]; *Tiqunei Zohar*, 69, 112a (see below).

has ceased from them. But with respect to the Torah in which they engage, its light shines in their minds and is almost a spark of prophecy. And this is as our Sages of blessed memory said: "A wise man is even superior to a prophet" [b. B. Bat. 12a]. (1993: 54–55)

The light of the Torah—namely, Moses' Torah—shines in the minds of those who study it, kindling a spark that is tantamount to prophecy.[25] This light is, of course, that of the sun, of Moses the man, who despite his sun having set, continues to illumine scholars throughout the generations with the light of his teaching, awakening in them virtually prophetic new interpretations. Although the illumination comes from intellectual engagement in Moses' Torah rather than from Moses himself, this fact does not blur the sharp outlines of the common religious tendency.[26] As in the *Zohar*, R. Moses promotes the radical view that the Torah is a secret living entity that in each generations sends out its rays, breaking into the world as new interpretations scholars discover through its light.

This idea, according to which all the innovations that have been made since the days of Moses through the exile are none other than dim and slender manifestations of Moses' prophetic spirit, immediately brings the story of Moses in R. Akiba's study hall to mind:

> Rab Judah said in the name of Rab, When Moses ascended on high he found the Holy One, blessed be He, engaged in affixing coronets to the letters. Said Moses, "Lord of the Universe, Who stays Thy hand? He answered, "There will arise a man, at the end of many generations, Akiba b. Joseph by name, who will expound upon each tittle heaps and heaps of laws." "Lord of the Universe," said Moses, "permit me to see him." He replied, "Turn thee round." Moses went and sat down behind eight rows [and listened to the discourse upon the law]. Not being able to follow their arguments he was ill at ease, but when they came a certain subject and the disciples said to their master "Whence do you know it?" and the latter replied "It is a law given unto Moses at Sinai" he was comforted. (b. Men. 29b)[27]

---

[25] The link between Moses' light and prophecy is made is explicit in *Tiqunei Zohar*, 18, 31b, where Moses is said to be like the sun whose rising produces the prophets' prophecy via its illumination and whose setting blocks it.

[26] A similar idea may be alluded to in *Tiqunei Zohar*, 69, 112a, where it is said that something of Moses is spread abroad into every righteous and wise person who engages in Torah-study. The disparity between this version and that cited above from the *Raya Mehemna* may be explained in terms of development. The moderate statement in the *Responsa* reflects an earlier stage in the evolution of the idea, according to which the spring that gives rise to the Torah innovations is the Torah itself and its study. In my opinion, however, R. Moses' version constitutes a later reduction of the radical version in the *Raya Mehemna*.

[27] For other aspects of the Jewish myth reflected in this midrash, see Liebes (1993a: 1–2).

Although the *Raya Mehemna* conveys the talmudic notion itself, it also seeks to expose the talmudic paradox.²⁸ All of R. Akiba's teaching is "law given to Moses at Sinai," the *Zohar* maintains, because everything derives from his spirit, which shines through his teaching and renews it through the scholars' overt activity. Hereby, Moses never ceases to deliver his Torah. The latter being none other than abundance perpetually emanated by Moses that takes form in the study halls in new interpretations and the illumination of those who shine therein, Moses' death is inconceivable. This view is also consistent with the *Zohar*'s attitude towards new interpretations and their value. As Liebes has evinced (2007b: 274–275), the reference here is not only to new kabbalistic interpretations but also to halakhic rulings.

The messianic context of this saying is very clear: "Thus you illumine through all the halakhists and kabbalists and they draw from you in secret as from a spring that waters the trees under their roots in secret until its waters burst out in the open." Even if now, during the exile, Moses' work is clandestine, it will eventually become overt, the light of the sun then becoming like the light of the seven days of creation. In this framework, Moses' light can be none other than a new, higher, and fuller manifestation of the Torah. All the new interpretations during this time will be absorbed and assimilated into the overflowing spring that will burst forth from the fountain. This brief but significant comment reveals the anarchic potential buried in the idea of Moses' immortality, the overt dimension of the Torah being understood as a slender and indirect ray of the great light to come that is the true and complete revelation of Moses' Torah. This notion is elaborated on in detail in *Tiqunei Zohar* 69:

> Said R. Shim'on: ... Happy is the generation in which this is revealed, for all this will be renewed by Moses at the end of days in the final generation in order to fulfil the verse *What has been is what will be* (Qoh 1:9) ... of whom it is said *A generation goes, and a generation comes* (ibid, 4). And something of him spreads through every generation in every righteous and wise person who engages in the Torah—up to sixty myriads—in order to repair all the damage done to them.

All the new interpretations are due to be made by Moses in the eschaton, up until that point something of him spreading and illumining through his Torah every righteous and wise man who preoccupies himself with Torah-study. Moses thus does not die at all because "What has been is what will be"— the

---

28 This passage appears to be an example of what Liebes (ibid) refers to as the relationship between talmudic and zoharic myth, the *Zohar*, in its attempt to simplify the poetic expression, in fact uprooting it.

first letters of this phrase alluding to his name: מה שיהיה הוא שיהיה. His activities must continue because his task is for "a thousand generations."

This idea is associated with the "Torah of the Tree of Life" that contains nothing permitted or prohibited that is said in the *Tiqunei Zohar* to be destined to replace the Torah of this world based on the Tree of Knowledge. Although the question of whether the Torah of this world will be completely abolished, as Scholem (1976a: 68–71) maintains, thus regarding it as antinomian, or will merely represent the ontological or epistemological eradication of evil, as Gottlieb (1976: 545–550) and Liebes (2007b: 270–279) argue is beyond our current brief, the *Raya Mehemna*'s approach appears very moderate and cautious in comparison.[29] Here, the dichotomy between the two Torahs—in this world and the one to come—is softened and transformed into an actual relationship between the light of the moon and stars and that of the sun. The moon's light possesses an independent status that allows a relative and partial association, thereby illuminating something of the future in the present.[30] Rather than a revolutionary vision this constitutes a developing consciousness anchored in a sort of periodic natural law of setting and rising. It thus seems closer to the idea found in the body of the *Zohar* regarding the "innermost soul of the Torah"—the innermost of the four aspects of the Torah (clothing, body, soul, and innermost soul). This is the inner core of the overt Torah, which at present is oblique and abstruse even to the scholars who serve the supernal king and will only be fully revealed in the future (*Zohar*, 3:152a).

The relationship between the *Zohar* and the early aggada

What are the roots of the notion that Moses continues to emanate his Torah after his death? Did it emerge in kabbalistic thought *ex nihilo* or can its origins be identified in earlier writings? Examination of the zoharic tradition in fact helps to shed light on the enigmatic talmudic tradition regarding Moses' death. This contains two views, the first—delivered in the name of R. Eliezer the Elder that a *Bat Kol* proclaimed "Moses died there" being countered by the second, according to which "Others declare that Moses never died." This rests on a *gezera shava* that applies the use of the word "there" in Exod 34:28 to its

---

29 For the former view, see also Tishby and Lachower (2:1103 n. 177).
30 For a similar link in relation to the various strata of the Torah, see Yisraeli (2005: 216–217). The well-known parable of the maiden in the palace evinces that the three lower levels of the Torah—the *pshat*, *drash*, and *remez*—all reflect the *sod* in diverse degrees, only differing from one another in the extent to which the latter can be inferred from them.

occurrence in Exod 34:5: just as in the former verse Moses was alive and serving God, so too he must be in our verse.

The homily further associates two Moses' ascent of Mount Sinai to receive the Torah and deliver it to Israel with his ascent of Mount Nebo prior to his death (Deut 34:1). On each ascent, Moses found himself in God's presence, "being with" Him on the first and dying 'על פי ה' on the second. Both occasions also involved the loss of a leader, the people only making the golden calf because "the man who brought us up out of the land of Egypt, we do not know what has become of him" (Exod 32:1) and Moses handing over the reins to Joshua because he was not allowed to enter the land with the people. In addition to the *gezerah shava*, the anonymous Sages who hold that Moses did not die thus also find substantive associations between the two verses related to Moses' life.[31] Just as Moses went up to "stand and serve" on Mount Sinai so also did on Mount Nebo. The enigmatic expression עומד ומשמש in relation to the latter event is clarified by the first occasion: Moses ascended Mount Sinai in order to receive the Torah and teach it to the people, not dying there despite not eating and drinking for forty days and nights. We may thus infer that since his ascent of Mount Nebo, he has continually been engaged in receiving the Torah from heaven in order to deliver it to the people.[32] The *Zohar* thus transpires to correctly interpret the original meaning of the talmudic dictum, expanding, exposing, and developing the meaning enfolded in it regarding the claim that Moses did not die.[33]

This exposition explains why R. Eliezer the Elder so vehemently resisted the view that Moses did not die but is still alive and active, the need to emphasize

---

31 The analogy between Moses' ascent of Mount Nebo and Mount Sinai is also found in *Tg. Ps.-Jon.* to Deut 32:49, which asserts that when Moses was commanded to ascend the former he "thought to himself 'Perhaps this ascent will be similar to the ascent of Mt. Sinai.' Therefore he said, 'Let me go and sanctify the people [like then, at the beginning].'"

32 *Inter alia*, rabbinic literature itself employs the root שמ"ש in the sense of a student learning Torah from his master: cf. *t. Sotah* 14:9; *y. Šhab.* 13, 3, 12a; *b. Hul.* 54a; et al. The parallel in *Sifre Deut.* 357 replaces the phrase with עומד ומשרת—which carries the same meaning, undoubtedly being influenced by the title משרת משה (Moses' assistant/servant) given to Joshua in Num 11:28 and Josh 1:1—Joshua of course being Moses' outstanding "student." Irrespective of the formula, the fact that the focus lies on Moses' activity upon the mountain here indicates that Torah-study is meant: see Aptowitzer (1931), who understands Moses' "ministering" as a priestly officiating in the heavenly temple. This exegesis is untenable, however, both because no other sources speak of Moses undertaking such a task (apart from the Samaritan *Tevat Marqa*: see ibid: 265–266 n. 1 on p. 266) and because the idea is adduced in the homily as though self-evident and in no need of any support.

33 The verb משמש applied to Moses here may have raised dual associations in the zoharic homilist's mind—the sun and the *shamash*, a rabbinic designation for the phallus. These two symbols are closely associated in the *Zohar* with Moses' teaching—*Tiferet*.

the fact that Moses' death is a well-known fact throughout Israel highlighting the radical nature of the counter-claim.[34] The discussion of the biographical question of whether Moses died or not thus forms the vehicle for a fierce polemical dispute over the status of the Torah after Moses' lifetime. The allegation that Moses did not die in effect undercuts both his prophecy and the Torah by asserting that the giving of the Torah is an ongoing process that will not end until the eschaton, when the sun will be revealed in all its glory. Then and only then will its revelation be full and unmediated. Although R. Eliezer the Elder's objection to this idea fits his status as a halakhic conservative opposed to Torah innovations — "I have never in my life said a thing which I did not hear from my teachers" (*b. Sukka* 28a)—it appears to derive primarily from a profound apprehension of its anarchistic and christological overtones. If the Torah has not yet been delivered in its final and complete version, it may be regarded as conditional rather than absolute, dependent upon the illumination of the spirit of the sages in every generation.[35]

This concern is evident already in *Deuteronomy Rabbah*: "*For this commandment ... it is not in heaven* (Deut 30:11). Moses said to Israel: 'Do not say: 'Another Moses will arise and bring us another Torah from heaven'; I therefore warn you, *It is not in heaven*, that is to say, no part of it has remained in heaven" (8:6). Although Urbach (1956: 308) maintains this homily was "directed against Messianic concepts that were current among the Rabbis, and to which the homilist was opposed," he adduces no explicit support for the existence of such an outlook. The above discussion indicates that it is the view propounded by the "some say" in the tannaitic dictum, perhaps already reflecting a sophisticated response to

---

34 In the Babylonian Talmud, R. Eliezer's statement is adduced prior to that which rejects the idea that Moses died. R. Eliezer's dictum suggesting a polemic as we noted above, however, the order in which the *baraita* is arranged and the citing of R. Eliezer's words before that of the anonymous counter view indicates that the passage reflects the outlook of the *baraita*'s author.
35 Cf. ibid, 27b; *b. Yoma* 66b. *b. Ber.* 27b cites the harsh dictum that "One who says something which he has not heard from his master causes the Divine Presence to depart from Israel." R. Eliezer in fact refrains from giving a halakhic ruling on several occasions on the grounds that "I did not hear it": cf. *m. Neg.* 9:3, 11:7. Elsewhere, it is stated : "Rabban Johanan ben Zakkai said to Eliezer: Expound to us something from the teachings of the Torah. He answered: I will tell you a parable. What am I like? I am like a well which cannot give forth more water than one put in it." To this Rabban Johanan replied: " I will tell you a parable. To what can this man be likened? To a well which bubbles up and produces water of itself. Similarly, you can expound more teachings of the Torah than were spoken to Moses on Sinai" (*'Abot R. Nat.* B 2:13) (cf. *m. 'Abot* 2:8: "Eliezer b. Hyrcanus is a plastered cistern, which does not lose a drop"). For R. Eliezer's conservatism, due to his possible belonging to Beit Shammai, see Yisraeli (2001: 275–277). For his figure and teaching in general, see Gilat (1968).

counter claims: "If we are not to expect 'another Moses,' then we may say that the historical Moses who gave the Torah in its essence never died but continued and still continues to deliver those parts of it that remain 'in heaven.'"

The declaration that Moses did not die in the Talmud and its echoes in the *Zohar* raise the question of the type of existence possessed Moses after his final ascent of Mount Nebo. Did he become an angel, like Enoch and Elijah? If he did not die, perhaps he was never buried? Although the *Zohar* does not appear to deny Moses' physical death and burial, it does regard his death as unusual and exceptional—"on another, upper side" (1:53a). Being gathered and ascended to the "supernal holy academy" where he was concealed from humanity (*Zohar*, 174a), what to human eyes—and thus what is recorded in the Torah—appeared to be his death was in fact merely the transfer of his spirit from the earthly to the mythical realm. Henceforth, he mediates between the supernal and lower worlds under the influence and emanation of the spirit of the Torah hidden away for the sages of future generations.

The rabbinic sources themselves do not demand such an interpretation, merely portraying Moses as standing and ministering on the mountain in his earthly, physical state. This conclusion also arises from a maximalist exegesis of the talmudic homily: just as Moses ascended to God on Mount Sinai in his physical, earthly body, so he ascended Mount Nebo in precisely the same fashion. While the Sages generally regard his first ascent not merely as an ascent to the top of the mountain but also as an ascent to the upper realms, he does not turn into an angel on the mountain or divest himself of his physical body because he must descend again in order to give the Torah to the people and continue to lead them in the wilderness.[36]

---

[36] There is thus no need to distinguish between the version in *b. Sotah* 13b ("standing and ministering") and that in *Sifre Deut.* 357 ("standing and ministering *above*"). Moses' ascent is depicted in this fashion in all the midrashic aggadot, in particular in those that open with the statement: "When Moses ascended on high." Here, Moses is portrayed as wandering amongst the ministering angels and debating with them: cf. *b. Šabb.* 88b–89a; *b. Men.* 29b; *Exod. Rab.* 28a; et al. The idea is articulated explicitly in *Deut. Rab.* 10:2: "God so created the world that the upper realms should be for the upper beings and the lower realms for the lower, for so Scripture says, *The heavens are the heavens of the Lord, but the earth hath He given to the children of men* (Ps 115:16). Moses came and changed the earthly into heavenly, and the heavenly into earthly, for so Scripture says, *And Moses went up unto God* (Exod 19:3), *And the Lord came down upon Mount Sinai* (ibid, 20) (cf. *Tanh. B.* Vayera 19). The view cited in the name of R. Jose in the *baraita* in *b. Sukka* 5a—according to which "Neither did the Shechinah ever descend to earth, nor did Moses or Elijah ever ascend to Heaven, as it is written, 'The heavens are the heavens of the Lord, but the earth hath He given to the sons of men' (Ps 115:6)—is therefore evidently non-representative: see also above, chapter 6. Moses' ascent to

All these facts indicate that Moses did not die any form of physical death nor was buried—this perhaps being the reason was his burial place is not known. Support for the conjecture may be adduced from Josephus, who states that

> Now as soon as they were come to the mountain called Abarim ... he dismissed the senate; and as he was going to embrace Eleazar and Joshua, and was still discoursing with them, a cloud stood over him on the sudden, and he disappeared in a certain valley, although he wrote in the holy books that he died, which was done out of fear, lest they should venture to say that, because of his extraordinary virtue, he went to God. (*Ant.* 4.8.48 [Whiston])[37]

According to this account, Moses "disappeared." What does Josephus mean by this, however? While he argues that the Torah's statement "Moses died" is a deliberate piece of "misinformation," he then proceeds to deny the possibility that Moses ascended to God (like Enoch and Elijah). We must thus assume that whether or not this passage reflects traces of the ancient midrashic tradition, it clearly propounds that Moses was gathered to a certain place, thus still being alive and on the mountain.

The midrashic homilies in the *Zohar* are thus linked to the early talmudic tradition not only formally but also substantively. This recognition both reveals the talmudic basis of the zoharic exposition and contributes to our understanding of the talmudic-midrashic texts. Although this insight must be applied carefully and critically, attention being paid to the divergent spiritual and religious contexts in which the ideas are cited and reworked, a direct thematic line can be drawn between the early aggadic tradition and its reworking in the *Zohar*.

Moses' light and soul in the *Tiqunim* literature

The idea that Moses delivers his Torah to the scholars in each generation even after his death as expressed in the parable and the sun and moon also recalls other early midrashic traditions, in particular that which maintains that Moses' face was "like the face of the sun" while Joshua's was "like the face of the moon": "*And thou shalt put of thy splendour upon him* (Num 27:20), but not *all* thy splendour. We thus learn: Moses' countenance was like that of the sun and Joshua's countenance was like that of the moon" (*Sifre Num.* 140). The homiletic context here suggests that the parable seeks to demonstrate the

---

heaven may in fact be alluded to in the notation that he "neither ate bread nor drank water" (Exod 34:28; cf. Deut 9:18).
[37] See Loewenstamm (1958: 149 n. 14). For the possible influence of Sophocles' *Oedipus* on Josephus here, see Feldman (1998: 174 n. 19, 395).

greater light Moses' prophecy gives than that of Joshua's. This is made explicit in the conclusion of the parallel in *b. B. Bat.* 75a, which adds the words: "Alas, for such shame! Alas for such reproach!"

As its wont, the *Zohar* "stretches" this tradition to the limit, perceiving the parable as not only comparing Moses and Joshua but also establishing the relationship between them. Just as the sun shines its rays on the moon, so the light of Joshua's Torah—which represents here all the sages of the generation after Moses—only contains what he received from Moses.[38] It is thus Moses who transmits the power of creativity to his disciple Joshua and the scholars in all subsequent generations.

The use of the image of the light to depict Moses' influence appears to be drawn from a midrashic interpretation of the extension of God's Spirit to the seventy elders in Num 11:17: "What was Moses like at that moment? To a candle placed on a lampstand from which many candles were lit, yet the light of the first did not diminish" (*Sifre Num.* 93).[39] The biblical source of the imagery undoubtedly derives from the well-known description of Moses' descent from Mount Sinai: "When Aaron and all the Israelites saw Moses, the skin of his face was shining, and they were afraid to come near him" (Exod 34:30). The early *Sifre Zuta* already places this verse in a cosmic context: "This teaches that the rays that went forth from Moses' face were like those that go forth from the sun" (27:2 [p. 321]). In light of the discussion above, if the biblical shining of Moses' face represents his special status on Mount Sinai the attribution of the same quality to Moses on Mount Nebo is hardly surprising. Additional—albeit relatively late—midrashic sources also assert, moreover, that the light of Moses' face was none other than the light of the Torah:

> Resh Lakish said: When Moses wrote the law he acquired a lustrous appearance. How [did this come about]? Resh Lakish said: The scroll that was given to Moses was made of a parchment of white fire, and was written upon with black fire and sealed with fire and was swathed with bands of fire, and whilst he was writing it he dried his pen on his hair, and as a result he acquired a lustrous appearance. (*Deut. Rab.* 3:12)

Moses' face was thus illumined by the Torah, this idea then being expanded to the transmission of the light to others and of Moses' splendour to Joshua on the eve of Moses' death, thence finding its way to the *Zohar* and its assertion of

---

38 This interpretation is also found in R. Moses de León's *Responsa* in a passage we have cited above. Here, too, it must be noted that while the expansive exegesis is not demanded it nonetheless possesses a firm base, the subject of the homily being the passing over of Moses' splendour to Joshua.
39 Cf. *Tg. Ps.-Jon.* to Num 11:25; *Num. Rab.* 15:19; *Zohar*, 2:86b, 3:220a; et al.

Moses' perpetual influence following his death—on Joshua and the scholars of Israel throughout the generations.

In the *Raya Mehemna* and *Tiqunim*—the latest stratum of the *Zohar*—this tradition appears in a slightly different version, namely, that something of Moses' soul spreads over the sixty myriads of Israel—i.e., over all of the people of Israel.⁴⁰ This can be learnt from one of the passages cited above, which interlinks the two traditions: "A halakhah Moses received on Mount Sinai—something of him spread over sixty myriads of Israel and illumines them with his Torah like the sun which is covered at night and illumines all the stars and constellations—and night is none other than exile" (*Zohar*, 3:238b [*Raya Mehemna*]). Here, the spreading of something of Moses' soul over the sixty myriads is associated with the illumination of the Torah via the parable of the sun. The motif of the illumination given by Moses' soul deriving from the tradition that Moses did not die in any form, it is thus related to the latter. This link leads to a better understanding of the nature of this "spreading," also allowing us to recognize that the Tiqunist view exemplified here regards Moses as a living celestial creature who exists and is active, perpetually influencing the scholars and the wise—or indeed all the people of Israel in a form of supernal inspiration that overrides human creativity.

This last passage also creates the impression that the notion of the spreading of something of Moses' soul in its original Tiqunist version is not identical with the idea of the reincarnation or transmigration of Moses' soul we find in Lurianic Kabbalah but is rather, as R. Moses Cordovero suggests in his *Pardes Rimonim*, "the presence of the light of his Torah, which shines upon the master of Torah and the sixty myriad who are suckled by them" (1962: 8, 22).⁴¹ In other words, Moses does not reveal himself in every generation in a specific figure or figures but is a real, living, and existing entity that perpetually emanates and influences via his Torah, light, or the spreading of something from his soul. The idea of his reincarnation or the transmigration of his soul we find in isolated places in the *Raya Mehemna* (cf. 3:216a–b, 273a) appears to constitute an "inner-*Tiqunist*" development and creative interpretation of the original notion, possibly also drawing from more distant fields.⁴² As Liebes (1993d: 29–30) notes in this regard, af-

---

40 This idea differs from and should not be confused with another—which also appears in the *Tiqunim*—according to which Moses' soul includes the sixty myriads of Israel.
41 See Scholem (1976a: 330 n. 54; 306 n. 54; 1997: 306 n. 53); Liebes (1977: 330; 1993d: 29–30); Zack (1995: 41).
42 Reincarnation as a general law—rather than a means of correcting specific offences—does not occur in the body of the *Zohar*, constituting one of the innovations introduced by the author of the *Tiqunei Zohar*: see Yisraeli (2005: 113–129 and the references cited therein).

finities exist between the zoharic passage and Averroes' theory of the Active Intellect embodied in every generation and the intellects of the scholarly.[43] The ancient talmudic idea of Moses' immortality nonetheless appears to lie at the basis of the later kabbalistic tradition, taking form in the zoharic kabbalistic idea of Moses' soul being "embodied" in the sages of Israel and the people as a whole. In its various guises, this notion undermines the spatial and temporal foundation of the revelation on Mount Sinai by transforming it into a continuous and ongoing process in which the concealed Torah gradually manifests itself up until the day of redemption—when it will reveal itself in its full glory.[44]

This insight into Moses' status in the *Tiqunei Zohar* and *Raya Mehemna* may aid in resolving one of the thorniest issues in relation to the literary framework of the *Raya Mehemna*—namely, whether Moses appears herein as a historical, concrete personage or as a celestial being. Does the encounter between the "faithful shepherd" and "holy lamp" take place on earth or in the heavenly academy and, most importantly of all, who is this Moses? Tishby and Lachower (1989: 1:155–156) have addressed some of these questions in a brief passage, Goldreich engaging in a more comprehensive discussion of them (1994: 477–481). Although according to the former most of the deeds described in the *Raya Mehemna* take place in the heavenly realms, Moses is portrayed as a flesh-and-blood personage in other dicta. Goldreich in contrast maintains that Moses is a real-life figure who works on earth. He, too, argues, however, that "It must be admitted that we also find descriptions in the *Tiqunei Zohar* whose explanation as the descent of the upper inhabitants to the Raya Mehemna living below is very difficult" (ibid: 479). We must therefore conclude that the rich world of the *Zohar* (and the *Tiqunim* literature in general) is aware of an intermediate sphere, populated by numerous figures—such as R. Hamnuna, Yenuka, or Saba de-Mishpatim—ranging from the concrete to the abstract on various levels of mythic tension.[45]

Even before the issue of Moses' nature can be determined, however, his literary role in the framing story must be addressed. This question is clarified by the view that regards Moses as a living and existing entity who spreads something of his soul to others and activates the kabbalists' creative spirit. Whatever the manner of its appearance, Moses' literary status embodies in the composition that bears his name that creative spirit illumined by the light of the concealed Moses. R. Shimon's discussions with the Raya Mehemna discursively-con-

---

[43] Liebes (1993d: 29–30) adduces various sources for the identification between the Active Intellect and Moses.
[44] For the relationship between the revelation of secrets in the zoharic *Idra* and the giving of the Torah on Sinai, see Liebes (1993d: 23); Zack (1995: 40).
[45] See Liebes (1995: 219–226); Yisraeli (2005: 72–76).

cretely reflect Moses' Torah revelation, the sun's illumination of the moon, the spreading of something from Moses' soul to R. Shimon, and the very innovative process. The concretization of the spirit and its personal embodiment in the zoharic literature are also evident in the *Saba de-Mishpatim*, where the Torah speaks through the mouth of the Saba to a pair of Companions, stimulating them to creativity (Yisraeli, 2005: 244–246). Like the *Saba de-Mishpatim*, here, too, the revelatory figures serve the *Zohar*'s *ars poetica* purposes, the conversations between R. Shimon and Moses reflecting via the concretization of Moses' spirit the creative process and introduction of new Torah interpretations.[46] From this perspective, the search for concrete historical personages is of only secondary importance, the rights to the name Moses belonging first and foremost to the historical Moses, who is also the mythic Moses who exists and lives because "Moses did not die."

Conclusion

The figure of Moses weaves a long path through from the ancient view according to which he did not die but is immortal, perpetually standing and ministering and receiving the Torah on Sinai, through to the zoharic presentation of him as spreading something of his soul to the scholars in every generation so that they can offer new interpretations of the Torah and finally to the post-zoharic idea in the *Tiqunei Zohar* in which he resumes a historical dimension, this time in a deliberate and self-conscious literary framework. The common denominator all these versions share is the rejection of the finality of the revelation of the Torah on Sinai and the "stretching" of this foundational event down through Jewish history until the last generation, when it will be fully revealed and give up all its secrets.

---

[46] In *Saba de-Mishpatim*, the artistic crafting, and primarily the striking harmony between the framing story and the homiletic contents, are far greater than the literary framework of the *Raya Mehemna*. This fact must be attributed, however, to the decline in the creative quality that occurs in the transition from the early zoharic literature to the *Tiqunim* literature.

Chapter 15:
Elijah the Zealot

Having examined the way in which the *Zohar* understands Elijah's—and Enoch's—ascent into heaven in Chapter 6, here I shall address another, more human, aspect of Elijah, namely, his zeal. As per my wont, I shall focus on the zoharic aggadic perspective.

Who is Elijah and what role has he played in Jewish literature down the ages? Very few of the biblical protagonists have gained such a prominent place in Jewish thought as Elijah the Tishbite. In contrast to such figures as the patriarchs, Moses, and David, however, Elijah's status as a historical and ahistorical figure alike is not self-evident, not being a function of his biblical biography or role in Israelite history. His extra-biblical personage far exceeds what we are told of him in the book of Kings (1 Kings 17–20). He reveals himself to the scholars and righteous of every generation, joining the upper and lowers realms, and, as heralder of the redemption, linking the past, present, and future. The biblical account of his life thus forms one brief episode within the broad spectrum of Jewish tradition that crosses time and space. The blending of the figure of the prophet, wonder-maker, and proclaimer of the redemption places Elijah at the heart of a vibrant, vigorous religious consciousness.

Although his post-biblical features have been extensively studied, little has been written, on his appearance in the *Zohar*—and even less on his zeal.[1] This quality is fundamental to his conduct. He attempts to control the rain (1 Kgs 17:1), destroys the prophets of Baal on Mount Carmel (1 Kgs 19:20–40), and on his own admission was "very zealous for the LORD, the God of hosts" (1 Kgs 19:10, 14). Aggadic literature down the ages having evaluated this attribute, the *Zohar*'s treatment of the subject forms a summary and response to a long debate of the issue in the midrashic tradition. Herein, I shall focusing on the classic midrashim and the *Zohar*, analysing the changes that occurred the assessment of Elijah's zeal and, of course, addressing related other issues that shed light on it.

---

[1] See Margoliot (1960); Gutman (1923); Ish Shalom (1902); Weiner (1978); Milikowsky (2001); Benedict (1980); Peli (1986); Zakovitch (2000); Martyn (1976).

Elijah's origin and identity

The enigmatic character of the stories told about Elijah in the biblical text is set by his very first appearance therein: "Now Elijah the Tishbite, of Tishbe in Gilead, said to Ahab ..." (1 Kgs 17:1). In contrast to its usual custom, Scripture does not tell us his father's name or tribe, only saying of him that he was a "Tishbite of Tishbe in Gilead." These lacuna demanding attention, the Sages gave them their full attention. On several occasions, we thus find that his biographical data arouse great interest—and various conjectures:

> And Leah said: Fortune is come—ba gad (Gen 30:11): the fortune of the house has come; the fortune of the world has come; he [namely, Elijah] has come who will overthrow (legaded) the foundations of the heathen. The Rabbis debated: To which tribe did Elijah belong? R. Leazar said: To Benjamin, for it is written, And Jaarashiah, and Elijah, and Zochri, were the sons of Jeroboam ... All these were the sons of Benjamin (1 Chr 8:27, 40). R. Nehorai said: To Gad, for it says, And Elijah the Tishbite, who was of the settlers of Gilead, said (1 Kgs 17:1) ... On one occasion our Rabbis were debating about him, some maintaining that he belonged to the tribe of Gad, others to the tribe of Benjamin. Whereupon he came and stood before them and said, "Sirs, why do you debate about me? I am a descendant of Rachel [hence of Benjamin]." (Gen. Rab. 71:9)

Other sources states that Elijah was one of Leah's sons.[2] According to another tradition, which occurs already in the Babylonian Talmud, Elijah was a priest. When he revealed himself to the amora Rabba b. Abbuha in a cemetery, the latter thus asked him: "Art thou not a priest: why then dost thou stand in a cemetery?" (b. B. Meṣ. 114b).[3] In another midrash, Elijah himself attests "I am a priest."[4]

This tradition is particularly striking in that it appears to allude to a far more well-known identification—namely, "Phinehas is Elijah." This rests on the clear parallels between these two zealots for the Lord. Just as Phinehas killed Zimri, Elijah killed the prophets of Baal, both intending in doing so to return the people's heart to their God. As we shall see below, Elijah's sudden appearance in the book of Kings also suggests that he was a familiar figure who needed no intro-

---

[2] *Mid. Ps. B.* 30:3. Cf. *Pes. Rab Kah.* Zot habracha (p. 442). For the discussion of whether Elijah was a son or Rachel or Leah, see Ish Shalom (1902: 5–6).

[3] *Seder Eliyahu Rabbah* 18 combines the two traditions: when Elijah declared "I am a descendant of Rachel," he was asked, "Are you not a priest [and thus a descendent of Levi, son of Leah]?" (ER, p. 98).

[4] *Mid. Prov.* 9 (p. 68). This text has several parallels in later midrashim: *Ma'aseh asara harugei malkut* (Jellenik, *Beit Hamidrash* 60 [B], p. 27); *Midrash eleh ezkara* (ibid, 2, pp. 68–69). Elijah is also referred to as a high priest in the Targums: *Tg. Ps.-Jon.* on Exod 40:10 and Deut 30:4; *Tg. Esther* (I), 4:1; *Tg. Lam.* 4:22; *Tg. Qoh.* 10:20.

duction to the readers. A link between Elijah and Phinehas may already be evident in Malachi's description of the priest as one whose lips "should guard knowledge, and people should seek instruction from his mouth, for he is the messenger of the LORD of hosts" (Mal 2:7) with whom God makes a "covenant of life and well-being" with God (v. 5) in light of Num 25:11–13:

> "Phinehas son of Eleazar, son of Aaron the priest, has turned back my wrath from the Israelites by manifesting such zeal among them on my behalf that in my jealousy I did not consume the Israelites. Therefore say, 'I hereby grant him my covenant of peace. It shall be for him and for his descendants after him a covenant of perpetual priesthood, because he was zealous for his God, and made atonement for the Israelites.'"

The beginning of the following chapter then speaks of God's messenger: "See, I am sending my messenger to prepare the way before me, and the LORD whom you seek will suddenly come to his temple. The messenger of the covenant in whom you delight—indeed, he is coming, says the LORD of hosts" (Mal 3:1). This is none other than Elijah: "Lo, I will send you the prophet Elijah before the great and terrible day of the LORD comes" (Mal 4:5).[5]

Rather strangely, the tradition that "Phinehas is Elijah" finds no explicit reference in either of the Talmuds or the early midrashic literature (Ayeli, 1994: n. 8). Even the late *Seder Eliyahu Rabbah* which, as its name suggests, focuses on the prophet, is silent on this issue. The earliest reference to it appears to be in *Pirqe R. Eliezer*, dated to ca. the eighth century: "R. Eliezer said: He called the name of Phineas by the name of Elijah" (47).[6] This identification also lies at the heart of another homily on Elijah's zeal:

> (The Holy One, blessed be) He, said him [Elijah]: Thou art always zealous! Thou wast zealous in Shittim on account of the immorality. Because it is said: 'Phineas, the son of Eleazar, the son of Aaron the priest, turned my wrath away from the children of Israel, in that he was zealous with my zeal among them' (Num 25:11). (*Pirqe R. El.* 29)

It is only in the medieval *Yalqut Shimoni*, however, transmitted in the name of Resh Laqish, that the identification is made directly and explicitly:

> Said Shimon ben Laqish: Phinehas is Elijah. The Holy One, blessed be He, said to him: I have made peace between Israel and Myself in this world. But in the world to come you will be the one who makes peace between Myself and My children, as it is written: "Lo, I will send you the prophet Elijah before the great and terrible day of the LORD comes,

---

5 In the MT, of course, Malachi 3 also includes the verses assigned in the English translations to Malachi 4 (3:19–24).
6 For Elijah in *Pirqe R. Eliezer*, see Adelman (2009: 185–205; 2014); Stein (2004: 150–151).

etc." (Mal 4:5) and "He will turn the hearts of parents to their children and the hearts of children to their parents" (ibid, 6). (Numbers 771 [p, 512])[7]

The silence of the classical talmudic sources on this theme naturally aroused many objections to the identification between these two figures so chronologically removed from one another during the Middle Ages, primarily amongst the rationalist commentators. Ibn Ezra, for example, remarks on the verse "It shall be for him and for his descendants after him a covenant of perpetual priesthood" (Num 25:13): "'After him' shows that he did in fact die. He could not, therefore, have been Elijah (as some think)." R. Moshe the Darshan similarly observes: "Everyone who says that Phinehas the son of Eleazar is Elijah says falsely, for slow is his way and twisted his path ... Phinehas is not Elijah" (Haberman, 1949–1956: 1:232). Those commentators who remained faithful to the aggadic tradition countered this position with their view.[8]

The rabbinic silence is all the more surprising in light of the fact that Elijah and Phinehas are explicitly identified in contemporaneous Jewish literature. Thus, for example, an ancient tradition reflected in *Targum Pseudo-Jonathan* explains the verse "The following are the names of the sons of Levi according to their genealogies: Gershon, Kehath, and Merari, and the length of Levi's life was one hundred thirty-seven years" (Exod 6:16) as: "And the years of the life of Kehath the saint, a hundred and thirty and three years. He lived to see Phinehas, who is Elijah, the Great Priest, who is to be sent to the captivity of Israel at the end of the days."[9] Rendering Num 25:12, he also associates the two: "Swearing by My Name, I say to him, Behold, I decree to him My covenant of peace, and will make him an angel of the covenant, that he may ever live, to announce the

---

7 Although the editor of the *Yalqut* attributes this dictum to "Yelammdenu," it is not found in our extant version of that world: see Wertheimer (1950: 1:296). The identification between Elijah and Phinehas also occurs in numerous *piyyutim*. Thus, for example, we read in one for Motzei Shabbat that deals entirely with Elijah: "A man who was zealous for God, a man associated with peace by Yequtiel [Moses], a man who approached and atoned for Israel." In another, recited at circumcisions, we read: "The Compassionate One will send us a righteous priest who was taken and concealed ... and his face with be covered in his splendour and be revealed. My covenant of life and peace was with him." The title "righteous priest" and the reference to "My covenant was with him" clearly allude to the identification of Elijah, who stands at the centre of this *piyyut*, with Phinehas.
8 Cf. Gersonides on 1 Kgs 17:1.
9 The dating of *Tg. Ps.-Jon.* is disputed: see Shinan (1979a: 193–198). Even if it is thought to be relatively late, however, the frequency with which it identifies Elijah and Phinehas attests that this was already a well-entrenched tradition.

Redemption at the end of the days." His frequent references to "Elijah the high priest" also doubtless reflect the identification between Elijah and Phinehas.[10]

Christian sources also attest to this tradition (Ayeli, 1994: 48–49). Of particular significance is Origen's statement regarding the tradition of the "Hebrews" in this regard:

> As for the change of name, a thing which reminds us of mysteries, I do not know how the Hebrews came to tell about Phinehas, son of Eleazar, who admittedly prolonged his life to the time of many of the judges, as we read in the Book of Judges (Judg 20:28) to tell about him what I now mention. They say that he was Elijah, because he had been promised immortality (Num 25:12), on account of the covenant of peace granted to him because he was jealous with a divine jealousy ... No wonder, then, if those who conceived Phinehas and Elijah to be the same person, whether they judged soundly in this or not, for that is not now the question ... (*Commentary on John*, 6.7 [Menzies])[11]

Even if they ignored it, the Sages were thus familiar with this tradition. Several homilies implicitly allude to Elijah's priestly status or Phinehas' immortality. In *Sifre Numbers* on Num 25:12 for example, we read that "*And made atonement for the Israelites*—for up until now he had not moved but stood and atoned until the dead lived" (131 [p. 173]). *Num. Rab.* 21:3 similarly states: "*Wherefore say: I give unto him my covenant of peace* (25:12). This implies that Phinehas is still alive at the present time." Other chronological dicta make no reference to this tradition at all, however.[12]

Despite its early origin, the Sages appear to have rejected this tradition in favour of the claim that Elijah as a Gadite or Benjaminite. The Elijah-Phinehas theory only resurfacing at a later stage, thence regaining its lost stature, we must ask what caused it to disappear during the early talmudic and midrashic period. Non-substantive sources and circumstances being of little help in this re-

---

10 Cf. Exod 40:10: "... for the sake of ... Elijah the high priest who is to be sent at the end of the exiles"; Deut 30:4: "Even though your dispersal will be to the ends of the heavens, from there will the *Memra* of the Lord gather you through the mediation of Elijah, the great priest, and from there he will bring you near through the mediation of the King Messiah."
11 Cf. Spiro (1953). The Hebrew root קנ״א is rendered by both "zeal" and "jealousy" in English.
12 Cf. *Tanh*. Pinchas (beginning). The phrase "is still alive" appears to be taken from *Seder Olam Rabbah* 1 or possibly *b. B. Bat.* 121b (although the text there is disputed [see *Diqduqei Sofrim*]). The latter text adduces a long "chain" of figures who lived long lives: "Our Rabbis taught: Seven [men] spanned [the life of] the whole world. [For] Methuselah saw Adam; Shem saw Methuselah, Jacob saw Shem; Amram saw Jacob; Ahijah the Shilonite saw Amram; Elijah saw Ahijah the Shilonite, and he is still alive." R. Samuel ben Meir (Rashbam) correctly comments on this dictum: "This tanna does not regard Elijah to be Phinehas, for were that to be the case it would have had to say: Moses saw Amram and Phinehas saw Moses and he still exists" (*ad loc.*, Ahijah the Shilonite saw Amram).

gard, we must approach the issue from a slightly different angle: why for a certain period of time did the Sages object to the identification between Elijah and Phinehas and allow it to fade into oblivion?

Victor Aptowitzer (1927) early on suggested that the two figures were linked as part of the Hasmonean strategy to gain a messianic role for the priestly clan, the Sages opposing such political messianic pretensions and even issuing a halakhic ruling in this respect: "Priests may not be anointed as kings" (*y. Hor.* 3, 2, 47c and the parallels).[13] For precisely the same reasons as the Hasmoneans promoted this tradition, the Sages thus rejected it. Even the general formulation of Elijah's assertion "I am a descendant of Rachel" indicates that it was intended to refute the claim that Phinehas was Elijah. Once the Hasmonean polemic had receded, he argues, this tradition could resurface.

The Hasmonean argument had already lost its relevance in the talmudic period, however, the messianic trends similarly long since having lost their vitality.[14] The attempt to attribute the rejection to an anti-Christian polemic in light of the Christian claim that Jesus was a priest suffers from a similar problem. The objection to Elijah's priestly status is also difficult to understand in light of the fact that the Sages frequently refer to Elijah as a messenger.[15]

It thus appears better to assume the locus of the debate to lie on an essentially ideological place, without attempting to force it into any specific historical context. I suggest that the disparities between the different midrashic strata in relation to the Phinehas-Elijah tradition are best understood as divergences in outlook concerning the common feature shared by the two men—i.e., their zeal. Despite the affinities between their modes of action and the fact that both were (the only ones!) zealous for the Lord according to Scripture, Elijah does not resemble Phinehas in any other way. While Phinehas was zealous for

---

[13] See Lorberbaum (2011: 80); Schwartz (1992: 50–51).
[14] Aptowitzer's argument (1927) is ostensibly supported by Trg. Ps.-Jon. rendering of Moses' blessing of Levi, which appears to constitute clear proof of the link between the Hasmonean polemic and the tradition regarding Elijah's priestly status: "Bless Lord, the sacrifice of the house of Levi, who give the tenth of the tenth; and the oblation of the hand of Elijah the priest, which he will offer on Mount Karmela, receive Thou with acceptance: break the loins of Achab his enemy, and the neck of the false prophets who rise up against him, that the enemies of Johanan the high priest may not have a foot to stand" (to Deut 33:8). In fact, however, not only is this verse probably corrupt (Shinan, 1979a: 195) but it is also clear that it is intended to identify the priests who are in his view in need and worthy of blessing. Elijah the priest who sacrifices on Mount Carmel is no more associated with Jonathan the High Priest referred to at the end of the passage than he is with the Levites who tithe mentioned at the beginning.
[15] The links between Elijah and Jesus in the Gospels lie beyond my present scope: see Ayeli (1994: 56–57); Poirier; Miller (2007).

the Lord, prompting God's blessing upon him—"Therefore say, 'I hereby grant him my covenant of peace. It shall be for him and for his descendants after him a covenant of perpetual priesthood, because he was zealous for his God, and made atonement for the Israelites'" (Num 25:12–13)—Elijah is not similarly praised, even for his deeds. This surprising divergence appears to reflect the attempt to apply what is said of Phinehas to Elijah. Henceforth, the covenant of peace given to Phinehas is also bestowed upon Elijah, the latter's actions—like those of Phinehas—therefore being worthy of explicit divine approval. The talmudic neglect of this tradition is thus to be understood as reflecting the Sages' reservations regarding the trend that sought to expand Phinehas' covenant of peace and apply it to zealotry as a norm.

Zeal and Elijah in rabbinic thought

The Sages' reluctance to accept Phinehas' deed as a norm is well documented, finding explicit expression in talmudic literature. A close examination of the rabbinic attitude towards his zeal reveals that while following the line set by Scripture that lauds the zealot for his commitment, resourcefulness, and boldness the Sages were cautious about presenting it as normative, taking care to erect clear fences around it. The problematics of his ardour are reflected in a rare halakhic ruling regarding the normative character of zeal: "If one … cohabits with a heathen [lit.: Syrian] woman, he is punished by zealots" (*m. Sanh.* 9:6). This effectively constitutes a retroactive coming to terms with an act that is fundamentally illegal—a fact elucidated by Palestinian and Babylonian amoraim alike:

> R. Hisda said: If the zealot comes to take counsel [whether to punish the transgressors enumerated in the Mishnah], we do not instruct him to do so. It has been stated likewise: Rabbah b. Bar Hana said in R. Johanan's name: If he comes to take counsel, we do not instruct him to do so. What is more, had Zimri forsaken his mistress and Phinehas slain him, Phinehas would have been executed on his account; and had Zimri turned upon Phinehas and slain him, he would not have been executed, since Phinehas was a pursuer [seeking to take his life]. (*b. Sanh.* 152b)[16]

---

[16] The Sages' attitude can instructively be compared with the way in which Philo cites the zealot halakhah: "And it is well that a charge should be given to all those who have any admiration for virtue to inflict all such punishment out of hand without any delay, not bringing them before either any judgment seat, or any council, or any bench of magistrates, but giving vent to their own disposition which hates evil and loves God, so as to chastise the impious with implacable rigour, looking upon themselves as everything for the time being, counsellors, and judges, and generals, and members of the assembly, and accusers, and witnesses, and laws, and the people;

The definition of the person who commits an act of zeal, who possesses the "covenant of peace" with God, as a "pursuer" demonstrates the lengths to which the Sages sought to avoid making such behaviour normative. Although this attitude may have arisen as part of an anti-Hasmonean polemic (Aptowitzer, 1927), it was no less relevant in the days of the Great Revolt in Jerusalem or in the wake of the failure of the Bar Kokhba revolt. We also cannot ignore the possibility, however, that it reflects a fundamental ahistorical worldview.

The Sages' view of Elijah and his zeal is self-evident, finding direct and explicit expression in several places. Thus, for example, we read in *Canticles Rabbah*:

> Similarly it is written of Elijah: *And he said, I have been very jealous for the Lord, the God of Hosts; for the children of Israel have forsaken Thy covenant* (1 Kgs 19:14). Said God to him: 'Is it My covenant or thy covenant?' He then said: 'They have thrown down thy altars.' Said God to him: 'Are they My altars or thy altars?' He then said, 'And slain Thy prophets with the sword.' Said God to him: 'They are My prophets; what concern is it of thine? He then said: 'And I, even I, only am left, and they seek my life to take it away.' See now, what is written there: *And he looked, and behold there was at his head a cake baked on the hot stones—reṣafim* (ibid, 6). What is meant by reṣafim? R. Samuel b. Nahman said: Ruṣ peh (break the mouth): break the mouths of all who calumniate My sons. (1.6.1)

Elsewhere, the midrashist highlights the disparity between the expected role of the classical prophet and Elijah's deviance from this:

> *Zeal is fierce as the grave* (Cant 8:6). Zeal was fierce that placed Elijah against Israel, as is written: *I have been very jealous for the Lord, the God of Hosts; for the children of Israel have forsaken Thy covenant* (1 Kgs 19:14). Elijah should have gone to the place where his ancestors had stood and asked for mercy on Israel but he did not do so. The Holy One, blessed be He, said to him: You have asked for what you need; go back to Damascus. (Mid. Zuta, Cant. 8:6 [p. 36])

Similar criticism is leveled against Elijah in *Pesiqta Rabbati*:

> *I went down to the nut orchard* (Cant 6:11): Whoever is not trusted to go up there immediately falls, protecting himself so that his property will not be stolen from under him. Just like Moses and Isaiah and Elijah ... Elijah—*because they have forsaken Thy covenant*. And it is written: *And you shall anoint Elisha son of Shaphat of Abel-meholah as prophet in your place* (1 Kgs 19:16). (11, 42b)

---

that so, since there is no conceivable hindrance, they may with all their company put themselves forward fearlessly to fight as the champions of holiness" (*Spec.* 1.55 [Yonge]): see Alon (1977: 89–137).

In the Babylonian Talmud, R. Jose is recorded as denouncing Elijah, calling him "Father Elijah the pedant" (*b. Sanh.* 113a). In some of the sources that decry his zeal he is said to pay a heavy price for it, the midrashists linking this restitution with the commission given him in the closely following verses—to anoint Elisha in his place. In other words, Elijah's zeal brings about the end of his own ministry. In similar fashion to the passage from the *Pesiqta* above, the *Mekilta* states:

> Elijah insisted upon the honor due the Father, but did not insist upon the honor due the son, as it is said: "And he said, I have been very jealous for the Lord, the God of Hosts" (1 Kgs 19:10). And thereupon what is said? "And the Lord said unto him: Go return on thy way to the wilderness of Damascus; and when thou comest, thou shalt anoint ... Elisha the son of Shaphat of Abel-meholah to be prophet in thy room." (Pischa 1)

A closely corresponding statement occurs in the late *Seder Eliyahu Zuta*:

> Then the Holy One asked Elijah: *What doest thou here, Elijah?* (1 Kgs 19:9). Elijah should have responded with an entreaty of mercy, saying: Master of the universe, Israel are Your children, the children of those who have been tested by You, the children of Abraham, Isaac, and Jacob, who have done Your will in the world. But this was not what Elijah said. Instead he dared to say to God: *I have been very jealous for the Lord, the God of hosts: for the children of Israel have forsaken Thy covenant, thrown down Thine altars, and slain Thy Prophets with the sword; and I, even I, only am left* (1 Kgs 19:10). (EZ, p. 186)

One of the most well-known passages in which this criticism is voiced is *Pirqe R. El.* 29:

> Elijah, may he be remembered for good, arose and fled from the land of Israel, and he betook himself to Mount Horeb, as it is said, "And he arose, and did eat and drink" (1 Kgs 19:8). There the Holy One, blessed be He, was revealed to him, and He said to him: "What doest thou here, Elijah?" (ibid, 9). He answered Him, saying: "I have been very zealous" (ibid, 10). (The Holy One, blessed be) He, said to him: Thou art always zealous! Thou wast zealous in Shittim on account of immorality. Because it is said: "Phineas, the son of Eleazar, the son of Aaron the priest, turned my wrath away from the children of Israel, in that he was zealous with my zeal among them" (Num 25:11). Here also art thou zealous. By thy life! Thy shall not observe the covenant of circumcision until thou seest it (done) with thine eyes. Hence the sages instituted (the custom) that people should have a seat of honour for the Messenger of the Covenant [who must be present at every subsequent circumcision to attest that the people are in fact observing the Covenant].

Although we shall discuss these homilies below in their evolution in the *Zohar*, here we may note that the approach reflected in the varied sources is clear and consistent—even if not demanded by a literal reading of Scripture and defaming of Elijah's character.[17]

The view that exhibits strong reservations regarding zeal in general and Elijah's in particular thus has deep roots in rabbinic literature, even in its early stratum. The tradition that "stretches" Phinehas' zeal to the days of Elijah therefore stands in contradiction to the fundamental anti-zealotry orientation that regards Zimri's execution as an exception to the rule that cannot be extended to other times or places. Properly understanding the meaning of the identification between Elijah and Phinehas, the Sages consequently shunned it.

They did not completely ignore Elijah's zeal, however, traces of it being evident in the role of revelator attributed to him in tannaitic and amoraic literature. In these texts, Elijah presents and argues for the fulfillment of the hasidic ethos of "within the margin of the law." In numerous cases, he appears to outstanding halakhists, reproving them for not remaining with the proper perimeters: "How long will you deliver the people of our God to execution!" (*b. B. Meṣ.* 84a). He ceased coming before one of the amoraim on the grounds: "Am I revealed to the informers?" (*y. Ter.* 8, 4, 46b). Once, he would not communicate with R. Joshua ben Levi for three days because three parsangs away a man had been devoured by a lion (*b. Mak.* 11a). On another occasion, he concealed himself from an amora because the latter treated his servant badly (*b. Ket.* 61a), similarly stopping conversing with a man after he made a porter's lodge, which prevented the cries of poor men from being heard within the courtyard (*b. B. Bat.* 7b). Elijah's sorties and messenger status, during which he returned to human company after having been "removed" from it in order to raise the human moral bar also appear to reflect a form of zeal that is the Sages regard as positive and essential for allowing room for the hasidic ethos in a normative, conformist, and gray world.[18]

---

17 Although another view exists, according to which Elijah did demand the honour due the son—"R. Eleazar also said: Elijah spoke insolently toward heaven, as it says, *For Thou didst turn their heart backwards* (1 Kgs 18:37) … R. Samuel b. Isaac said: Whence do we know that the Holy One, blessed be He, gave Elijah right? Because it says, *And whom I have wronged* (Num 11:2)" (*b. Ber.* 31b)—with respect to zealotry as a norm it is irrelevant whether criticism of Elijah's zeal is voiced or whether he is depicted as non-zealous.

18 *Contra* the view held by other scholars that rabbinic literature exhibits a sharp change in its attitude towards Elijah, the zealous prophet being replaced by a compassionate man who intercedes on Israel's behalf: see Kaminka (1944); Samet (2003: 533f). In my opinion, the talmudic aggada illustrates, highlights, and isolates various elements of Elijah's zealotry rather than rejecting other sides of his character. Some of the talmudic and midrashic narratives are stories of miracles that reflect a wonder-making figure. Others are based on his ascent to heaven, these including some in which he appears as an angel who reveals the goings on in the heavenly academy or court to his interlocutor (see below). Another type—directly relevant to our present

Elijah and Phinehas in the zoharic tradition

The *Zohar*, whose links with Pirqe R. Eliezer are well known and documented, relates to the identification between Elijah and Phinehas as self-evident:

> Of Elijah, what is written? *He came and sat under* רתם (*rotem*), *a broom bush* ... (1 Kings 19:4) ... the blessed Holy One revealed Himself to him and said, *"What are you doing here, Elijah?"* (1 Kings 19:9). At first, you were accusing zealously on behalf of the covenant, and when I saw that you were zealous for Me regarding that covenant, I took it with the consent of Moses and gave to you, so Moses said, *I hereby grant him My covenant of peace* (Numbers 25:12) ... Phinehas is Elijah, surely on a single rung. (*Zohar*, 2:190a)[19]

This tradition is alluded to, explicitly or implicitly, on numerous occasions in the *Zohar*.[20] As its wont, the book anchors it in the context of the sefiric world, thereby raising it to kabbalistic heights: "Phinehas is Elijah, surely on a single rung." According to several passages, the two men belong to the Judgment associated with the Fear of Isaac—i.e., *Gevura*.[21]

---

purposes—are hasidic stories in which Elijah's zeal represents the demand for a lofty moral norm. Nor does Malachi's description of Elijah's future role affect his character, all that is said about him there being that he will turn the hearts of the parents to their children without any detail of the way in which this will occur—whether through the zeal with which he returned Israel to God on Mount Carmel or by some other means (according to Sirach, "At the appointed time, it is written, you are destined to calm the wrath of God before it breaks out in fury" [48:10] —just like Phinehas!). In *Seder Olam Rabbah*, Elijah's appearance is strikingly associated with the eschaton and the war of Gog and Magog: "And in Ahaziah's second year, Elijah was hidden and will not be seen again until King Messiah will come, then he will be seen, then hidden a second time until God and Magog come. But now he writes down the deeds of all generations" (10.7). In *Yalqut Shimoni* (originally attributed by the compiler to *Midrash Abkir*), he is portrayed as a militant: "Immediately, the Holy One, blessed be He, grasped [Esau's] prince by the fringes of his head and Elijah slaughtered him, the blood running down over his clothes" (Genesis 133 [p. 675]. The view in *m. Eduy.* 8:7, according to which Elijah comes "to make peace in the world," is thus an unusual and innovative one, intended to dispute the ancient tradition ("R. Joshua said: I have received a tradition from Rabban Johanan b. Zakkai, who heard it from his teacher, and his teacher [heard it] from his teacher, as a halachah given to Moses from Sinai").

19 Cf. Tishby and Lachower (1989: 1:222–223).
20 See 1:209a, b, 3:210a; *Raya Mehemna* 3:227b, 238a. In *Zohar Hadash* (Ruth), 84c, two talmudic opinions are adduced in relation to Elijah's origins side by side: "R. Johanan says [he is] from Gad ... R. Eliezer said: Elijah is Phinehas."
21 Cf. *Zohar*, 3:215a: "Phinehas is Isaac and Phinehas arose and exercised judgment, clothing himself in mighty *Gevura*, which is Samael." Although the addition "surely on a single rung" refers to the same *sefira*, it also already appears to contain echoes of the medieval difficulty with the identification between Elijah and Phinehas due to their historical-biographical remove. In

The Zohar also feels that Elijah's zeal must be explained (Hellner-Eshed, 1997). An examination of the various homilies that address this issue reveals that even though some of them remain faithful to the central trend with rabbinic literature and criticize him—primarily in line with the version transmitted in *Pirqe R. Eliezer*—others exhibit a more moderate approach. We shall discuss one of these. While its general tenor is one of fierce objection to Elijah's zeal, it weaves into its paraphrase of the "Elijah the Messenger of the Covenant" homily in *Pirqe R. Eliezer* additional midrashic elements:

> Come and see what is written: *suddenly a chariot of fire and horses of fire appeared [and separated the two of them ...] ...* (2 Kings 2:11)—for then body was stripped from spirit, and he ascended, unlike the rest of the earth, and endured as a holy angel, like other holy supernal beings. He carries out missions in the world, as has been established, for miracles performed in the world by the blessed Holy One are performed by him ... *And behold, a voice addressed him, saying, "Why are you here, Elijah?" He replied, "I have been very zealous"* (1 Kings 19:13–14). The blessed Holy One said to him, "How long will you be zealous for Me? You have locked the door so that death has no dominion over you, and the world cannot endure you along with human beings." He replied, *For the Children of Israel have forsaken Your covenant* (ibid, 14). He said, "By your life, wherever My children fulfil the holy covenant, you will be present there!" As has been said, because of this a chair is prepared for Elijah, who appears there. Come and see the consequences of Elijah's word, as is written: *I will leave in Israel seven thousand—all the knees that have not knelt to Baal ...* (ibid, 18). The blessed Holy One said to him, "From now on, the world cannot endure you along with human beings. *And Elisha son of Shaphat of Abel-meholah, anoint as prophet in your stead* (ibid, 16)—here is another prophet for My children. As for you, ascend to your site!" Come and see: Every person who is zealous for the blessed Holy One cannot be dominated by the Angel of Death as can other human beings. Peace endures for him, as they have established, as is written concerning Phinehas: *I hereby grant him My covenant of peace* (Numbers 25:12). (*Zohar*, 1:209a–b)

The novelty of this interpretation in relation to the rabbinic midrashim lies in the fact that if in the *Mekilta*, for example, the command to anoint Elisha is perceived as tantamount to Elijah's deposal due to his zeal ("because your prophecy is impossible"), the *Zohar* also associates with Elijah's ascension in the whirlwind, wherein it finds the fierce "sanction" of him due to his zealous deeds. This reworking of the aggadic tradition of Elijah's dismissal is very significant, not constituting simply the blending of two literary motifs. If Elijah's "laying

---

other words, the fact that they both belong to the same supernal *sefira* in the primary arena of events according to kabbalistic theory is likely to bestow an ahistorical interpretation upon the tradition identifying them.

off" also forms the background to his heavenly ascent it cannot be his disposal itself, as we shall discuss in the following section.

Elijah's zeal: Between earth and heaven

Having discussed Elijah's ascent in Chapter 6, here my attention lies specifically with the fact that the *Zohar* customarily regards Elijah as an angel:

> "Rabbi Nathan asked Rabbi Jose bar Hanina. One day he said to him: Did Elijah the prophet have a son or not? He said to him: He had something else, as is written *Do not touch my anointed ones; do my prophets no harm* (Psalm 105:15) ... You ask about one who is an angel in heaven?" (*Zohar Hadash* [Ruth], 76a).

Elsewhere, Elijah is explicitly said to be an "angel, carrying out missions" (*Zohar*, 1:151b), serving as "one of the servants of the blessed Holy One who minister before him" (*Zohar Hadash*, 25c [*Midrash Ne'elam*]).[22] One passage that occurs in close proximity to the homily on Elijah's zeal specifies his status after his ascension, linking it to his well-known manifestations as a wonder-worker:

> "... he thus ascended, unlike the rest of the earth, and endured as a holy angel, like other holy supernal beings. He carries out missions in the world, as has been established, for miracles performed in the world by the blessed Holy One are performed by him" (*Zohar*, 1:209a).

This is precisely the way in which the text in the zoharic passage on Elijah's zeal, the subject of our inquiry here, is to be understood: "... for then body was stripped from spirit and he thus ascended, unlike the rest of the earth, and endured as a holy angel, like other holy supernal beings. He carries out missions in the world." Here, the *Zohar* regards Elijah's angelic status as the key for understanding his revelation to later generations—the "missions he carries out in the world."

It is precisely Elijah's human past that ensures his special place in the between the realms whence he speaks with human beings. In various guises, he skips from world to world, revealing himself, and rebuking and delivering, continuing this role into the eschaton. In talmudic literature and the *Zohar*, Elijah belongs to the life of every generation as a figure whose miraculous appearances draw a thread of piety and mystery through their universes and a form of mes-

---

22 Cf. also *Zohar*, 1:209a, 2:197a, 3:68b; et al.

sianism envisioned by Malachi.²³ Elijah's angelic status is the inner kernel of his figure, joining together his various appearances in the past, present, and future into a colourful, glowing mosaic.

Beyond these general characteristics Elijah bears in the *Zohar*, however, in the "zeal midrash" we are discussing here the book raises him and his ascent into the heavens to new heights. Here, his breaking through the boundaries of human reality takes on a profound anthropological significance, being regarded as a human victory over the Angel of Death: "The Angel of Death could not dominate him." Thus, for example, we read in the *Midrash Ne'elam*:

> R. Nehemiah and R. Judah said: When the blessed Holy One raised Elijah to the heavens, the Angel of Death opposed him. Said the blessed Holy One to him: "For this purpose did I create the heavens, so that Elijah would ascend to them." Said the Angel of Death to him: "Master of the Universe, now the creatures will have reason to open their mouths." Said the blessed Holy One to him: "He is not like the rest of the creatures; he can remove you from the world and you know not his power." Said the Angel of Death to him: "Master of the Universe, give me authority and I shall go down to him and tell him: descend." Immediately he descended. When Elijah saw him, he placed him under his feet and sought to remove him from the world, but the blessed Holy One would not allow him to do so. He immediately bound him underneath him and ascended to heaven, as is written: *Elijah ascended in a whirlwind into heaven* (2 Kgs 2:11). (*Zohar Hadash* [Ruth]. 66a)

In another clear and explicit statement the *Zohar* asserts of Phinehas (whom it identifies with Elijah): "This is what is written of Phinehas: *I hereby grant him my covenant of peace* (Num 25:12)—peace from the Angel of Death, who does not dominate him forever and is not judged by his judgments" (*Zohar*, 3:214a).

The *Zohar*'s enhancement of the figure of Elijah raises the question of why Elijah merited this status out of all the biblical protagonists. This inquiry appears to lead us to an even greater innovation in the *Zohar*'s "zeal midrash"—namely, its association of zeal with death: "Come and see: Every person who is zealous for the blessed Holy One cannot be dominated by the Angel of Death as can

---

23 Scholem (1976a: 25) has demonstrated that the early kabbalists—R. Abraham ben David of Posquières and R. Isaac Sagi-Nahor—were already said to have been visited by Elijah. Cf. also the tradition cited in the preface to *Sefer Hapliya*. Lurianic kabbalah exhibits the same consciousness, as evidenced by *Shivchei Haari*: "He did not engage solely in studying the Talmud and the plain interpretation of the Torah but for seven years he also sat alone ... and there merited the Holy Spirit and Elijah of blessed memory, who manifested himself to him in every time and age and revealed the secrets of the Torah to him" (Shlomo Shlomiel ben Hayim, *Shivchei Haari* 30b–31a). Cf. also Naftali Hertz ben Kacob Elchanan, *Emeq hamelech*, 10a. Many kabbalists—including the authors of the *Zohar*—believing the revelation of the mysteries of the Torah to form part of the messianic vision, Elijah's activity is thus consistent with "before the great and terrible day of the LORD comes."

other human beings. Peace endures for him ..." Rather than his zeal leading to the decree that he must be removed it is precisely because of it that he merited being lifted up. His zeal thus reflects his distinction from other men, raising him to the level of an immortal angel.

This elucidation of Elijah's ascent into heaven returns us to the covert polemic regarding the status of zeal, revealing the complex and profound dimension of the zoharic ideology. As we noted above, although a clear link exists between the *Zohar* and the *Mekilta*'s assertion that Elijah was deposed on account of his zeal, the two dicta differ radically in meaning, being virtually antithetical. While the *Zohar* rejects zeal as a norm, it does so not because it is fundamentally wrong but because its purposes are unattainable in a flawed human world.[24] Fanatic zeal is regarded here as an "inhuman" quality—not in the normal sense of this term but referring to a super-human quality belonging to other realms of existence, to which he is "drawn up" due to his zeal. The decree "and you, go to your site (אתר)" is not a rejection of Elijah but his raising up to his proper level in the supernal realms.[25]

The *Zohar*'s attitude towards Elijah's zeal thus differs from both preceding views, perhaps blending them both. While it does not laud his zeal it does not denounce it, relating to both traditions alike on the grounds that both have a place in Jewish thought. Zeal is an expression of religious perfection, in and of itself a lofty and praiseworthy quality. It is so noble, however, that there is no room for it on earth, in a world dominated by the Angel of Death. Elijah conquers the latter not by virtue of his qualities as a miracle worker but precisely because of his zeal. Thus "Every person who is zealous for the blessed Holy One cannot be dominated by the Angel of Death as can other human beings.". In other words, the zealous do not die but live forever. The *Zohar* therefore rejects zeal in the normative-social context because the world cannot tolerate it on the one hand and lauds it as a noble sentiment and a lofty religious-spiritual attribute on the other.

The *Zohar*'s positive attitude towards zeal here is not accidental. In *Parashat Sotah*, which deals with a husband's jealousy of his wife, it also determines this

---

24 The text preceding this homily suggests that Elijah's zeal derives from his too-close identification with the masculine aspect of the godhead, his approach to the heterogeneous human world built upon couple relations and the complementary nature of male and female thus being deficient: see Hellner-Eshed (1997: 109–114).

25 The root סל"ק occurs in *Tg. Onqelos* already in the sense of "go up." The *Zohar* regularly employs this root and meaning in the *hithpael* for emphasis and stress when it refers to a mystical ascension. אתר in zoharic terminology signifies "rung" or *sefira*. As we observed above, Phinehas-is-Elijah's "rung" is the *sefira* of "harsh Judgment"— *Gevura*.

"zeal" to be a virtue, something that should not be dependent upon his discretion or anger.[26] In this context, it takes a strikingly favourable stance with regard to zeal:

> *Zeal is fierce as the grave* (Cant 8:6). Everyone who loves but does not join it with zeal, his love is not love. When he is zealous then his love is complete. Hence we learn that a man must be zealous for his wife so that she will be joined to him in perfect love, for out of this he does not lay his eyes on any other woman. (*Zohar*, 1:245a)

According to the *Zohar*, jealousy/zeal is the other side of love—in fact, none other than its most perfect and elevated expression: "... jealousy exists only in love: out of love comes jealousy; whoever is jealous of a beloved one finds this harder than the level called Sheol, the cruelest level of Hell" (*Zohar*, 3:54b). No need exists—certainly not with respect to the *Zohar*—to note that what is good and right between a man and woman is also fitting for human relations with God.[27] In both instances, however, the fire of zeal burns and consumes to such a degree that there is no place for it in fragile and flawed human existence.

Conclusion

Can two antithetical dimensions be held together? How can we say one thing and the opposite of biblical zeal? Here, we touch on the distinctive quality of the zoharic midrash, the perspective through which it examines reality embracing both the upper and lower realms. The zoharic lens reveals a richness that goes beyond those not immersed in the world of the kabbalists, capable of crossing the homiletic horizon in its elaboration and enhancement of remote vistas and fields and thereby providing a broader, multidimensional picture. This opens new hermeneutical options for the zoharic homilist that are foreign to the person only familiar with those of space and time and unaware of the mystical heights and depths of the story. This literary three-dimensionality also allows him to analyse and evaluate the subjects to which he devotes himself from diverse perspectives, letting them stand side by side. While it is indeed possible to have reservations

---

26 The tannaim dispute this issue in the Talmud: see *b. Sotah* 3a; *Sifre Num.* 7.
27 The *Zohar* extols and exalts Phinehas' zeal well above and beyond what is written of him in Scripture and rabbinic literature: see 3:213b–214a. Moses is also noted for his zeal (in other circumstances): see 2:13b. For a husband's jealousy for his wife and God's for the Shekhina in the *Zohar* and kabbalistic thought in general, see Liebes (1978: 107–108 n. 171; 2007d: 323–324 n, 171).

regarding Elijah's zeal as depicted in Scripture it may also be viewed as a lofty religious ideal. Religious zeal is "removed" in both senses of the word—denied in human existence but also raised above it to the mystical heights of the ideational world of the *sefirot*.

In summary, alongside the classical midrashic tradition that finds expression in the *Zohar*, which completely rejects zeal (hereby providing us with nothing new), we also encounter a new midrashic approach that feels no compunction to decide between diverse opinions regarding the biblical and midrashic perception of Elijah's zeal, holding onto both simultaneously. "The earth is one block" (*b. Ket*. 27b)—like Phinehas' zeal, Elijah's is for the "covenant of peace" and cannot be divided between those who hold onto it. The fire of zeal is the essence of devotion to the religious ideal. As with all fire, however, when it burns fiercely it consumes and destroys. It thus cannot exist in a flawed and defective reality, only being able to fully come into its own on the "great and terrible day of the LORD."

Epilogue

The Study of Aggada and Midrash in the *Zohar:* Expectations and Future Trends

In the twelve central chapters of this volume, I have examined the way in which the *Zohar* treats various biblical episodes interpreted and elaborated upon within the early rabbinic and midrashic corpus. As the book's title indicated, these inquires are "windows" through which, like the lover seeking the maiden in the palace, I have sought to catch a glimpse of the zoharic aggada, its literary qualities, and the way in which it conducts conversations with the early talmudic aggada and contemporaneous kabbalistic exegesis.

Through the diverse perspectives that have been opened up herein, we have gained a clearer and sharper picture of the zoharic authors and their spiritual and religious world. In some of the chapters, for example, we have seen a profound longing for what lies beyond the mystical horizon, towards the gaining of the heart's desire that, according to the ancient tradition, can only be attained in the future or remains a utopian ideal. The idea of the "hidden light," for instance, reflects a tendency to draw the light stored up for the righteous in the world to come into this world and present reality. The representation of the Exodus as the liberation of the kabbalistic spirit similarly demonstrates the way in which the *Zohar* identifies those who took part in it as being liberated from the need to eat and drink, regarding the kabbalistic band as the prime exemplars of those who have gained such status. The *Zohar*'s outlook also gains clear outlines from an investigation of its treatment of Adam's sin, which indicates its call for transcendence and mystical ardor. Here, several homilies evince that the *Zohar* regards the essence of Adam's sin as religious shallowness and the theosophic willingness to suffice with a little, exemplified in Adam's preference of the Tree of Knowledge over the Tree of Life. This spirit also finds expression in the book's attitude towards Moses' death and the sin of Nadab and Abihu. The traditions relating to Moses' death allow the *Zohar* to posit that the Torah will be renewed and full revealed through his messianic light given to the kabbalistic scholars as they study his Torah. The sin of Nadab and Abihu similarly becomes the vehicle for exhibiting tolerance towards and even of a measure of covert idealization of anarchistic religious fervor, the two figures merging, in a homily on reincarnation, with that of Phineas son of Eleazar, upon whom God bestowed a "covenant of peace." On the other side of the coin, the zoharic exegesis of Abraham's origin reveals a more balanced approach to mystical longing that, in contrast to other trends within rabbinic and medieval literature, recognizes the limitations of human achievement and the need to combine the effort to gain intimacy with God with lower and upper "awakenings." Another type of balance arises from the the *Zohar*'s discussion of Elijah and Enoch. This sharpens the essential reservation the zoharic homilists exhibit towards the "man-angel" figure.

Two further chapters examined the *Zohar*'s attitude towards magic. In looking at the war against Amalek, we noted the transition from a thaumaturgic understanding of "Moses' hands" to the theurgic kabbalistic conception. In looking at the comparison between Moses and Balaam we see the homilist's particular interest in the ethical aspects of the magical act. Ideological and mental trends can also be identified in the discussion of Elijah's zealotry, which illustrates the way in which the *Zohar* treats the zealous intuitions suppressed in rabbinic literature. These are particularly evident in the chapter on "Esau's suppressed cry," which demonstrates how the *Zohar* seeks to argue that Esau has been maltreated. Finally, the investigation of the *aqeda* reveals the first buds of a trend towards shifting the focus of interest from the theosophic to the psychological, the theoretical to the existential.

The study of the way in which the *Zohar* reworks ancient midrashic material is still in its infancy. Here, I have sought to pave the way for future research, shedding light on various aspects of the task. At the heart of this enterprise lies the recognition that the *Zohar* flourished within a creative tradition that drew its roots from the ancient aggada on the one hand and medieval kabbalistic thought on the other. This premise dictated and defined the methodology adopted , which blended a search for the history of the talmudic/midrashic tradition and its evolution within the *Zohar* with an attempt to locate the background to its embodiment and consolidation within the kabbalistic environment, and frequently the broader religious context, of the medieval period. Awareness of the complexity of the "terrain" requires a cautious approach and measured steps combined with a close and sensitive attentiveness to the nuances in order to reveal not only the spirit of the homily but also diverse streams and polemics within the zoharic enterprise and its environs.

These scholarly directions must be applied to additional material. The broader the scope covered, the better we shall be able to determine the nature of the aggada in the *Zohar* and the spirit of its authors. At the same time, however, in order to fully grasp and understand the spirit of the zoharic treatment of ancient midrashim and aggadot we must also open up new avenues and vistas, some of which we have touched upon in this volume. Let me note here the most prominent examples.

Future studies should focus in particular upon the literary and ideational links between the *Zohar* and the early/earlier sources. In this context, the association between the *Zohar* and Nahmanides' Torah commentary is of great interest. In the introduction to this contribution, I suggested that the *Zohar*'s choice of the midrashic genre may be perceived as "improving upon" Nahmanides' hermeneutical endeavours. A comprehensive examination of Nahmanides' influence upon the zoharic homiletics may well produce important insights. The way in which the *Zohar* makes use of exegesis that followed Nahmanides' approach should prove to be a fruitful avenue of investigation, revealing what parts of his kabbalistic exegesis it accepted and which it rejected—or was perhaps unaware of.

At a more advanced stage, the horizons may be expanded to provide a fuller picture of the interpretive traditions relating to the biblical text in the writings of the early kabbalists from the end of the twelfth through to the end of the thirteenth century, on the eve of the *Zohar*'s appearance. Here, we must first identify all the exegetical traditions relating to the biblical text that lie scattered throughout the kabbalistic literature of this period—published works and manuscripts alike. This step must be followed by an analytic mapping of all these witnesses and the outlining of the links and associations they reflect, the history of the various traditions, and the changes they underwent over time and space. This endeavour will contributed greatly to our understanding of the *Zohar*'s interpretive and homiletical creativity, in particular the differentiation within the hermeneutical / homiletical material between the early aggadic traditions and those composed by the zoharic authors themselves.

The *Zohar*'s affinities with Philo constitute another avenue of research that has been neglected to date. This issue, which has arisen on several occasions in the present volume, has been addressed primarily in relation to the dating of *Midrash Ne'elam*. It is also of great importance in its own right, however. If we discover that Philo's thought exerted a direct influence upon the zoharic literature—or *Midrash Hane'elam* at the very least—we may then seek to trace the channels through which it flowed. From a broader perspective, we must also examine the affinities between the zoharic corpus and hellenistic sources—a subject to which Liebes has devoted several studies. On occasion, zoharic motifs appear to have been drawn directly from hellenistic texts that left no trace in other pre-zoharic Jewish writings. Here, too, the extent and weight of such influence must be investigated.

The broader cultural context of the aggada in the *Zohar* also requires more extensive and in-depth study. Although numerous scholars have examined the book's relationship to its non-Jewish cultural and religious environment, the question of the extent to which these insights are valid in relation to the kabbalists' exegetical activity still remains to be properly investigated. Can any sign of influence or affinities with contemporary or earlier Christian interpretation be discerned in the zoharic aggada? Do the zoharic aggadic traditions display any correspondence with Islamic versions of the same aggada? Can traces of a polemic with foreign interpretive approaches of this kind be discerned in the *Zohar*? Some of these questions have arise on the margins of the discussion in this volume, these—and others—demanding more comprehensive study.

As I noted in the introduction, in order not to stray too far from the book's thematic framework I have chosen not to focus in anything but a general way upon the *Zohar*'s hermeneutical techniques. Future research elucidating the nature of the zoharic homily will undoutbledly contribute to our understanding of the relationship between the zoharic literature and rabbinic corpus from another, unique perspective. A better comprehension of the zoharic homiletic method, as perhaps also its *Sitz im Leben*, can also clarify the ways in which the ancient aggada was incorporated into the zoharic corpus.

The study of zoharic aggada also demands investigation of the later strata of the historical kabbalah. Thus, for example, the "historical" doctrine of reincarnation or transmigration, which associates various and diverse figures with "reincarnatory" lineages, should in my view be regarded as a sub-genre of exegesis. Although this hermeneutical premise lay at the heart of the discussion of Nadab and Abihu, whose sin I discussed in relation to the exegetical-ideological significance of their identification between Phinehas, it only occurs in isolated places. At the same time, in the pre-zoharic kabbalah onwards up through the Lurianic kabbalah of the sixteenth century these links grew and spread into a "reincarnatory dynasty." In my opinion, this doctrine contains within it an important key for understanding the kabbalistic reading of the biblical text, forming a new type of kabbalist homiletics. We must also examine this midrashic language and how the aggadic and hermeneutical dicta delivered in it should be interpreted. From this perspective and many others, we also need to investigate the Lurianic corpus of biblical aggadot, which in turn calls for an examination of this aggada in the Hasidic and Lithuanian tradition of homiletics of the eighteenth and nineteenth centuries.

In his "*Halacha* and *Aggadah*," Bialik observes: "The *Halachah* is the crystallization, the ultimate and inevitable quintessence of the *Aggadah*; the *Aggadah* is the content of the *Halachah*. The Aggadah is a plaintive voice of the heart's yearning as it wings its way to heaven" (2000: 46). To a large degree, we may apply the same definition to the relationship between kabbalistic thought and aggada in the *Zohar*. If the kabbalah—as a fundamental corpus or theoretical discussion of God, humanity, and the world is also the "ultimate and inevitable quintessence of the *Aggadah*," then the zoharic aggada exemplifies the zoharic book's living and breathing spirituality, the dynamic and human reflections of religious life within the spiritual realms of the kabbalah. If so, the Zohar's "splendour" must be understood not only in terms of dogma, myth, and ethos but also via its personality, beliefs, deliberations, sensitivities, and editing. I hope that a trace or echo of this spirit has shone through in these pages.

Bibliography

Abrabanel, Isaac. *Perush al ha-nevi'im ha-achronim*. Jerusalem, 1954.
Abrabanel, Isaac. *Perush al ha-nevi'im ha-rishonim*. Jerusalem, 1954.
Abrams, Daniel. From Divine Shape to Angelic Being: The Career of Akatriel in Jewish literature. *JR* 76 (1996): 43–63.
Abrams, Daniel. Knowing the Maiden Without Eyes: Reading the Sexual Reconstruction of the Jewish Mystic in a Zoharic Parable. *Daat* 50–52 (2003): 487–511.
Abrams, Daniel. *Kabbalistic Manuscripts and Textual Theory: Methodologies of Textual Theory and Editorial Practice in the Study of Jewish Mysticism*. Jerusalem: Magnes, 2010.
Abulafia, Todoros. *Otzar ha-kavod ha-shalem*. Warsaw, 1879. Ed. C. Erlanger. Bnei Brak, 1987.
Abulafia, Todoros. *Sha'ar ha-razim*. Ed. Michal Oron. Jerusalem, 1989.
Afterman, Adam. *Devekut: Mystical Intimacy in Medieval Jewish Thought*. Los Angeles: Cherub, 2011 (Hebrew).
Aggadat Bereshit. Trans. and annotated by Lieve M. Teugels. Leiden: Brill, 2001.
Albo, Joseph. *Sefer ha-iqarim*. Lemberg, 1866.
Alon, Gedalyahu. *Jews, Judaism, and the Classical World: Studies in Jewish history in the Times of the Second Temple*. Trans. I. Abrahams. Jerusalem: Magnes, 1977.
Alon, Gedalyahu. *The Jews in their Land in the Talmudic Age (70–640 C.E.)*. Trans. G. Levi. Jerusalem: Magnes, 1980–1984.
Altmann, Alexander. *A Note on the Rabbinic Doctrine of Creation*. In *Studies in Religious Philosophy and Mysticism*, 128–139. New York: Routledge & Kegan Paul, 1969.
Altmann, Alexander. Sefer or zarua le-R. Moshe de Leon: Mavo text criti ve-he'arot. *Kovetz al Yad* 9 [19], 1980: 243–44.
Aminoff, Irit. The figures of Esau and the kingdom of Edom in palestinian midrashic-talmudic literature in the tannaitic and amoraic periods. PhD diss., Melbourne University, 1981 (Hebrew).
Angelet, Joseph. *Sefer livnat hasapir*. Jerusalem, 1913.
Aptowitzer, Avigdor. The Heavenly Temple in the Agada. *Tarbiz* 2.2 (1931): 137–153; *Tarbiz* 2.3 (1931): 257–287 (Hebrew).
Aptowitzer, Victor. *Parteipolitik der hasmonaerzeit im rabbinischen und pseudoepigraphischen schrifttum*. Vienna, 1927.
Asulin, Shifra. The mystical commentary of the Song of Songs in the *Zohar* and its background. PhD diss., Hebrew University of Jerusalem, 2006 (Hebrew).
Avi-Yonah, Michael. *The Jews under Roman and Byzantine Rule: A Political History of Palestine from the Bar Kokhba War to the Arab Conquest*. Jerusalem: Bialik Institute, 1984 (Hebrew).
Ayali, Meir. Elijah—Whence Did He Come: The Ancestry and Origins of Elijah in the Midrash of the Sages. *Tura: Studies in Jewish Thought* 3 (1994): 43–64 (Hebrew).
Azriel of Gerona. *Perush ha-aggadot le-rabbi azriel me-gerona*. Ed. Isaiah Tishbi. Jerusalem, 1945.
Bachya ben Asher. *Perush rabbeinu Bachya la-torah*. Ed. Chaim Dov Chavel. Jerusalem, 1982.
Baer, Yitzhak. *Israel Among the Nations*. Jerusalem: Bialik Institute, 1955 (Hebrew).
Baer, Yitzhak. *A History of the Jews in Christian Spain*. 2 vols. Philadelphia: Jewish Publication Society, 1961.

Baer, Yitzhak. *Studies in the History of the Jewish People.* Jerusalem: Historical Society of Israel, 1985 (Hebrew).

Baer, Yitzhak. The Historical Background of the "Raya Mehemna." *Zion* 5 (1940): 1–44 (Hebrew).

Baine Harris, R. *Authority: A Philosophical Analysis.* Alabama: University of Alabama Press, 1976.

Bar Sheshet, Jacob. *Meshiv devarim nekhohim.* Edited by G. Vajda. Jerusalem, 1968.

Belkin, Samuel. *Midrash Ha-Ne'elam* and its Sources in Early Alexandrian Midrashim. *Sura* 3 (1958): 25–92 (Hebrew).

Belkin, Samuel. *The Midrash of Philo.* New York: Yeshiva University Press, 1989 (Hebrew).

Ben David, Abraham. *Perush ha-rab"ad al sefer yetzira.* Warsaw, 1884.

Ben Elimelech, Abraham. *Liqutey shikhcha u-pe'ah.* Ferrara, 1555.

Ben Gershom, Levi. *Perush le-sefer melakhim.* Miqra'ot gedolot he-keter 8. Ramat-Gan, 2114.

Ben Gershom, Levi. *Perushey ha-torah.* Ed. Ya'akov Lieb Levi. Jerusalem, 1996.

Ben-Chaim, Shlomo Shlomil. *Shivchey ha-ari.* Peremyshlyany, 1869.

Benedict, Benjamin. Eliyahu ha-navi: Navi ha-shalom. *Kovetz hakinus la-torah she-be-al pe* (1980): 101–112.

Berdyczewski, Micha Josef. *Mi-maqor yisrael: Ma'asiyot ve-sipurey-am.* Tel Aviv: Bialik Institute, 1939–1945.

Berger, David. Miracles and the Natural Order in Nahmanides. In *Rabbi Moses Nahmanides (Ramban): Explorations in his religious and literary virtuosity*, Isadore Twersky (ed.), 107–128. Cambridge: Harvard University Press, 1983.

Bialik, Haim, Rawnitzki, Yehoshua (eds.). *Sefer ha-aggada.* Tel Aviv, 1948.

Blidstein, Yaakov. The Blood of the Binding of Isaac: Notes on the Spiegel-Urbach Debate. In *Judaism: Topics, Fragments, Faces, Identities—Jubilee Volume in Honor of Rivka*, Haviva Pedaya and Ephraim Meir (eds.), 431–437. Beersheba: Ben-Gurion University Press, 2007 (Hebrew).

Bohak Gideon. *Ancient Jewish Magic.* Cambridge: Cambridge University Press, 2008.

Boyarin, Daniel. *Intertextuality and the Reading of Midrash.* Bloomington: Indiana University Press, 1994.

Brodie, C. Piyyutim bilti noda'im. *Kovetz al yad* 11 (1936): 7–23.

Brody, Seth. Human hands dwell in heavenly heights: Worship and mystical experience in thirteenth-century kabbalah. PhD diss., University of Pennsylvania, 1991.

Brody, Seth. Human Hands Dwell in Heavenly Heights: Contemplative Ascent and Theurgic Power in Thirteenth-Century Kabbalah. In *Mystics of the Book: Themes, Topics, and Typologies*, Robert A. Herrera (ed.), 123–158. New York: Peter Lang, 1993.

Brown, Michael. Biblical Myth and Contemporary Experience: The "Akeda" in Modern Jewish Literature. *Judaism* 3 (1982): 99–111.

Buber, Martin. *The Hidden Light—Hassidic Tales.* Jerusalem: Schocken, 2005 (Hebrew).

Cohen Eloro, Dorit. *Sod ha-malbush u-mareh ha-malakh be-sefer ha-zohar.* Jerusalem: Magnes, 1987.

Cohen Eloro, Dorit. Magic and sorcery in the Zohar. PhD diss., Hebrew University of Jerusalem, 1989 (Hebrew).

Cohen, Gerson D. Esau as a Symbol in Early Medieval Thought. In *Jewish Medieval and Renaissance Studies*, Alexander Altmann (ed.), 19–48). Cambridge: Harvard University Press, 1967.

Cordovero, Moshe. *Sefer Pardes Rimonim.* Jerusalem, 1962.

Crescas, Hasdai. *The Light of the Lord*. Ed. S. Fischer. Jerusalem: Sifrei Ramot, 1980 (Hebrew).
Dan, Joseph. *Torat ha-sod shel chasidut ashkenaz*. Jerusalem: Bialik Institute, 1968 (Hebrew).
Dan, Joseph. Samael, Lilith, and the Concept of Evil in Early Kabbalah. *AJS Review* 5 (1980): 17–40.
Dan, Joseph. Midrash and the Dawn of Kabbalah. In *Midrash and Literature*, Geoffrey Hartman and Sandford Budick (eds.), 127–139. New Haven: Yale University Press, 1986.
Dan, Joseph. *The Ancient Jewish Mysticism*. Tel Aviv: MOD, 1993.
Dan, Joseph. *On Sanctity, Religion, Ethics, and Mysticism in Judaism and Other Religions*. Jerusalem: Magnes, 1997 (Hebrew).
Dan, Joseph. Samael and the Problem of Jewish Gnosticism. In *Perspectives on Jewish Thought and Mysticism*, Elliot Wolfson and Allan Arkush (eds.), 257–267. Amsterdam: Harwood Academic Publisher, 1998.
Dan, Joseph. *History of Jewish Mysticism and Esotericism*. 11 vols. Zalman Shazar Centre, 1999–2015 (Hebrew).
Dan, Joseph. Ottiot De-Rabbi Akiva and its Concept of Language. *Daat* 55 (2005): 5–30 (Hebrew).
Efrati, Jacob Eliahu. *Parashat ha-aqeda: Ha-miqra'ot u-midrashey ha-aggada shel chazal kifshutam*. Petach Tikva, 1983.
Ehrlich, Uri. *The nonverbal Language of Jewish Prayer: A New Approach to Jewish Liturgy*. Tübingen: Mohr Siebeck, 2004.
Eisenstein, Yehuda D. *Otzar midrashim*. New York: Reznik Menschel, and Co., 1915.
Elboim, Jacob. More on the *Akedah* Legends. *Jerusalem Studies in Hebrew Literature* 9 (1986): 341–356 (Hebrew).
Elboim, Jacob. *Yalqut Shim'oni* and the Medieval Midrashic Anthology. In *The anthology in Jewish literature*, David Stern (ed.), 159–175. Oxford: Oxford University Press, 2004.
Elboim, Jacob (ed.). *Lehavin divrey chakhamim*. Jerusalem: Bialik Institute, 2000.
Elchanan, Naftali Hertz ben Yaakov. *Emeq ha-melech*. Amsterdam, 1648.
Elimelech of Lizhensk. *Sefer noam elimelech*. Lemberg, 1788.
Elior, Rachel. Jacob Frank and His Book *The Sayings of the Lord:* Religious Anarchism as a Restoration of Myth and Metaphor. In *The Sabbatian Movement and its Aftermath: Messianism, Sabbatianism and Frankism*, Rachel Elior (ed.), 2:451–547. Jerusalem: Institute for Jewish Studies, 2001 (Hebrew).
Elior, Rachel. *Temple and Chariot, Priests and Angels, Sanctuary and Heavenly Sanctuaries in Early Jewish Mysticism*. Jerusalem: Magnes, 2003 (Hebrew).
Elior, Rachel. "You Have Chosen Enoch from Among Human Beings": Enoch "The Scribe of Righteousness" and the Scrolls' Library of "The Priests of the Sons of Zadok." In *Creation and recreation in Jewish thought: Festschrift in honor of Joseph Dan on the occasion of his seventieth birthday*, Rachel Elior, Peter Schäfer (eds.), 15–64. Tübingen: Mohr Siebeck, 2005 (Hebrew).
Elizur, Shulamit. The Influence of the Crusades on the *Piyyutim* of the *Aqeda*. *Et haDa'at* 1 (1997): 15–35) (Hebrew).
Emden, Jacob. *Sefer she'ilat ya'avetz*. Lemberg, 1884.
Epstein, Jacob. *Introduction to Tannaitic Literature: Mishna, Tosephta and Halakhic Midrashim*. Jerusalem, 1957 (Hebrew).
Even Chen, Alexander. *The Binding of Isaac: Mystical and Philosophical Interpretation of the Bible*. Tel Aviv: Miskal, 2006 (Hebrew).

Farber-Ginat, Asi. On the Sources of Rabbi Moses de Leon's Early Kabbalistic System. *Jerusalem Studies in Jewish Thought* 3 (1984): 67–94 (Hebrew).
Farber-Ginat, Asi. "The Shell Precedes the Fruit": On the Question of the Origin of Metaphysical Evil in Early Kabbalistic Thought. In *Myth and Judaism*, Haviva Pedaya (ed.), 118–142. Jerusalem: Bialik Institute, 1996 (Hebrew).
Feldman, Louis. *Josephus' Interpretation of the Bible*. Berkeley: University of California Press, 1998.
Felix, Irit. Chapters in the kabbalistic thought of R. Joseph Angelet. MA thesis, Hebrew University, Jerusalem, 1991 (Hebrew).
Fishbane, Michael. *Biblical Interpretation in Ancient Israel*. Oxford: Clarendon, 1985.
Fishbane, Michael. *The Kiss of God: Spiritual and Mystical Death in Judaism*. Washington, DC: University of Washington Press, 1994.
Flusser, David. Nadab and Abihu in the Midrash and in Philo's Writings. *Milet* 2 (1985): 79–84 (Hebrew).
Frankel, Yonah. *Darchei ha-aggadah ve-ha-midrash*. Givatayim: Massada, 1991.
Friedman, Richard E. *The Bible with Sources Revealed: A New View into the Five Books of Moses*. New York: HarperCollins, 2003.
Funkenstein, Amos. *Perceptions of Jewish History*. Berkeley: University of California Press, 1993.
Galanti, Abraham. Zoharey Chama. Munkatsh, 1881.
Garb, Jonathan. Models of Sacred Space in Jewish Mysticism and their Impact in the Twentieth Century. In *The Land of Israel in 20th Century Jewish Thought*. Aviezer Ravitzky (ed.), 1–25. Jerusalem: Yad Ben-Zvi, 2004 (Hebrew).
Garsiel, Moshe. Literary Structure and Message in the Jacob and Esau Stories. *Hagut ba-miqra* 4 (1983): 63–81 (Hebrew).
Gavarin Martelle. The Problem of Evil in the Thought of Rabbi Isaac Sagi Nahor and his Disciples, *Daat* 20 (1988): 29–50 (Hebrew).
Gelander, Shamai. Strange Fire. *An Annual for Biblical and Ancient New Eastern Studies* 9 (1985/87): 73–81 (Hebrew).
Gikatilla, Joseph. *Sha'arey tzedeq*. Cracow, 1881.
Gikatilla. Joseph. *Sha'arey ora*. Ed. Joseph ben Shlomo. Jerusalem, 1981.
Gikatilla, Joseph. *Ginat egoz*. Jerusalem, 1989.
Gilat, Yitzhak Dov. The Teachings of R. Eliezer Ben Hyrcanos. Tel Aviv: Dvir, 1968 (Hebrew).
Giller, Pinchas. *Reading the Zohar: The Sacred Text of the Kabbalah*. Oxford: Oxford University Press, 2001.
Ginzberg, Louis. *Legends of the Jews*. 7 vols. Trans. Henrietta Szold and Paul Radin. Philadelphia: Jewish Publication Society, 2003.
Goetschel, Roland. The Conception of Prophecy in the Works of R. Moses de Leon and R. Joseph Gikatilla. *Jerusalem Studies in Jewish Thought* 8 (1989): 217–237 (Hebrew).
Goldberg, Abraham. Ha-drashot ha-kefulot be-mekhilta de-miluim. *Sinai* 89 (1981): 115–118.
Goldberg, Abraham. Be'ayot arikha ve-sidur be-bereshit rabba u-ve-vayikra rabba she-terem ba'u al pitronan. *Mehqerei Talmud* 3 (2005): 30–152.
Goldreich, Amos. "Clarifications in the Self-Perception of the Author of *Tiqqunei Zohar*." In *Massu'ot: Studies in Kabbalistic Literature and Jewish Philosophy in Memory of Prof. Ephraim Gottlieb*, Michal Oron, Amos Goldreich (eds.), 459–496. Jerusalem: Bialik Institute, 1994 (Hebrew).

Goldreich, Amos. *Automatic Writing in Zoharic Literature and Modernism*. Los Angeles: Cherub Press, 2010 (Hebrew).
Goldreich, Amos. *Sefer Mei'rat Einayim* by R. Isaac of Acre: A critical edition. PhD diss., Hebrew University of Jerusalem, 1981 (Hebrew).
Goldschmidt, Daniel (ed.). *Seder ha-selichot: Ke-minhag polin ve-rov ha-qehilot be-eretz yisrael*. Jerusalem: Mossad Harav Kook, 1965.
Goldschmidt, Daniel (ed.). *Machzor leyamim nora'im: Lefi minhagey bnei ashkenaz le-khol ha-anafim*. Jerusalem: Koren, 1984.
Goshen-Gottstein, Alon. The Myth of the Act of Creation in the Amoraitic Literature. In *Myth in Judaism*, Haviva Pedaya (ed.), 58–77. Beersheba: Ben Gurion University Press, 1996 (Hebrew).
Gottlieb, Ephraim. *The Kabbalah in the Writings of R. Bahya ben Asher ibn Halawa* (Jerusalem: Qiryat Sefer, 1970 (Hebrew).
Gottleib, Ephraim. *Studies in the Kabbala Literature*. Tel Aviv: Tel Aviv University, 1976 (Hebrew).
Green, Arthur. *Rabbi Nahman of Bratslav: a critical biography*. Tel Aviv: Am Oved, 1979.
Greenstein, Edward. Deconstruction and Biblical Narrative. *Prooftexts* 9 (1989): 56–61.
Greenstein, Edward. An Inner-Biblical Midrash of the Nadab and Abihu Episode. *Proceedings of the Eleventh World Congress of Jewish Studies*. Jerusalem: World Union of Jewish Studies, 1994), A*71–*78 (Hebrew).
Gries, Zeev. Mati meged: Ha-or ha-nechsakh—Arakhim asteti'im be-sefer ha-zohar. *Qiryat Sefer* 55 (1980): 373–378.
Gries, Zeev. The Commentaries on Song of Songs in Early Kabbalah. *Mar'eh* 1 (2006): 18–24.
Grossman, Abraham. *The Early Sages of France, Their Lives, Leadership, and Works (900–1096)*. Jerusalem: Magnes, 2001 (Hebrew).
Gruenwald, Ithamar. The Midrashic Condition: From the Derashot of the Sages to the Derashot of the Qabbalists. *Jewish Studies in Jewish Thought* 8 (1989): 255–298 (Hebrew).
Haberman, Abraham. *Chelqat mechoqeq: Divrey misrash ve-aggada al moshe rabbeinu u-petirato*. Jerusalem/Tel Aviv: Schocken, 1947 (Hebrew).
Haberman, Abraham (ed.). *The Literary Works of Abraham Epstein*. 2 vols. Jerusalem: Mossad Harav Kook, 1949–1956 (Hebrew).
Halbertal, Moshe. *By Way of Truth: Nahmanides and the Creation of Tradition*. Jerusalem: Shalom Hartman Institute, 2006 (Hebrew).
Halevi, Elimelech. *Parshiyot ba-aggada le-or meqorot yevani'im*. Tel Aviv: Dvir, 1973.
Halevi, Judah. *The Kuzari*. Trans. H. Hirschfeld. New York: Pardes, 1946.
Hallamish, Moshe. Towards an Assessment of the Influence of *Sefer Ha-Bahir* on the Kabbalist R. Joseph Joseph ben Shalom Ashkenazi. *Bar-Ilan Year Book* 7–8 (1969–1970): 211–224 (Hebrew).
Hallamish, Moshe. *The Kabbalistic Commentary of Rabbi Yoseph Ben Shalom Ashkenazi on Genesis Rabbah*. Jerusalem: Magnes, 1984 (Hebrew).
Harari, Yuval. *Early Jewish Magic: Research, Method, Sources*. Jerusalem: Bialik Institute, 1998 (Hebrew).
Harari, Yuval. La'asot Petichat Lev: Magical Practices for Knowledge, Understanding and Memory in Ancient and Medieval Judaism. In *Shefa Tal: Studies in Jewish Philosophy and Culture Dedicated to Beracha Zack*, Zeev Gries, Chaim Kriesal, and Boaz Huss (eds.), 303–347. Beersheba: Ben-Gurion University Press, 2005 (Hebrew).

Har-Shefi, Avishar. The early kings: The myth of the Edomite kings in the literature of the *Idrot*. MA thesis, Bar-Ilan University, 2007 (Hebrew).
Heinemann, Isaac. *Darkhei ha-aggada*. Jerusalem: Magnes, 1974.
Heinemann, Joseph. The Structure and Division of Genesis Rabbah. *Bar-Ilan* 9 (1972): 279–289 (Hebrew).
Heinemann, Joseph. *Aggadot ve-toldoteyhen: Iyunim be-hishtalshalutan shel mesorot*. Jerusalem: Keter, 1993.
Hellner-Eshed, Melila. Nefesh ha-qana ba-zohar. *Elu va-Elu* 4 (1997): 98–116.
Hellner-Eshed, Melila. *A River Flows from Eden: The Language of Mystical Experience in the Zohar*. Stanford: Stanford University Press, 2009.
Herr, Moshe David. Roman rule in tannaitic literature: Its image and conception. PhD diss., Hebrew University of Jerusalem, 1970 (Hebrew).
Hirshfeld, Nurit. From Which Tree did Adam and Eve Eat in the Garden of Eden? In *A Garden Eastward in Eden: Traditions of Paradise*, Rachel Elior (ed.), 191–204. Jerusalem: Magnes, 2010 (Hebrew).
Hirshman, Marc. *Midrash and Mikra: A Comparison of Rabbinics and Patristics*. Tel Aviv: Hakibbutz Hameuchad, 1992 (Hebrew).
Hoffman, David. Le-cheqer midrashey ha-tana'im. In *Mesilot le-torat ha-tana'im*, Alexander Susskind Rabinowitz (ed.). Tel Aviv: Achdut, 1928.
Horowitz, Isaiah. *Shney Luchot Habrit*. 3 vols. Trans. Eliyahu Munk. Brooklyn: Lambda Publishers, 2000.
Hurowitz, Avigdor V. What Did Balak's Messengers Bring to Balaam? *Eretz Israel* 22 (1993) 83–86 (Hebrew).
Huss, Boaz. Rabbi Joseph Gikatilia's Definition of Symbolism and its Influence on Kabbalistic Literature. *Jerusalem Studies in Jewish Thought* 12/1 (1996): 158–176 (Hebrew).
Huss, Boaz. A Sage is preferable than a Prophet: Rabbi Shim'on Bar Yohai and Moses in the Zohar. *Kabbalah* 4 (1999): 103–139 (Hebrew).
Huss, Boaz. Nisan, the Wife of the Infinite: The Mystical Hermeneutics of Rabbi Isaac of Acre. *Kabbalah* 5 (2000): 155–181.
Huss, Boaz. *Sockets of Fine Gold: The Kabbalah of R. Shimo'n Ibn Lavi*. Jerusalem: Magnes/Yad Ben-Zvi, 2000 (Hebrew).
Huss, Boaz. *Like the Radiance of the Sky: Chapters in the Reception History of the Zohar and the Construction of its Symbolic Value*. Jerusalem: Yad Ben-Zvi/Bialik Institute, 2008 (Hebrew).
Ibn Ezra, Abraham. *Commentary on the Torah*. Ed. Asher Weiss. Jerusalem, 2005.
Ibn Gabbai, Meir. *Avodat ha-qodesh*. Warsaw, 1883.
Ibn Gaon, Shem-Tov. *Keter shem-tov*. Jerusalem, 2001.
Ibn Janah, Jonah. *Sefer ha-rikma*. Trans. J. Ibn Tivon. Ed. Michael Wilensky. Berlin, 1929.
Ibn Lavi, Shimon. *Sefer ketem paz*. Jerusalem, 1981.
Ibn Shuaib, Joshua. *Beur le-perush ha-ramban al ha-torah meyuchas le-ha-rav meir b"r shlomo abusaulla*. Warsaw, 1875.
Ibn Shuaib, Joshua. *Sefer ha-drashot al ha-torah u-mo'adei ha-shana*. Ed. Zev Metzger. Jerusalem, 1992.
Idel, Moshe. The Evil Thought of the Deity. *Tarbiz* 49.3–4 (1979/1980): 356–364 (Hebrew).
Idel, Moshe. The Concept of Torah in Hekhalot Literature and its Metamorphosis in Kabbalah. *Jewish Studies in Jewish Thought* 1 (1981): 23–84 (Hebrew).
Idel, Moshe. The Sefirot Above the Sefirot. *Tarbiz* 51 (1982): 239–280 (Hebrew).

Idel, Moshe. We Do Not Have a Kabbalistic Tradition on This. In *Rabbi Moses Maimonides (Rambam): Explorations in his Religious and Literary Virtuosity*, Isadore Twersky (ed.), 51–73. Cambridge: Harvard University Press, 1983.

Idel, Moshe. The Worlds of Angels in Human Form. In *Studies in Jewish Mysticism, Philosophy and Ethical Literature, Presented to Isaiah Tishby on his Seventy-Fifth Birthday*, Joseph Dan and Joseph Hacker (eds.), 1–66. Jerusalem: Magnes, 1986 (Hebrew).

Idel, Moshe. *Kabbalah: New Perspectives*. New Haven: Yale University Press, 1988.

Idel, Moshe. Enoch is Metatron. *Immanuel* 24/25 (1990): 220–240.

Idel, Moshe. Preliminary Observations on the Variety of Kabbalistic Exegesis. In *Rabbi Mordechai Breuer Festschrift: Collected Papers in Jewish Studies*, M. Ahrend et al. (eds.), 2: 773–784. Jerusalem: Academon, 1992 (Hebrew).

Idel, Moshe. Midrashic Versus Other Forms of Jewish Hermeneutics: Some Comparative Reflections. In *The Midrashic Imagination: Jewish Imagination, Thought and History*, Michael Fishbane (ed.), 45–58. Albany: SUNY Press, 1993.

Idel, Moshe. Kabbalah and Elites in Thirteenth-century Spain. *Mediterranean Historical Review* 9 (1994): 5–19.

Idel, Moshe. Rabbi Moshe ben Nahman: Kabbalah, Halachah and Spiritual Leadership. *Tarbiz* 64 (1995): 535–580 (Hebrew).

Idel, Moshe. ParDeS: Some Reflections on Kabbalistic Hermeneutics. In *Death, Ecstasy and Other Worldly Journeys*, John Collins, Michael Fishbane (eds.), 249–268. Albany: SUNY Press, 1995 (1995a).

Idel, Moshe. *Hasidism: Between Ecstasy and Magic*. Albany: SUNY Press, 1995 (1995b).

Idel, Moshe. Metatron: Hearot al hitpatchut ha-mitos ba-yahadut. In *Myth in Judaism*, Haviva Pedaya (ed.), 22–44. Beersheba Ben Gurion University Press, 1996.

Idel, Moshe. *Menahem Recanati the Kabbalist*. Tel Aviv: Schocken, 1998 (Hebrew).

Idel, Moshe. From the "Hidden Light" to the "Light Within the Torah": A Chapter in the Phenomenology of Jewish Mysticism. In *Migvan de'ot ve-hashqafot al ha-or*, A. Zion (ed.), 23–62. Jerusalem: Ministry of Education, 2003 (Hebrew).

Idel, Moshe. *Absorbing Reflections*. New Haven: Yale University Press, 2008.

Idel, Moshe. The Image of Man Above the Sefirot: R. David ben Yehuda He-Hasid's Theosophy of Ten Supernanal *Sahsahot* and its Reverberations. *Kabbalah* 20 (2009): 181–212.

Irshai, Oded. R. Abbahu Said: If a Man should Say to you: 'I am God' - He is a Liar (Hebrew). *Zion* 47 (1982): 173–177.

Ish Shalom, Meir. *Mavo le-seder eliyahu*. In *Seder eliyahu rabbah ve-seder eliyahu zuta*. Vienna, 1902.

Jellenik, Aaron. *Bet ha-midrash*. Leipzig, 1878. Repr. Jerusalem: Wahrman, 1967.

Joseph Hamekaney. *Sefer yosef ha-mekane*. Ed. J. Rosenthal. Jerusalem, 1970.

Kahalani, Ezra. *Aggadat Bereshit*: Introduction, proposal for a critical edition and discussion of its content and structure. PhD diss., Hebrew University of Jerusalem, 2003 (Hebrew).

Kahana, Menahem. *The Two Mekhiltot to the* Amalek *Portion*. Jerusalem: Magnes, 1999 (Hebrew).

Kam, Matia. Ha-acher itanu ve-ha-acher be-tokhenu: Gilgulav shel sipur ya'aqov ve-esav min ha-miqra ve-ad la-et ha-hadasha. In *The Other Within and Without*, Haim Deutsch and Menachem Ben-Sasson (eds.), 342–366 Tel Aviv: Yediot Ahronot, 2001.

Kaminka, Aaron. *Essays in Historical Criticism*. New York: Qeren le-Tarbuth of Cincinnati, 1944 (Hebrew).

Kaufmann, Yehezkel. *The Religion of Israel: From Its Beginnings to the Babylonian Exile.* Trans. Moshe Greenberg. Chicago: University of Chicago Press, 1960.

Ketterer, Eliane. Alphabet of Rabbi Aqiba (version A–B). PhD diss., Hebrew University of Jerusalem, 2005 (Hebrew).

Kister, Menahem. Observations on Aspects of Exegesis, Tradition, and Theology in Midrash, Pseudepigrapha, and Other Jewish Writings. In *Tracing the Threads: Studies in the Vitality of Jewish Pseudepigrapha*, John C. Reeves (ed.), 1–34. Atlanta: Society of Biblical Literature, 1994.

Kister, Menahem. Ancient Material in Pirqe De-Rabbi Eli'ezer: Basilides, Qumran, the Book of Jubilees. In *"Go Out and Study the Land": Archaeological, Historical, and Textual Studies in Honor of Hanan Eshel*, Aren Maier, Jodi Magness, and Lawrence Schiffman (eds.), 69–93. Leiden: Brill 2012.

Klein-Braslavi, Sarah. *The Rambam's Understanding of the Stories of Adam in the Book of Genesis.* Jerusalem: Reuven Mass, 1986 (Hebrew).

Klein-Braslavi, Sarah. Solomon's "Prophecy" in the Works of Maimonides. In *Tribute to Sara, Studies in Jewish Philosophy and Kabbala Presented to Professor Sara O. Heller Wilensky*, Moshe Idel, Devora Dimant, and Shalom Rosenberg (eds.), 57–81. Jerusalem: Magnes, 1994) (Hebrew).

Krauss, Samuel. *Qadmoniot hatalmud.* 4 vols. Odessa/Berlin/Tel Aviv, 1914–1923.

Kulik, Alexander. *Retroverting Slavonic Pseudepigrapha: Toward the Original of the Apocalypse of Abraham.* Leiden: Brill, 2005.

Kushelevsky, Rella. *Moses and the Angel of Death.* New York: Lang, 1995.

Kushelevsky, Rella. A Chiastic Phenomenon in the Narratives on the Death of Moses. In *Encyclopedia of the Jewish Story*, Rella Kushelevsky and Yoav Elstein (eds.), 135–167. Ramat-Gan: University of Bar-Ilan Press, 2004–2013 (Hebrew).

Lasker, Daniel. Saadia Gaon on Christianity and Islam. In *The Jews of Medieval Islam: Community, Society and Identity*, Daniel Lasker (ed.), 165–177. Leiden: Brill, 1995.

Lasker, Daniel. Against Whom Did Rav Saadia Gaon Polemicize in his Discussion Concerning the Abrogation of the Torah? *Daat* 32–33 (1997): 5–11 (Hebrew).

Lederberg, Netanel. Darka shel haqdamat ha-zohar be-veur ma'aseh ha-aqeda. *Maagalim* 4 (2005): 175–194.

Leon, Moses de. *Mishkan ha-edut.* Paris ms. NNL HEB 12/719 (n.d.).

Leon, Moses de. Sod bil'am. *Sefer ha-nefesh ha-chachama*, 53. Basila, 1608.

Leon, Moses de. *Sefer sheqel ha-qodesh.* Ed. Charles Mopsik. Los Angeles: Cherub, 1996.

Leon, Moses de. She'elot ve-teshuvot le-rabbi moshe de-leon be-inyeney qabala. In *Studies in Kabbalah and its Branches*, Isaiah Tishby (ed.), 1: 36–75. Jerusalem: Magnes, 1993.

Levenson, Jon. *The Death and Resurrection of the Beloved Son: The Transformation of Child Sacrifice in Judaism and Christianity.* New Haven: Yale University Press, 1993.

Levi, Herman Zvi (ed.). *Sons: Myth, Theme, and Literary Topos.* Jerusalem, 1991 (Hebrew).

Levinson, Joshua. *The Twice-Told Tale: A Poetics of the Exegetical Narrative in Rabbinic Midrash.* Jerusalem: Magnes, 2005 (Hebrew).

Lieberman, Saul. Chazonut yannai. In *Studies in Studies in Palestinian Talmudic Literature.* Jerusalem, 1991, 123–152.

Liebes, Esther. Lay not Thy Hand Upon the Lad – The Highest point of Abraham's Experience. In *Judaism: Topics, Fragments, Faces, Identities—Jubilee Volume in Honor of Rivka*, Haviva Pedaya and Ephraim Meir (eds.), 439–452. Beersheba: Ben-Gurion University Press, 2007 (Hebrew).

Liebes, Yehuda. *Chapters in the dictionary of the book of the Zohar*. PhD diss., Hebrew University of Jerusalem, 1977 (Hebrew).
Liebes, Yehuda. The Author of the Book *Tzaddik Yesod Olam:* The Sabbataian Prophet. Rabbi Leib Prossnitz. *Daat* 1 (1978): 73–120 (Hebrew).
Liebes, Yehuda. The Angels of the Shofar and Yeshua Sar ha-Panim. *Jerusalem Studies in Jewish Thought* 6 (1987): 171–195 (Hebrew).
Liebes, Yehuda. *The Sin of Elisha: Four Entered the Orchard and the Nature of Talmudic Mysticism*. Jerusalem: Magnes, 1990 (Hebrew).
Liebes, Yehuda. "Two Young Roes of a Doe": The Secret Sermon of Isaac Luria before his Death. In *Lurianic Kabbalah: Proceedings of the Fourth International Conference on the History of Mysticism*, Rachel Elior and Yehuda Liebes (eds.), 113–169. Jerusalem: Hebrew University of Jerusalem, 1992 (Hebrew).
Liebes, Yehuda. *De Natura Dei:* On the Development of the Jewish Myth. In *Studies in Jewish Myth and Jewish Messianism*, 1–64. Albany: SUNY Press, 1993 (1993a).
Liebes, Yehuda. Christian Influences on the Zohar. In *Studies in the Zohar*, 139–162. Trans. Arnold Schwartz, Stephanie Nakache and Penina Peli. Albany: SUNY Press, 1993 (1993b).
Liebes, Yehuda. How the Zohar was Written. *Studies in the Zohar*, 85–138. Trans. Arnold Schwartz, Stephanie Nakache and Penina Peli. Albany: SUNY Press, 1993 (1993c).
Liebes, Yehuda. The Messiah of the Zohar. In *Studies in the Zohar*, 1–84. Trans. Arnold Schwartz, Stephanie Nakache and Penina Peli. Albany: SUNY Press, 1993 (1993d).
Liebes, Yehuda. Zohar and Eros. *Alpayyim* 9 (1994): 67–115 (Hebrew).
Liebes, Yehuda. Myth versus Symbol in the Zohar and in Lurianic Kabbala. In *Essential Papers on Kabbalah*, Lawrence Fine (ed.), 212–242. New York: New York University Press, 1995.
Liebes, Yehuda. *Ars Poetica in Sefer Yetsira*. Tel Aviv: Schocken, 2000 (Hebrew).
Liebes, Yehuda. The Zohar as Renaissance in Castile. *Daat* 46 (2001): 5–11 (Hebrew).
Liebes, Yehuda. Introduction: Magic and Kabbalah. In *Demons, Demons and Souls: Studies in Demonology by Gershom Scholem*, Esther Liebes (ed.), 3–7. Jerusalem: Yad Ben-Zvi, 2004 (Hebrew).
Liebes, Yehuda. The Shaker of the Earth: The Uniqueness of Rashbi. In *Judaism: Topics, Fragments, Faces, Identities—Jubilee Volume in Honor of Rivka*, Haviva Pedaya and Ephraim Meir (eds.), 337–357. Beersheba: Ben-Gurion University Press, 2007 (Hebrew) (2007a).
Liebes, Yehuda. Zohar and Tiqqunei Zohar: From Renaissance to Revolution. In *New Developments in Zohar Studies*, Ronit Meroz (ed.), 251–301. Tel Aviv: Tel Aviv University Press, 2007 (Hebrew) (2007b).
Liebes, Yehuda. Of God's Love and Jealousy: The Dangers of Divine Affection. *Dimuy* 7 (1994): 30–36 (Hebrew).
Liebes, Yehuda. *The Cult of the Dawn. The Attitude of the Zohar towards Idolatry*. Jerusalem: Carmel, 2011 (Hebrew).
Liver, Jacob (ed.). *The Military History of the Land of Israel in Biblical Times*. Jerusalem: Israel Defense Forces Publishing House, 1964 (Hebrew).
Loewenstamm, Samuel. The Death of Moses. In *Studies on the Testament of Abraham*, George Nickelsburg (ed.), 185–217. Missoula: Scholars Press, 1976.
Loewenstamm, Samuel. Nachalat ha-shem. *Studies in Bible, 1986*, Sara Japhet (ed.), 155–192. Jerusalem: Magnes, 1986 (Hebrew).

Loewenstamm, Samuel. *The Evolution of the Exodus Tradition*. Jerusalem: Magnes, 1992.
Ma'arekht ha-elohit im perush ha-chayat. Mantua, 1558.
Mack, Hananel. *The Mystery of Rabbi Moshe Hadarshan*. Jerusalem: Bialik Institute, 2010 (Hebrew).
Maimonides, Moses. *The Guide of the Perplexed*. 2 vols. Trans. Shlomo Pines. Ed. Leo Strauss. Chicago: Chicago University Press, 1963.
Maimonides, Moses. *Mishneh Torah: Maimonides' Code of Law and Ethics*. New York: Hebrew Publishing Company, 1974.
Maimonides, Moses. *Mishna im perush rabbeinu moshe ben maimon*. Ed. Joseph Kapach. Jerusalem: Mossad Harav Kook, 1964.
Mandel, Pinchas. "Bira" as an Architectural Term in Rabbinic Literature. *Tarbiz* 61 (1991): 195–217 (Hebrew).
Margoliot, Eliezer. *Elijah the Prophet in the Literature, Faith, and Spiritual Life of Israel*. Jerusalem, 1960 (Hebrew).
Martyn, J. Louis. *We Have Found Elijah*. In *Jews, Greeks and Christians: Religious Cultures in Late Antiquity*, Robert Hamerton-Kelly and Robin Scroggs (eds.), 181–219. Leiden: Brill, 1976.
Matt, Daniel. Matnita Dilan: A Technique of Innovation in the Zohar. *Jerusalem Studies in Jewish Thought* 8 (1989): 123–145 (Hebrew).
Matt, Daniel. New-Ancient Words: The Aura of Secrecy in the Zohar. In *Gershom Scholem's Major Trends in Jewish Mysticism: 50 Years After*, Peter Schäfer and Joseph Dan (eds.), 181–207). Tübingen: Mohr Siebeck, 1993.
Matt, Daniel. *The Zohar Pritzker Edition*. 10 vols. Stanford: Stanford University Press, 2004–2009.
Meged, Mati. Sipurey ha-zohar: Miyunam, meqorotehem, ziqotehem ha-pnimi'im u-mashma'utam legabeh ha-zohar atzmo ve-legabeh demuto shel ha-mistiqa'i. MA thesis, Hebrew University of Jerusalem, 1963.
Meir, Ofra. *The Homiletical Story in* Genesis Rabbah. Tel Aviv: Hakibbutz Hameuchad, 1987 (Hebrew).
Meir, Ofra. Ma'aseh ha-arikha be-bereishit rabba u-ve-vayiqra rabba. In *Mechqarim be-midrashey ha-aggada: Sefer zikaron le-zvi meir rabinovitz*, M. Lerner and M. Friedman (eds.), 61–90. Tel Aviv: Tel Aviv University Press, 1996.
Mekhilta De-Rabbi Ishmael. 3 vols. Ed. Jacob Lauterbach. Philadelphia: JPS, 1933.
Menahem Nahum of Chernobyl. *Upright Practices, The Light of the Eyes*. Ed. Arthur Green. New York: Paulist Press, 1982.
Menn, Esther. Inner-Biblical Exegesis in the Tanak. In *A History of Biblical Interpretation*, A. Hauser, D.F. Watson (ed.), 55–79. Grand Rapids: Eerdmans, 2003.
Meroz, Ronit. Zoharic Narratives and their Adaptation. *Hispania Judaica* 32 (2001): 3–63.
Meroz, Ronit. "And I Was Not There?": The Complaints of Rabbi Simeon bar Yohai according to an Unknown Story of the Zohar. *Tarbiz* 71 (2002): 163–193 (Hebrew) (2002a).
Meroz, Ronit. On the Time and Place of Some Paragraphs of Sefer Ha-Bahir. *Da'at* 49 (2002): 137–180 (Hebrew) (2002b).
Meroz, Ronit. The Weaving of a Myth: An Analysis of Two Stories in the Zohar. In *Study and Knowledge in Jewish Thought*, Haim Kreisel (ed.), 2:168–205. Beersheba: Ben-Gurion University Press, 2006 (Hebrew).
Meroz, Ronit. R. Joseph Angelet and his "Zoharic Writings." *Te'uda 21–22* (2007): 303–404 (Hebrew).

Meroz, Ronit. *Yuvaley zohar: Mahadura biqortit shel zohar parashat shemot* (forthcoming).
Milikowsky, Chaim. Trajectories of Return, Restoration and Redemption in Rabbinic
    Judaism: Elijah, the Messiah, the War of Gog and the World to Come. In *Restoration: Old
    Testament, Jewish, and Christian Perspectives*, James M. Scott (ed.), 265–280. Leiden:
    Brill, 2001.
Mirsky, Aaron. *Piyyutei Yosi ben Yosi*. Jerusalem: Bialik Institute, 1977.
Mopsik, Charles. Introduction. *Sefer sheqel ha-qodesh*. Los Angeles: Cherub, 1996.
Nahmanides. *Ramban (Nachmanides): Commentary on the* Torah. 5 vols. Ed. Charles Chavel.
    New York: Judaica Press, 2005.
Niehoff, Maren. Questions and Answers in Philo and Genesis Rabbah. *JSJ* 39 (2008): 1–30.
Nissim of Marseilles. *Ma'aseh nissim: Perush la-torah le-rabbi nissim ben rabbi moshe
    mi-marsey*. Ed. H. Kriesel. Jerusalem, 2000.
Oron, Michal. The Narrative of the Letters and Its Source: A Study of a Zoharic Midrash on
    the Letters of the Alphabet. In *Studies in Jewish Mysticism, Philosophy, and Ethical
    Literature Presented to Isaiah Tishby on his Seventy-Fifth Birthday*, Joseph Dan, Joseph
    Hacker (eds.), 97–109. Jerusalem: Magnes, 1986 (Hebrew).
Oron, Michal. Artistic Elements in the Homiletics of the Zohar. *Jerusalem Studies in Jewish
    thought* 8 (1989): 299–310 (1989a).
Oron, Michal. The Doctrine of the Soul and Reincarnation in 13th-century Kabbalah. In
    Studies in Jewish Thought, Sarah Heller-Wilensky, Moshe Idel (eds.), 277–289.
    Jerusalem: Magnes, 1989 (Hebrew) (1989b).
Oron, Michal. "Place Me as a Seal upon Your Heart": Reflections on the Poetics of the Author
    of the Section of *Sabba de-Mishpatim*. In *Massu'ot: Studies in Kabbalistic Literature and
    Jewish Philosophy in Memory of Prof. Ephraim Gottlieb*, Michal Oron, Amos Goldreich
    (eds.), 1–24. Jerusalem: Bialik Institute, 1994 (Hebrew).
Oron, Michal. Midrash ha-Ne'elam: Old and New. *Kabbalah* 22 (2011):109–148 (Hebrew).
Pechter, Mordechai. Between night and morning: Zohar II 36b–38b. *Jerusalem Studies in
    Jewish thought* 8 (1989): 311–346.
Pedaya, Haviva. "The Provencal Stratum of *Sefer ha-bahir*. *Jerusalem Studies in Jewish
    Thought* 9 (1990): 2:139–164 (Hebrew).
Pedaya, Haviva. Or ke-tokh ve-or ke-ma'ateft. In *Lights in Literature, Art and Jewish Thought*.
    Emily D. Bilski, Amital Mendelsohn, and Avigdor Shinan (eds.), 565–636. Tel Aviv: Am
    Oved, 1996.
Pedaya, Haviva. *Vision and Speech: Models of Prophecy in Jewish Mysticism*. Los Angeles:
    Cherub, 2002 (Hebrew).
Pedaya, Haviva. *Nahmanides, Cyclical Time and Holy Text*. Tel Aviv: Am Oved, 2003 (Hebrew).
Pedaya, Haviva. *Name and Sanctuary in the Teaching of Rabbi Isaac the Blind: A Comparative
    Study in the Writings of the Earliest Kabbalists*. Jerusalem: Magnes, 2005 (Hebrew).
Peli, Pinchas. Eliyahu ha-navi be-veit midrasham shal chazal. In *Mechqarim be-tarbut yisrael
    mugashim le-aharon mirski bimlot li shivim shana*, Zvi Malachi (ed.), 141–168. Lod:
    Machon Haberman le-mechqarey sifrut, 1986.
Pĕsikta Dĕ-Rab Kahăna. Trans. William Gordon Braude. Philadelphia: JPS, 1975.
Pesiqta rabbati. Ed. Meir Ish Shalom. Tel Aviv, 1968.
Philo. Trans. F. Colson and G. Whitaker. Loeb Classical Library. (Cambridge: Harvard
    University Press, 1929–1962.
Piekarz, Mendel. *Polish Hasidism: Ideological Trends Between the Two Wars and During the
    Shoah*. Jerusalem: Bialik Institute, 1990 (Hebrew).

Pines, Shlomo. Nahmanides on Adam in the Garden of Eden in the Context of Other Interpretations of Genesis, Chapters 2 and 3. In *Galut achar gola*, Aharon Mirsky et al. (ed.), 159–164. Jerusalem: Yad Ben-Zvi, 1988 (Hebrew).
Posen, Raphael. *The Consistency of Targum Onqelos' Translation*. Jerusalem: Magnes, 2014 (Hebrew).
Rabinovitz, Tzvi Meir. *Mahzor piyute rabbi yanaai la-torah ve-la-mo'adim*. Jerusalem, 1985.
Recanti. Menachem. *Perush hatorah*. Jerusalem, 2003.
Rembaum, Joel. Medieval Jewish Criticism of the Christian Doctrine of Original Sin. *AJS Review* 7–8 (1983): 353–382.
Rippin, Andrew. Saadia Gaon and Genesis 22: Aspects of Jewish-Muslim Interaction and Polemic. In *Studies in Islamic and Jewish Traditions*, William Brinner and Stephen Ricks (eds.), 33–46. Atlanta: Scholars Press, 1986.
Rofé, Alexander. *The Book of Balaam (Numbers 22:2–24:25)*. Jerusalem: Simor, 1979 (Hebrew).
Rokeach, David. Philo of Alexandria, the Midrash and the Ancient Halakha. *Tarbiz* 55.3 (1985–1986): 433–439 (Hebrew).
Rokeah, David. *Justin Martyr and the Jews*. Leiden: Brill, 2002.
Rosensohn, Israel. Edom: Ha-piyyut ha-midrash ve-ha-historiya. *Masoret hapiyyut* 3 (2002): 45–75.
Rubin, Zvia. *Ha-muva'ot mi-sefer ha-zohar be-perush al ha-torah le-rabbi menachem recanati*. Jerusalem: Academon, 1992.
Saadia Gaon. *Sefer hanivchar baemunoth vehade'oth*. Ed. Joseph Kapach. Jerusalem, 1970.
Saadia Gaon. *Perushey ha-rav saadia gaon la-torah*. Ed. Moshe Zucker. New York: 1984.
Safrai, Shmuel and Safrai, Zev. *Haggadat chazal*. Jerusalem, 1998.
Safran, Bezalel. Rabbi Azriel and Nahmanides: Two Views of the Fall of Man. In *Rabbi Moses Maimonides (Rambam): Explorations in his religious and literary virtuosity*, Isadore Twersky (ed.), 75–106. Cambridge: Harvard University Press, 1983.
Samet, Elchanan. *Pirkey eliyahu*. Ma'ale Adumim, 2003.
Sandmel, Samuel. *Philo's Place in Judaism: A Study of Conceptions of Abraham in Jewish literature*. New York: Ktav, 1971.
Schäfer, Peter. *Synopse zur Hekhalot-Literatur*. Tübingen: Mohr Siebeck, 1981.
Schlossberg, Eliezer. R. Saadia Gaon's Attitude towards Islam. *Daat* 25 (1990): 21–51.
Schlossberg, Eliezer. The Binding of Isaac in Rabbi Saadia Gaom's Polemic Against Islam. In *The Faith of Abraham: In the Light of Interpretation throughout the Ages*, Moshe Hallamish, Hannah Kasher, and Yohanan Silman (eds.), 115–129. Ramat-Gan: Bar-Ilan University Press, 2002 (Hebrew).
Scholem, Gershom. The Kabbalah of R. Jacob and R. Isaac Hacohen. *Madaei Hayahadut* 2 (1927): 165–293 (Hebrew).
Scholem, Gershom. The Author of the Commentary on the Sefer Yetzirah attributed to Rabad and His Works. *Kiryat Sefer* 4 (1928): 286–302 (Hebrew).
Scholem, Gershom. *Manuscripts in Hebrew on the Kabbalah*. Jerusalem, 1930 (Hebrew).
Scholem, Gershom. An Inquiry into the Kabbalah of R. Isaac ben Jacob Hacohen: The Evolution of the Doctrine of the Worlds in the Early Kabbalah. *Tarbiz* 2 (1931): 415–442; 3 (1932): 33–66. (Hebrew).
Scholem, Gershom. *Major Trends in Jewish Mysticism*. Jerusalem: Schocken, 1941.

Scholem, Gershom. Seridim hadashim mi-kitvei r. azriel mi-gerona. *Studies in Memory of Asher Gulak and Samuel Klein*, Simcha Assaf and Gershom Scholem (eds.), Jerusalem: Academon, 1942.
Scholem, Gershom. Studies in the Doctrine of Transmigration in 13th-Century Kabbalah. *Tarbiz* 16 (1945): 135–150 (Hebrew).
Scholem, Gershom. *Reshit ha-qabala*. Jerusalem, 1948.
Scholem, Gershom. *Jewish Gnosticism, Merkabah Mysticism and Talmudic Traditions*. New York: Jewish Theological Seminary of America, 1965.
Scholem, Gershom. *Elements of the Kabbalah and its Symbolism*. Jerusalem: Bialik Institute, 1976 (1976a).
Scholem, Gershom. Two Treatises of R. Moses De Leon. *Qovetz al Yad* n.s 8 (1976): 325–384 (Hebrew) (1976b).
Scholem, Gershom. *Kabbalah*. Jerusalem: Keter, 1977.
Scholem, Gershom. *Reshit ha-qabala ve-sefer ha-bahir: Hartza'otav shel gershom shalom bishnat 1962*. Ed. Rivka Schatz. Jerusalem: Academon, 1986.
Scholem, Gershom. *Origins of the Kabbala*. Trans. Allan Arkush. Ed. Zwi Werblowsky. Philadelphia: Jewish Publication Society, 1987.
Scholem, Gershom. *One More Thing: Chapters in Heritage and Revival*. Tel Aviv: Am Oved, 1989 (Hebrew).
Scholem, Gershom. *Gershom Scholem's Annotated Zohar*. Jerusalem: Hebrew University, 1992.
Scholem, Gershom. Te'udah chadasha le-toldot reshit ha-kabbalah. In *Gershom shalom: Studies in Kabbalah (1)*, Joseph ben Shlomo and Moshe Idel (eds.), 1:7–38. Tel Aviv: Am Oved, 1998.
Scholem, Gershom. Beliar the King of the Devils. In *Devils, Demons and Souls: Essays on Demonology by Gershom Scholem*, Esther Liebes (ed.), 9–53. Jerusalem: Yad Ben-Zvi, 2004 (Hebrew).
Schwarz, Dov. *Amulets, Properties, and Rationalism in Medieval Jewish Thought*. Ramat-Gan: Bar-Ilan University Press, 2004 (Hebrew).
Sefer habahir. Ed. Daniel Abrams. Los Angeles: Cherub, 1994.
Sefer habahir. Ed. Reuben Margoliot. Jerusalem, 1984.
Sefer hapli'a. Jerusalem, 1997.
Sefer haqana. Jerusalem, 1998.
Sefer hatmuna. Lemberg, 1892.
Sefer hayashar. Ed. Joseph Dan. Jerusalem, 1986.
Sefer hazohar al chamisha chumshey torah. Ed. Reuben Margoliot. Jerusalem, 1984.
Sefer hazohar al hatorah. Mantua, 1558–1560.
Sefer hazohar. Cremona, 1559.
Sefer tiquney zohar. Ed. Reuben Margoliot. Jerusalem, 1978.
Sefer tiquney zohar. Mantua, 1558.
Segal, Eliezer L. The Exegetical Craft of the "Zohar": Toward an Appreciation. *AJS Review* 17 (1992): 31–49.
Septimus, Bernard. Open Rebuke and Concealed Love: Nahmanides and the Andalusian Tradition. In *Moses Nahmanides (Ramban): Explorations in his Religious and Literary Virtuosity*, Isadore Twersky (ed.), 11–34. Cambridge: Harvard University Press, 1983.
Sermoneta, Joseph. Ha-or: mahuto ve-tafqido be-perush le-parashat bereshit shel rabbi yehuda ben moshe Daniel romano. In *Massu'ot: Studies in Kabbalistic Literature and*

Jewish Philosophy in Memory of Prof. Ephraim Gottlieb, Michal Oron, Amos Goldreich (eds.), 459–496. Jerusalem: Bialik Institute, 1994 (Hebrew).
Shapira, Natan. *Megaley amuqot*. London, 2008.
Shechterman, Deborah. The Doctrine of Original Sin in Jewish Philosophy of the Thirteenth and Fourteenth Centuries. *Daat* 20 (1988): 65–90 (Hebrew).
Shinan, Avigdor. *The Aggadah in the Aramaic Targums to the Pentateuch*. Jerusalem: Makor, 1979 (Hebrew) (1979a).
Shinan, Avigdor. The Sins of Nadab and Abihu in Rabbinic Literature. *Tarbiz* 48.3–4 (1979), 201–14 (Hebrew) (1979b).
Shinan, Avigdor. Aqedatei de-yitzhak: Aqedat yitshak be-re'i ha-targum ha-arami. In *The Binding of Isaac for His Generations Throughout: An Israeli Perspective*, Israel Rosensohn and Benjamin Lau (eds.), 197–204. Tel Aviv: Isaac Hirschberg Memorial Foundation, 2003 (2003a).
Shinan, Avigdor. Chava ve-chivia: Al ha-isha ve-ha-nachash be-pardes ha-aggada. In *Migvan de'ot ve-hashqafot al ha-or*, D. Kerem (ed.), 49–65. Jerusalem: Ministry of Education, 2003 (2003b).
Shochetman, Eliav. Halakha she-eina halakha. *Sinai* 102 (1997): 184–186.
Shuchat, Raphael. Abraham's Faith according to the School R. Elijah of Vilna: Intellectual Versus Revelationist faith. In *The Faith of Abraham in the Light of Interpretation Throughout the Ages*, Moshe Hallamish, Hannah Kasher, and Yochanan Silman (eds.), 193–203. Ramat-Gan: Bar-Ilan University Press, 2002 (Hebrew).
Sifra. Ed. Isaac Hirsch. Vienna, 1862.
Sifra: An Analytical Translation I–III. Trans. Jacob Neusner. Atlanta: Scholars Press, 1988.
Sifre al sefer bamidbar vesifri zuta. Ed. Chaim Shaul Horowitz. Jerusalem, 1966.
Sifre al sefer dvarim. Ed. Eliezer Arie Finkelstein. New York/Jerusalem, 2001.
Silman, Yohanan. Abraham in the Kuzari in its Systematic Contexts. In *The Faith of Abraham: In the Light of Interpretation throughout the Ages*, Moshe Hallamish, Hannah Kasher, and Yohanan Silman (eds.), 131–142. Ramat-Gan: Bar-Ilan University Press, 2002 (Hebrew).
Speigel, Shalom. From the Legends of the Aggadah: A *Piyyut* on the Slaughter of Isaac and His Resurrection by Rabbi Ephraim of Bonn. In *Alexander Marx Jubilee Volume*, 471–547. New York: , 1950 (Hebrew).
Swetnam, James. *Jesus and Isaac: A Study of the Epistle to the Hebrews in the Light of Aqedah*. Rome: Loyola Press, 1981.
Ta-Shma, Israel. *The Revealed in the Hidden*. Tel Aviv: Hakibbutz Hameuhad, 1995 (Hebrew).
Tene, Naomi. The mystic narrative in the *Zohar*. PhD diss., Bar-Ilan University, 1992 (Hebrew).
Tishby, Isaiah. *Commentary on Talmudic Aggadoth by Rabbi Azriel of Gerona*. Jerusalem: Mossad Harav Kook, 1945 (Hebrew).
Tishby, Isaiah and Lachower, Fishel. *The Wisdom of the Zohar*. 3 vols. Trans. David Goldstein. Oxford/New York: Oxford University Press, 1989.
Tishby, Isaiah. *Studies in Kabbalah and its Branches*. 2 vols. Jerusalem: Magnes, 1993 (Hebrew).
Touitou, Elazar. *Exegesis in Perpetual Motion: Studies in the Pentateuchal Commentary of Rabbi Samuel Ben Meir*. Ramat-Gan: Bar-Ilan University Press, 2003 (Hebrew).
Turner, Masha. The Portial of Abraham the Patriarch in the Guide of Perplexed. *Daat* 37 (1996): 181–192 (Hebrew).

Urbach, Efraim E. Homilies of the rabbis on the prophets of the nations and the Balaam stories. *Tarbiz* 25 (1956): 272–289 (Hebrew).

Urbach, Efraim E. *The Sages*. 2 vols. Jerusalem: Magnes, 1975.

VanderKam, James. *Enoch and the Growth of an Apocalyptic Tradition*. Washington, DC: Catholic Biblical Association, 1984.

VanderKam, James. *Enoch: A Man of All Generations*. Columbia: University of South Carolina Press, 1995.

Walfish, Avraham. The literary method of redaction in the mishnah based on tractate rosh ha-shanah. PhD, Hebrew University of Jerusalem, 2001 (Hebrew).

Weinberg, Zvi. Lidmuto shel esav: Al hora'at dmuyot miqrayot be-veit ha-sefer. *Shema'atin* 78 (1984): 5–10.

Weiner, Aharon. *The Prophet Elijah in the Development of Judaism: A Depth-Psychological Study*. London: Routledge & Kegan Paul, 1978.

Weiss, Hillel. Ha-ayil Ba-sevakh: Le-nose ha-aqeda be-sifrut dorenu. In *The Binding of Isaac for His Generations Throughout: An Israeli Perspective*, Israel Rozenson and Benjamin Lau (eds.), 263–273. Tel Aviv: Memorial Fund for Yitzhak Hershberg, 2003.

Werblowsky, Zwi. Philo and the Zohar: A Note on the Method of the "Scienza Nuova" in Jewish Studies. *JJS* 10 (1959): 113–135.

Wertheimer, Shlomo. *Teshuvot rabbeinu sa'adia gaon z"l le-chivai ha-balkhi*. Jerusalem, 1931.

Wertheimer, Shlomo. *Batey midrashot*. Jerusalem: Moshe Lilienthal Press, 1950.

Wieder, Naftali. *The Formation of Jewish Liturgy in the East and the West: A Collection of Essays*, 2 vols. Jerusalem: Yad Ben-Zvi, 1998 (Hebrew).

Wijhnhoven, Jochanan. *Sefer HaMishkal*: Text and study. PhD diss., Brandeis University, 1964.

Wisblit, Shlomo. Yetziat mitzrayim ke-avtipus la-ge'ula ha-atidit ve-ke-musa hizdahut le'umit. *Morashteynu* 14 (2010): 109–117.

Wolfson, Elliot. Left Contained in the Right: A Study in Zoharic Hermeneutics. *AJS Review* 11 (1986): 26–52.

Wolfson, Elliot. *The Book of the Pomegranate: Moses de Leon's Sefer Ha-Rimon*. Atlanta: Scholars Press, 1988 (1988a).

Wolfson, Elliot. The Hermeneutics of Visionary Experience: Revelation and Interpretation in the Zohar. *Religion* 18 (1988): 311–345 (1988b).

Wolfson, Elliot. Light Through Darkness: The Ideal of Human Perfection in the Zohar," *Harvard Theological Review* 81 (1988): 73–95 (1988c).

Wolfson, Elliot. Anthropomorphic Imagery and Letter Symbolism in the Zohar. *Jerusalem Studies in Jewish Thought* 8 (1989): 169–701 (Hebrew) (1989a). (141–181)

Wolfson, Elliot. By Way of Truth: Aspects of Nahmanides' Kabbalistic Hermeneutic. *AJS Review* 14 (1989): 103–178 (1989b).

Wolfson, Elliot. Beautiful Maiden Without Eyes: "Peshat" and "Sod" in Zoharic Hermeneutics. In *The Midrashic Imagination: Jewish Exegesis, Thought and History*, Michael Fishbane (Ed.). 155–203. Albany: SUNY Press, 1993 (1993a).

Wolfson, Elliot. Images of God's Feet: Some Observations on the Divine Body in Judaism. In *People of the Body: Jews and Judaism from an Embodied Perspective*, Howard Eilberg-Schwartz (ed.), 143–181. Albany: SUNY Press, 1993 (1993b).

Wolfson, Elliot. *Through a Speculum that Shines: Vision and Imagination in Medieval Jewish Mysticism*. Princeton: Princeton University Press, 1994.

Wolfson, Elliot. *Luminal Darkness: Imaginal Gleanings from Zoharic Literature*. Oxford: Oneworld Publications, 2007.

Yahalom, Joseph (ed.). *Priestly Palestinian Poetry: A Narrative Liturgy for the Day of Atonement.* Jerusalem: Magnes, 1996 (Hebrew).
Yahalom, Joseph and Sokoloff, Michael. Aramaic Piyyutim from the Byzantine Period. *JQR* 75.3 (1985): 309–321.
Yassif, Eli. *The Sacrifice of Isaac: Studies in the Development of a Literary Tradition.* Jerusalem: Makor, 1978 (Hebrew).
Yehuda ben Barzillai ha-Barzeloni. *Perush sefer yetzira.* Ed. S.Z.H. Halberstam. Jerusalem, 1971.
Yisraeli, Oded. Chutz mi-sha'arey ona'a: Iyun be-sipur ha-aggada tanuro shel aknai. In *Al derekh ha-avot: Shloshim shana le-mikhlelet ya'aqov Herzog*, Amnon Bazak, Samuel Vigoda, and Meir Munitz (eds.), 269–281. Alon Shvut: Tvunot, 2001 (Hebrew).
Yisraeli, Oded. *The Interpretation of Secrets and the Secrets of Interpretation: Midrashic and Hermeneutic Strategies in Sabba de-Mishpatim of the Zohar.* Los Angeles: Cherub, 2005 (Hebrew).
Yisraeli, Oded. The Tree of Life and its Roots: A History of a Kabbalistic Symbol. In *A Garden Eastward in Eden: Traditions of Paradise*, Rachel Elior (ed.), 269–289. Jerusalem: Magnes, 2010 (Hebrew).
Yisraeli, Oded. Halakhic Conflicts in the Zohar. In *And This is for Yehuda: Studies Presented to our Friend, Professor Yehuda Liebes, on the Occasion of his Sixty-fifth Birthday*, Maren Neihoff, Jonathan Garb, and Ronit Meroz (eds.), 202–221. Jerusalem, Bialik Institute, 2012 (Hebrew).
Yisraeli, Oded. From Heavenly Palaces to the Palace of the Torah: Characteristics of Zoharic Mysticism. In *Jewish Spirituality*, M. Idel (ed.) (forthcoming) (Hebrew).
Yuval, Israel. *The Sages in their Generations: The Spiritual Leadership of German Jewry at the End of the Middle Ages.* Jerusalem: Magnes, 1988 (Hebrew).
Yuval, Israel. *Two Nations in Your Womb: Perceptions of Jews and Christians in Late Antiquity and the Middle Ages.* Berkeley: University of California Press, 2006.
Zack, Bracha. Eretz and Eretz Yisrael in the Zohar. *Jerusalem Studies in Jewish Thought* 8 (1989): 239–253 (Hebrew).
Zack, Bracha. *The Kabbalah of Rabbi Moshe Cordovero.* Beersheba: Ben-Gurion University Press, 1995 (Hebrew).
Zack, Bracha. The Land of Israel, The Zohar and the Kabbalah of Safed. In *Zion and Zionism among the Sephardi and Oriental Jews*, Zev Harvey et al. (eds.), 51–79. Jerusalem: International Congress for the Study of the Legacy of Sephardi and Oriental Jewry, 2002 (Hebrew).
Zacuto, Moses. *Sefer derekh ha-emet: Hagahot al sefer ha-zohar ve-al sefer tikkuney zohar le-ha-ari z"l.* Venice: 1662.
Zakovitch, Yair. Elijah and Elisha in the "Praise of Israel's Great Ancestors' (Ben Sira 47:36–48:19). In *Studies in Bible and Exegesis* 5 (2000), 163–177 (Hebrew).
Zakovitch, Yair. Or ha-bri'ah ve-or acharit ha-yamim. In Aaron Zion (ed.), *Migvan de'ot ve-hashqafot al ha-or*, 63–74. Jerusalem: Ministry of Education, 2003.
Zakovitch, Yair. *Inner-Biblical and Extra-Biblical Midrash and the Relationship Between Them.* Tel Aviv: Am Oved, 2009 (Hebrew).
Zakovitch, Yair and Shinan, A. *That's Not What the Good Book Says.* Tel Aviv: Yediot Aharonot/ Sifre Hemed, 2004 (Hebrew).
Zimmer, Eric. *Society and Its Customs: Studies in the History and Metamorphosis of Jewish Customs.* Jerusalem: Zalman Shazar Centre, 1996 (Hebrew).
Zion, Menachem. *Sefer zioni: Perush al ha-torah.* Lemberg, 1882.

Zohar Chadash u-midrash ha-ne'elam. Thessaloniki, 1597.
Zohar Chadash. Ed. Reuben Margoliot. Jerusalem, 1978.
Zunz, Yom-Tov Lipman. *The Sermons of the Jews and Their Historical Evolution*. Jerusalem, 1974.

Chapters first published elsewhere

Chapter 6: The Ascent of Enoch and Elijah in the Kabbalah of the Thirteenth Century. *Pe'amim* 110 (2007): 31–54 (Hebrew).
Chapter 7: The Emergence of Abraham according to the Zohar. *Daat* 60 (2007): 51–70 (Hebrew).
Chapter 8: The Binding of Isaac in the *Zohar:* From Trial to Experience. *AJS Review* (2011): 1–24.
Chapter 9: The Suppressed Cry of Esau: From Early Midrash to the Late Zoharic Literature. *Te'uda* 21–22 (2007): 165–198 (Hebrew).
Chapter 10: The Memory of the Exodus in the *Zohar*. *Derekh Efrata* 13 (2009–2010): 13–34 (Hebrew).
Chapter 11: Did Moses' Hands Wage War? The War Against Amalek in the Zohar—From Human to Higher Needs. *Kabbalah* 23 (2010): 161–180 (Hebrew).
Chapter 12: Holy Revolt: The Act of Nadab and Abihu in the *Zohar*. In *Spiritual Authority: Struggles Over Cultural Power in Jewish Thought*, Howard Kreisel, Boaz Huss, and Uri Ehrlich (eds.), 83–101. Beersheba: Ben-Gurion University Press, 2009 (Hebrew).
Chapter 14: Moses did not Die: Traces of a Rabbinic Tradition in the *Zohar*. In *Moses the Man, Master of the Prophets: In the Light of Interpretation Throughout the Ages*, Moshe Hallamish, Hannah Kasher, and Hanokh Ben-Pazi (eds.), 381–406. Ramat-Gan: Bar-Ilan University Press, 2010.
Chapter 15: Elijah's Jealousy in Midrashic Tradition and the *Zohar*. *Derekh Aggada* 6 (2003): 103–124.

Index of Zoharic Sources

1:21b	210	1:157a	165
1:22a	62	1:157b	165
1:31b	45	1:160a	145
1:35b	18, 54	1:166a	145
1:36a	54, 61	1:168a	227
1:36b	65	1:171a	145
1:37b	229	1:172b	145, 146
1:39a	120	1:177a	145
1:47a	83	1:177b	146
1:52a	62	1:192a	61, 191
1:53a	238	1:203b	45
1:56b	70	1:208a	17
1:59b	120	1:208b	17
1:65a	146	1:209a	79, 254, 255, 256
1:65b	122	1:209b	254
1:68b	209	1:221a	62
1:73a	191	1:221b	62
1:75a		1:237a	18, 61
1:75b	65	1:245a	259
1:76b	130	2:10b	70
1:77a	88	2:13b	259
1:77b	18, 97	2:18a	163
1:80a	99	2:26b	197
1:81b	18	2:33a	109
1:83a	59, 60	2:34a	59
1:86a	101	2:37a	22
1:99b	219	2:37b	191
1:107a	83	2:40a	163
1:110b	150	2:50a	165
1:119b	125, 126	2:57b	171, 182
1:120a	128, 129	2:61b	18, 166
1:120b	121	2:65b	174
1:124b	122	2:66a	179
1:125b	209, 211	2:69a	211
1:126a	211	2:69b	209
1:131b	228	2:86b	240
1:133b	125	2:99a	10
1:137b	18	2:111a	151
1:138b	145, 146	2:111b	152
1:139b	127	2:112a	152, 154
1:144b	145	2:147b	47
1:146b	145	2:148b	46
1:148a	18	2:157a	228
1:151b	256	2:166b	47

2:174a	228, 238	3:210a	209, 254
2:181b	153	3:211b	209
2:190a	254	3:213b	259
2:194b	176. 177	3:214a	257
2:197a	79, 80, 256	3:215a	254
2:218b	122	3:215b	197
2:220b	47	3:216a	232, 241
2:254b	148	3:217a	197
2:257a	125	3:220a	240
2:265b	122	3:227b	254
2:267b	61	3:236b	19
3:5b	191	3:238a	232, 254
3:33b	191, 192	3:238b	232, 241
3:37b	191, 192	3:256a	232
3:54b	259	3:273a	241
3:55b	121	3:284a	231
3:56b	192		
3:57a	197	**Zohar hadash**	
3:60a	192, 200		
3:64a	145	15b	44
3:68b	256	18c	61, 62
3:71b	17	22b	191
3:72b	17	25c	256
3:92b	179	31a	158
3:107a	62	40a	146
3:112a	209	48b	61
3:113a	211	54a	145, 209
3;142b	17	66a	257
3:143a	17	76a	79, 256
3:145a	179	78a	145
3:146a	179	84c	254
3:152a	235	85a	47
3:153b	232	87a	145
3:155b	23	122b	120
3:156b	231		
3:181b	229	**Tiqunei Zohar**	
3:184b	209		
3:185a	145	31b	233
3:192a	209	69a	61
3:192b	146, 211	81a	61
3:193b	211	85b	61
3:200a	211	103a	61
3:204a	36	112a	232, 233
3:206b	209, 211	115a	61
3:207b	201	139a	124

Index of subjects

Angel   29, 41, 54, 67f., 71, 73, 76–86, 89, 109, 111, 114–118, 121, 128, 132, 142, 146, 166f., 169, 176, 203–205, 224, 226, 238, 247, 253, 255f., 258, 262
Angel of Death   54, 71, 73, 77, 79, 111, 146, 223–226, 228f., 255, 257f.
Antropomorphism   180
Arousal from above   88, 90, 98f.
Arousal from below   88, 90, 98
Asceticism   75, 78, 217
Ashmadai   163f.
Astrology   22, 101, 103, 206
Axis mundi   89

Book of Adam   13, 82
Book of Enoch   13
Book of Solomon   13

Chariot   39, 67f., 73, 79, 162, 226, 255
Christianity   50, 69, 71, 134–136, 138f., 225, 237
Commandment   7, 51, 54, 58f., 64, 93, 105, 111, 130, 142, 153, 158, 161, 164, 168, 219, 237
Crown   68, 210f., 215
Cutting down the shoots   17, 24, 54f., 57, 60f., 64, 192f., 196

Death   25, 52, 55, 59, 61f., 69–71, 73–77, 79, 83f., 96, 111, 114f., 117, 121–123, 138, 149, 186, 188–192, 194, 197, 199f., 222–232, 234–241, 255, 257, 261
Death by a kiss   76, 226f.
Destruction   27, 135, 136, 137, 190
Din benei chalof   82
Din (sefirah)   18, 25, 84, 118, 123–128, 131–133, 179, 194
Divination   202–204, 206, 209f., 212f., 216f., 219, 221
Divine world   8, 16f., 55, 175, 180, 182, 184f.
Duma   163

Emanation   145, 148f., 154, 175, 178, 211, 214, 216, 231, 238
Evil   25, 27, 34f., 52–64, 68–70, 83f., 94, 113f., 125, 134–136, 138, 143, 145–155, 162, 165, 170, 177, 185, 194, 202, 209, 212f., 235, 250
Exile   60, 123, 138, 145, 158, 173, 230–234, 241, 248

Garden of Eden   7, 12, 17, 34, 57, 61, 68, 71, 75, 144, 224f.
Garment   9, 22f., 29, 31, 73, 80, 89f., 106, 118, 120, 137, 163f., 183
Gates of impurity   27, 159, 164
German Pietists   11, 84

Hasidism   19, 24, 48f., 131–133, 146, 201, 253f., 264
Hesed (sefirah)   18, 25, 42, 47f., 83f., 118, 122–127, 130–133, 179, 181
Hidden light   29, 33, 35, 37–39, 41–43, 45–49, 172, 261
Hokhma (sefirah)   167
Holiness   63, 139, 150, 152–154, 164, 196, 203, 211–214, 216f., 220, 251
Human evil   27, 136, 139
Human soul   19, 51, 56, 59, 61, 63f., 128, 133, 150

Idolatry   90f., 94f., 112, 144, 159, 219
Immortality   69f., 77–79, 223, 225, 229f., 234, 242f., 248, 258
Impurity   27, 158f., 164, 167, 177, 211–214, 217, 220, 228
Islam   102, 264

Land of Israel   17, 60, 65, 72, 89f., 97, 162, 252
land of Israel   17
Light   3f., 6, 14–16, 20, 24, 29–31, 33–50, 61, 67, 75, 80, 82, 87, 91–93, 95, 99, 101, 103f., 108, 110, 114, 130–132, 137, 143, 147, 151, 155, 158, 161, 166, 169f., 175, 184, 192, 198, 200–202, 206, 213,

218, 220, 222, 230–235, 239–242, 244, 246 f., 249, 261 f.
light of creation   39
light of prophecy   38
Light of the seven days   33, 34, 42, 48, 234
light of thought   37, 39 f.
Light of wisdom   39, 44 f.
Lower Crowns   210–212, 216, 220
Lurianic kabbalah   35, 132 f., 146, 149, 191, 193, 195, 241, 257, 264

Magic   14, 17 f., 29, 62, 65, 85, 168 f., 171 f., 175, 178, 183–185, 204, 206, 208 f., 214, 218–221, 262
Malkut (Sefirah)   17 f., 24, 27, 53, 64 f., 118, 126, 162, 165 f., 192 f., 195 f., 245
Messianism   34, 71, 73, 138, 148, 157, 173, 222, 230 f., 234, 237, 248 f., 254, 257, 261
Metamorphosis   26, 76, 128
Metatron   68 f., 71–73, 79–82, 86, 176, 226
Miracle   78, 84, 97, 169 f., 253, 255 f., 258

Netzach (sefirah)   152, 172

Original sin   50, 57, 60 f., 64

Philosophy   6, 22, 35, 37, 39, 74, 85, 91, 99, 101, 103, 204 f., 207, 227 f.
powers of impurity   158, 164
Prayer   29, 94, 114, 171, 174 f., 178, 182
Priest   121 f., 174, 178–181, 189 f., 194, 196 f., 200, 245–249, 252
primordial light   33, 35–42, 44 f., 47
Prophecy   13, 26, 38–40, 46, 75, 78, 84, 99, 104, 136, 142, 150, 152, 159, 184, 189, 202–220, 225, 227, 232 f., 237, 240, 244–246, 249, 251–253, 255 f.
Prophetic Kabbalah   19, 81

Rationalism   70, 74, 76, 118, 226 f., 247
Redemption   115, 138, 157–159, 178, 185, 206, 208, 230 f., 242, 244, 248
Reincarnation   82, 196–199, 241, 261, 264
Resurrection   72, 77, 120 f., 144, 166, 229

Revelation   6, 10, 13 f., 18, 26, 29, 41, 43, 77, 87, 90, 92–98, 100 f., 103, 105, 215, 234, 237, 242 f., 256 f.

Sabbateanism   60
Sacrifice   27, 108–114, 116–124, 127–129, 132, 153, 161, 174, 193 f., 200, 249
Samael   146, 151–154, 162 f., 173, 176, 254
Satan   16, 52, 63, 109 f., 127, 146, 224
Secret   5, 7, 9 f., 12–14, 17, 28, 42, 45, 82, 118, 155, 172, 215, 219, 230–234, 242 f., 257
Sefirot   17 f., 24, 53, 61, 81 f., 84, 99, 118, 122, 127, 162, 167, 171, 176, 178 f., 181 f., 184, 191, 193, 195, 260
Shekhina   17 f., 38, 59, 61, 73, 98, 187, 189, 195, 209, 227, 230, 232, 259
Sin   17 f., 24, 30 f., 34 f., 38, 44, 50–65, 68 f., 75, 78, 116, 144, 149, 153, 179, 181 f., 186–189, 191–193, 195 f., 198 f., 212, 261, 264
Sitra achra   17 f., 27, 53, 58, 60, 122, 134, 145 f., 149–153, 159, 162–164, 177, 179, 181, 194, 210–212, 215 f., 220
Sod aliyat ha-shelach   82
Soul   7, 10, 12, 18 f., 25, 31, 37, 39, 42, 51 f., 54, 70, 74–78, 80 f., 95, 97 f., 100 f., 103 f., 115, 119 f., 122, 127 f., 131, 133, 141, 149, 165–167, 196–199, 202, 204, 211, 223–225, 227 f., 235, 239, 241–243

Temple   5, 27, 95, 121, 134, 137, 189 f., 201, 236, 246
Theurgy   17 f., 53–55, 61, 64, 169, 172, 176, 184, 262
Tiferet (Sefirah)   17 f., 24, 27, 53, 62, 64, 118, 165, 167, 171, 174, 181, 192 f., 196, 217, 229 f., 236
Tiqla   149
Torah   1, 5–7, 9 f., 13 f., 21–23, 26, 28, 39, 45–49, 53, 55, 74 f., 77, 80, 83, 96, 98, 111, 117, 131, 136, 139, 142, 152, 155, 157–159, 162, 166 f., 171 f., 190, 194, 198, 200, 208, 213 f., 219, 222, 225, 227, 229–243, 257, 261 f.
Transfiguration   70, 76, 81

Transmigration 12, 82, 197–199, 241, 264
Tree of Knowledge 24, 50–55, 57, 62–65, 235, 261
Tree of life 7, 24f., 51–54, 62f., 65, 222, 229, 235, 261
Trial 16, 110, 130, 212
Tzimtzum 35, 132

Unio mystica 81
Upper realms 5, 17, 19, 52, 73, 75–80, 85, 98, 133, 179, 238

Upper soul 52, 54

World to come 36, 40–42, 44, 47–49, 77f., 120f., 144, 151, 166, 223, 231, 246, 261

Yesod (Sefirh) 17, 81

Zoharic circle 25, 28, 46, 79f., 98, 123, 133, 149, 172, 179, 182, 185, 211

Index of persons

Aaron of Karlin 48 f.
Abraham b. David (Rabad) 14, 182 f., 187
Abrabanel, Isaac 75, 76, 136
Abrams, Daniel 1 f., 25, 28, 31, 180
Abulafia, Abraham 19, 48, 81, 91
Abulafia, Todros 5, 28, 30, 53, 174, 193
Adelman, Rachel 246
Afterman, Adam 205
Al Barceloni, Judah 38, 44
Aminoff, Irit 135, 145
Angelet, Joseph 2, 124, 131, 185
Aptowitzer, Victor 236, 249, 251
Ashkenazi, Joseph b. Shalom 28, 82, 108, 114, 182 f.
Asulin, Shifra 2
Azikri, Eleazar 97
Azriel of Gerona 5, 28 f., 39–41, 45–47, 54–56, 201, 204 f., 227

Baer, Yitzhak 30, 37, 106
Bahya b. Asher 28, 65
Belkin, Samuel 70, 106
Berdyczewski, Micha Josef 3
Bezalel b. Solomon of Kobryn 109
Blidstein, Yaacov 108, 113, 201
Bohak Gideon 214
Boyarin, Daniel 8 f.

Cohen Aloro, Dorit 2
Cordovero, Moses 84, 241
Crescas, Hasdai 99, 105, 204

Dan, Joseph 5 f., 11, 44, 53, 71, 83 f., 146, 153, 194
De Leon, Moses 1, 6, 8, 23, 26, 28, 30, 42, 47, 57, 60, 61 62, 63, 64, 66, 83, 84, 126, 180, 11, 185, 209, 211, 212, 214, 215, 216, 217, 218, 219, 220, 240
Del Medigo, Elijah 1

Efrati, Jacob Eliahu 108, 115
Elboim, Jacob 5, 108, 129
Elimelech of Lizhensk 48 f.

Elior, Rachel 69, 155
Ezra b. Solomon 5, 28, 41, 51–57, 63 f., 201, 204 f.

Felix, Iris 124
Fishbane, Michael 3, 226
Flusser, David 71, 199
Frank, Jacob 155
Frankel, Yonah 3–5, 8, 12

Galanti, Abraham 60
Garb, Jonathan 89
Gersonides 38, 74 f., 204, 227, 247
Gikatilla, Joseph 1, 6, 28, 53 f., 91, 123 f., 162 f., 181, 185, 217, 220
Giller, Pinchas 2
Ginzberg, Louis 3, 87, 94 f., 135, 169, 209
Goetschel, Roland 213 f.
Goldreich, Amos 2, 11, 14, 30, 118, 172, 193, 222, 230, 242
Gottlieb, Ephraim 46, 54, 78, 179, 235
Green, Arthur 2, 230
Gries, Zeev 3, 43
Gruenwald, Ithamar 3, 11, 72 f.

Hacker, Joel 2
Harari, Yuval 14, 169, 214
Heinemann, Isaac 4, 8
Heinemann, Joseph 3, 8, 96
Hellner-Eshed, Melila 2, 15, 23, 46, 98, 255, 258
Horowitz, Isaiah 231
Huss, Boaz 1 f., 4, 7, 14, 17, 21, 23, 31, 35, 222

Ibn Ezra, Abraham 75, 111, 117, 138, 142 f., 161, 171, 206, 247
Ibn Gabbai, Meir 82, 91
Ibn Gaon, Shem-Tov 118, 172
Ibn Janah, Jonah 111
Ibn Shuaib, Joshua 172, 177, 184
– Idel, Moshe 2, 5–7, 9, 12, 17 f., 23, 28, 42, 48, 69, 72, 81, 106, 148, 169, 176, 180, 201, 205

Isaac Hacohen   28, 53, 145, 214
Isaac of Acre   78, 118, 172, 193

Jacob bar Sheshet   28, 104
Jacob Hacohen   28, 211
Joseph of Shushan   1
Josephus   75, 94f., 143, 187, 204, 207, 209, 225, 239
Judah Aryeh of Modena   1
Judah Halevi   70, 75f., 78, 92, 101, 157, 207

Kaufmann, Yehezkel   93, 110
Kimchi, David   74
Kister, Menahem   71, 94, 101, 115, 226

Lasker, Daniel   111, 124
Levi b. Abraham   74, 76f., 226
Levinson, Joshua   3f., 8, 16
Lieberman, Saul   95, 223
Liebes, Yehuda   1–3, 5, 13, 15, 18, 21, 26, 28, 30, 42f., 69, 72, 85, 87, 89, 91, 93, 96, 100f., 103–106, 109f., 118, 121–124, 148f., 153, 169, 180, 182, 185, 191, 197, 209, 222, 227, 230, 232–235, 241f., 259, 263

Mack, Hananel   5
Maimonides   6, 50, 63, 76f., 91–93, 96f., 99, 104–106, 139, 157, 183, 204, 219, 227f., 230
Margolies, Reuvein   21
Matt, Daniel   2, 13, 21, 23, 44, 62, 136, 179
Meged, Mati   2
Meir, Ofra   4, 91, 96, 135
Menachem Nachum of Chernobyl   131
Menn, Esther   3
Meroz, Ronit   2, 28, 31, 200, 210, 217
Mopsik, Charles   214
Moses of Burgos   28, 53

Nahmanides   6–8, 28, 31, 53, 55f., 59, 77–80, 82, 88–91, 108, 110, 117f., 138, 145f., 153, 159, 161, 163, 166, 171f., 177f., 192–195, 201, 205–208, 210, 212, 215, 218f., 262f.
Niehoff, Maren   106

Oron, Michal   2, 43, 53, 198

Pachter, Mordechai   2
Pedaya, Haviva   2, 5f., 28, 39, 51, 53, 84, 89, 159, 176f., 179–182, 205
Philo   37, 70, 76, 94, 103–107, 116f., 119f., 170, 199, 203f., 207, 209, 225, 250, 263
Pines, Shlomo   56

Recanti, Menahem   39

Sa'adia Gaon   111, 138
Safran, Bezalel   53, 55
Sagi-Nahor, Isaac   14, 28, 51, 176, 177, 180, 257
Samuel ben meir (Rashbam)   171, 248
Schäfer, Peter   69, 74
Scholem, Gershom   1, 5f., 9, 13f., 20f., 23, 28, 32, 50f., 53–55, 57, 61, 63, 69, 82, 84, 106, 120, 125, 145, 163f., 180, 183, 193, 198, 201, 205, 211, 216, 235, 241, 257
Segal, Eliezer   3
Shapira, Kalonymus Kalman   109
Shinan, Avigdor   50, 93, 108, 115, 166, 187, 190, 247, 249
Simeon bar Jochai   1, 5, 14, 21f., 30f., 77
Speigel, Shalom   108, 112, 119, 120
Stein, Dina   51, 246

Ta-Shma, Israel   20, 179
Tene, Naomi   2

Urbach, Efraim   33, 50, 96, 105, 108, 112, 119, 169, 208, 214, 237

Walfish, Avraham   169f.
Werblowsky, Zwi   106

Wolfson, Elliot   2, 5, 14, 28, 42f., 57, 180f., 185

Yisraeli, Oded   2, 7–10, 12f., 15, 20, 23f., 51, 53, 98, 100, 131f., 149, 189, 194, 235, 237, 241–243

Zakovitch, Yair   3, 33, 93, 166, 244
Zakut, Moses   193
Zion, Menachem   84, 131, 162, 172, 179
Zunz, Yom-Tov Lipman   3, 5

www.ingramcontent.com/pod-product-compliance
Lightning Source LLC
Chambersburg PA
CBHW030749250426
43673CB00059B/1331